This book is dedicated to Colleen.

Contents

Acknowledgments

I'd like to thank

Alanna Coyne for her untiring assistance
Matt Culter of Customer Centric for turning me on to Web analytics
Mark Gibbs for his wit, intelligence, and friendship
Mellanie Hills for her shining example
Anne Holland for her excellent work with MarketingSherpa
Jakob Neilson at Useit.com for doing what he does so I don't have to
Karl Sterne, my father, for his encouragement and editorial skills
Kristin Zhivago for her insight and friendship

My thanks also go to people like Phil Gibson at National Semiconductor, Seth Romanow at Compaq, Rob Sherrell at Delta Airlines, and the dozens of professionals who spent the time to tell me about how they measure their Web site success.

About the Author

Jim Sterne (Santa Barbara, CA) is a pioneering expert on Internet marketing. He specializes in Internet marketing strategies for business. Sterne produced the world's first seminar series on Internet marketing in 1994 and is an internationally recognized speaker. Information about his company, Target Marketing of Santa Barbara, can be found at www.targeting.com.

The Web Is Great:
Get Over It, Get On with It

**"Not everything that can be counted counts,
and not everything that counts can be counted."**
Albert Einstein

How about a World Wide Web simulator? Just submit your Web site design and implementation plans to this rule-based, artificially intelligent, neural-networked interpretation of 513,410,000 surfing people; it thinks about it for a while, and out comes a 3-year analysis. Will your site get lots of traffic or be a ghost town? Generate sales or cause very unpleasant PR? All the anguish and nail-biting done away with. Everything fully automatic, with no risk of public humiliation.

Why do we want such a tool? Because we're clueless.

Our Web sites were created in a volcanic eruption of bombastic enthusiasm and visionary expectation in an era when all things were possible and we just made it up as we went along. Was it worth it? Of course. Are we grateful for the Era of Experimentation and Learning? Absolutely. How do we take our sites to the next level? Will the changes we propose have a positive or negative impact? There are several popular methods for answering those questions:

Wait and see

Trial and error

Give it a shot

Presumption, supposition, hypothesis

Wild conjecture

Reading tea leaves

But my 11-year-old son likes it

The Magic 8-Ball

We're clueless.

The Thrill Is Gone

"Get online or go out of business" was a line I never used. I heard it enough times between 1994 and 2001 to convince me that the world didn't need to hear it yet again, so I focused on the practical side.

Was the Web going to change the way we live, work, communicate, shop, pay, and play? Sure. But I took those truths to be self-evident. Every other keynote speaker at the sometimes three-per-week conferences I was ping-ponging between shook the rafters with threats of "Dot Com or Be Gone!", "Be Digital or Be Toast!", "Get Web or Be Dead!" You remember the rhetoric. I figured they could have the spotlight calling for the new millennium while I plowed away in the background helping companies figure out how to get some actual value out of all this Internet stuff.

Oh sure, I was on the advisory boards of numerous Internet-only startups (still am, in fact—it keeps me young). But I'm of an age where I never forgot the value of rigid systems (stagnant business models) and the wisdom of defined processes (bureaucracy), so I decided early on to focus my efforts on helping large firms figure out how to use the Internet to best advantage.

While the venture capitalists were busy pouring kerosene on anything that looked even slightly incendiary, I stuck with my white shirt and rep tie and charged off to preach to the multinationals. That, as Willie Sutton would have said, was where the money was, is, and ever shall be.

I consulted. I gave workshops. I wrote books. I advised, presented, and published about advertising on the Internet, marketing online, and customer service in a wired world. The Web was on a roll and I was keeping pace.

But come the new millennium, a hush fell over the Internet landscape. The voices extolling the new economy and e-everything were quieted by those muttering, "Show me the money." Now that we're actually airborne, the question is whether we're flying in the right direction and doing it in a fuel-efficient manner.

What Are You Measuring?

One of the wonders of the Internet is instant gratification. I just experienced this at The Benchmarking Exchange (TBE) site (www.industrymetrics.com), which offers an impressive range of business surveys that let you see the results as soon as you're finished taking whichever quiz captures your fancy. There are surveys about procedures management, supplier management, crisis management, call center employee training, customer service information systems, human resources, vacation policy, and a bunch more.

The E-business Strategy survey on the Benchmarking Exchange site, originally sponsored by General Management Technologies, caught my eye. Today, "this survey is now a part of the permanent and ongoing Surveyor Library on TBE and everyone is encouraged to participate. As more responses are collected, richer results will be realized." From 579 responses (as of January 2002), question 10 about the success of the respondents' sites created a pretty typical bell curve, leaning just a little toward the not convinced, but it was question 11 that really caught my attention (see Figure 1.1).

When asked how companies measure their Web sites, most people selected two choices from the list of six options. It comes as no surprise that the vast majority chose "Meeting subjective goals and objectives." This answer is pretty much close to the last one on the list, "We do not/have not measured e-business initiative success." In other words, we squint at it every now and then, lick a finger and hold it up in the breeze to figure out if it's okay, and then go on about our business.

Some look at sales, some look at savings, and at least *some* look at profitability. Thank heavens.

It Is Time for an Accounting

We've enjoyed experimenting—now it's time to face the facts.

PricewaterhouseCoopers talked to 78 large companies across most industries to find out enough to publish their "Electronic Business Outlook for the New Millennium" white paper, and the results were a bit alarming. Among the five top barriers to the development of e-business was a lack of key standards. While they were lamenting the absence of outside criteria, 44 percent of those firms had no specific, internal measures in place of their own.

We know it is time to face facts. The problem is that we're not sure which facts to face. The dot-com bubble has burst and we're grateful to those with the arrows in their backs, but it's time to get serious. It's time to get to work. We know there's value there—but where *exactly* do we find it? What *exactly* do we measure?

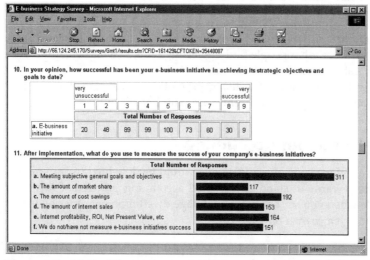

Figure 1.1   Most of those surveyed at Industrymetrics.com felt their sites were less than successful, and more than one-quarter measure nothing.

The singular goal of this book is to give you the broad scope of Web metrics possibilities. It's intended to be a guide through the labyrinth of viable measurement methods so that you can determine what you wish to measure, and what you are technically, economically, and politically *able* to measure.

What Kind of a Book Is This?

Good question. Let's start with what this book is *not*.

This Book Is Not about Statistical Analysis

Granted, you're going to need some statistical analysis smarts before you tackle half of this stuff, but you're not going to get pummeled with it here. There are plenty of places to learn the fine and mystical arts of higher mathematics and how they apply to the Web. This is not one of them. If that's your thing, take a look at *The Laws of the Web* by Bernardo A. Huberman (MIT Press, 2001).

This Book Is Not about Technology

I've written a slew of books about the Internet and I do my best to steer clear of which products are the most robust and which platforms offer the most features. That's a moving target, and this is a printed book after all.

While I will cover the basics in layman's terms, I will not be investigating the intricate inner workings of various servers, applications, databases, or networking software any more than necessary.

This Book Is Not about the Size of the Web

There are plenty of companies like Nua.com (www.nua.com) stretching the limits of their ability to keep track of how many people are online at this very moment. There are many ways to measure what people find interesting on the Web, such as the Buzz Index Weekly from Yahoo! (see Figure 1.2).

If you're looking for your next advertising promotion to cater to the statistical Yahoo! user, then the Buzz Report is the right place. This book is not.

This Book Is Not about Accounting

There are many prestigious halls of academe that would be delighted to enthrall you with the rigors and rewards of standard accepted accounting practices. Sadly, they have a little trouble when you start asking about page dwell time per order by visitor with a recency factor greater than once a week.

Figure 1.2 Yahoo!'s Buzz Index keeps track of what people are searching for week after week.

This Book Is Not about Internal Operations or Procurement

The Internet can save astonishing amounts of money by being a tool for internal communications, communications with suppliers, and generally running a company. Descriptions of the best ways to measure your intranet for maximum effectiveness or your acquisition systems for best value are not to be found in these pages.

Okay, so what *is* this book about?

Another good question. Keep this up and we'll get along just fine.

This Book Is about Measuring Your Success with Customers

This book looks at the Web as a business tool for communicating with your customers.

I have been in sales and marketing for 20 years and have been an online marketing and customer service consultant for the past 9 of them. Therefore, this book is about measuring those places where the customer and the company come together:

Advertising: Raise awareness

Marketing: Educate and persuade

Sales: Complete the transaction

Customer Service: Answer questions and solve problems

This is a business book for business people. This book takes a commonsense approach to what *can* be measured and a business perspective about what *should* be measured.

The Catalyst: Why Another Book?

Few practice what they preach. Matt Cutler, cofounder of NetGenesis (purchased in 2002 by SPSS, the 30-year-old business analytics company), preaches what he practices and is a top-notch public speaker. I had heard him present at an Internet World conference in New York back in 1995 and was immediately impressed.

Later, we met up in the speaker's lounge. Jack Powers, Internet World's conference chair and majordomo at the time (and another whose presentation skills I hungrily study), found the two of us talking and congratulated both of us for being tapped for the upcoming Internet World conference in Sydney.

These were Matt's salad days. NetGenesis was only a couple of years old and still a few years from going public. So I was happy to pick up the tab for our dinner at one of those very nice restaurants at The Rocks, overlooking the Circular Cove in Sydney Harbor.

Matt described the purpose of NetGenesis and I was hooked. He was creating software and services that reached into the recorded history of a Web site's activity and shaped the raw data into valuable meaning. Earlier Web log analysis software was out there but hobbled. NetGenesis took off where the others stopped. "Why settle for what you can get out of the logs when there are a bunch of other tools you can put in place to watch what happens on your site?" he asked. "Why not use data from cookies and packet sniffers and transaction servers?"

I was offering advice on how to improve the value of a Web site to those who were spending great gobbets of money floundering around in the primordial TCP/IP soup, and Matt was offering proof, validation, and documentation.

The synergy between us—our mutual enthusiasm, our mutual desire to get to the bottom of this wild, new Web phenomenon, and our mutual commitment to make a difference—led to an immediate personal bond and a periodic working relationship. We would meet at various conferences; I was invited to speak at a number of Net Genesis User Group Meetings, and we stayed in touch via email.

I stayed interested in Web metrics because it was an opportunity to get closer to the truth. It was obvious that mere log file analysis wasn't enough. We were just paving the cow paths. "Listen, we've got paths and we've got asphalt. Let's put them both together and the paths will be significantly better." That may be true, but it only codifies an ad hoc means of getting from point A to point B.

If, instead, we look at where we want to go, we can devise a much better means of getting there. An interstate highway system beats the pants off of interconnected, paved cow paths every time.

At the beginning of 1999, Matt invited me to help write a white paper for his company about e-metrics. "We'll talk to top Web sites and find out what they're measuring and how," Matt said. "We'll tie it all together in a neat 'best practices' package and have something that will be more than just a marketing piece for NetGenesis—it'll be a guidebook for Web sites everywhere." I was intrigued.

Twenty-five interviews with the managers of major Web sites, dozens of phone calls, hundreds of emails, and countless revisions later, we published "E-Metrics: Business Metrics for the New Economy" (available at both www.netgen.com and www.targeting.com).

Bottom line? Everybody was collecting huge volumes of information and nobody had a clue what to do with it. We learned that expectation and reality were not quite on speaking terms.

Jump to 2001. Time to do another round of interviews to see if we'd learned anything. This time, I tackled them on my own and I was no longer interested in a formal study. I wanted to find out how people were *feeling* about Web metrics. How they were *coping* with the problem.

Everybody I interviewed (fifty large companies, running multiple Web sites) was (and still is) begging for more information—not more data, but more usable information. Some of these people had been assigned the task or were self-selected. Some of them were clearly identified as the go-to people for the duty. Their job titles included:

- Head of Strategic Planning, Services, and Programs
- Director, E-marketing and User Experience E-business Systems, Global Business Solutions
- EVP, Chief Marketing Officer
- General Manager, E-business Development
- Manager, Interactive Marketing
- Manager, Online Communications Corporate Brand Office
- Performance Manager, E-business
- Group Vice President, E-business and Internet Operations
- Director of Information Services
- Vice President, E-business
- Senior Manager, E-business
- Director of Digital Marketing
- Vice President, Online Marketing
- Internet Content Manager
- E-commerce Marketing Specialist
- Manager, Measurement and Analysis E-marketing /Corporate Strategy and Marketing Group

I learned a lot from them.

Who Is This Book For?

This book was written by talking to people whose titles look something like the above, but it was written for those who have to testify to the veracity of the value attributed to their Web sites.

Whether you are part of a central Web team, a member of middle management, a corporate executive, or one of dozens of organizations offering services to them, this book is intended to help you understand what's possible to measure, in order to figure out what you should do about it.

This book is for people like Terry Lund at Eastman Kodak, who won't learn much by reading it (he lives and breathes this stuff) but who will benefit greatly by handing it out to those who count on him and his people to keep Kodak.com working well. It will help him improve the services he can offer to the business by enlightening the consumers of those services. Lund knows that it's only through education that he'll be able to really help the company: "I've been kind of poking people a little bit saying we need to figure out a way to assign a value to a visit, or assign a value to a clickstream segment. And my own opinion is that we are too bashful about assigning a dollar sign.

"A few years ago," he says, "we tried something we called a 'value creation model.' We tried to build one and we were embarrassed at the numbers because they were just too big, you know? We were trying to equate it to brand impressions. We were trying to show that you could place a brand value on page views and take credit for it. But no matter how you convert it into dollars—television eyeballs, or print media eyeballs—you go get these numbers and then cut them in half or cut them by a third, and you still have millions and millions of dollars in value."

Lund can't make a business case out of numbers that don't seem real. They won't be believed. So he's been on a quest to find specific metrics that can be easily explained and understood.

This book is for an executive (who will remain unnamed) who said, "Jim, I have a $4 million budget and about twenty direct reports. They're all working their tails off every day and I can't for the life of me figure out if they're working on the right projects. They're all doing what they're told, but who the heck knows what to tell them to do? How the heck do I determine whether more investor relations content is worth more than a new product configuration system? How do I tell if a 20 percent increase in the banner ad budget is going to impact sales?"

This book is for the manager responsible for the success of one product line who is faced with a company Web site run by people who have 5 years of Web experience but no business experience.

This book is for the woman looking to be just a little bit more prepared than the others when it's time to present budgets to the board for approval.

This book is for the Web site design team that just *knows* a new navigation system can improve the site's effectiveness tenfold but needs hard numbers to prove it.

You already know that measuring things is important. This book is intended to help you choose *what* to measure, *how* to measure it, and what action to take based on the results. If you find yourself drawn to the topic but I haven't listed you here, send me an email at jsterne@targeting.com and straighten me out, because this book is for you.

The Web Metrics Continuum

Not every company should or can measure everything. What you measure depends in part on the goals of your Web site and the size of your budget. It also depends on where you are now and where you aspire to be on the Web Metrics Continuum (see Figure 1.3).

No Logs—Flying Blind

"Oh, yeah, I'm sure we have server logs somewhere. I mean, every server makes a log, right? But our customers seem happy—most of them. You know, they tell us if any of the pages are broken, and so far it seems to be working fine."

Occasional Log File Report—Map in Hand, Window Open

"We're getting daily reports that our hosting service sends. It shows . . . let's see . . . oh, here it is. It shows us total hits, total files, total pages, total visits, total kbytes (whatever *that* is), and some other stuff. We take a hard look at these about once a month to see if there's anything going on we should know about."

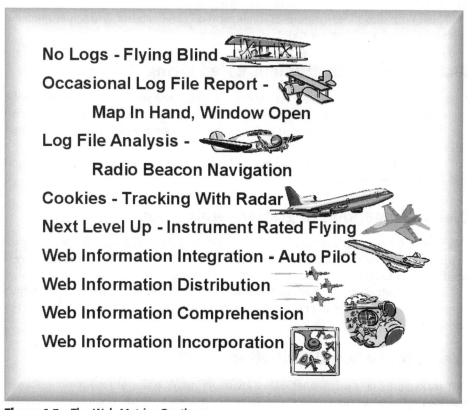

Figure 1.3 The Web Metrics Continuum.

Log File Analysis—Radio Beacon Navigation

"We have our logs crunched and we do a formal review every week. We know that people come to our site more on Mondays and Tuesdays and traffic peaks at about 10:00 A.M. We know which pages are the most popular, and we watch for changes in that sort of traffic when we do special promotions.

"We know which pages people most often use as entry pages, and we know where they leave. We know where they're coming from, although the majority are still coming from AOL, so I don't know how useful that is, really. We know that we get the most traffic from Yahoo! and Google, and which search phrases they're using to find us. But we're *still* trying to figure out why so many find us by searching for 'dancinghamsters.' Weird.

"Once a month, we print out a huge color graph that shows our progress and pin it to the wall where everybody can see it. It's really neat."

Cookies—Tracking with Radar

"We're using cookies to track sessions and do path analysis. We've got a good picture of how people navigate the site differently from one visit to the next. We've got a registration page and determined that sales do, indeed, go up when we welcome people back to the site by name. We know which promotions are bringing in the most visitors and which are bringing in the most repeat visitors.

"Those with direct Web responsibility depend on these reports, and upper management asks about our progress about once a month."

Web Analytics—Instrument Rated Flying

"Using a variety of tools, we're tracking exactly which ads are turning into sales in the short term and which are boosting loyalty in the long run. We know where to spend our time in order to either increase traffic to the site, increase visit duration, increase sales, or lower costs.

"There's an executive committee every 2 weeks that looks over our progress and makes recommendations."

Web Information Integration—Auto Pilot

"We've tied our analytics and e-commerce systems together with our offline order processing and inventory control systems and can clearly forecast how much stock we'll need on hand to meet the needs of various promotions.

"Representatives in our customer service call center/email center can see which pages callers have looked at and can advise them according to their particular level of knowledge."

Web Information Distribution

"We make sure that the information we glean off our Web site and from our customer relationship management systems is disbursed throughout the organization. Executives and managers have access to near real-time numbers about what's happening on our site."

Web Information Comprehension

"We have mandatory weekly meetings to ensure that the data we send out is fully understood and becomes part of the decision-making process. These numbers are good, but only if the people making decisions on a daily basis can fathom them.

"We also get feedback from the Executive Web Team about the changes they see in sales and customer satisfaction. Our compensation is tied to these reports, so we have them audited once a quarter by an outside firm."

Web Information Incorporation

"It's a completely closed-loop system. We used to control the whole Web site—the content, the look and feel, the online store—all of it. Now, we're responsible for carrying out the work orders from the business unit managers who are responsible for profit and loss.

"They have their fingers on the pulse of our site, our catalogue sales, and our store sales, and they can tell in an instant if a new product line, promotional campaign, or product photograph is dong what it's supposed to do. We're here to help them."

What Do You Measure?

With so much data available from Web servers, what's the most important thing to measure? The most important metric is that which helps improve your site. But what improves one site does not necessarily improve all sites.

Web Site Deconstruction: Measuring Bit by Bit

"The primary role of traditional measurement systems . . . is to pull 'good information' up so that senior managers can make 'good decisions' that flow down. To that end, each relatively independent function has its own set of measures, whose main purpose is to inform top managers about its activities."
Christopher Meyer, "How the Right Measures Help Teams Excel,"
Harvard Business Review, May–June 1994

That's the role of *traditional* measurement systems. Here are Meyer's first two guiding principles and I agree wholeheartedly:

1. **The overarching purpose of a measurement system should be to help a team, rather than top managers, gauge its progress.** If you work with metrics that help you do your job better, then the results can be rolled up into management reports that will help executives steer the supertanker. When management starts asking for reports that have nothing to do with the team's goals and objectives, things start getting wonky.

2. **A truly empowered team must play the lead role in designing its own measurement system. Let upper management set the goals for the company.** Each department must set its own goals that will help the corporation move in the right direction. In other words, you should pick up a copy of this book for each Web team you have.

Different Expectations for Different Sites

Yahoo! is a portal. It's also a directory, a free email service, a news outlet, a weather station, a shopping center, and, well, a portal. Their sole purpose in life is to get more and more people to click on more and more internal links so they can show more and more advertisements and earn more and more advertising revenue. Simple. So what do they measure? People and pages.

Companies that have based their business models on Web-based advertising are finding it rough going. It turns out that running an ad-supported Web site is a lot like running a controlled-subscription magazine. You've got to constantly be remodeling your site to cater to the fickle whims of the surfing public. Tricky.

If you're running an e-commerce site such as Amazon.com, your goals are a bit different. More people is nice, but more sales is what it's all about.

The majority of small businesses have marketing-only Web sites. Miller Manufacturing (see Figure 1.4) sells the Silent Servant dumbwaiter (www.silentservant.com). It's not available in stores. It's not available online. But you can get one if you call them on the phone.

The Silent Servant Web site is perfectly serviceable for its purpose. There's a persuasive description of how manual dumbwaiters have been used for years to carry household items up from and down to the ground floor. They are a major convenience for the transportation of groceries, laundry, firewood, and seasonally used items you'd rather store when they're not needed. Miller Manufacturing offers advice on how to choose the correct dumbwaiter for your needs and divulges complete specifications, dimensions, and detailed schematics for each model. You can request more information from the company. You can call their 800 number and get one for yourself.

What does Miller Manufacturing measure to determine the success of this site? Leads. They want to know how many people called them up to talk to a sales rep. They want to know if the Web is working better than newspaper ads or direct mail for getting the attention of the right prospects.

What you measure depends on your goals.

Where Do You Start?

Marketing marvel Kristin Zhivago (www.zhivago.com) asked me something very similar in an interview for her *Marketing Technology* newsletter (August 2001): "Let's assume that I want to get into this metrics stuff. What choices do I have? Where do I start? What would happen to me after I started down the road?"

I answered with the following map.

Step One: Self-Assessment

Where are we at the moment? What tools do we have? What expertise do we have? What level of commitment do we have from upstairs?

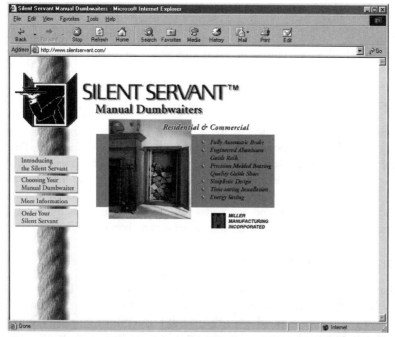

Figure 1.4   You can learn about Silent Servants online, but they won't sell you one.

Step Two: The Vision Thing

Where do we want to be in 5 years? Yes, I know it's the Internet and everything changes at a moment's notice, but give it a try. Look over the horizon and imagine a better future. With a destination in mind, you'll be wary of creating new projects that take you further away from the Big Picture.

Step Three: The Numbers You Need

What do you *really* need to know? Measuring everything isn't a good idea just because you can. You don't need to know the temperature of the windshield washing liquid in your car, but the oil pressure is pretty important.

Step Four: Low-Hanging Fruit

What are the three or four metrics that, if you had them today, would only take one small step for a programmer and end up as one giant leap for business kind? (*And* won't take you further away from the Big Picture?)

Step Five: Prioritize

A gas gauge is more important than an oil pressure gauge and the oil thermometer is much more important than a tachometer. Work out a plan of attack based on your priorities.

Step Six: Find the Money

The Web team should not have to fund e-metrics projects except for those things for which the Web team is directly responsible: server performance, network load, uptime stats—that's their bailiwick. Everything else belongs to the different business units. If HR wants to know how many people looked at a given job offer, it's up to them to pay for the privilege. If marketing wants to know about the cost of eyeball acquisition, then they can pony up for the reports. In time, the Web team develops cross-discipline tools that lower the cost and lessen the time it takes to eke out and deliver useful information.

Step Seven: The Master Plan

Now that you have a couple of wins in your pocket, take a look over the landscape of data systems, Web servers, and applications, and map out a master plan. Which Web sites should be torn down and recoded from the ground up? Which only need a few patches? How are you going to tie your legacy systems into the customer-facing applications? How are you going to retrofit all of your number-crunching capability so that you can actually tell what your company is doing, and what that means?

I didn't say that any of this stuff was going to be easy. But it *is* important.

How This Book Is Organized

Chances are excellent that your goals are not as voluminous as the metrics covered in this tome, so take a look to see which chapters cover your situation.

Ways to Measure

The fundamentals never go away. When all is said and done, you want to know if your Web site was worth the effort. Did it provide a decent return on investment?

Chapter 2, "Measuring Measurement," looks at what we're trying to accomplish with an understanding that we're going to have to communicate our Web findings with those who hear the word *metrics* and think of return on investment, return on assets, and return on equity. So this chapter is a bridge from their world to the world of servers and page views, and how we make the leap from one to the other.

How to Get Funding

Chapter 3, "Raising the Flag, Convincing the Boss," is an exploration of what you need to say and do to get the additional people, equipment, and software you'll need to take your Web metrics efforts to the next level.

Ed Yourdon, editor of *Cutter IT Journal* and a software maven from way back, likes to tell the story of a large project kickoff meeting. As people are getting settled around the table, one of the attendees asks, "Before we dive down into the technical details, is there a way to measure how we'll know if the project is a success?" There's a slight pause while everybody looks at each other. "In fact," he continues, "do we even know *who* is allowed to declare this project a success?" They realized that nobody could say the project was a winner, but any of three top executives could pull the plug for a wide variety of reasons. How the project got approved in the first place is a tale of political intrigue and favor mongering.

The people who hold the power of thumbs up or thumbs down, of life and death, are people who like numbers. They feel secure with finite calculations and specific outcomes. This aversion to making decisions based on gut feel is a point well made by Joel Maloff, executive vice president for Fusion Telecommunications International, in his lecture, "Getting Top Management to Sign Off on Internet" (see Figure 1.5).

When approaching the executive budget committee, speak in terms of money made and money saved before you try to intrigue them with visions of a 360-degree view of your customers.

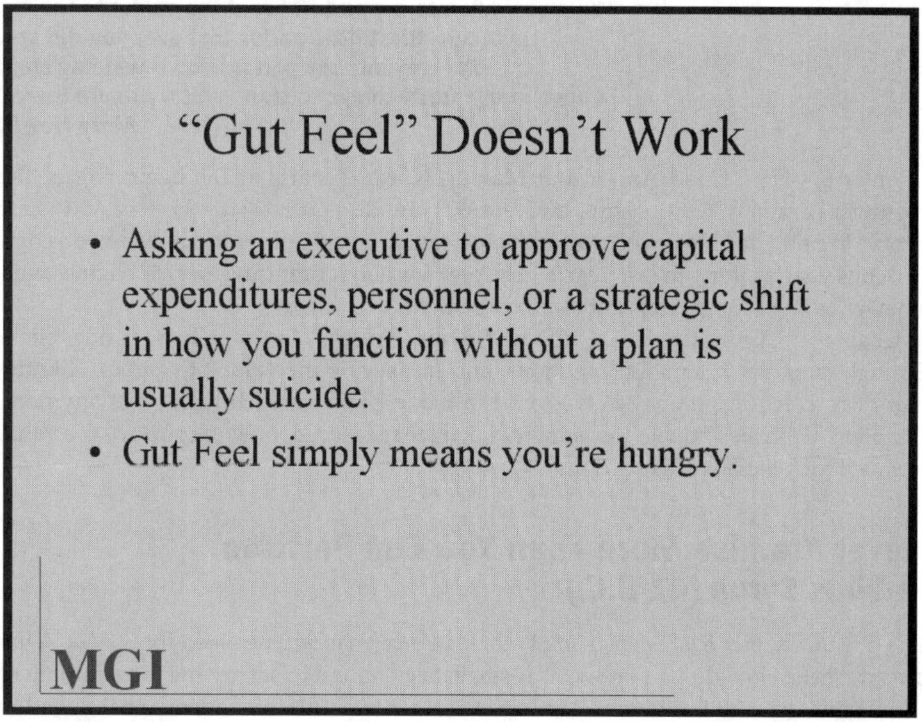

"Gut Feel" Doesn't Work

- Asking an executive to approve capital expenditures, personnel, or a strategic shift in how you function without a plan is usually suicide.
- Gut Feel simply means you're hungry.

MGI

Figure 1.5   Maloff has been instrumental in helping many managers get funding for their Internet initiatives.

Setting the Standard

Benchmarking is a fine old tradition, and Web sites are a fine new phenomenon. While the prospect of a standard set of predefined Web site attributes is still out of reach, there is some progress being made and it's important to know what the first steps look like. That's what Chapter 4, "Web Measurement Standards," is for.

Log Files: Love 'Em or Hate 'Em

Whole books have been written about log files and, unless you're directly responsible for rolling those log files into meaningful reports or have a penchant toward the technically arcane, those books are great for helping you sleep.

Chapter 5, "Sawing Logs," is the requisite rudimentary look at log files. What are they? What do they contain? It's about how server logs were never intended to be the font of all Web wisdom and how to work with and around them. Again, this is not a technical book. The information in this chapter will give you the information you need to communicate effectively with those who manage the log files and generate the reports.

Step into My Parlor

"Will you walk into my parlor?" said the spider to the fly;
"'Tis the prettiest little parlor that ever you did spy.
The way into my parlor is up a winding stair,
And I have many pretty things to show when you are there."
Mary Howitt

Chapter 6, "How Good Are You at Making Noise?," starts at the beginning of the customer-company relationship: awareness. How do you measure how easy it is for people to find you? How well do you manage your brand online and how do you compare this year's efforts to last year's? Chapter 6 is about branding, search engines, and a newer online concern: reputation management.

Chapter 7, "How Good Are You at Buying Noise?," looks at banner ads, click-through rates, reach, email promotions, and measuring the value of visitors. "I know half my advertising money is wasted, I just don't know which half." Not anymore. Chapter 7 describes how to measure it and, once measured, how to improve the value received for your advertising dollar.

Never Promise More Than You Can Perform: Publius Syrus (42 B.C.)

The title of Chapter 8 is "Measuring Web Site Performance: The Need for Speed." That puts it nicely. How do you know your site is fast enough to satisfy the most impatient site visitor on a 28.8 modem? You need three things: the awareness that speed is important, an understanding of the various ways to measure your site, and the ability to discuss that importance with the variety of organizations within your company that slow your site down, whether they know it or not.

Speed is a critical factor in online customer satisfaction. It's one thing to know it, and another to keep your eye on it.

Content Conundrum

Every Web site is different, yet they all contain content. Do you know the value of the content on your site? Can you easily evaluate whether you should add more product specification pages or flesh out the description of your return policy? Should another article about your CEO take precedence over updating your calendar-of-events page? How do you tell if the content you have is any good?

Chapter 9, "Calculating the Caliber of Content," feels your pain and explains various ways to go about totting up the value of content on your site.

Helping Visitors Blaze a Trail

You know most Web sites are hard to get around. You know most Web site designers spent too much time in art school and too little time in software functionality class. But you're so close to your own site, you know the structure and the layout so well, how on earth do you go about improving it? You measure.

Chapter 10, "Well-Marked Trails: Measuring Web Site Navigation," looks at home pages, landing pages, and multiple browsers, and then dips into the world of human perception, both visual and cognitive. What *is* the optimal path on your site? When is stickiness a no-no? How do you calculate a migration rate and determine visitor focus? How do you judge the output of a usability study? What can you glean from the way visitors use your on-site search engine?

Making the Sale

Unless your site is intended to get votes, start a revolution, convert heathens, or simply sit there and look pretty, chances are excellent that you're online in order to sell stuff.

Tracking how much stuff you sell isn't the issue—you do that as a matter of course. The question is: What should you measure in order to sell more stuff? Recency, frequency, navigation, seducible moments, abandonment, and what you can learn from peering into peoples' shopping carts—it's all in Chapter 11, "Calculating Conversion."

Getting Personal

Since I tripped over the Internet in 1994, I've been intrigued by the fact that Web sites run on computers and computers can remember everything. Therefore, they should be able to remember who I am, what I usually buy, and then some. But how do you get the most out of personalization systems? They're not cheap and they're not easy. So what's the payback?

Chapter 12, "Maximizing Customer Information: The Personalization Continuum," walks through the numerous levels of personalization from segmentation all the way through customer relationship management (CRM). There's a great deal of attention paid to retention, loyalty, and customer lifetime value. This is the area where the Web is truly unique, but is still quite mysterious in terms of measuring value and success.

Customer Self-Service and Beyond

What a great idea! Customers can just bloody well take care of themselves, thank you very much. We won't have to answer the phone or anything. We'll just let 'em go to the frequently asked questions page on our Web site and be done with it!

Cost avoidance isn't a bad goal, as long as it's not your sole means of patting yourself on the back. Chapter 13, "Measuring the Value of Online Customer Service," certainly looks at measuring the cost reductions you can enjoy by way of an FAQ, a knowledge base, a chatterbot, and more, but it also focuses on measuring the value of your person-to-person online interactions. Even further, it looks at the value of having your customers talk directly to one another and how to measure who's doing a good job of it.

Chapter 13 then delves into the fine art of measuring customer satisfaction. The Web offers an inexpensive way to gather information directly from customers. Because new technologies are springing up all the time, there are many different ways to go about opinion gathering, and doing it well has a significant impact on getting accurate and useful input.

Life in the Real World

Throughout this book, you'll find quotes from a great many of the corporations I interviewed—a comment here, a wise warning there, an anguished cry of frustration everywhere else. But Chapter 14, "Field Studies," is a tale of two corporations. I start off the chapter explaining that these are not formal case studies but more documentary looks at two firms with different levels of success.

The first is a large company with lots of divisions, lots of Web sites, lots of Web metrics, and lots of headaches. This company (which shall remain nameless) experiences many of the common problems encountered by so many of those I spoke with. They are truly representative of the majority of companies that care but can't quite get their act together.

They are filled with good intentions. They are serious about doing a good job. They are willing to assign resources to get the job done. But for all their effort, they are falling woefully behind. Their problems may simply be due to their size, but they act as an excellent cautionary tale. Read and be warned.

The flip side of the coin is Compaq. Compaq is doing so many things right that they are a wonderful example of what's possible. Given a clear set of goals and a serious, focused effort to accomplish them, Compaq may not be perfect, they do not make the right decisions at every turn and, most interesting, they are not using any secret software, special equipment, or witchcraft to make things happen. In other words: This Could Be You.

The Big Finish

The last chapter of a book like this is supposed to be a summary, a reminder of all that's come before, and there's a *little* of that in Chapter 15, "Making It Work by Bringing It All Together." For the most part, however, this chapter contains some warnings that didn't belong elsewhere in the book, some additional opportunities for Web site measurement from the outside, and a cosmic lament about the difficulties we face as we strive toward what is *going* to be possible.

I'm still enthralled by the dream of a three-dimensional, 360-degree view of each and every customer. The Web has turned dream to hope. As we get closer and closer to that hope becoming a reality, we discover just how hard it will be to achieve.

Measuring Measurement

When Matt Cutler stands before an audience of technical and marketing professionals who are there to learn about the company's innovative Web analytics tools and services, he makes them uneasy right off the bat. People are intrigued at first by his jet-black hair caught up in a neat ponytail and signature goatee framing a mischievous grin, heightened by the intelligent twinkle in his eyes. Then he hits them with, "Am I tall or short?"

The audience immediately becomes uncomfortable. The answer is painfully obvious. Since Randy Newman isn't in the room, silence reigns. Matt lets the self-consciousness grow for a bit.

Finally, he says, "I'm 5-foot-6." A pause. "Is that tall or short?"

Somebody, usually in the back of the room, will finally break the ice and verbally admit that Matt is, indeed, short. Matt invariably responds with a smile. "Yes! I'm short! But 5-foot-6 is a measurement. By itself it means nothing. It's just a number. Whether or not I'm short is a matter of circumstance, isn't it?

"I recently spent a couple of weeks in Japan," he tells them, "and I can't tell you how unique it was to stand in the middle of the subway and look out over the tops of all the heads. But I was *still* 5-foot-6.

"Five-six is a measurement. Short or tall is a metric; it only has meaning in comparison with other numbers."

You say you got a million page views yesterday. Is that good or bad? That depends on how many page views you got the day before. In fact, it's much more complicated than that. Sometimes, a lot of page views can be a sign of faulty navigation.

Measurement is a tricky business, so let's get it into perspective before we try to tackle the relationships between page views, sessions, and customer loyalty.

Income and Expense: The Usual Suspects

Since you can measure absolutely anything, measuring the right things is what matters. In business, we can fall back on Generally Accepted Accounting Principals. These are the methods used to help us gauge our corporate progress and compare it to our past, to the competition, and to industry benchmarks. So let's just get as high-level as we can and take it from there.

What matters the most in business?

Profits.

Sometimes stating the obvious is so grounding.

Tot up how much comes in and subtract how much goes out. Revenues and costs are the two most important things you can measure. They are the final tally of any business, the magic bottom line.

Of course, figuring out the value of your company is another matter. Fixed assets, market capitalization, and price-to-earnings ratios are very useful, but whether you should hang onto your assets, whether your company share price goes up or down, and whether that price is where it should be depends a lot on whether you're making or losing money. Yes, the dot coms tried ditching that idea for a while in the late 1990s, but we've come back to our senses.

Your task is to figure out which processes impact revenues and costs so you can manipulate them in favor of higher profits. Is your cash flow healthy enough to take advantage of opportunities and protect you from adversity? Does your inventory turn over fast enough to mitigate the cost of storing it and the time-value of the money locked up in ownership? Are you retaining your customers and building your base or suffering from client churn?

If you track your share of the market, the growth of your industry, the ratio between the value of booked orders and open invoices, you can get a feel for whether the changes made in the running of your company are helping or hurting. Calculating the amount of revenue you generate per employee and per customer helps you compare your firm to others across the board.

The only drawback to all the possible things to measure is that there are so many of them.

A Wealth of Measurement Methods

There's no end to the things you can measure. Studies can correlate employee punctuality to manufacturing output, press release flamboyance to investor turnover, and frequency of at-desk massages (remember those?) to grammatical errors per email. So let's start simple and start with the Four R's: ROI, ROA, ROE, and ORI.

Return on Investment (ROI)

I first heard the words return on investment when I opened an account at Palo Alto Savings with a $25 birthday fortune received from my grandmother. I'd never seen so much money before and felt the bank was the best place to keep it. To my mind, it was just like my piggy bank at home, except it would be much tougher to sneak out a nickel for a candy bar without my parents knowing about it.

The woman behind the counter explained that I could get a better ROI if I was willing to let the bank hang onto my money for a longer time. Do you want your money anytime? You'll get a smaller return on investment. Let the bank play with it a while longer; they'll give you more back. That made sense, even to a 7-year-old.

Return on Assets (ROA)

Return on assets didn't make sense to me until I was 10 years old and set up a lemonade stand on the street corner. I grabbed an old card table and a couple of lawn chairs. I used the honest-to-goodness Kool-Aid pitcher with the smiley face on it. I picked lemons from the backyard and bought (no freebies on this one) 1 pound of sugar. Total investment: 53 cents. So at the end of the day, I was very proud of the $1.22 I had in my hand. That would buy a delightfully unhealthy number of candy bars. I was delighted.

When Rich from across the street (he was 13 years of age) offered to buy my stand the next day for $2, I thought I'd struck it, well, rich. I'd have to work more than 2 days in a row for that! All on a meager investment of 53 cents. That seemed like a great return.

Fortunately, Doug , my older brother, was on hand to explain that Rich would then be allowed to keep the table, the chairs, and our favorite Kool-Aid pitcher. The furniture and the pitcher were my assets. I didn't have to pay for them. I didn't have to buy them every day. But they would belong to Rich after I took his $2.

Not only that, my natural-marketing-whiz brother explained, I had built up some recognition in the neighborhood. People who had seen me the day before would remember me and come back the next day. My very first lesson in brand equity. By the time Doug had explained that I was likely to earn even more this day—being Saturday—Rich had lost interest and hustled up a whiffle ball game down the street. He was not the consummate entrepreneur.

Return on Equity (ROE)

The ROE lesson was short and sweet. I had borrowed the 53 cents from my father, making him a primary shareholder in my little enterprise. On Sunday evening, when he asked for payment in full plus the 5 cents interest we had agreed to, I had to admit that all of the equity had found its way down to the corner store with the large candy counter.

Dad was not pleased that I had forgotten about him and explained that the nickel was his return on equity. He had not put any energy into the enterprise, only money. His pre-agreed ROE was now AWOL. Fortunately, Dad consented to payment in unconsumed Nestlé Crunch bars.

Online Relationship Improvement (ORI)

Thirty-six years later, when I was sitting as a member of the board of directors of the Swiss consulting firm Omaco (www.omaco.com), the term online relationship management, or ORI, originated. The firm was working with a large publisher looking to implement a customer relationship management (CRM) system. The publisher wanted to know how much money the company was going to see returned from its investment. We realized that the answer was not to be clearly tabulated in Swiss francs.

As a consulting firm, we wouldn't be able to help until the publisher understood the value was to be realized in terms of goodwill, stronger brand affinity, and higher customer retention. There was also the value of ongoing direct market research to consider. So we created ORI and began to ponder ways to measure it for this particular client.

As you can see, once you get past measuring money in and money out, things get esoteric quickly. So let's start with the simple metrics. The days of depreciating a computer to zero within months or expecting double-your-money-back within weeks are over. I'm also going to stick with the idea that if you get a return on your technology investment within a couple of years, you're doing well.

Measuring the Value of Technology

If you run your own servers, you're going to have to buy them, house them, feed them, and keep caretakers within reach 24 hours a day. If you outsource the care and feeding of your Web server, you've got expenses. Either way, you're going to be playing with the total cost of ownership. Sure, there's hardware, software, personnel, and electricity to buy. But there's more: lost productivity when the server goes down; converting to the new systems when that server doesn't come up again; training your people to care and feed the new systems.

In his white paper entitled "Calculating ROI for Business Intelligence Projects" (Base Consulting Group, December 12, 2000, www.baseconsulting.com), Jonathan Wu spelled out how to estimate the cost of implementing a business intelligence project. He felt that cost could be classified into one of three categories: hardware, software, and labor. They are defined as follows:

Hardware costs   relate to the information system devices that are required by the project such as server system(s), client systems, and network communication.

Software costs   include the software applications required by the project such as the business intelligence (BI) application and the Relational Database Management System (RDBMS) license fees.

Labor costs   pertain to the use of internal and external resources dedicated to the project. Individuals working on the BI project fill the following roles: project manager, business analyst(s), BI application specialist(s), database administrator, systems administrator, and trainer(s).

The total cost of implementing a BI project can be divided into two categories— initial and recurring:

Initial costs are those costs an organization incurs for the BI project once. These costs include hardware costs for the project, software license fees, and labor costs to configure and implement the system as well as train users.

Recurring costs are those costs an organization incurs for the BI project that will continue to be incurred after the project has been completed.

Understanding the total cost of implementation is imperative to stay within the organization's budget.

Understanding costs can also help determine the phases of implementing the BI application. An estimate of the cost components of a BI project such as software costs, maintenance or support fees, and average configuration cost can be obtained from external resources such as software vendors/resellers and professional services firms. The estimated cost of implementing a BI application will be used in the ROI calculation.

Be prepared to compute the cost of having a network connection that's too slow once a week. Accept the fact that your revenue projections are going to falter periodically due to completely unforeseeable problems like the weather, the competition, or your whole Web team ordering the same entree at a local, substandard seafood restaurant and being out of commission for 2 days.

You're never going to be able to report back to upper management on the exact ROI of your entire Web site. But if you're good, you can manage a portfolio of Web initiatives over time, something suggested by Robert Scheier in an article in the May/June issue of *Computerworld* (www.computerworld.com/ROI).

Quick riddle: *What's the difference between a 250,000-square-foot warehouse in Singapore, an upgrade to your firm's Web site, and 10,000 shares in Genetech?*
The answer: *Nothing. They're all investments you make after weighing their risks and returns. As conditions change, you buy, sell, or hold the overall rate of return on your risk.*

The question is always the same: How are you going to measure success? If those shares of Genetech go up 9 percent, is that enough? If your Web initiative saves $25,000 per week for 6 weeks, is that considered "successful"? So pick a target and pick a date. Watch how things run and be ready (here's the hard part) to drop the project like a hot rock when it falls below a predetermined threshold of acceptable progress and profit.

In the end, it all boils down to revenues and costs. Yes, improvements in customer satisfaction can increase sales per order, order per customer, and overall income. And increased employee satisfaction can lower the cost of doing business by reducing the costs of recruiting and training. But they both point back to the triple-threat question: How much did you make? What did it cost? What's the difference?

The big difference is that we've been accustomed to following the money since cuneiform was scratched into rocks. We understand, on a very instinctual level, that if I have five apples and you take away two, something very important has happened and we want to record that event for posterity.

On the Web, our knowledge of metrics began with server log (see Chapter 5, "Sawing Logs"). Look at all that data! Is there any information in there?

Web servers were created by programmers, not business analysts. A Web server spits out *massive* amounts of data, and we business types have been trying to make sense of it ever since. Instead, we should have told the programmers what we needed, so they could build the proper information-gathering mechanisms into the servers.

Back when servers were being brought into existence, we didn't have a clue how important our Web sites were going to be. As it stands, businesspeople are tugging on the technicians' sleeves, begging for scraps of relevant knowledge.

With more investment, we can take advantage of more intelligent technology. In the meantime, we can impact the knowledge we glean by carefully constructing our approach to measurement.

Method to the Madness

In his book *Keeping Score* (Quality Resources, 1996), Mark Graham Brown boils down Web metrics to its bare essentials quite well:

- Fewer is Better: Concentrate on measuring the vital few key variables rather than the trivial many.

- Measures should be linked to the factors needed for success: key business drivers.

- Measures should be a mix of past, present, and future to ensure that the organization is concerned with all three perspectives.

- Measures should be based around the needs of customers, shareholders, and other key stakeholders.

- Measures should start at the top and flow down to all levels of employees in the organization.

- Multiple indices can be combined into a single index to give a better overall assessment of performance.

- Measures should be changed or at least adjusted as the environment and your strategy changes.

- Measures need to have targets or goals established that are based on research rather than arbitrary numbers.

In his book, *The Agenda* (Crown Press, 2001) Michael Hammer offers several pieces of management advice. First, measurement should be the responsibility of every manager; don't leave it up to the accounting department. Next, don't hang onto your old metrics just because they exist. Then, map out the links between your overall goals and those things you can actually control, and establish specific targets as your goals. Make sure your measurements are "objective, timely, and easy to understand." Create a disciplined process based on metrics that ensures continuous improvement. Trust the facts and the measurements over opinions and seat-of-the pants intuition.

Hammer's advice is easier said than done. Just finding good, solid business data in the first place is a significant challenge.

Of course, things are a little different on a Web site compared to general business metrics. We have a great deal more data to work with, from page view and click-streams through individual profiles and CRM aggregations. A great deal of your success in this area will depend on whether your site is built to be measured.

Design Your Web Site with Measurement In Mind

There are about a dozen serious sellers of Web-analysis software systems. They educate prospective customers, identify which of their software applications best fit the specific prospect's needs, install said software, and then do their best to make sure their clients get the information they're after. But all vendors tend to run into the same two problems before they're finished: The Web site under scrutinization has been constructed without regard to eventual measurement and the approach to measurement wasn't thoroughly constructed.

Building Better Sites

A simple example of a design more difficult to measure than necessary might be a frequently asked questions (FAQ) document. If there are ten questions and answers on a single page, then you can tell how many times that page was viewed. But if you have a main FAQ page with ten questions that are linked to their respective answer pages, then simply by reading your logs files, you can tell which are your *most* frequently asked questions. As I said—simple.

Can you reengineer a large, existing Web site that's been growing organically for several years across multiple divisions inside recently merged companies? No; don't even think about it. Instead, you can only advise future generations of Web builders to be cognizant of the need to measure as they go about their information architecting.

When a content owner comes up with a new datasheet, when a promotions manager wants to launch a sweepstakes, when a customer service manager wants to implement the latest in simulated virtual humanoid customer interaction, get them all to stop for just a bit and add a few words about success metrics into their proposals. How will they measure success?

Then post those success metrics in plain view of everybody building the site. Have those measurability goals as clear and understandable and ingrained to the site builders as gravity is to cathedral architects. That way they won't try to retrofit gauges into the system; instead, those gauges will be part of the system.

For the meantime, we have to survey and weigh and grade the sites we have at the moment. You can't change the past, so try and have an impact on your future by taking the right steps when creating a Web-measurement process.

Manage Your Approach to Measurement

In their white paper, "Design for Analysis: Delivering the Promise of E-Business Intelligence" (1998), NetGenesis offers an approach for creating a system of measurements. In their terms, "design for analysis" consists of four major phases (see Figure 2.1). The team at NetGenesis defines each of these phases as follows:

Consider site design as a tool for improving e-metric analysis. Creating your site and your reporting systems to be quantifiable requires considerable time and attention.

Determine Your Needs

Scope out the "who, what, and where" of your Web project. Perform a needs assessment with the goals of evaluating your current environment and available resources, determining what actions you want users to take on your Web site, deciding what functionality on the Web site supports the desired action, and clarifying your high-level objectives. This will allow you to chart out the path that will lead to those goals from your current situation. What will you need in the way of people, training, equipment, and software? How much time will it take? What will it cost?

Understand Your Online Customer

Your business metrics are driven by the relevant data you collect and store. They enable you to establish a baseline that will provide context and serve as the foundation on which you build e-business intelligence. Identify the information available in your Web data that you are not yet using to full potential. Utilizing information about site navigation, product interest, and promotional success measurements all leads toward an improved Web experience for your users. Focus on your current inventory of customer knowledge and map out the next level of customer attributes to collect. What information can be collected the fastest—and with the least amount of customer disturbance—that will allow you to provide new customized online services? Work through the collection, normalization, and data application process to ensure a smooth operating environment.

Optimize Your E-Business

Once you have successfully applied customer information back into Web design and content management, your e-business intelligence solution will be producing, with clockwork regularity, baseline business e-metric reports that reflect your core business achievements. With this solid contextual foundation in place, it is time to put the analytical infrastructure to practical use in your tactical business management activities. Apply the e-metric calculations described in the Research Study to create a new set of baseline figures. These are the new numbers to beat. These are the stage-one results that will guide you toward increased income, lowered costs, and higher customer satisfaction.

Quantify Success

A methodology is successful only if it is repeatable and measurable. Make sure your efforts are an iterative process. It is essential to review the methodology itself to ensure that it continues to meet your e-business intelligence needs. Once you have built a solid foundation of long-term e-metrics and have engaged in extensive tactical refinement of your e-business programs, it is time to engage in the process of extracting new business directions from actual customer interaction data. You will be setting new e-metrics standards and creating new e-metrics to measure your future success.

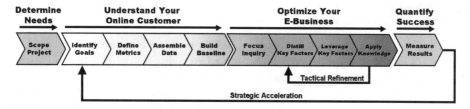

Figure 2.1   NetGenesis's Design for Analysis Framework distributes the e-metrics development process into multiple classifications.

Once you have a handle on why you're measuring, how you're measuring, who is responsible for measuring and how often, all you have to do is figure out *what* to measure.

What, Exactly, Do You Want to Know?

Asking what you want to know is simple, but the answer is elusive. We keep looping back to the chorus: How do you define success? What specific questions are you trying to answer? You might be wanting to find answers to any of the following questions:

Are you attracting new people to your site?

Is your site "sticky"? Which regions are not?

What is the health of your lead qualification process?

How proficient is your conversion of browsers to buyers?

What site navigation do you wish to encourage?

What behavior indicates that a prospect is ready to buy?

How do customer segments differ?

What attributes describe your best customers?

How can they help you target other prospects like them?

How can profiling help you cross-sell and up-sell?

What is your churn rate?

How do you measure loyalty?

Getting a handle on what's important to you is the first step. It's all about setting goals. Be very clear about what you set out to accomplish. This becomes more and more important when you start to consider the challenge of getting your e-metrics projects funded. So start with the goals that matter to the people who have their hands on the purse strings.

Summary

There are many ways to measure your success in running a business. And there are many ways to measure your success in running a Web site. Knowing *how* to measure is almost as important as knowing what you want to measure.

But first, you'll need to get upper management to understand the need for Web metrics and agree on their value. Otherwise, you won't get the necessary funding for the tools and processes you'll need to get the most out of your site. That deserves an entire chapter.

Raising the Flag,
Convincing the Boss

You want to dig deep into the rich vein of ore of your Web site statistics. You want to mine that data for all it's worth. You want to venture into the great data unknown and bring back out untold riches of information, leading to customer knowledge and, thereby, profit enlightenment. Good for you!

Of course, it's going to cost you.

That means explaining yourself to the committee upstairs. Chances are, they know all about restricting resources, bisecting budgets, and pruning projects. They know nothing about Web site management, advertising campaign management, or customer relationship management. Your job, should you decide to accept it, is to teach them.

Hope they've read a little Tom Peters. Trust that some of them have allowed the *Harvard Business Review* into their lives now and then. Pray that the likes of forward thinkers and Web gurus Nicholas Negroponte, Michael Dertouzos, Don Tapscott, and Paul Gilster have appeared on their nightstands at some point in the past. But don't count on it. Count instead on the fact that, from the budget committee members' perspective, you, with your request for Web metrics funding, are yet another beggar, crawling to them on hands and knees with your hand out asking, "Please, Sir. May I have some more?" The answer is always and immediately a resounding "No!" even before they realize that you actually bothered to put on a business suit to make the request.

The question should be rephrased somewhat differently: "How would you like to increase revenues in the flapjack department by 12 percent and lower costs by 23 percent within an 11-week period?" The response is going to be a lot more positive. And it probably also will include a lunch at the club and a key to the executive washroom.

Aligning Web Goals with Corporate Goals

The people occupying the executive suite are looking from the top down. Approach them in terms of revenues, not page views, and operational issues rather than operating systems. Bill Heerman at the electric utility Southern Company understands how to approach the top brass. He says: "I know our CEO isn't really that interested in anything that's 'gee whiz,' He's more interested in how these automated tasks can make us a more profitable organization."

As in all sales situations, figure out what's important to *them*. And *then* go for the bag of gold.

Synchronous Goals

Pam Ingersoll is the director of Digital Marketing at the Niagara Mohawk utility in upstate New York. There, marketing goals are completely in line with corporate directives: *Employ digital marketing as an additional medium to communicate current messages, increase satisfaction, and decrease cost.* She says the plan is working: "We actually do a satisfaction survey quarterly—it's a random survey; it's not just people who've called in—and we see a significant increase in the satisfaction of people who say they have visited our Web site versus [those who] haven't, so that's one [measurement] that we track on a quarterly basis."

When Ingersoll worked with her management team, she made sure not to leave them out of the picture. Another one of her specific goals is to *educate managers and employees in the uses of digital systems and their advantages, and leverage the power of the Internet for enhanced relationships and additional revenue.*

We're not talking about efforts to deploy virtual e-commerce, repurpose viral technologies, facilitate global B2B infomediary communities, or anything else you might come up with at the Web Economy Bullshit Generator (http://www.dack.com/web/bullshit.html). Pam gets the support of her organization because the goals are clear and the progress measurable.

According to Robbie Hudec, director of E-Tizing Strategy and Communications at BellSouth, the southern telecommunications company, they've identified four strategic imperatives for 2001, which were displayed on the wall for all to see: "achieve financial excellence, roll out DSL, get into long distance, and improve service."

It was clear to Hudec that funding for any Web project would depend on clear metrics, including funding for the Web metrics project: "Every Web initiative has measures for success defined as part of the business case development for the project. Each initiative is responsible for tracking to those success measures. The measurements were developed with BellSouth's imperatives and the overall e-tizing success metrics in mind."

Living in the corporate communications side of the house at the chemical giant DuPont, Juan-Francisco "Kiko" Suarez is zeroed in on efficiency:

> I want to be as efficient as I can fulfilling our mission which is to "Protect the DuPont brand and to promote the DuPont brand by increasing the brand's perceived value, contributing to increase business value, and then enhancing the reputation of the company worldwide."

Our first objective is to find more efficient ways to conduct public affairs activities using digital technologies and the Internet. Second is to fulfill the needs of our stakeholders. That means communicating with customers, investors, influencers, and employees via what I call "online self-services." So if there is no self-service, it's not good enough.
And then, last, create leading brand building tools for DuPont. Those are the three main objectives that I have. One is conduct public affairs in a more efficient way, second is build self-services for the stakeholders, and third is build brand-building tools that allow us to increase the value of our brands."

Bend Your Goals to Their Will

Goals like Ingersoll's, Hudec's, and Suarez's are very straightforward. Like mother-hood and apple pie, they're very hard to argue against. But sometimes even the most judicious, most reasonable, most agreeable goals are brushed aside. Why? Because they're not on the menu as one of the goals du jour. Before you go to the executive suite, take a moment to check the wind and test the waters.

The wind is as easy to read as the bright orange sock atop the airport control tower. Just take a look through the last couple of months of internal memos, public speeches, and published interviews. What words come up again and again? What pet phrases are getting the most exposure? Is the fuss all about breaking ground with new research? Is it focused on mergers and acquisitions? Are the bigwigs still banging the drum about cutting costs? Then there's your script.

Only do yourself a favor: Don't quote the sources verbatim. If you play the exact same tune right back to them, their eyes will glaze over. At worst, they'll recognize their own words and your ploy. A better strategy is to restate and rephrase so that the theme is the same but the melody is slightly different. This way, they get to pat themselves on the back for spotting something new that just happens to fit right in with the goals of the Big Cheese the way he or she wants things to run. Well done!

Testing the water requires a bit more courage. Rather than surfing the corporate intranet for opportunities for plagiarism, you need to get right in front of the powers that be on an individual basis and ask for their help.

"Wendy? I just have a quick question. Which of these paragraphs do you think works better?"

"Doug? I'm trying to prioritize between these two initiatives. Which do you think should get top billing?"

Keep it simple. Keep it short. Make sure they see enough of what you're trying to do to understand the implications of their answers. Then, when it's time for the committee to discuss your proposal, several of them will have already had a hand in its development. Nothing like a little pride of ownership to help them steer another little appropriation your way.

Get Real

Joel Maloff has been actively involved in leading-edge telecommunications since 1973. Currently executive vice president for Fusion Telecommunications International, Joel was once vice president, Client Services for Advanced Network & Services (ANS), one of the originators of the commercial Internet, bringing it from the world of education into the world of business—from .edu to .com.

Maloff is one of the few people on the planet who speaks publicly as much or more than I do about Internet business issues. We meet at least biannually at Internet World conferences, sometimes as far away as Hong Kong and New Delhi. While I'm on stage trumpeting the finer points of Web metrics or online marketing and customer service, his perennial audience-pleaser is entitled "Getting Top Management to Sign Off on Internet."

Maloff offers some "Specific Strategies for Getting Top Management to Sign Off" that may seem academic, but we've both seen projects fall into oblivion for lack of prudence. His strategies are straightforward:

- Identify and enlist an executive sponsor; alliances and opened doors are critical.
- Have a clearly articulated message and plan with specific action steps, anticipated results, timetable, investment requirements, and potential benefits.
- Use external experts for credibility where needed.

The best-laid plans don't stop short. The best-laid plans have the details worked into them. "Reduce the cost of customer care" is all well and good, and many executives will simply sign off on the concept. But not most. Most high-level managers got that way by knowing that the devil (or God—you decide) is in the details. Have the details at the ready, if needed.

Setting Specific Goals

Knowing whether you're successful depends on your definition of success—a point that is often missed by many who are in the throes of running a Web site. And clearly, different sites have different goals at different times. Identifying your specific goals is good not just for getting the money but also for ensuring that you have a good idea of what you're trying to accomplish. It's always a prerequisite to success.

Bill Heerman manages Web content in the corporate communication department at Southern Company. For those of you not familiar with this firm, they are ranked at 76 on the 2001 Fortune 500, up from number 153 the year before. They provide electricity to something like 4 million people in, you guessed it, the South. They also dabble in power plants and wireless communications services.

For Bill, the goals are clear. "I mean it's sort of a cliché, the low-hanging fruit for our company is bill payment. Southern Company is a holding company for five major utilities. And we are not in competitive markets, and our business primarily is pricing, service, sign up for service, and pay your bill. We wanted those elements translated to the Web. We want to do a better job of making it work perfectly, but it's pretty good and we're on to the next phase, which is more product-oriented."

Low-hanging fruit became something of a mantra among the e-metrics connoisseurs I spoke with. "No one needs a Web presence," Bill says, and he has a point. "No, there's no value to that. I tell them to look at their routines and ask, 'what is my sales cycle?' This is what we do to get a customer, this is how we contact them, this is how we close the deal, this is what we sell them, this is how much money we make. Lay that out and then look at ways to automate that process. Are there places in there where you could take out intermediaries? Can you do things without people? Can you move people to a different place where they might be more effective?" But he doesn't stop there.

"How can the Web take the pressure off you in order to move through that sales cycle? Depending on the product, it can impact in different places. In some cases it's just simply the payment of the bill. In some places it's the qualification of the lead. And every different part of our business is different. We sell generation capability to large companies and we sell surge protection to residents. It's much different.

"You are not going to be able to close the deal when you're selling power plant output to a bottling factory, because they're going to need more information and there's going to be more personal involvement. But that doesn't mean there's not any point in there where you couldn't use the Web, because at some point in their actual energy consumption certain bells and whistles go off that automatically notify us that it's time for another phone call or another meeting."

While Southern is pumping electricity into the Southeast, Pinnacle is doing the same thing into the Southwest, specifically through their subsidiary, Pinnacle West. Kim Sweeny describes herself as "sort of the Web mistress" for APS and she also focused on one, clear aim: "The goal was, move transactions to the Web site. We redesigned the site to do just that and we have accomplished it. Our numbers reflect that. We try not to let every Tom, Dick, and Harry who has a content suggestion get in the way. And it's really hard when you have a limited amount of real estate to say to the people who are promoting safety, for instance. You know, it's really important that we tell customers about safety but that is not the current goal of this Web site. It's moving transactions. So, I'm sorry, but I can't put that on the home page." Don't worry, Kim has a velvet glove as well.

Sue Fullman is the corporate vice president/director of Motorola DIRECT, the part of the company that sells mobile phones off its Web site. She clearly identifies the group's objectives: "Basically there are five different things we measure. Conversion rate would be the first and that's probably one of the most sensitive in terms of drivers. Second is number of unique visitors. Third is proportion of repeat customers. Then number of orders per year, per customer. And then the ratio of repeat order revenue to first-time order revenue and the average order. And those are the ones that we're honing down to, to give us the answer in terms of how are we doing."

But what are your goals if you're selling crayons?

Binney & Smith is the wholly owned subsidiary of Hallmark Cards that you've never heard of. But you certainly know their products: Crayola and Silly Putty (see Figure 3.1). Gregg Dixon is the vice president of Internet Services at Binney & Smith, which puts him high enough up the chain to be a goal setter on both sides of the fence, Internet *and* corporate. Gregg has a laserlike focus on what he wants the Web to do for him. "Stated very simply, our strategy is to increase the consumption of our core products by having a presence online and encouraging consumers to do more arts-and-crafts activities."

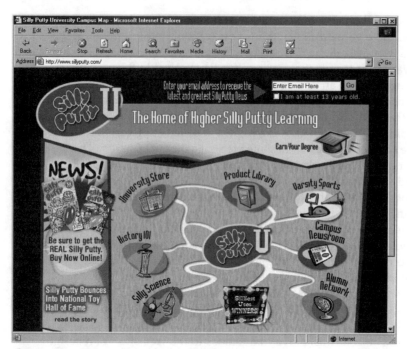

Figure 3.1 Binney & Smith decided that getting people to use Silly Putty more would result in more sales.

It sounds simple, but, says Gregg, "There are many factors to that strategy. It is not necessarily about online sales or advertising, and sponsorships. The fundamental reason we are online is because we believe that if we put good content in front of people, they will do the activity more and we will benefit from our highly profitable core business."

This is the same philosophy Lego adopted when they went online years ago: Create fun stuff for people to do and they will do more and buy more stuff to do it with. Lego even went so far as to look the other way when their Mindstorms Lego control software was hacked. What the heck—let the kids be creative—it'll sell more Legos.

Gregg knows the folks at Hallmark care about value: "They care about how much revenue we have generated both directly and indirectly as well as efficiencies that we create by doing things digitally. Our strategy has always been directly tied to our corporate strategy. We knew that if it was simply going to be Internet for technology's sake or Internet as a direct revenue or profit generation machine in and of itself, it wouldn't be something that we would be interested in. We had to recognize that there were many values from the Internet. Stuff like cost savings and communicating to customers and communicating to consumers.

"We have this motto: 'Think big, test small, and scale up.'"

These people know where they're headed.

What's the ROI of Measuring ROI?

Even with hardware getting cheaper and analytic software becoming more prevalent, there comes a point of diminishing returns when your returns are being measured. If your Web site is generating 2 gigabytes of server and transaction logs every day and you need machines twice the size of the servers to keep up with the analysis of that data, at some point you have to throw up your hands and say, "Either give me another number cruncher or stop asking for new reports!"

Motorola ran a spreadsheet last year that resulted in a cost of $120 per person to analyze sufficient detail to satisfy upper management. That might have been fine if they were looking at prospects considering the purchase of satellite and broadcast network systems. Unfortunately, this was the mobile phone division. "It was obvious that the economics were not aligned with our business," one spokesperson told me.

The problem is one of desire versus ability. If I promised to tell you what percentage of products get put in the shopping cart but never purchased and which ones they are, you'd be thrilled—until I told you it was going to cost a quarter of a million dollars. Each month.

Sampling is the solution of choice for a great many large Web sites. Take a picture every now and then rather than making a movie all day long. Track a handful of people as they wander through the site, rather than track each and every individual. This is an area of keen frustration for marketers and analysts alike. The promise of the Web was to get to that one-to-one relationship—to be able to keep tabs on people on an individual basis.

So how do you make the determination of which data is worth saving and which calculations are worth running? Kris Carpenter, vice president of Excite Products and Services at Excite, got creative. When dealing with a Web site that attracts so many people every day (15 million per month, according to Nielsen//NetRatings), creativity is a must.

"Well, what we've actually done," Kris explained, "is sort of twofold. We have the core data that gets archived and then often stored, not necessarily in a live database but in various archived formats that we can go back in and do time-based analysis against, if it makes sense. For specific products, where we have additional data products, we just need to understand some fundamental trends.

"For example, with the search engine, you don't want to know every query that's ever been performed, but to understand the top thousand queries. How is that changing in terms of frequency? What types of categories are consumers looking for most frequently? So that you can do the best job possible of delivering the right body of information in that database.

"So, that kind of information we end up archiving on a by-product basis because we also correlate it back to things like advertising inventory or consumer demand for specific subject."

I picture what used to be called the smoke-filled room, with executive types sitting around, scratching their heads, saying, "You know, folks, it would be really interesting to find out if . . ." and dream up some correlation between subject matter, frequency, recency, and so on. At the other end of the table, the IT representative says, "Yeah, but that would cost us $2 million to run the data, and what's the value of that kind of a calculation?"

Excite runs through an ROI business requirement analysis each time a new Web initiative is proposed. Kris describes it this way: "Every quarter there's a review of specific research we create, partnering with a third party like a Harris or a Jupiter or a Nielsen. We have specific budget allocated for those things. Every project is then evaluated based on the ROI. The same thing occurs for internal reporting. We make a case that says we need to have this type of data warehousing in place, we need to have everybody in the business be able to access and look at trends, and understand them."

One of the things that has come out of that approach to investment analysis is something Excite calls "cow pathing," their term for clickstream analysis. But we'll get to that in Chapter 9, "Measuring Web Site Performance."

If you find yourself dealing with a ragtag group of big-band leaders who are marching to the beats of conflicting goals, do not despair. There is a tune you can play that will be music to their ears no matter what their personal predilections. Even if they cannot fathom the Web and it's potential enlightenment, they will understand the words "Economies of Scale."

Appeal to Their Wallets: Centralization

If the executive committee you must face is simply too disjointed or too lofty to understand or vote for *your* goals, then revert to a goal they can all share. Your company isn't going to have a clue about which Web projects are really paying off unless and until there is a common way to measure them. A common gauge for Web initiatives generally requires some form of central control.

Critical mass is required to garner the benefits, of course. The larger the company, the bigger the benefits, and the benefits of central Web management are many.

At this point your executive committee would be nodding their heads. This sounds reasonable. Centralizing Web services makes sense for most large firms, and measuring *that* does not require an advanced degree in higher mathematics. Still, some will want to debate the issue.

Centralization and Economies of Scale

I was all set to pick a fight with the cowardly Anonymous who had written an article in the September 15, 2001, issue of *CIO Magazine* (www.cio.com) about the hopelessness of centralization. In it, he or she wrote:

> It is true that in the hands of an exceptionally skilled CIO, operating within a highly autocratic headquarters structure and servicing a mature business in a mature industry, highly centralized structure works well enough. And a Yugo will get you to work in the morning.
>
> Centrally managed IT (information technology) organizations are a holdover (or return to) a far less user-centric and, frankly, far easier time when all processing power in a company resided in the data center and the devices on desks were as dumb as a sack of rocks.

Centralizing IT in this era of distributed capabilities is a mistake justified by, among other things, the unsubstantiated notion that it is less expensive. The pressure to recentralize functions in this slow economy as a means to eliminate redundancy is absolute nonsense, at least in the case of IT, because for every dollar saved, $2 will be spent (secretly) in uncoordinated, non-standard, unstoppable IT efforts in the field.

Slap a handkerchief on my head and call me Gumby, I simply couldn't figure out how to make a centralized model work.

Okay, Gumby, let me find a handkerchief. First of all, we're not really fighting eye-to-eye, since you're going on about IT as a whole and I'm focused on all things Webbish. There are *some* things that should be handed over to the business units—the content owners, if you will—and some things that can clearly enjoy an economy of scale. But to just say that everybody should be in charge of their own fiefdom is fiscally foolhardy.

To one extent or another, I broke the department into pieces and gave them away, budget and all, to the division and department heads they were servicing . . . . The department head and his team were responsible for chattering projects, establishing priorities and levels of investment, and overseeing functional requirements and implementation—the "what" of the systems development and support process. I, on the other hand, owned the "how" — how it would be developed, using which tools and which standards, and how it would integrate with other systems.

Well, hell's bells, Gumby, why didn't you say that in the first place?

Gumby is trying to right an old wrong and I'm trying to right a new one. Between the two of us we agree mightily. Gumby describes the old problem well enough—that a central team of programmers cannot adequately know enough about the operations of all the arms of the octopus to properly encode those processes into software applications. Fair enough. But in larger companies, the Web did not start out as a centrally controlled project that all and sundry needed to try and roll out of the data center. Web sites started out as skunk works undertakings after hours when nobody was looking—in multiple places at the same time—all inventing different solutions to the same problems.

The glory of the Web at its inception became the bane of almost every corporate Web manager. The Web started off below the radar, and everybody who created their own Web site had complete control and autonomy. A few were lucky. Some companies have one purpose in life instead of many.

An airline, for example, is out to put people on airplanes. That's it. No, it's not easy, but it's easier than a company that makes communications systems, mobile phones, cable modems, pagers, power conversion components, global positioning systems, emergency dispatch systems, automotive engine test software, customer service request management systems, and simultaneous streaming audio services.

That's what Sue Fullman found out when she went to work at Motorola. I asked her how many Web sites and servers Motorola had across their various business units and departments.

"You really don't want to know that," was her instant reaction. "That was the biggest shock to me coming from United Airlines where we did it from scratch, one site, and cleanly too. Here [at Motorola], I would say in Europe alone they have eighteen consumer sites and Asia, they have fifty, I believe. I could definitely have over a thousand. We're in the process of massive consolidation. We've finally got everybody to focus on it and we're getting each of the regions to shut them down."

I asked Sue if there was a central, core Web team.

"Yes. It's like an e-business group. There are five different sectors, but I would say three are pretty much driving it and basically have started the first stages of consolidating the back end so you have the same security, you know, all the same architecture being integrated, you have the content publishing being consolidated, you have a common look and feel. So, all the pieces are coming together."

It was a Herculean effort that was tantamount to rolling back the hands of time.

Centralization: Forward, into the Past

Centralization was a given in the 1960s and 1970s, when owning a computer meant having a room to house it in, a team of white-lab-coated systems engineers to run it, and an excellent relationship with your banker—to the tune of millions of dollars.

In the 1980s, minicomputers broke out of the glassed-in data center and found their way into divisional headquarters. By the late 1980s, workstations could shoulder a great deal of local processing responsibility, and in the early 1990s, a PC was powerful enough to run a small department. Distributed computing was off at a gallop and never looked back.

By the time the Web showed up as a commercially accessible and viable tool in 1994, everybody was running their own show—and soon, their own Web server.

David Wright is the Web site director at Unisys, another company that sells more different kinds of products than you can count on both hands and both feet. He faced the same Web site proliferation challenge as Sue at Motorola.

Says Wright: "Everybody was doing their own thing. It was a toy, and the engineers—particularly computer engineers in our company—just thought this was the neatest thing and they could show their creativity, their individuality. Unfortunately, it didn't do Unisys much good."

They let a thousand flowers bloom and everybody got hay fever. But Unisys recognized and started rectifying the problem way back in late 1995.

"It probably took a year and a half to two years to get it all under control around the world," continued Wright. "It was fairly easy to do with the big stuff, you know, especially the things that were hosted on the servers that were locally controlled. The ones that were under people's desks and in numerous countries were a little harder to ferret out."

The Ability to Centralize

With so much computing power available to so many, why push for central control now? Because it's possible.

Throughout the distributed computing era, there was always a desire to connect up with the mainframe. Minicomputers were tied to the mainframe to update the corporate general ledger. PCs were hooked up to access corporate databases and act as the front end to corporate applications. But getting these disparate systems to speak the same language was always hard work. Controlling a PC from a mainframe was tough, and the payback was insufficient in most cases.

Today, the Web is the glue that ties all systems together. A Web browser on any machine, large or small, can access the data and applications on any server. We now have the opportunity to take advantage of centralization—if we do it carefully.

Gumby has a point.

The Trouble with Centralization

Cost is the major theme here, but politics are the hammer blow to making a centrally organized structure work properly. As Gumby put it:

> Centralizing IT is a "teamwork is a lot of people doing what I say" approach to managing resources and priorities. . . . The distrust and frustration of users in the field who are too far removed to participate in or even understand how or why development and support decisions are being made will, in the end, derail the best laid strategic plans and intentions . . . . Nameless, faceless IT people in far-off places make for ready-made villains and highly useful scapegoats when things don't go as planned.

A walk in the park? No. What's the solution? Knowing what to control from the center and what to leave in the hands of those at the edge. You control the *how* and let the content owners control the *what*. They'll decide what to say about their products, what services to offer, and what price to set. You help them accomplish the task by offering them the carrot of *best practices*.

Value of Best Practices/Best Processes

Want to save more money? Get people to do the same things the same ways.

Let's say I'm launching a new product, and along with creating printed material, a trade show booth and posters, press releases, and tchotchkes to hand out at seminars, I need to get some fresh content online. I need to schedule how long it's going to take to get that content from concept to live hosting in time for the launch. If I have a standardized approach, I'm a happier camper. I can get the job done faster with fewer headaches.

Al Sacco, performance manager in e-business at First Energy, gets serious about productivity. He likes the idea of a standard method that can shave a few minutes off a process. "Let's say so many minutes per week equates to so many productive minutes per year that results in a savings based on an average annual rate within your company." Eventually it all adds up.

Kristin Zhivago, publisher of the *Marketing Technology* newsletter (www.zhivago .com) and temporary vice president of marketing to her many Fortune 500 clients, is a marketing process aficionado. She's got a seven-point plan to measure marketing efforts, which is extremely applicable to any business team. How do you know you have a good process? By evaluating how successfully the following metrics are achieved:

Volume.   How much gets done

Timeliness.   How promptly it gets done

Quality.   The relevance and excellence of what gets done

Team involvement.   The extent to which everyone is part of the process

Internal acceptance.   Recognition and approval by superiors, peers, and staff

Bottom line.   The revenue and profit that your company earns as a result of your efforts

Customer satisfaction.   The ultimate yardstick

Mats Rene, manager of Ericsson.com, the international telecommunications company's online presence, uses a metric as an extension to Zhivago's team involvement: "We measure how happy our people are with the processes we're implementing and with the work we're doing. It is very valuable."

Mats looks at the way the company publishes information on the Internet, and he notes:

> You can save a lot by having, for example, a content management process in place. So, we're doing that. We would like to reduce the number of sites from 1,000 down to maybe two or three hundred sites. They're all going to work on the same platform, all using the same processes, using the same templates, design, and so on.
>
> The same process is key. So that's what we're trying to achieve. You can estimate how much it costs to maintain a site with a content management system and without. How much does it take to build a new site with or without templates? If you look at those figures, it actually creates a pretty good business case for having a corporate template system in place. That's how we are trying to measure it right now.
>
> There's also just the other savings, for example, time to publish, which we also use as one of our metrics. And then the process to get something up on the Internet with a content management system in place. It should be as convenient as possible. From days to a half a day or a few hours.
>
> The cost of content management is not too difficult to measure. Buy the license, develop the templates, develop the portal. Those costs are quite basic. The difficult thing is to create the business case for doing that investment and saying how much will we save by having this in place instead of having all rivers just run individually. It's very difficult.
>
> We think that having a common method or process in place saves an average percentage of about 25 percent. The payback time as we see it now is around 6 months.

Getting the Most Out of Centralization

I asked Rene Bonvanie, vice president of Online Marketing at Oracle, if they had suffered from the let-a-thousand-flowers-bloom, open-handed Web development philosophy and allowed each group and department to create their own Web initiative. If so, were they trying to get control again?

> We used to have that [problem] until I came to this position. Not only is it expensive but it is very hard for me to control headlines across the board. If I have to shift the work to a thousand places—actually it was sixty-three places, there was an oracle.it in Italy, one in Spain, in Korea, and so on—and not a single content management system for them to do the work in, I'm going to die. It's not going to happen. Consistency is very important for us. And economies of scale.
>
> So we actually saved the company forty million dollars last year by moving from a decentralized environment with individual servers and contracts to a single Web site running everything. Now that was a pretty big challenge because no one, not even the guys at Apache (the server software), who we have actually used for some of the technology, had

ever run a Web site that was running in Chinese and Korean and Hebrew and what have you at the same time. They had no idea how to do that. Their view of integration is to just run another Web server.

We have a couple of hundred thousand pages, which, from a management perspective, was a challenge. So we built a content management system. The first day I got on the job here, that was the first project I made. We needed something to manage all these pages.

Lots of managers will sit up and notice when you throw around numbers like 25 percent savings in 6 months. But $40 million has a nice ring to it, doesn't it?

Okay, so centralization saves money—but what does all this have to do with metrics?

Managing for Metrics

Best practices are a boon to those of us who like to count things. If everybody is going about their business in the same way, it's significantly easier to compare and contrast. If they all eat their apples by taking bites around the core, you can see who eats quickly, noisily, efficiently. But when the guy on the end is peeling an orange, dividing it into sections, and popping them into his mouth one at a time, comparisons become a bit muddled. Common process means common metrics. A common technical platform might be as important as common processes.

While United Airlines flies a single Web site, Delta Airlines has a handful of sites to manage. Says Rob Casas, general manager of Delta's e-Business Development: "Delta.com is the main part of our Web effort, but we have Mind Your Own Business Travel as well. And there are a couple of variations of delta.com, one for corporations and one for travel agencies."

But, like the folks at United, Casas knows that keeping all those parts flying in close formation makes for smoother operations. Says he, "All these reside in the same server areas, so all of our content management systems and all the server logs and so forth, are all under the same infrastructure. So when we measure things, we're able to measure them across the board for all of these sites.

"In terms of standardizing reports, some of the sites have different objectives, but the primary objectives like customer service or selling tickets online, that kind of thing, some of those are common across all those different sites. When we report on them, on whatever metrics we're looking at, whether it's cost per acquisition or clickthrough rates or conversion rates, all of those kinds of things are looked at through the same scope."

The other benefit to standard metrics is intellectual cross-pollination. Steve Robinson is the director of Web Development and Technology in the Ecare group at Xerox. "Once you create the metrics," says Steve, "it starts providing you the information on questions you never even thought to ask. And there is this feedback loop that is saying, 'Wow, there is a bunch of new questions we should be asking now.'"

While the power of return on investment in terms of money is enormous when convincing an executive to part with some, don't forget the other types of returns with which you can entice them. You can appeal to their hearts as well as their wallets.

Nonfinancial Value

All that glitters is not gold. Money doesn't buy happiness. A good reputation is more valuable than money. Money is a terrible master but an excellent servant.

Now that you're in the right frame of mind, there *are* some incentives for funding an e-metrics project beyond the fiscal.

Those of us who've been at this Web thing for a while and those of us born with an extra what-if gene just *know* that there is a world of mysteries to be unfolded if we only look at the psychedelic poster long enough for the picture of the unicorn to appear.

Okay, so maybe that's not the strongest argument when dealing with the top brass. But consider the possibility that one of them *was* born with that extra gene. Take that one aside and spend a few minutes brainstorming the possibilities of up-sell and cross-sell, the wonders of providing services that customers didn't even know they wanted, and the glory of knowing exactly what people are going to want to buy for Christmas next year.

Use this technique only on a closed course with a professional driver while wearing your seat belt and helmet. In other words, make sure you don't out-brainstorm the guy with budgetary signature.

Is your entire executive audience made up of nonimaginative types? It's possible. Then come back down to earth and talk about another reason for a big, fat e-metrics project that can't be measured directly in dollars: customer satisfaction.

Customer Satisfaction

Gary Bird, vice president of e-business at Honeywell, agrees that there's money to be saved, but that's not all.

According to Gary: "The primary benefits of centralization are probably twofold. Reducing the costs by an economy of scale both in the ongoing support as well as applying standards across P and Ls, of course. The other benefit is really the bigger one: more consolidated experience for our customers; a one-face, one-place viewpoint where you take a user-centric approach. Rather than [having] a bunch of shopping carts and different product lines and capabilities up on the Web and allowing our organizational structure to bleed through, we want to organize around markets and communities—the customer. We want to provide a user-centric view to our customers versus the business unit structural view. And single-user sign-on is important for a B2B customer across multiple business units."

Oh, sure, you're doing customer surveys already. Sure, you're asking them all about what they like and don't like on your site. But chances are superb that you're asking them after-the-fact questions about their latest experience rather than focusing on the questions that can (here comes the chorus again) raise revenue and lower costs.

Customer surveys are a critical part of a balanced e-metrics diet, and few are doing it, with many fewer doing it well. This is a big issue, and therefore, worthy of its own chapter. If this is a hot issue for you, turn at once to the "Measuring Customer Satisfaction" section in Chapter 13, "Measuring the Value of Online Customer Service."

The View from On High

"The top-down approach works by starting with the CEO and her direct reports to develop a set of macro metrics for the entire organization."
Mark Graham Brown, Keeping Score (Productivity Inc., 1996)

It sounds simple, but it quickly becomes a case of the tail wagging the dog if your firm doesn't already have some sort of predefined metrics in place.

What Are Web Managers Sending Up the Chain?

Of all the collected statistics and information, what gets reported upstairs? What do senior managers look at to determine whether the Web is successful?

Rob Sherell, Delta Airlines' manager of Interactive Marketing, says it depends:

We'll pass along consistent metrics associated with every program on the marketing site that we do: You know, what did we spend and what were the results for return on investment against our initial projections and what are next steps. So we may launch a program related to, let's say, email address acquisition from existing Sky Miles members. So we can do a direct-mail piece to existing Sky Miles members; we'll say we spent X, we received X new enrollments, the cost per enrollment was X.

Primarily we're doing ticket-purchase activities, activities designed to drive ticket purchase, so on a consistent basis we'll report up things like 'This month we ran four promotions, the cost was this, the cost per ticket for this program was $4, this one was $7,' that kind of thing. We also report the aggregate information. We kind of roll up the chain to our VPs and Senior VPs. We'll only send stuff up the chain if it's a large impact.

Rob Casas, general manager of Delta's E-Commerce Development, says Delta's upper management focuses on a number of things:

"One is obviously on the service aspect. Let's take the handling of upgrades online as an example. An overall number that says this is what we're doing online is great, but what gets their attention is the impact it has on the offline pieces. For instance, we're tying that and other service-related queries at the Web site desk to the sales factor in our call centers, which has actually in the last two or three years consistently gone up proportional to the volume of Web-related service calls that we're doing. That gets their attention, so we're showing this graph that goes up proportionally on the number of arrival/departure queries and online upgrades that we do and the sales factor in our reservation call centers is also going up in the same proportion, and that ties a correlation between the two."

It's pretty clear that people are going online to get flight information and not bothering the Delta call center until they're ready to make a purchase. "That's one of the things that we're seeing pretty tight correlation to," says Casas. "And it's great to show that the call centers are in fact producing revenue while we know we will never be able to sell everything through the Web site. So to have a strong, supporting distribution model on our call centers as well is a pretty powerful message for [upper management]."

At Eastman Kodak, Terry Lund, director of Web Site Capabilities, says he's lucky:

"The good news is we've got a chief marketing officer for Kodak.com, Sharon Delmin. She came out of the packaged-goods industry at Kraft foods and is a very experienced, data-driven, consumer-marketing person."

Of course, there's a downside there as well. Sharon *wants* the information and wants to interact with it in real time. Lund doesn't mind:

"For the very first time we've got somebody driving very specific questions: 'I want to be able to understand this, this, and this.' She knows how she wants to drive the effectiveness of the Web site from her marketing perspective in terms of repeat visitors, new visitors, time they spend and where they go, all those kinds of questions. She's the one who's driving us nuts trying to aggregate the data in the right way, so it's a very healthy interaction. You know, there's a tension there because we can't easily deliver, but it's also refreshing because finally we've got somebody asking the right questions."

What Executives Need

Peter F. Drucker summarizes nicely what executives really need:

"The ability to gather, arrange, and manipulate information with computers has given business people new tools for managing. But data processing tools have done more than simply enable executives to do the same tasks better. They have changed the very concepts of what a business is and what managing means. To manage in the future, executives will need an information system integrated with strategy, rather than individual tools that so far have been used largely to record the past." ("The Information Executives Really Need," Harvard Business Review, *January-February 1995).*

What Executives Want: The Dashboard

Chances are, your situation falls somewhere between the Clueless Pointy-Haired Boss and Kodak's Chief Marketing Officer. You have a team of executives who understand the premise but are not so data-driven. They want the live, dynamic summary. They want the dashboard on their desktop.

They want the dashboard with the built-in navigation system and all the dials and gauges and warning lights that allow them to take a quick peek on a weekly basis and say, "Okay, everything looks normal."

Learning what's important on a dashboard takes time. Put a teenager in a car and it takes a flashing red light in the rearview mirror to make him understand the value of the speedometer. Stranded on the edge of the desert with only a half a can of warm soda teaches the lesson about the value of the gas gauge. If it's his own car, then the words "blown head gasket" and the associated cost of repair will make him forever remember the need to look at the oil-pressure readout now and again.

At the moment, most senior executives are curious but not schooled. How should they react when the visitors-per-hour needle hovers dangerously close to zero or pegs at the highest number allowed? Executives are flying with a map, a compass, and the position of the sun.

How often does that dashboard need to be updated? Depends on who's looking and why.

Sue Fullman at Motorola looks at the dashboard for some stats more often than others: "We're using this pretty much on a monthly basis and, where we can, on a weekly basis in our staff meetings to review it. So we get an idea if anything changes. We know what's changed on the site, and we know pretty quickly if the conversion is impacted. So in March they put a [new] front page on Motorola.com; it was a different look and feel and the navigation was not linked properly. It was linked, but it was not the best navigation for a consumer from a pathing standpoint and the conversion rate was cut in half—almost immediately, so we knew something was wrong."

What do you put on *your* dashboard and how do you roll that data up to the powers that be? It depends. That answer requires some investigation, which is why they invented consultants. My approach to e-metrics consulting is to start with an audit that strives to answer the following questions:

- What information are you getting now?
- What additional information could you be getting with a very small investment?
- What information do those above you want to see?
- How much time and money will it take to give them what they want?
- What's the quickest-win/lowest-hanging fruit?
- What's the fastest way to get those numbers on their desktops?

That last question is a matter of technology, and that's where I turn it over to professionals— people like Dan Harper and Bob Fetterman at iDashes.net, who risk their lives (or at least their careers) on a daily basis.

I think of iDashes.net as the company with the glass-bottom boat. Once you tell them what you want to accomplish, they'll don the wetsuits and scuba gear, place the coral just where you want it, and make the whole thing enticing to the fish you want to see.

In other words, they look at the data you want to display, figure out how to extract it from your various data systems, and whip up the appropriate dials and graphs so it displays nicely. They make it look like a dashboard (see Figure 3.2).

In a car, you don't need to know much more about the gasoline than how much you've got left. If you really want to drill down, onboard computers will tell you your average miles per gallon and how far you can drive at your current rate of consumption, and that's about it. In a company, the ability to see the numbers as trends over time (see Figure 3.3) and to drill down to the spreadsheet that generated the numbers in the first place are critical to staying on top of a changing environment.

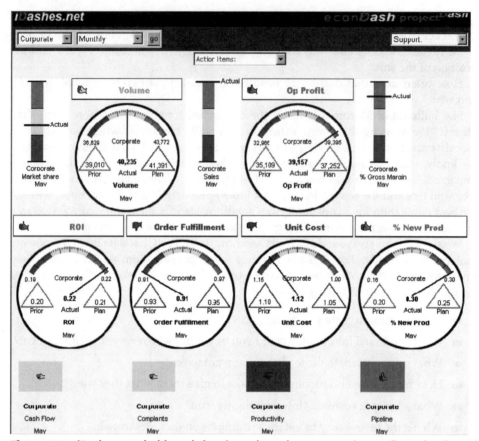

Figure 3.2 iDashes.net dashboard showing sales volume, operating profit, and a slew of other company-health-at-a-glance metrics.

Trends Are Your Friends

The reason you want to drill down is that numbers aren't nearly as important as trends. It doesn't matter at all if your Web site got 2 million visitors this month. It only matters if that is an improvement over the previous month, or the same month of the previous year.

Showing the numbers to your executives will pay off if you can clearly show what's working and can run on its own, and what's floundering and needs some attention. Heck, you might even beat them at their own game with a little management-speak of your own: the balanced scorecard.

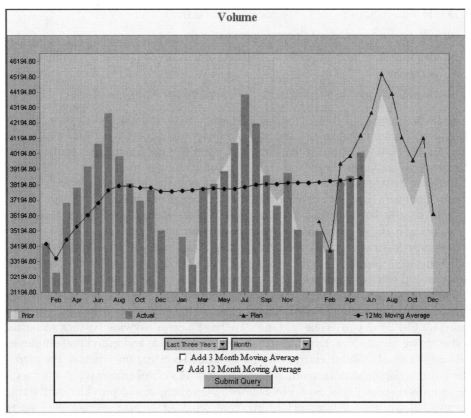

Figure 3.3   A single click on the iDashes gauge brings up a chart comparing current figures to the past.

The Balanced Scorecard Approach

In the January-February 1992 issue of the *Harvard Business Review*, Robert Kaplan and David Norton published an article entitled "The Balanced Scorecard: Measures that Drive Performance." They claimed that finance is simply not a wide enough measurement to determine the health of a company.

Mind you, finances are not forgotten. They are included to keep track of the past—actions already taken. Kaplan and Norton also included operational measures on customer satisfaction, internal processes, and improvements processes because these, they said, were the drivers of future financial performance. The duo said that the Balanced Scorecard provides answers to four basic questions:

- How do customers see us? (customer perspective)
- What must we excel at? (internal perspective)
- Can we continue to improve and create value? (innovations and learning perspective)
- How do we look to shareholders? (financial perspective)

First, the scorecard brings together, in a single management report, many of the seemingly disparate elements of a company's competitive agenda: becoming customer oriented, shortening response time, improving quality, emphasizing teamwork, reducing new product launch times, and managing for the long term.

The idea caught on because this sort of tabulation would reveal where improvements in one area may have been achieved at the expense of another.

How do customers see us? Kaplan and Norton spotted four ways customers measure companies: time, quality, performance, and service. How quickly do you deliver orders or release new products? Quality is measured by the number of defects in the products received. Service and performance are determined by how well your products and services create value for your customers.

The idea is catching on and is used in running Web sites as well. Just ask Dorothy Paleologos, head of Strategic Planning at e.Aetna, the Web side of the big insurance company. She'll tell you as she told me: "We have a companywide balance scorecard and what we call the level twos, which are departmentwide and individual-employee balance scorecards. And of course they are all nested one into the other. At the corporate level, we have metrics around the Internet and we've broken down our work with the Internet by constituent. So it's by member, plan sponsor, and provider. At the corporate level, we measure Internet inquiries completed. At the plan sponsor level, we're measuring new electronic plan sponsors. At the provider level, we're measuring electronic transactions as a percentage of total transactions."

At Delta Airlines, Rob Casas understands the difference between the monetary metrics and the rest:

> "I think there are two different things you can look at: financial value or the direct benefit, which is measured by the Net Present Value (NPV) of the program, but you've also got to look at the strategic value and indirect value, which is measured by the value to the customer, the competitive environment, and you've also got to look at implementation risks and time to implement. We look at a combination of those."

Rob Sherell agrees:

> "At the end of the day we have to go back to our finance folks who ultimately look at the first factor as more important than the others. We're trying to show how the satisfaction measurements and ultimately the customer-centric strategy that we need to establish do end up impacting that bottom line. And how measurements in general can help us pinpoint that element of force."

Show the boss a varied enough picture, and the funding makes more sense than just on the basic idea of ROI. If all else fails in your efforts to convince the top brass of the value of your e-metrics proposal, don't head to Monster.com just yet. Instead, work the grassroots angle.

Lead by Example

Chances are excellent that you do not have a chief marketing officer for your Web site like they do at Kodak. So you have to find the data-driven individuals in the bowels of your organization and get them working with you.

How do you find them? By showing that the types of tools you propose to use are, indeed, useful. Look to the access logs of the reports you're generating now and keep track of who's keeping track.

One high-profile manufacturer I spoke with is keeping a sharp eye on who's reading the Web reports that are already available. "It tends to be the marketing professionals right now," he told me. "If I look at WebTrends to see who is drilling and who is asking the right questions, I've got some good-news areas and I've got some areas that are out to lunch. We have a marketing university coming up; we'll do some retraining. We have some areas that are pretty sophisticated in their use."

Find those who are already reaching out. If you can get a hold of two or three tuned-in people, be they product-line managers, human resources maestros, or advertising authorities, you can help them in small, specific projects that offer proof of concept.

National Semiconductor (www.national.com) keeps an eye on the interest generated by pages describing new product ideas they host on their site—new products that aren't in production yet. When the trend starts to rise faster than traffic to the other areas on their site, National has an idea that something's up and it's time to ramp up production. That way they are ready to ship out samples at a moment's notice, rather than waiting for the orders and telling would-be customers that they'll have to wait 6 to 8 weeks.

The folks who occupy the larger offices at your firm are just like the rest of us. They thrive on stories like that one. They want to hear about the other companies that are doing well and how they're doing it. But they especially want to hear stories about how their own company is succeeding. A couple of low-hanging fruit, quick-win stories like that, and funding more e-metrics projects becomes easier and easier.

In the meantime, remember that you're not just standing on the street corner in the snow selling pencils out of a cup. You're also trying to alter the course of the supertanker called Your Company. You want the powers that be to look at the Web as a source of valuable business intelligence? A couple of industry experts and a few PowerPoint presentations can make them see the light. You want them to actually look at the results and take action based on what they see? You've become a change agent. Again.

When asked about the most difficult part of e-metrics, Larry Bunyard, director of the Internet Business Group *and* Director of Applications at Tektronix, pinpointed the hard part: "Changing behavior. Technology is the easy part."

Follow the Leaders

Now that the dot-com excitement has come and gone, you really don't want to get caught up in being a change agent for the sake of change. People (especially management types) are no longer thrilled by the prospects of the new, new thing. They don't want to boldly go where no one has gone before.

As the times change, Joel Maloff, vice president for Fusion Telecommunications International, quoted near the beginning of the chapter, changes his presentations, but his theme remains the same: Don't shoot for the stars when you're just trying to hit the front door. His message is pretty simple when it comes to asking for money (see Figure 3.4).

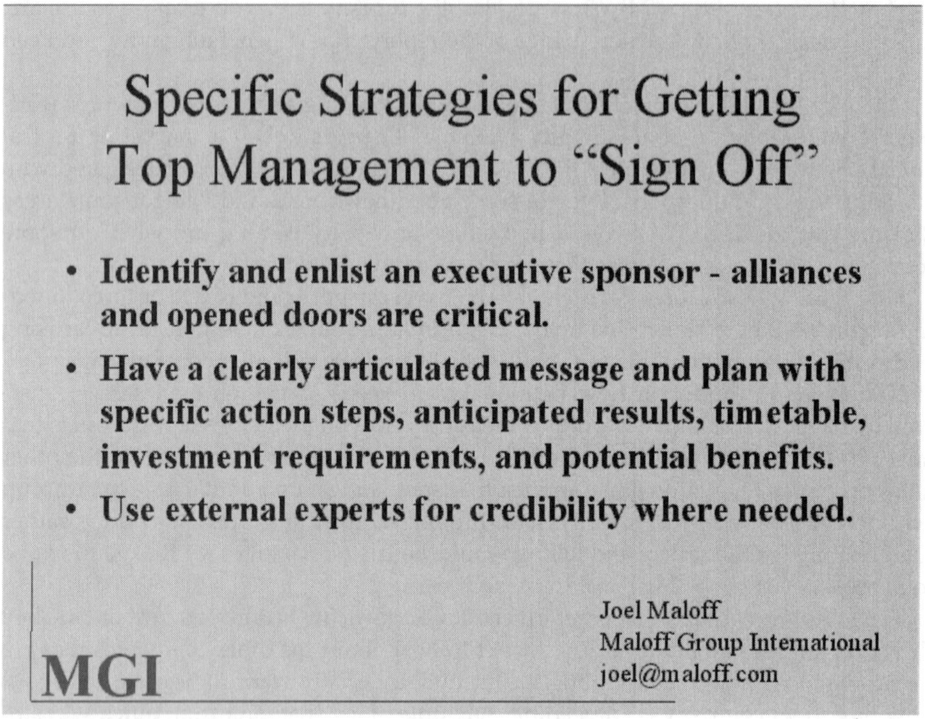

Specific Strategies for Getting Top Management to "Sign Off"

- **Identify and enlist an executive sponsor - alliances and opened doors are critical.**
- **Have a clearly articulated message and plan with specific action steps, anticipated results, timetable, investment requirements, and potential benefits.**
- **Use external experts for credibility where needed.**

Joel Maloff
Maloff Group International
joel@maloff.com

MGI

Figure 3.4   Joel Maloff knows that realism is your best ally.

Today's executive wants to let others dive into the pool first. That's the best way to tell the difference between the deep end and the shallow end without hitting bottom or getting in over your head. So they want to see what the standards are. They want to know what the basic benchmarks look like. Why bother measuring the number of users searching your site for fourth-quarter earnings data with wireless devices if you can't compare the results to others?

What's the state of Web metrics standards? It's not pretty, but there's hope.

Web Measurement Standards

If you grabbed this book off the shelf in the bookstore and immediately turned to this chapter, you're my kind of Web businessperson.

"Great!" you think. "Benchmarks!" you hope. "Standards!" you imagine, as those around edge away in that suggestive manner that indicates you may have actually spoken the words aloud. Well, there's good news and bad news, and let's get the bad news out of the way: When it comes to benchmarks, there aren't any.

Wait! Don't close the book and put it back on the shelf upside down and backwards just yet. There *is* some good news. There are a handful of measurement standards out there. And they couldn't possibly come soon enough.

The woman who heads up the e-metrics process at one large manufacturer pleaded for the death of an old metric and its replacement by one we all know and love. She asked: "Wouldn't it be great if we could just all agree that when we say 'hits,' what we really mean is page views? Then, I wouldn't have to spend half of my waking life trying to explain the difference to all the low-level managers in the company when they come to me asking about hits."

The Need for Standards

We use standard definitions and measurements to help make sense of a complex world. It's confusing to head over to Team VMAX, the official British Women's 4-Way

Skydiving Team site (see Figure 4.1) (www.vmax.org.uk) and read up on Sacha Chilton.

If you happen to be British, hang out with a lot of British people, like to visit Great Britain often, or just watch a lot of *Masterpiece Theatre*, you *might* know that a "stone" is 14 pounds. That's pounds as in weight, not pounds sterling as in currency. So 9-stone Sacha is a very svelte 126 pounds, which is just right for a "slight frame" according to the good people at MetLife Online who pay attention to such things (www.metlife.com/Lifeadvice/Tools/Heightnweight/Docs/women.html).

But if you can't tell a pound of plummeting professional chef from the cost of a nice, safe train ride from London to Liverpool, then you understand the problem that happens when Web managers talk to marketing people about the traffic they're getting on their sites.

One airline Web metrics manager lamented to me about how hard it is to be clear: "We have internal difficulties communicating what the difference is between a page view, a hit, a session, or a unique visitor—so we have some internal guidelines to communicate to our internal constituents about what the media people are talking about. We would certainly support any standardization of terms in the travel industry to significantly reduce some of the confusion going around. Conversion in the travel industry means a different thing to an Amazon.com."

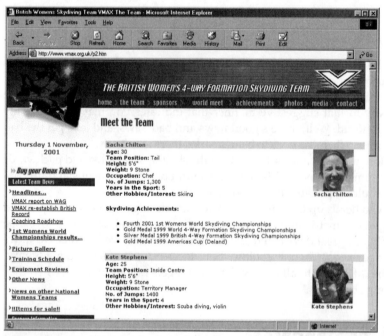

Figure 4.1   We know Sacha isn't an Amazon at 5-foot-6, but how much does she weigh?

They take the bull by the horns at Eastman Kodak, where Director of Site Capabilities Terry Lund wants to be sure that everybody is on the same page. "I give a 2-hour Introduction to Web Traffic Analysis internal training course. I spend at least the first hour trying to do a level set—you know, definition of terms and what some of the issues are around measuring things."

But Lund is certain that he doesn't have all the answers. "One of the things I say is I haven't figured out how to express Web traffic as a single number. You know, if I tell you Kodak's Web traffic is 17.6, what the hell does it mean? And so I settled in on people, pages, and time."

Lund understands that just because you have a known definition of traffic doesn't mean you know what action to take because of a given result: "You have to decide, is this good traffic? Or is the traffic getting better? The definition of 'good' or 'better' or 'bad' is very contextual. Because sometimes more people is good and sometime more time is good. Sometimes more time is bad."

So we must start at the very beginning and come to terms with the terms we're using. Simple definitions are easy to come by. Look no further than the, "E-Metrics Glossary of Terms," courtesy of the NetGenesis Web site. For more complex standards, we turn to those who have come before us to see what is being measured in any sort of a consistent way.

The Broadest of Standards

How many people are online? Doesn't really matter anymore. The good people at Nua (an authoritative online source for information on Internet demographics and trends) take a periodic "educated guess" as to the extent of the global Internet user population (see Figure 4.2).

What are they doing online? According to Nielsen//NetRatings (www.nielsen-netratings.com), they are, on average, getting online six times per week, looking at eighteen sites, for over 3 1/2 hours, and looking at each page a little under a minute.

Remember that all of those estimates and averages are from the Nielsen//NetRatings Audience Measurement Service, which bases their numbers on a sample of households that have access to the Internet using Windows 95/98/NT and MacOS 8 or better.

Averages are fine for ideal height to weight, but averages on the Web are tremendously misleading. According to the Webmaster at Microsoft, people wander around on their site for an average of 6 minutes per visit. In August 2000, Nielsen//NetRatings clocked the average eBay visitor at 1 hour and 42 minutes on the site per visit during that month, viewing 256 pages per session. Is the on-site individual viewing time an average of 6 minutes or 102 minutes? Which is the right average for your site?

The two questions we *do* seem to be able to answer in a common way are: Who's going where? How did they get there?

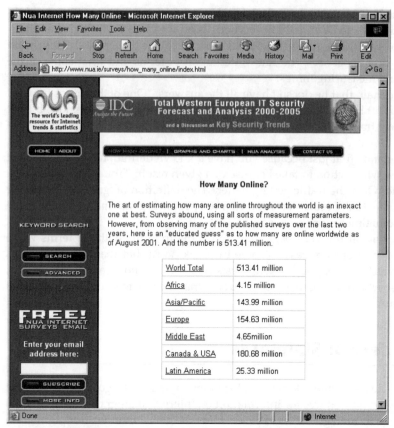

Figure 4.2   As of August 2001, Nua guessed there are 513.41 million people online in the world.

Who's Going Where?

NetRatings (www.netratings.com) keeps an eye on where people go online. At their site, they describe their services this way:

> *The basis for the audience measurement data and analysis, which is the foundation of the NetRatings services, is actual click-by-click Internet user behavior measured through a comprehensive, real-time meter installed on the computers of over 225,000 individuals in 29 countries worldwide, both at home and at work.*
>
> *The company has strategic relationships with Nielsen Media Research, the leading television-audience measurement company in North America, and ACNielsen Corporation, the global leader in providing market research and analysis to the consumer products and services industries.*
>
> *Jointly developed and offered by NetRatings, Nielsen Media Research and ACNielsen, the Nielsen//NetRatings services have set the benchmark for best practices in panel-based research and real-time tracking and collection of Internet audience behavior. The services, marketed globally under the Nielsen//NetRatings brand, enable customers to make informed business-critical decisions regarding their Internet strategies.*

In essence, this is the same approach as the ACNielsen measurement of television watchers. They keep an eye on a handful of people and suppose that everybody else is doing the same. There's something to be said for a sufficiently large panel. There's also something to be said for having, for the sake of argument, a quarter of a million people in their panel. If Nua is right, then NetRatings has their finger on the pulse of a little under 1 ½ percent of the online world. Statistically significant? Let's just say this is as good as it gets for knowing which site gets the most visitors (see Figure 4.3)

These numbers by themselves are good for bragging rights and for setting the price of advertising, but not much else. NetRatings gets really interesting however, because they know something about the individuals they're tracking—quite a bit in fact.

As a client, you'll get the full report of just what sort of people are coming to your site (see Figure 4.4).

If you're in the consumer world, this information becomes very compelling. If you're selling shoes to teenagers, and you're Property 5 in Figure 4.4, you've got your work cut out for you. You're getting a hair shy of 8 ½ percent of the target audience's attention, whereas the second-to-last competitor is getting nearly twice the traffic from the target audience. Time to sponsor an MTV show.

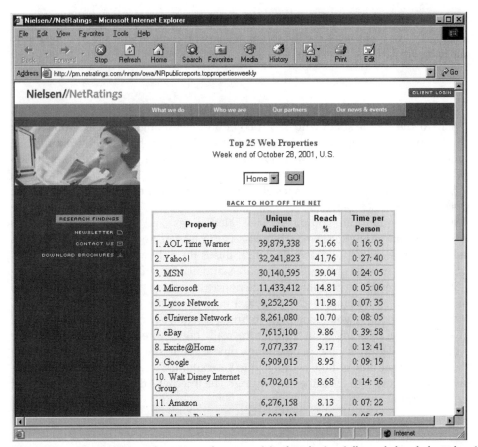

Figure 4.3 NetRatings ranks AOL as *the* most visited Web site, followed closely by Yahoo!

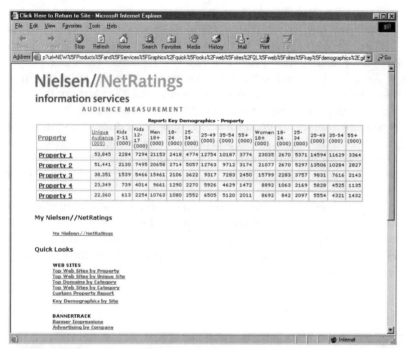

Figure 4.4   As a client, you'll see the sort of people who come to your site as compared to your competitors.

Want to know more about who these people are? NetRatings will be only too happy to tell you, by gender, by age, by income, by education, by race, by occupation. Remember, this is a panel of known individuals, and NetRatings makes a living by following them around all day. So if you're Disney, it's encouraging to note that there's a big block of visitors between the ages of 2 and 11, bested only by the block between the ages of 35 to 49—their parents.

But do reports from companies like NetRatings and Jupiter Media Metrix (www.jmm.com) represent standard methods of measurement? Yes, if only de facto standards. They are standards by default. If this is the only way to measure the massive numbers of people online, then they are standards by definition.

But you are certain to get more accurate figures by asking your visitors directly; the online survey, the qualitative call to actual customers, the occasional focus group. Nothing like talking to your customers to find out who your customers really are.

Okay, so there are sources out there for the really big picture and they're useful as far as they go in identifying the people who come to your site versus the competition. Fine. The next question is, how do they *get* to your site? Is there a standard way of measuring the effectiveness of online advertising? The Internet Advertising Bureau would like you to think so.

How Did They Get There?

The first place anybody started wrestling with standards is where the money hits the Web: advertising. Why bother coming to terms with standardized terms? Because money is changing hands and we want to be darned sure we know what we're talking about. I learned that lesson in the second grade when I was promised five dollars in exchange for my favorite *Man From Uncle* communicator pen and received five doll hairs and a punch on the arm. Predetermined definitions make the wold of commerce go 'round.

The Interactive Advertising Bureau (www.iab.net) was founded in 1996 as a booster organization. Its job was to convince Big Business to spend lots of money on Internet advertising. This is not a secret mission. They're very up front about it. In fact, their mission statement reads, "The IAB is the only association dedicated to helping online, wireless, interactive television, and other emerging platform media companies increase their revenues by promoting the benefits of interactive media."

So they spend their time "evaluating and recommending guidelines and best practices, fielding research to document the effectiveness of interactive media, and educating the advertising industry about the use of interactive advertising and marketing. Membership includes companies that are actively engaged in the sale of interactive advertising and marketing."

In order to do that with any coherence, the IAB has published a glossary (http://www.iab.net/main/glossary1.htm) with more than 275 terms of art spelled out for those of us trying to understand each other as we write and sign contracts. In doing so, the IAB takes a stab at filling a very empty void.

Kris Carpenter, vice president of Excite Products and Services, says the IAB is better than nothing: "The IAB is by definition the de facto standards provider for some of those metrics today. There is more than one way of interpreting these metrics and maybe the advertising ones alone are not sufficient for understanding the full scope of the business, but in the absence of having that kind of vehicle, the IAB plays that role."

HIT

When users access a Web site, their computer sends a request to the site's server to begin downloading a page. Each element of a requested page (including graphics, text, interactive items) is recorded by the site's Web server log file as a "hit." If a page containing two graphics is accessed by a user, those hits will be recorded once for the page itself and once for each of the graphics. Webmasters use hits to measure their servers' workload. Because page designs and visit patterns vary from site to site, the number of hits bears no relationship to the number of pages downloaded, and is therefore a poor guide for traffic measurement.

From the IAB Glossary (: www.iab.net/main/glossary1.htm)

HIT

A single entry in a server log file, generated when a user requests a resource on your Web site. Requests are often referred to as "hits." A request can result in an error or a successful transmission of any data type. Hits are not a useful comparison between Web sites or parts of the same Web site, as each Web page is made up of an arbitrary number of individual files.

From the NetGenesis Glossary (www.netgen.com/index.cfm?section= solutions&file=emetrics_glossary)

Most of the problem is education. We all ran around talking about *hits* without really agreeing to a definition. Take a look in the sidebars at how hits are defined by the IAB and then by NetGenesis.

If you've got the authors of these two glossaries in the same room, they would very quickly agree with each other on the fine points. But as a practitioner of Web measurement, you have to deal with an ambiguity. Is a hit recorded when the request is made by the user, or by the server? One click by the user equals one hit? Or one request for the shipment of a file by the server? Do we record when the file is requested or actually sent?

The bottom line on hits is that an individual hit is recorded when a file is actually sent by the server. If a request is made for a page with two graphics, there are three requests: one for the page, and one each for the graphics. If, however, the page cannot be found, the response that is sent is an error message, which can (if you're not paying strict attention) be recorded as a single hit.

So we all agree that hits are a poor form of measurement by anybody's standards. But they are an excellent example of just how easy it is to misinterpret reports generated by those who work with the technology on a daily basis and then throw the "results" over the wall to those who do not. When you start with numbers that are not well defined, like hits, and then use them to calculate metrics that are not well defined, like frequency, all you can do is compare today to yesterday, this week to last week, and month to month.

Heaven help you try to look at industry standards, or benchmarks.

Benchmarking

The Agile Virtual Enterprise (H. T. Goranson, Quorum Books, 1999, p. 77) refers to benchmarks as *downstream metrics*:

> *Benchmark [is] an after-the-fact snapshot metric whose utility is in the comparison with other snapshots. A downstream metric might have some utility for benchmarking a process against other instances of itself, but in order to be useful to another process in another organization, a thorough normalization must take place, making sure the process and general context is similar between the two cases.*

Here's where we run into difficulty. Benchmarking as commonly applied is the process of comparing many companies, identifying the best in class, and then presumably comparing your organization with the purpose of improvement.

Benchmarking assumes that there is a well understood set of characteristics that are being benchmarked and that there is a meaningful sample size.

Computerworld (www.computerworld.com) does a great job with their Quick-Study Dictionary (see Figure 4.5).

For *benchmarking,* Computerworld offers a very straightforward definition: "Benchmarking is a measurement tool used to gauge a company's operating performance against that of competitors to identify best practices and make improvements. Examples within corporate IT include measuring the costs of supporting a data center or network infrastructure."

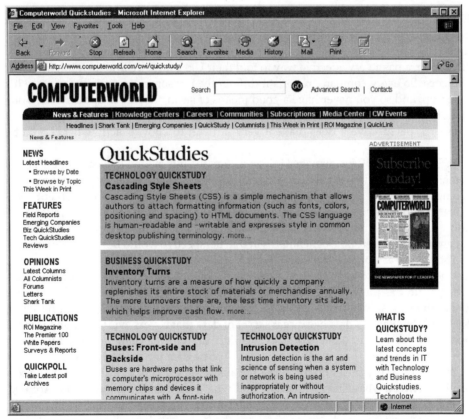

Figure 4.5   Computerworld offers more than 250 detailed definitions for IT terms.

But then they address *e-commerce benchmarking* as a separate entity: "E-commerce benchmarking is used to help companies compare the costs and performance of their online operations with those of other companies."

In the Computerworld article defining e-commerce benchmarking, Mark Czarnecki, president of The Benchmarking Network, Inc., says, "All the concepts and principles of e-commerce are still not set," making benchmarks very difficult:

> *Normally, there's a set of "anchors" that companies can rely on when they do benchmarking—a defined measure of performance, such as transactions per second or monthly sales, Czarnecki says. "Defining it means there's some kind of stable business process. [With e-commerce], there's not a stable business process," he adds.*
>
> *The top priority for electronic businesses is turning a profit, says Jim Sample, a consultant at Reston, Va.-based benchmarking service provider Compass America Inc. "The drive toward profitability then trickles back to having to put in some traditional measurement system," he says.*

Benchmarking Specifics

Comparing two advertising venues is extremely difficult due to the vagaries of the language used by different venues. Kris Carpenter from Excite wishes we could come up with some hard-and-fast, non-vendor-oriented, truly consortium-level definitions: "Lycos Terra has a very effective way to fold their U.S. audience into their international audience. So every company reports it differently. For some it's distinct, for some it's rolled-up, and so you never have a good means of seeing apples to apples. That's one of the advantages that companies have in putting the best light on everything, but from a research perspective it does make it very difficult to know exactly what should be communicated."

In Sweden, Mats Rene manages Ericsson.com, the international telecommunications giant. He wants to know how his site and his processes for managing it measure up: "Sometimes you feel a bit alone, especially when you get into the area of content management, which is extremely complex. I don't really think that anyone can understand how complex it is until you are in the middle of it. I mean it's so much work and it's expensive too. To get some benchmarks in that perspective would be really interesting."

The picture at Kodak is the same. Terry Lund wants to know how some features on his site compare to competitors of all stripes: "There were some 137 startup dot coms trying to do this [new photographic feature] as well. And the perception from senior management was they were going to eat our lunch. So we started reporting using Nielsen//NetRatings data because it's a set of data that covers everybody and is independently derived. In other words, we can't really use the data we collect with our Accrue software because we don't have any Accrue data for anybody else."

Terry finds it very frustrating, and he's not alone. "There's not a particularly strong correlation between what Nielsen measures and what we measure ourselves with Accrue," he says. "The absolute numbers are off by a big factor." Apples to apples indeed.

In the advertising marketplace, there are the Web sites that sell ad space, there are the brokers that serve the ads, there are the Webmasters who receive the clickthroughs, and there are the NetRatings types that report on who's getting the most traffic. Talk to anybody running a Web site of any size and you hear the same lament. None of those four numbers match in any way. There's not even a formula to relate them to each other. They're not normally within 20 percent, or a multiple of 3. Those numbers are consistently all over the map.

Why the frustration? Everybody's got a different methodology. Nobody's got a standard definition. What we're measuring is still misunderstood. Everybody is delivering numbers that will allow them to bill as much as possible, instead of looking for accuracy or coming to some approved agreement.

How then do you compare yourself to your competitors? With a little help.

Competitive Analysis

Larry Bunyard at Tektronix would love to do more comparison between his firm and his competitors to see where he stands next to industry leaders. He has an overwhelmingly practical perspective: "I want to spend a dollar more to beat Intel or to beat Agilent. I don't need to spend a hundred thousand dollars more, I just need to spend that one more so I'm at parity or beyond them depending upon strategy. That's impossible to determine today."

As it turns out, there are a number of services out there that offer competitive Web intelligence.

Classic Business Intelligence

There's classic competitive intelligence about those who would beat you at your own game. If you want the lowdown on the enemy, there are dozens of sites that will give or sell you access to their database of deep, dark, not-terribly-secret info on public companies:

Corporate Information	www.corporateinformation.com
CompanySleuth	www.companysleuth.com
Hoover's Online	www.hooversonline.com
EDGAR Online	www.edgaronline.com
LexisNexis	www.lexisnexis.com
Thomas Register	www.thomasregister.com

There are also companies like RivalWatch (www.rivalwatch.com), which, in its own words, uses the Web to compile "critical competitive information dealing with pricing, product assortment and promotions and presents this information as actionable intelligence to increase sales, profits, and customer satisfaction for both online and offline businesses." These services will help you keep an eye on the competition. Keeping an eye on your competitors' Web sites is another matter.

Change Notification

Under the headline "Change Happens," Mind-it (see Figure 4.6) (mindit.netmind.com) offers a watchful eye on whatever pages you wish. Want to keep track of a competitor's price list? No problem. Want to be notified when a competitor's "executive team" page changes? Happy to be of service. Want to know when there's a new question on their FAQ? Delighted.

Mind-it is brutally simple to use. Surf to the page you want to keep on top of, and hit the Mind-it button. You then have the choice of tracking any change to the page, selected text, images, links, or specific keywords.

Another way to keep on top of what your competitors are up to is to invest in an intern. They work cheap, they're thrilled when you slide a pizza under the door, and they'd love to be able to put your company name on their resumé and point out that they were doing important Web work for you. They're also a lot brighter than you'd expect and can come up with off-the-cuff observations that can keep you at the head of the class.

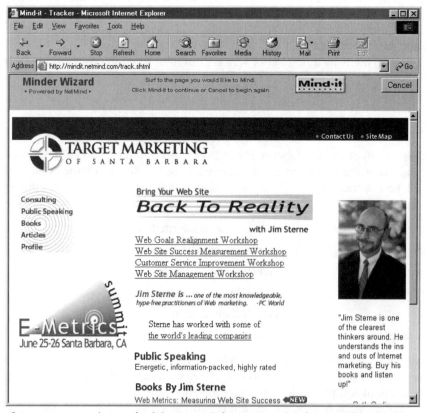

Figure 4.6   Keeping track of Jim Sterne's home page is a breeze with Mind-it.

The Nitty Gritty

What I'm personally interested in is the idea of industry-standard numbers. If you think in terms of direct mail, the standard industry expectation is for a 2 percent response. Spend a little, spend a lot, you still get a 2 percent response. So where did that number come from? Says who? We may never know, but 2 percent has been ground into our direct-response psyches for lo, these many years and has come to be considered fact.

Where are the facts for the online world? True or not, superstition or solid research, I don't care. I'm just looking for a number to hold up as a mirror to my efforts to see if I am worthy. If I'm on the Web, what should my clickthrough rate be on a banner ad? What should the proper, optimal number of clicks be to make an e-commerce purchase? Well, I know the answer to that one already and Amazon.com patented it. The correct number is 1.

Whether I'm doing e-commerce or publishing information for people who are doing research or I'm interacting with them at a customer service level, each one of these needs its own metrics. We have to come up with some industry standards, so eventually we can come up with some best practices that allow us to compare.

When two different departments attempt e-commerce, we need a way to say "We did it this way and you did it that way. We came up with 17.5 and you came up with 18.3; therefore, your way is better. We'll adopt your method."

We have to agree on definitions of terms and agree on methodologies of measurement. We have to find a way to discuss best practices to determine how to collect the numbers, what formulas to use, and which results are common enough to be called benchmarks.

A Call to Arms

This book is an attempt to get the conversation started. I'll do my best to roll out an approach to measurement, and you send the feedback to metrics@targeting.com. If you think I've described something inaccurately, it is your duty to report it to me. If you see something I missed, I want to know about it.

If you have a standard measure, a standard result, a benchmark that we can all use as a yardstick—then let me know about it at once!

So far, we've talked about *why* to track what happens on your site. Now it's time to talk about *how*. First stop, the unavoidable dive into the ubiquitous server log file.

Sawing Logs

Matt Cutler knows what people want: the Big Red Metrics Button.

The Big Red Metrics Button doesn't require the user to have an education. It doesn't require any detailed investigation into technology. It doesn't require a working knowledge of the insides of your Web site. It doesn't require a firm grasp of the goals for your Web site. It does, however, require a make-believe, artificial fairyland to live in because it's not something you're ever going to find on the planet Earth.

What you'll find instead is a range of products and services that will help you extract information from your Web site, all of which require a bit of tweaking, altering, and looking at sideways to get the information you need to accomplish specific goals.

The Gartner Levels of Ambition

The Gartner Group (www.gartner.com) has an interesting way of dividing tools into four levels:

Level 1: Monitoring. The focus is on Web site optimization. You look at server logs to figure out how to get people to stick around longer and give them more of what they want.

Level 2: Feedback. Here you pay attention to the site visitor and try to improve the user experience. You look at the amount of time people spend on the site, and you use visitor segmentation to alter the content for different types of visitors.

Level 3: Leverage.   The focus shifts from the visitor to the customer, and the goal is to increase customer profitability. Customer profiling, dynamic up-selling and cross-selling, and customer satisfaction reporting all come into play.

Level 4: Strategic.   Now the spotlight is turned around to shine on the company itself in order to optimize the business model: channeling low-margin customers to the competition, tracking lifetime value, and getting into some serious business intelligence analytics.

Before you rush off to find the best tool for the job, it behooves you to understand the basics. You just can't get any more basic than a log file.

Your Web server generates a great deal of information. It creates logs. Mountains of data are collected in your server logs every day. The assumption is that this information is generated to help you determine how well you're doing. Nice thought, but not the case.

Log files are merely the result of good, solid engineering. If you create a system that does something, it's a good idea to record what happened. That way you've got something to look at when things go wrong. So log files are the result of a Web server doing its job, and not the map to the Big Red Button.

The business management side of companies using the Web went to the Web-heads and asked for reports. The log files were it. Ever since, man has been trying to interpret log files like astrologers, phrenologists, and readers of the I Ching. Log files do, indeed, contain more data than, say, the configuration of the bumps on your head, but it's a matter of torturing usable information out of them.

Your Server Log: Up Close And Personal

Now it's time to dissect a typical log report to see what's inside. Those of you who get queasy at the sight of insides turned out are assured that all diagrams are in black and white and that no animals were harmed in the listing of this file.

When a client machine connects to your Web server, the server writes a line to the log file. The log file collects a dense clot of data (see Figure 5.1).

A single line of that data looks something like this:

```
63.173.190.16 - - [05/Nov/2001:19:46:42 -0800] "GET /classic.html
HTTP/1.1" 200 22838 "-" "Mozilla/4.7 (compatible; WhizBang)"
```

Starting from the left, the first set of numbers indicates who asked for the file. A reverse DNS lookup reveals that it belongs to the folks at www.whizbang.com. That means this entry was made by somebody or some*thing* (more on that in a minute) on November 5, while looking for a file called classic.html—part of my Full Sterne Ahead archives.

The time is calculated from Greenwich Mean Time and the -0800 points to the Pacific time zone.

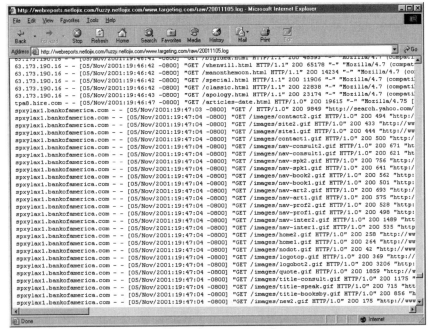

Figure 5.1 A typical log file does not make for light reading.

The request was sent using version 1.1 of the Hypertext Transport Protocol (HTTP) and the server responded by saying "200," which indicates it was only too happy to grant the request. If it couldn't find the file in question, it would have replied with a "404" or any of several other codes (more on error codes below).

Next, we are told that the server sent back 22,838 bytes. Next comes a quoted hyphen ("-"). That's where the referral link belongs. The hyphen tells us that the URL was entered directly, rather than clicked. At the end, we see that the user is running a Netscape 4.7-compatible browser called WhizBang.

What does this discrete line tell us? Not much, without having some context around it. Looking back at Figure 5.1, you can see that this IP address asked for four pages within the same second. That either represents more than the maximum daily allowance of Jolt Cola or these requests were not made by a person, but by a machine. The lack of a referring URL bolsters that assumption. Finally, who's ever heard of a browser called "WhizBang"? This calls for investigation.

At their site, we learn that "WhizBang! Labs began in 1999 when Dallan Quass, Bob Sherwin, and Berkeley Geddes decided to build a company around software that could be trained to automatically find, categorize, and extract specific data fields or records from unstructured text." I'd say that was the proof we were looking for.

You can see where the line-by-line analysis of a server log might be a bit too tedious to be useful. Fortunately, we have computers.

Number Crunching: It Takes a Lot of Horsepower

Omar Ahmad managed the servers at Netscape for several years. They have rooms and rooms of servers. They serve millions and millions of pages every day. But the biggest machines they have, the real bruisers, are used exclusively for server log analysis. Why? Because it takes muscle.

If you serve a million pages and each page is made up of ten files and each file is about 20 kbytes, then your server has to find, read, and send 200 terabytes of data. It makes a record of each transaction along the lines of:

```
207.77.91.38 - - [06/Mar/2001:09:25:28 -0600] "GET products/
tools/wrenches/left-handed/crescent5.html HTTP/1.1" 200 132
```

That line of text is 120 bytes. Multiply that by a million pages and ten files and you only have 1.2 terabytes of data. That's much smaller than the 200 terabytes that was served. So what's the problem?

The problem lies in the fact that serving data is one thing, analyzing it is quite another. To analyze data, the software needs to categorize it, hold it in memory, compare it, and report on the findings. Sifting through a terabyte of data is not something you want to do on the same machine you are using to serve those pages. The amount of CPU saturation would render visiting your site frustratingly slow.

Given a mountain of hardware to scale a mountain of data, this rich information will let you redesign your site and reevaluate your marketing strategy at will. Unfortunately, the numbers are not infallible.

Number Crumbling: Easy as Falling Off a Log File

Just in case you hadn't noticed already, Web site logs are not easy to read, do not accurately reflect what's really happening on your site, and cannot consistently give you the insights you were hoping for. There are several things that upset and bewilder a log file; all of them have to do with how the Internet works.

Cache Files Cause Undercounting

Cache files were a brilliant solution to two pressing Internet problems that stem from the same issue: speed. From the macro view, the designers of the Internet worried about the whole system being able to carry the load of all that data going back and forth. From the micro view, waiting for Web pages is as much fun as waiting in line at the bank.

The solution was to move the information as few times as possible.

When you click on a link and ask for a Web page for the first time, your browser looks in the cache file on your hard disk to see if you've already seen that page recently. If it doesn't find it there, it looks in the cache file on your ISP's proxy server. It doesn't find it there, so it reaches out across the Web to the host server and asks for the page. The host finds the desired page, sends it to you, and records the event in its log file.

On the way back to you, the file is copied into your ISP's cache and into the cache on your own hard disk. You see the page, find a link you like, and start the whole process over again.

After several clicks, you feel a need to go back a few pages, so you hit the Back button. Your browser looks in your cache file and immediately displays the page. It didn't have to go out on the Net at all. You put no additional strain on your ISP's system, no additional strain on the Internet at large, and you were instantly served the information you wanted.

Shortly thereafter, another customer of your ISP is interested in seeing that very same page. They click on a link or type in the URL and their browser repeats what yours did. It looks in the local cache file and finds nothing, so it looks in the ISP's cache file. Since the page was previously recorded when you originally fetched it, it's available for your fellow surfer to grab directly from the ISP. This added no additional traffic to the backbone and made the retrieval that much faster for the second viewer.

There's only one problem. The host server—the Web site you went to—had no idea that you looked at the page again and no idea that somebody else at the same ISP looked at that page. The action is never reported in the server log file.

Modern cache systems are said to be configurable to handle most kinds of e-commerce and advertising models without problems. Even so, some advertisers say up to 75 percent of page views are from cached versions, which don't record a new ad view. While this seems high, it's clear caching does have a significant impact on the validity of reported page views. AOL recently reported page view reports may be short by up to 30 percent because of caching practices.
"Caching on the Web," Webtools (www.webtools.com/story/servers/
TLS19981021S0004)

You can play with refresh tags, redirect commands, and nocache tags. You can randomize your URLs or add one dynamic object to your page so that the majority of the static content may be cached. But be careful. You don't want to break the cardinal rule of Web site design: Do Nothing to Slow Down the Customer Experience.

For a more in-depth look at caching and ad serving, take a look at the Appendix, "How Interactive Ads Are Delivered and Measurement Implication," written by Dick Bennett of ABC Interactive.

Now then, do you still remember our friend from WhizBang? The spider/robot/automated surfer that came by for a visit? You don't really want to include those creatures in your analysis, do you?

Robots Run Up the Numbers

You track your server logs and you chronicle the access trend over time. One day you launch a banner ad campaign and you see an astonishing jump in the number of visits to your site. Time to celebrate? Not yet.

First you have to be sure the additional hits weren't some new search spider (or an old one come back for a return visit) simply looking at every single page and "clicking" on every single link you have.

This is an ongoing issue, and several people have tried to keep on top of it. The Web Robots Pages at www.robotstxt.org/wc/robots.html has an impressive list, but alas, it's dated—a common problem.

That's why the IAB and ABCi figured it was newsworthy enough for a press release when they announced their monthly amended Master List of Spiders and Robots in October 2001:

> *The Interactive Advertising Bureau (IAB) has reached agreement with ABCi, an industry leader in the online third party verification arena, for ABCi to create and maintain the ABCi/IAB master industry list of spiders and robots. The list will be updated monthly and is available to IAB members and ABCi clients free of charge. It is the third step in a chain of recommendations, which will culminate in guidelines that the IAB will issue by the end of the year, all geared to improving the quality of online ad campaign measurement.*
>
> *As the IAB strives to provide its members, and the industry at large, with the tools that are necessary to streamline and improve the accuracy of online campaign measurement, the use of the ABCi/IAB master list of spiders and robots will go a long way towards eliminating inconsistent counts. The primary benefits of the list will be to reduce the time, effort, and cost to publishers, third party ad servers, and agencies associated with report reconciliation, and to provide advertisers with accurate measurement metrics," noted Robin Webster, president and CEO of the IAB. "By utilizing this approved and constantly updated master list, publishers will be able to filter out robot traffic from their reporting to advertisers, instilling greater confidence in the medium.*

Okay, so let's suppose you *are* able to filter out the automated clickers. All that's left will be real, live humans that you can count one by one, right? If only it were that simple.

How Many People on a Computer?

We are not yet living in the era of one person, one computer.

Once you've removed the robots from your reports, you now have to sift through and determine how many people are represented by all those clicks. By lumping all of the requests made from the same computer (207.154.137.4, for example), you can assume they all came from the same person. Except for two things: dynamic assignment of IP addresses and gateways.

When you dial into your local ISP, you are assigned an Internet Protocol (IP) address. That number is going to be drawn from a pool of numbers the ISP has on hand and you can be pretty sure you won't get the same number each time you dial up. Let's say you go to a certain site and then hang up your modem. Somebody else dials in, gets assigned the same IP address you were just using, and goes to the same site. The server logs for that site would think the two of you were one and the same.

The home computer is used by the whole family, so even if it *does* maintain the same IP address, your server log can't tell the difference between Mom, Dad, Wendy, or Doug.

The office computer used to be for the use of one individual, but the issue became clouded with the advent of notebook computers and wireless networks. Here, the local area network is doling out those IP addresses as needed, just like the dial-up ISP. Turn your notebook off and the IP address is sucked back into the pool for the next wandering employee.

Another log-baffling situation comes as the result of gateway computers. These are the systems that protect internal corporate networks and control the large number of users on online services such as America Online. Everybody surfing via America Online comes through an AOL gateway to your site. That means ten different people can look like one.

Is that somebody from Microsoft who seems to be *very* interested in your Web site? Or is it 200 people from Microsoft who were incorrectly told they could find a funny picture of Bill Gates on your site, found out there wasn't, and left? Due to the firewall hiding the final IP address, they all look like one person.

How Many People on a Web Site?

Your log file mixes together every click by every person. If your log shows 10,002 lines, they might have been made by one woman looking at two pages and one boy looking at 1,000 pages ten times. That's why the IP address is so important. It is the network node identification of the computer on which the requests were made.

Now we enter the Land of Assumptions. We assume that only one person was using each IP address that day. We assume each IP address only belonged to one computer that day. We assume that each person came to the site only once during that day. That's a lot of assumptions, and yes, we will tackle them in due course. First, a bit of good news—at least you can tell where those people came from.

Where Did They Come From?

Your server also keeps track of the links people clicked on to get to you. This information goes into the referer (sic) log file. If they type in the URL directly, there is no referral record in the file. If they come back by selecting a bookmarked page, no record is made. But all the rest, all those people who found you on Yahoo! or clicked on a banner ad or a link from a cooperative marketing partner will be duly noted in the log. That information is golden.

Which Page Had the Link?

The referer file holds part of the information you need to figure out which of your efforts is paying off. It will tell you how much traffic is coming from which attention-getting methods you have in place at any given point in time. This file is actually legible. The format for each entry is:

```
The page they were on -> the file they asked for
```

All that remains is to crunch the numbers and start tracking them over time. You'll very quickly determine that you get a certain percentage of visitors from Yahoo!, a certain percentage from MSN, from cooperative marketing partners, and from peoples' pages you didn't even know were pointing to you.

Once you know what the averages are, you can start to track the changes over time. When you launch a new ad banner campaign or trade a link with a new marketing partner, you'll know (almost) exactly what sort of response you provoked.

Knowing where the people were when they clicked over to your site is useful, but knowing *why* they did can be a serious competitive edge. The referer log holds more gold.

What Were They Looking For?

The very best part of what's locked up in your referer logs are the very search terms visitors typed into Excite, or Yahoo!, or Lycos. The URL of the page they were on is duly recorded, and that URL includes the long string of data the search engine used to produce the page, including the search term itself. A typical record might look like this:

```
empr2-29.menta.net - - [05/Nov/2001:02:23:09 -0800] "GET
/whitepaper.html HTTP/1.1" 200 8543
"http://www.google.com/search?q="business+metrics+for+the+new+economy"
&hl=es&lr=" "Mozilla/4.0 (compatible; MSIE 5.01; Windows 98)"
```

It doesn't take much to understand what people are looking for on my site (see Figure 5.2).

Knowing what people are looking for makes it possible to tabulate how many people found you generically ("running shoes") and how many found you using your brand name ("Nike"). An ongoing review of the terms people use can tell you which of your offline marketing efforts are working as well as your online promotions. It can give you a clue as to the changes in the language that the public uses to find your type of goods and services.

More important, you'll learn how to turn that language around for communicating back to your audience. The copy you write for your ads and brochures, the words you use on the buttons and links on your site, and even new product development should be sensitive to the words your prospects use.

Your referer log can also alert you to problems, because you are able to draw a correlation between the link clicked and the resulting actions.

Did They Stick Around?

If a large percentage of your visitors are dropping in, looking at one page, and leaving immediately, then you have a problem with how they are finding you. Let's say you run a Web site all about dogs. One of the pages you have up on your site talks about caring for canines in locations that often experience high temperatures. Playfully, you call this page Hot Dogs. You might notice that there are lots of people clicking through from AltaVista searches for "hot dogs." You're offering medical advice for man's best friend and they're looking for frankfurters. It's time to change your page so it doesn't attract the wrong kind of attention.

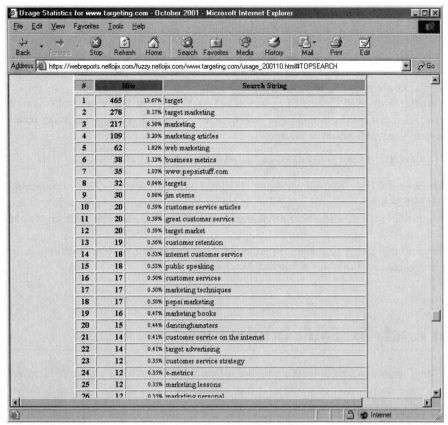

Figure 5.2 Yes, I did use the phrase "dancinghamsters" in one of my newsletters (#20), but most people find me because of some intersection of marketing and the Internet.

Your server logs can show the most-used entry and exit pages on your site. These are the pages most people use as a door into your site and the last page they looked at just before they left. A close scrutiny of those pages can tell you where people become disillusioned. Discovering where people decide to leave your site can give you valuable pointers to problem areas.

In between the entry and exit pages is the path most people take to get around. Is it direct? Is it painful? Do people wander around until they get fed up? How long do they stay on each page? Which pages are most popular? We'll get into this area in Chapter 9, "Calculating the Caliber of Content." We are not yet living in the era of one person, one computer, and in just a moment, we'll skip right over that era into the one that sees each person accessing your site from multiple computers, or mobile phones, or PDAs, or microwave ovens.

So you don't really know how many people looked at your site, and you don't really know which ones looked at what. Bummer. That's why they invented cookies, and we'll get to those soon enough. First, we have to deal with some more problems. Errors, to be precise.

Know the Code

Besides noting approximately how many people came to your site and where they came from, server logs also record server errors, and it's your job to make sure that incoming links are pointing to valid pages.

The World Wide Web Consortium (www.w3.org) is one of the organizations that publishes Web standards. You know one of their standard codes with total recall because you see it at least once a day:

Not found 404—The server has not found anything matching the URL given

Head over to the "Status codes in HTTP" page at www.w3.org/Protocols/HTTP/HTRESP.html to become familiar with what your Web server is trying to tell you. Especially if it's sending you anything in the 400 to 500 range—those codes are cries for help.

It's beyond my ability to probe the outer limits of the technical tools. I leave that to people more qualified than I. People like Mark Gibbs.

Error Analysis: Fault Intolerance

Mark Gibbs, must-read columnist on Web applications for the *Network World Newsletter* (www.nwfusion.com/newsletters/), has identified well the ways to track down and fix failures in code, as he shows in the following newsletter:

```
Date: Wed, 07 Nov 2001 17:30:02 -0600
Subject: Tracking down failures
To: jsterne@targeting.com
From: NW on WebApps <WebApps@bdcimail.com>
NETWORK WORLD NEWSLETTER: MARK GIBBS on WEB APPLICATIONS
11/07/01 Today's focus: Tracking down failures


Today's focus: Tracking down failures
By Mark Gibbs
Instrumentation--the measurement of something's operational and failure
states--is an area of Web applications design and management that has
been overlooked.
While you might know the details of your Web server's performance, you
probably aren't able to track down Web application failures if all that
exists to help you are the diagnostics in the operating system.
Have good heart, gentle reader--here's a plausible solution: the Halo
Application Fault Management system from InCert Software
(http://www.incert.com/). Halo is an add-on solution that can monitor
applications written in Java, C/C++ and Visual Basic, or third-party
code. Different applications require different Halo components to be
instrumented.
```

The first component is TouchBack for applications based on common development systems, such as Java under Windows NT, Windows 2000, Solaris and Linux; or C/C++, Visual Basic and Component Object Model under Windows NT, Windows 2000 and Solaris, where instrumentation can be added in at development time. TouchBack listens for the activation of selected processes and watches them for exceptions or hung conditions. When a fault occurs, TouchBack produces a "trace" file that shows information about the machine (CPU type and operating system version) and the environment, such as which versions of which modules are loaded. The trace file also provides details about memory and variables at the time of failure, as well as the line of code being executed at that time. This report can be e-mailed or sent automatically using File Transfer Protocol.

But TouchBack requires that you build it into the code. Many of us already have running applications and the prospect of going back and re-engineering our Web applications so we can get this kind of insight into our systems is merely a dream--there's neither the time nor the money to do so.

The other component, TraceBack, addresses the problem of instrumenting existing applications for Windows NT and Windows 2000. TraceBack is installed with reference to the source code after building for a given binary image. Once instrumented, the application can be deployed and will function as normal.

Upon failure, TraceBack creates a log file that includes all the information produced by TouchBack, plus a history of the program's execution correlated with the source code.

The Halo system monitors the TraceBack and TouchBack instrumented applications status with a Monitor Console that integrates with BMC's Patrol network management system to give a real-time view of application faults and fault history.

http://www.incert.com/solutions/incert_agentspring_solution.htm

Pricing is not cheap. For example, TraceBack starts at $20,000. Contact InCert for specific pricing for your environment.

To contact Mark Gibbs:

Mark Gibbs is a consultant, author, journalist, and columnist. He writes the weekly Backspin and Gearhead columns in Network World (http://www.nwfusion.com/columnists/gibbs.html). Gibbs is also president of Gibbs & Co. (http://www.gibbs.com/), a consulting organization for high-tech companies trying to get to grips with what they sell and how to talk about it. Gibbs can be contacted at mailto:webapps@gibbs.com.

What to Look for in a Log Sawing Tool

Getting the most out of your server logs will take more than a college intern and a case of Mountain Dew. You're going to need some tools. Be forewarned: There are many of them and they're not all readily comparable. Is a log-analysis-only tool enough for your needs? The following are a few things to consider.

Who Is the Software for?

Some tools are designed to help the Webmaster keep track of the raw numbers. These are good if you are worried about the strain placed on your server—sort of like worrying about the torque on your transmission linkage and the amount of horsepower your car produces. But a marketing manager is more interested in the miles per gallon and is looking for assurances that the car is not overheating and is headed in the right direction.

As you climb up the scale of cost for these packages, you'll find that the free ones will do some of the grunt work like the basic elimination of extraneous data, but the more expensive ones are more focused on delivering useful, business-oriented information. Decide what you want to know before digging into the specifications lists for these products or you'll be perpetually confused.

Flexibility

The more powerful the tool, the more you'll be able to create reports that are tailored to your needs. Generic reports are good as far as they go, and the more types of reports you can get, the more you'll find specific ones that are the most useful. But the real power of a superior piece of software shows up in your ability to create reports that specifically address your industry's needs, your Web site's peculiarities, and your promotional campaign nuances.

Archiving

One of the major drawbacks with log files is that they become more useful over time. The longer you keep them, the more you can refer back to historical data to get a bigger picture of traffic trends on your site. The downside is that log files are large and storing them is not a simple matter.

The better analysis tools also offer compression and archiving to shrink the size of the files and classify them for future use.

Output

A report is a report is a report. Right? Not so.

Some tools kick out reports that are merely rows of numbers. Most will draw charts and graphs. The better ones will do both, so that you can put the resulting data into other data visualization tools for even more informative manipulation. The upper-end tools let you compare month over month and integrate back-end data into your reports for a view of your e-business. Top-of-the-line tools give you reports that include non-Web data for a view of your business.

Scalability

Just how big *is* your site anyway? Just how much data are you recording in your logs? How many days are you going to add to your data before crunching some numbers?

When you add it all up, we're talking about a lot of information, and that means software that's up to the task. The major players in the Web analytics marketplace can almost certainly handle your needs (*almost* certainly), but when you're looking at some of the free stuff that's out there, ask the scalability question before getting in too deep.

Auditability

You're familiar with the idea of having your ad serving process and procedures audited, but don't forget that they can only do the job if they get the right data. Auditing services like ABCi need to see specific file types with specific data sets to render their unbiased certification. If you're going to sell ad space on your site, be sure the output from your metrics tools is compatible with your auditor's input requirements.

Speed

The biggest difference between getting your log analysis reports right away and getting them next week will be the power of the computer you use. But the log analysis tool vendors know faster reporting is a competitive edge. The better tools use special indexing techniques to perform their functions faster.

When it's time to compare the speed of different tools under consideration, be sure to try them out with your data, on your machine, in your office. This combination of factors has a large impact on how well each software package will operate, and you owe it to yourself to test them all on an even playing field.

Now let's run through the range of analysis tools to give you a feel for the landscape. We'll start with the basics after a few words of warning.

What to Look Out for in a Tool

You can read all about how wonderful these tools are at each of their Web sites. They're only too happy to tell you all their features, how easy they are to install and use, and how happy their customers are. The real world is a little bumpier than that. What speed bumps and potholes are down the road for you? Here are a few reports from the driver's seat to help you steer clear of jolts and jounces.

No Communicative Reports

"What bothers me is that the language of their fields is so complicated," complains the manager of a very large Web site with a lot of traffic. He says:

What is the real difference between "unique page views" versus "unique image views"? What's the difference between a "visit" and a "session"? I like to share this information with the product marketing managers. They give me some new content they want on the site and I report back to them on a weekly basis. I can't just send them raw reports because I'd have to spend days educating them how to read them.

I have to pull out the information that I know they are interested in, make some decisions on whether they want to see sessions rather that visitors or those kind of things. It takes more overhead to do manipulations to those reports so I can share them publicly. I'd never want to, although my boss is very analytical; she loves to look at spreadsheets and the numbers—we tried sending her a WebTrends report and she just got so bogged down in it, we spent hours going through it with her. We couldn't answer her questions.
So we agreed that OK, let's talk about what things we are really interested in and see what elements of WebTrends we can pull out. But that's frustrating.

Be prepared to do some massaging of those reports. The Web metrics managers at BellSouth send out a monthly Web Server Statistics Report, but they also send out a monthly Web Status Report that shows a specific page and includes an interpretation of the metrics collected and calculated for that page.

For a given month, they'll tell the recipients—in English sentences, rather than just spreadsheets and charts—that they had so many visitors, and how different that number is from the previous month. They then add some spin, some explanation. For example, people might get worried about a decline in visits from January to February, when the numbers simply reflect a shorter month. Instead of just averaging the visits per day, the BellSouth gang calculates the additional 3 days on the end of the month as an extrapolation of the previous trends. That way, they can give a more credible month-to-month comparison.

These reports will also include observations that don't pop out at the casual reader. Perhaps they'll note that it took longer for people to find a given page, or that the visits to the press release area and the product descriptions went up while the trend of visits to the home page flattened out, indicating that people are finding new ways to reach the site other than through the home page.

The Web metrics managers will comment on the traffic pulled in by email versus banner advertising, how many new registrants there are, and how much traffic is coming to the site from their Cingular Wireless site. Sure, the numbers go out. But this sort of interpretation is what really piques the interest of businesspeople.

The magic sauce in all of this is being able to tell what you're looking at, rather than expecting the software to hand you the answers. Gregg Dixon, vice president of Internet Services for the Crayola brand at Binney & Smith, says: "I think that the very best way to determine what you really need for data and how to use it is as business experts—people who have lots of experience and who are bright at seeing trends and noticing certain consumer behaviors. It takes those people basically doing lots of tests on things and then determining what really works best and having the technical ability to measure performance. You can't say we're going to lay this solution on top of all our data and it's going to do all the data mining for us and tell us what things matter most on the site. At the end of the day it takes bright people thinking creatively to determine what sort of things to test and analyze."

So, I asked him, we haven't found the technical replacement for intuition yet?

"No," answered Dixon, "and we never will. Frankly, I'm not sure that we ever should because intuition is what gets at the greatest gems."

No Overnight Success

If you want to download a log analysis tool and start getting reports immediately, you won't face a lot of problems. But if you're interested in garnering some serious business intelligence from a serious analysis tool, then be prepared for an installation, implementation, and interpretation proposition.

Kara Heinrichs, chief customer experience officer at Fry Multimedia (www.fry.com), has used a whole host of e-metrics tools on behalf of her clients:

> *If you have a good data analyst working with the software they can do good things. But the development and implementation curve is so long that sometimes we're just kind of watching helplessly and trying to help out with regards to making sure that the metrics are matching up with the ones they used to get.*
>
> *A lot of what we're doing these days with our clients is in lieu of the tools actually being there in a package and good-to-go is to encourage them to think about their business questions and then allow us to use whatever simple minded tools or complex tool we have to get them to an answer.*
>
> *If we want to know about buyer behavior versus non-buyer behavior and we happen to be doing that out of log files, we'll just run a script against the log files and pull out all the sessions of a buyer, sample that across the server farm, and run an analysis across that smaller data set.*

No Guarantees

One well-known manufacturer was about to unload his woes when he brought himself up short: "I'll trust you will hold it in confidence . . ." I assured him I would, as indeed I am.

He continued:

> *They came in and gave this beautiful presentation to us and it was great and we were drooling because we knew that we could build the system ourselves, but it would take our best developers months to do it. And they came in and basically said here's what we can do. They showed us an example running on a laptop and we were like wow, this is what we need. And for x thousands of dollars worth of investment per month, we don't even need our other tools any more.*
>
> *We don't need an entire server to support our reporting, we simply dump the user log to them every night and we get this beautiful reporting and analytics tool to use that solves all these problems. Everybody's talking about how we're not a difficult site, our data structures are very clearly defined, we know very clearly what we want—it all looked great.*
>
> *But the implementation of it was four times longer than what we expected and what we got back was nowhere near what was demonstrated for us.*

Buyer beware.

No Instant Gratification

Only some of the tools on the market today are able to kick out reports in real time. If you want to know how many people looked at your latest press release in the last 10 minutes, you definitely need to open your wallet. Standard log analysis tools are of the after-the-fact variety, crunching yesterday's numbers. Since these are the least expensive, we should start with them.

What You Can Learn from Log Analysis: The Basics

Any software you might use to make sense of your Web site is likely to find its way onto a list of log analysis tools. There are a lot of tools and many more become available every day. The last time I looked, there were nineteen of them at this Yahoo! category: http://dir.yahoo.com/Computers_and_Internet/Software/Internet/World_Wide_Web/Servers/Log_Analysis_Tools/.

But there were another forty-three at this site: http://dir.yahoo.com/Business_and_Economy/Business_to_Business/Communications_and_Networking/Internet_and_World_Wide_Web/Software/World_Wide_Web/Log_Analysis_Tools.

Most of the products on those lists are actually log analysis tools: the tools that take in your server logs and hand back reports of various kinds. These tools don't know about your back-end legacy systems. They don't know about registrations, purchases, customer service emails, or things that are served up dynamically from a database. Everything they know and report on they learn from your server logs.

WebTrends

Probably the most well known of the log analysis tools is WebTrends (www.webtrends.com). They've been at it the longest. "Log Analyzer," says their site, "is the web traffic analysis software package that introduced the WebTrends brand to web administrators and marketing managers everywhere. It's the ideal entry-level package for any small business ready to apply insights into visitor behavior to improve overall site performance." You can download a free trial version and pay the $500 if you like what you see, so the price is right.

The basic version of WebTrends delivers a healthy amount of information for the money and tracks the following information:

Hits

　Entire site (Successful)

　Average per day

　Home page

Page Views

　Page views (impressions)

　Average per day

　Document views

Visitor Sessions

Visitor sessions

Average per day

Average visitor session length

International visitor sessions

Visitor sessions of unknown origin

Visitor sessions from United States

Visitors

Unique visitors

Visitors who visited once

Visitors who visited more than once

WebTrends comes with some useful prepackages reports (see Figures 5.3 to 5.8).

Figure 5.3 shows the overall number of visits. The people who come to your site in a given time period are counted based on sessions. If they go get a cup of coffee, take a phone call, head off to a meeting, or go home at night, and are gone for more than 30 minutes, their session is considered closed. The very next time they click, WebTrends considers it a brand-new session.

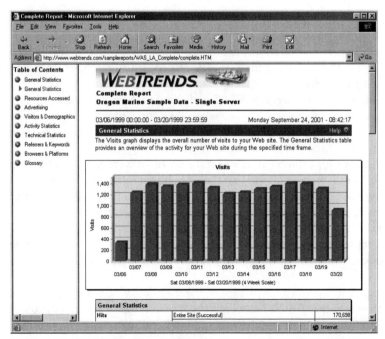

Figure 5.3 WebTrends report showing the overall number of visits.

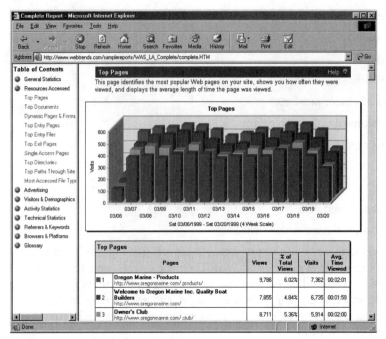

Figure 5.4 WebTrends Top Pages report.

Figure 5.4 is a graphical view of what people find interesting on your site. Which pages are most popular? How often are they looked at by the surfing public? How long did people ogle each page before moving on?

Keeping track of the top entry pages, as WebTrends does in the report shown in Figure 5.5, is crucial, as the first pages visitors see when they come to your site can make a serious first impression. You might very well think that your home page is the front door to your site, and you might very well be wrong.

How many times were ads seen on your site and how often were they clicked? You may think the report of views and clicks, like the one shown in Figure 5.6, is only of interest to those who sell advertising on their sites. Rest assured, they care. But this report can also be very interesting if you post special offers, closeout specials, or other promotions on your site that point to other areas within your site.

Knowing how people find your site is crucial if you're trying to attract the attention of more people. So, keep track of referring sites with a report like the one shown in Figure 5.7.

WebTrends is happy to draw you a picture of the popularity of search terms that drew people to you (see Figure 5.8). What were people searching for when they found you?

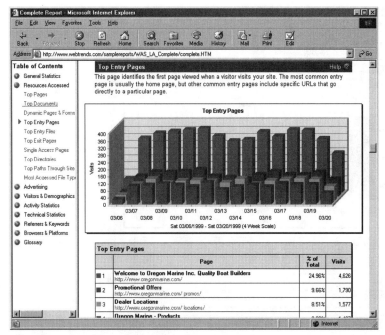

Figure 5.5   WebTrends Top Entry Pages report.

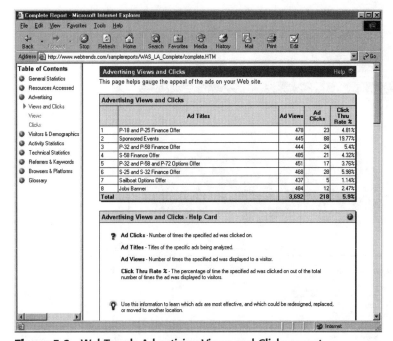

Figure 5.6   WebTrends Advertising Views and Clicks report.

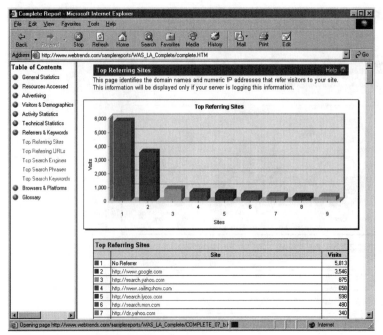

Figure 5.7   WebTrends Top Referring Sites report.

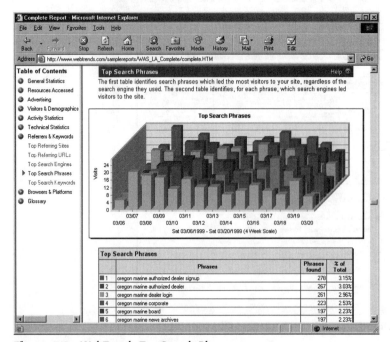

Figure 5.8   WebTrends Top Search Phrases report.

Record Only What You Need

By the time you reach the end of this book, you'll see that there are lots and *lots* of data-points available for capture, storage, and analysis. The intention here is to help you choose *what* to measure and what action to take based on the results. But there is one conundrum that's come up in almost every conversation I've had with Web managers, Web executives, and clients that we should address first: How much measurement can you afford?

Sites can choose to store or not store most types of information. For example, most sites choose to store only page views, excluding graphics. Sites can also choose to store important query parameters and search keywords while ignoring the rest, or whether or not to store complete referring URLs or just the name of the site.

The real problem shows up when you want to look at trends over time. Year-on-year analysis becomes very difficult if you don't have last year's data. And it gets exponentially more difficult when you consider all the changes you've made to your site over time.

How to Get the Best Site Traffic Numbers

In a Business 2.0 article entitled "Why Your Site Traffic Numbers Are Out of Whack" (March 2001) (www.business2.com/articles/mag/print/0,1643,9319,00.html), Brian Caulfield included a section called "How to Get the Best Site Traffic Numbers," which states:

> *Even with high-end site analytics software, it's impossible to get dead-on traffic counts. But with some care, you can get reasonably good numbers. Here's what to do.*
>
> 1. *Stomp out spiders. To distinguish spiders' hits from those created by real users, look for unusual activity on your logs. Spiders do things no normal person would, like visit every single page on your site in an hour. Once you think you've found a spider, comb through Web logs to locate its IP address, then direct your analytics software to ignore future hits originating from that address.*
>
> 2. *Watch out for masked IP addresses. Not every address represents an individual user. Corporations and dial-up ISPs (notably AOL) can show your server a single IP address for many, many actual users. Look for high traffic from a single address; it may indicate that you have more users than your data suggests.*
>
> 3. *Avoid cookie monsters. Don't expect accurate visitor counts from cookies. An unknown number of Web users set their browsers not to accept cookies. Cookies also can't distinguish between multiple people using the same computer—for example, PCs in libraries and schools.*
>
> 4. *Bust those caches. The most common way to defeat the problem of cached pages is to generate as many pages as possible "on the fly," using scripts to assemble them from a database, says Scott Hanson, vice president for auditing services at ABC Interactive. Dynamic pages are extremely difficult to cache.*

5. *Know your audience.* *Since Media Metrix and Nielsen//NetRatings track users only in homes and at work, ask your IT department to filter out users coming from libraries and schools before comparing trends in your site's traffic with Media Metrix's figures.*

Nothing brings the eCompany Now Web team closer to blows than the issue of traffic. Our server log files, ad banner logs, and tracking software give numbers that can vary 25 percent, and everyone who needs that data—from sales to editorial to marketing—is miffed about the absence of reliable numbers. Here are some lessons we've learned.

- *Decide in advance exactly what data you want to collect.*

- *Pick the right site-metrics software. Because we lacked clear expectations about what data we wanted, we chose a $10,000 version from WebTrends when we probably needed the deluxe version that cost 15 times as much.*

- *Dedicate a powerful piece of hardware to run the software, and have a technical person learn it, tweak it, and field requests for custom data runs.*

The above is what you get when you look at a pile of data (server logs) and ask, "What does it mean? What can it tell us?" The next step is to ask, "What do we want to know and how much information is there about that?"

As I am always trying to promote looking at the world from the customer perspective, I've organized this book that way. That's why the next chapter delves into the way most people hear of your company or product for the first time.

The obvious question is: How do you determine if you're doing a good job at getting people to come to your Web site?

How Good Are
You at Making Noise?

There are many books about *how* to get people to come to your Web site. I've even written a few of them. The question on the table for this book is, how do you measure how *well* you're attracting attention?

Attention comes in many forms, and the first thing people usually think of is banner advertising. Don't worry—we'll get there soon enough. But when you look at all of this from the customer perspective, the first way people find your site is because they already know you. If not, they find you through a search engine. Or maybe, just maybe, you were adroit enough to capture their attention with a banner. You may have enticed them back with an email. You might even have managed to get others to attract attention on your behalf.

So let's follow this vision of customer-centric perspective, starting with managing your brand.

Tending Your Brand

DuPont looks at brand management in two ways, according to the manager of online communications at DuPont's Corporate Brand Office, Kiko Suarez, "One is what we call direct. We control the timing and the message and the audience and the placement and the delivery." The rest of the world calls that marketing and advertising.

"And then," he continues, "we have what we call indirect where we do not control but we influence the time and the message, the audience, place, and delivery. Direct communications for us are both external and internal. External communications are things like publications, contributions to local communities, and speeches.

"The Internet is one of the channels we control and everything that has to do with advertising, promotion, etcetera, etcetera. Internally, we have also an intranet (which we control) and then email communication, publications, et cetera. The indirect, as you can imagine, is everything else. So we also keep an eye on government, media relationships, crisis management—that kind of thing."

Your brand is not something you manage. Yes, I hear cries of outrage from tens of thousands of people who have "Brand Manager" on their business cards and the people who have posted 256 brand management job opportunities at Monster.com. But just get in line behind those people who ascribe themselves software engineers. These terms are not so much oxymorons as misnomers.

You don't engineer software. You write it. You author it. You create it. You invent it.

You don't manage a brand. You coddle it. You influence it. You protect it. You nurture it. So how on earth do you measure your brand? Glad you asked. Kiko Suarez has part of the answer:

> Unique visitors is a useful metric because that gives you an idea of how visible your brand is and how many more impacts you are having. DuPont is a B to B company, but we still have a lot of consumer pull. DuPont.com is getting a lot of consumers. So the Web is an excellent way for us to expose our brand to the consumer audience.
>
> We're still sponsoring the NASCAR, but we have less and less opportunities to do that kind of thing except at the point of sale. DuPont.com is becoming one of the three top brand building tools for consumers. So we highlighted to management that over 65 percent of customers get in touch with brands and companies on the Web for the first time.

Merely keeping track of how many people type in your URL directly is as valid a way to track the vigor of your brand as DuPont's methods—and not just your corporate brand, but your product brands as well. "Another thing that we are doing, "says Suarez, "is offering sub-domains of DuPont.com to our own business units; www.kevlar.com, www.corian.com, www.lycra.com, that kind of thing. So we [are] measuring success in how we reinforce our corporate brand. We measure the number of visits that we get to a very specific section of DuPont.com that we call the interactive channel. That's like a window with the home page where we're going to be providing any page about our brands and that's an opportunity for us to provide an educational tool for lines and brands to consumers."

Suarez works in corporate communications at DuPont. That means his group is responsible for the image that the company projects into the world and for communicating with those people who want to talk to the company.

"We own investors. When they talk to DuPont they talk to DuPont, they do not talk to Lycra. We own employees together with HR. Then we own the other stakeholder that we call 'society,' where we have influencers. The only one that we do not own is customers because [they] are interested in things like buying a product and that is the responsibility of the business unit."

If you work in corporate communications, then you'll want to be measuring your online success by how often people use the pages you've created for them. Are people reading up on the company history? Do they show interest in the Letter from the Chairman? Are they looking through your archive of press releases? Do they click on the links to reports about the company's charity work?

And by the way, are you serving the journalistic community as well?

Media Relations

As director of media relations at BellSouth, Bill McClosky made enough noise early on about the need for a Web presence that they handed him the job of managing the Corporate Information Center at www.bellsouth.com.

He looks over the figures and finds that traffic is a function of what was always a traditional offline means of getting attention. "Frankly what we see as driving traffic is an interesting press release," he says. "When we push a press release out, we find that often we'll get people to come to the site or follow a link in the press release back to the site. It does give us the traffic, and if you use the word 'Internet' in the headline in the release, it really draws traffic. So Internet people care about Internet things."

McClosky keeps his eye on more than page views: "We've got a registration page where you can sign up to receive all releases we put out or just in a specific area. So if you only care about wireless things in Alabama, that's all you're going to get. You won't get anything about ADSL in Georgia."

What is the press interested in? What does the public want to be notified about? Knowing the answers can make a big difference in what information you offer in the future.

There's one other measurement that Bill finds valuable: "I know it gets a lot of traffic off my telephone. It saved me some late-night phone calls from reporters who all of a sudden at ten o'clock need a factoid for a story running the next morning." You can quantify cost-avoidance, but don't forget annoyance-avoidance. That's a great return on investment as well.

But does good public relations really drive traffic? Yes. How can you tell? Kodak undertook a measurement project that's as pretty as a picture, as described in this article from "Interactive Public Relations," produced by Lawrence Ragan Communications (www.ragan.com):

How much should your PR contribute to your Web site?
Answer: Five percent of weekly traffic and 4 percent of page views. That's what Kodak.com and agency Shandwick Interactive PR found after a 53-day beta measurement project to determine how PR and other traffic-driving tools affect Web site traffic.
"This project's goal was to determine if PR moves the needle, and yes, it does. Now, we'll look to continue this effort with all online PR programs, not only to determine what works and what doesn't but also to make accurate predictions on what we do. Such a model will justify our role and increases our credibility," says Kodak.com's PR manager Kristine Thompson.

Here's how the measurement project shook out:
Kodak.com promoted its May 19 (2000) launch of the Picture Playground section via aggressive media relations, Business Wire announcement, press releases to news and regional sites, hot sites, search engines/directories, and a small online briefing with 15 key reporters—all considered part of Kodak's PR for the section launch.

From May 19 to July 10, Kodak and Shandwick manually checked the top 100 referral links each day to determine where Web site visitors originated. The team visited each URL to ensure the referral was, indeed, generated because of the PR push. They discounted those that were not. This research took roughly 300 hours.

The Picture Playground section provides users with several photo-manipulating and sharing applications. For example, the Cartoon Maker takes uploaded pictures and turns them into cartoons. The Super Saturator drowns pictures in several colors. The Flower Power feature makes any face into a blooming flower.

Once the picture has been altered, users can play with photo-sharing applications, such as the Kodak PhotoQuilt Project, which weaves personal pictures into a virtual patchwork quilt. The Kodak Picture This postcards allow visitors to add a border, greeting, and personalized message to send to friends and family.

Pictures also can be made into prints and photo gifts such as mugs, sweatshirts, puzzles, and mouse pads.

During the eight-week PR launch and measurement period, the average number of weekly visitors was 11,923, or 5 percent, of total visitors and 120,155, or 4 percent, of total page views. PR really kicked in during the second week when it drove 18,524, or 7 percent, of total visitors and 200,365, or 6 percent, of total page views.

For the entire eight-week program, the top traffic generators—with referral links in the top 100 for one week or more—by category were:

> ***Search engines and directories** like Yahoo! Photography: Drove roughly 45 percent of visitors and 66 percent of page views.*
>
> ***Reviews on leading news/community sites** like USA Today and Project Cool (e.g., hot sites): Drove roughly 39 percent of visitors and 27 percent of page views. For example, USA Today was the top referral for two consecutive days and remained in the top 100 for 12 days. It generated 2,596, or 14 percent, of visitors and 25,664, or 12 percent, of page views.*
> *Project Cool was listed in the top 100 referral links for more than 20 days.*
>
> ***ISPs:** Drove roughly 14 percent of visitors and 4 percent of page views.*

For example, SSi Micro and Cybertours Inc. resulted in SSi ranking in the top 100 referral links for 16 consecutive days and generated 1,608, or 9 percent, of visitors and 3,357, or 2 percent, of page views.

Cybertours ranked in the top 100 for a total of 33 days and generated 934, or 5 percent, of visitors and 7,309, or 3 percent, of page views.

Roughly three percent of visitors came from regional news sites, which typically generate short-term traffic—these sites were listed in the top 100 referrals for two days maximum. Examples include The Rochester Business Journal, Cincinnati Inquirer, and Electronic Telegraph. Similarly, wire services, like Business Wire, generate short-term traffic; most were listed in the top 100 referrals for only one to two days, then available only via archived searches.

Overall, Yahoo! was the top traffic generator, delivering 45 percent of overall traffic and 57 percent of page views. Yahoo! referral links included:

- *Yahoo! Picks, generated 2,249 visitors and 110,855 page views.*

- *Yahoo! Cool links generated 2,417 visitors and 41,147 page views.*

- *Yahoo! directory links generated 1,747 visitors and 21,048 page views.*

- *Yahoo! Finance generated 326 visitors and 4,730 page views.*

- *Yahoo! UK, Cool links generated 28 visitors and 1,350 page views.*

- *Yahoo! Canada Cool links generated 88 visitors and 439 page views.*

For some serious, in-depth research into public relations metrics in general, the "Guidelines and Standards for Measuring and Evaluating PR Effectiveness" takes a look at the following:

Awareness and comprehension measurements

Recall and retention measurements

Attitude and preference measurements

Behavior measurements

You can find this article at The Institute for Public Relations (Figure 6.1) (www. instituteforpr.com).

It's good to watch what interests the media to save time and aggravation, but when it comes to brand management, you have to ask people for their opinion of your company.

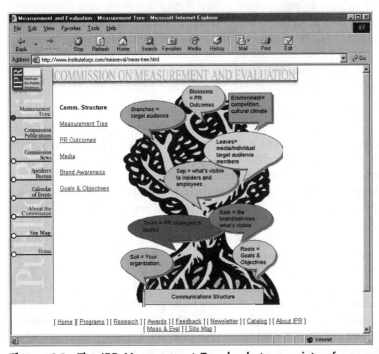

Figure 6.1 The IPR Measurement Tree leads to a variety of papers of public relations metrics.

Measuring Public Opinion

In a press release (www.jmm.com/xp/jmm/press/2001/pr_062501.xml) dated June 25, 2001, Jupiter Media Metrix (www.jmm.com) reported that the actual return on investment (ROI) from online advertising is at least 25 percent to 35 percent higher than most marketers believe. Why? Because most marketers are forgetting to add in the value of online branding.

The Jupiter Executive Survey found that only 15 percent of marketers were conducting formal online branding measurement, favoring direct-response metrics, which we'll cover in a following section.

Rudy Grahn, Jupiter analyst, suggests that "marketers will learn that they must begin quantifying online branding by measuring users' actual experience instead of gauging only their attitudes. Not everything is intended to be branding, but everything brands."

Key findings reported in the press release included the following:

According to Jupiter analysts, marketers who are looking to correlate ad spending with an increase in traffic are taking the wrong approach. In fact, Jupiter case studies show that while online advertising is more effective than marketers believe, it is still secondary to other factors in driving traffic to Web sites. Online advertising only contributes to 17 percent of the traffic to a Web site, while seasonality and an increase in Internet adoption contribute to 46 percent and 37 percent of the growth, respectively. Jupiter analysts suggest that marketers can measure branding value by correlating behavioral data (including individual user click-streams, repeated surfing patterns and aggregate user behavior) with the flights of specific ads. While there are not yet standards for determining this correlation, marketers have begun experimenting with calculating the relationship between aggregate spending and the corresponding volume of users' behavior such as hits on store locator pages, information requests and hits on phone-ordering information pages.

Okay, measuring brand impact is good. You knew that, But how do you *do* it? The same way you've always done it. You ask a panel of target market people about what they know/think about your company/product. You then show them some ads. Then you ask them again. For some, you wait until the next day to ask them and sometimes you wait a week to see if they still remember.

Kris Carpenter keeps track of frequency of return to help indicate how well the people at Excite are managing brand stewardship. But Excite also pays a lot of attention to public opinion. Even when they make changes to their navigation, they measure the impact of those changes by interviewing people. Using a third-party marketing research company, they keep tabs on how people feel about the site.

Using third-party marketing is like being in high school again and asking your friend to ask that cute person you're interested in if he or she likes you. If you ask people directly, they'll always respond with "of course I like you. I mean, it's not like I *like* like you, but of course I like you. Everybody likes you." Valuable, useful content is equal to zero. But when a third party asks, the response could be anything from nerd-dork-loser to cute-attractive-dreamboat. Now you know whether to make your move or move out of the country. Very useful.

In the world of branding, you're dealing with unassisted recall (Do you remember anything?), assisted recall (Do you remember the gorilla?), and attitudes (How do you feel about the company/product now?). That middle part, about the gorilla, is much more important than it seems.

In 2001, Christopher Chabris, a Harvard researcher, asked a group of people to watch a videotaped basketball game and count the passes made by one team or the other. In the middle of the action, a guy in a gorilla suit comes on the scene, scratches himself under the arms, and walks off. He was on the video for about 5 seconds. Forty percent of those watching simply did not see the gorilla and accused the researcher of making it up (archive.newscientist.com).

The moral of the story is that it's hard to get people to remember something. That's why "recall" is one of the important measurements of a branding campaign. As for attitude, that's a statistical issue as well. You just need that third party—somebody like Dynamic Logic (www.dynamiclogic.com).

In their own words, "Dynamic Logic is an online research company that specializes in measuring the impact of online communications." That means they ask the right questions—they even let *you* ask a couple of questions. Here's what they cover:

> *Awareness Levels. Are people more familiar with a brand or product as a result of exposure?*
>
> *Message Association. Can people connect a message or slogan with a specific brand?*
>
> *Purchase Intent. Are people more likely to buy a given product or service?*
>
> *Custom Yes/No Question. Determined by the client*
>
> *Custom Open-Ended Question. Determined by the client*
>
> *In addition to gathering data in a blind environment, the respondents are subsequently re-shown the banner and asked to give feedback, specifically about:*
>
> *Banner Recall. Do respondents remember seeing the banner?*
>
> *Visual Appeal. Do they like it?*
>
> *Message Appeal. Does the message convey the value of the good or service well?*

Many advertisers use multiple channels to communicate with consumers—some of which are offline and some are online. In addition to gathering attitudinal feedback from those who were exposed to a banner, AdIndex recruits a control sample to discount all attitudinal influences other than the banner. The sample is collected at the same time using the same targeting of the media buy to isolate the impact that the banner had on the minds and perceptions of web site visitors.

After you set up your banner and questions, AdIndex displays the results online (see Figures 6.2 and 6.3).

Knowing that branding is a soft subject, Dynamic Logic is very strict in the science of its methodology: "Dynamic Logic measures consumer perceptions and attitudes toward an advertiser's brand by capturing consumer opinions through an online survey. AdIndex gathers this data while the online campaign is running. To isolate the impact of advertising exposure on consumer attitudes, two groups of online consumers are sampled at the same time and from the same Web sites on which the campaign is running. As the only difference between the groups is the presence of the advertising, any attitudinal differences between the two groups can be attributed to the exposure to the ad campaign."

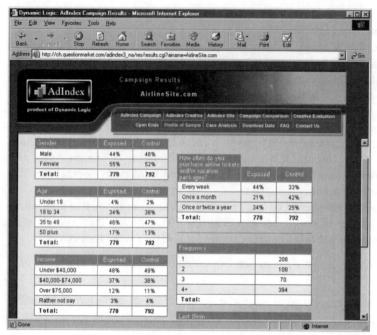

Figure 6.2   The Dynamic Logic's AdIndex service shows you whom they're testing.

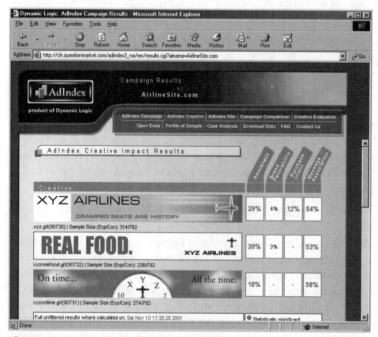

Figure 6.3   . . . and whether they remembered the ad and whether they feel better about the brand and are more likely to buy it.

You can learn a lot about which banners have the most impact from Dynamic Logic. Given the aggregate information the company collects from multiple advertisers, you can also learn the tips and tricks of improving your branding efforts. Tip 1: Don't forget your logo (see Figure 6.4) (www.dynamiclogic.com/beyond_1_7.html).

Dynamic Logic also measures the brand impact made by frequency ("Four or more exposures doubles impact of online branding" and "The branding value of online advertising plateaus after five exposures") and cleanliness ("Uncluttered banners lifted awareness by 14 percent, whereas cluttered banners lifted awareness by only 3 percent").

For a great deal more on online branding measurement and how it compares to offline branding measurement, take a look at "Branding 101: An Overview of Branding and Brand Measurement for Online Marketers" at www.dynamiclogic.com/site/Branding_101.doc.

It's important to keep in mind that branding doesn't happen in a vacuum. If your product is below par or if your customer service sucks, there's just no way that a great banner is going to help much. Remember that the Internet is a big place and there are sites out there where your reputation is being discussed. Are you paying attention?

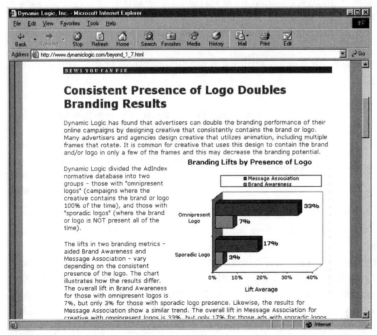

Figure 6.4 Dynamic Logic reports that you can double the branding performance of your online campaigns by consistently displaying your logo.

Reputation Management

Here's how Jakob Nielsen describes an online reputation manager (from www.useit. com/alertbox/990905.html):

> *A reputation manager is an **independent service** that keeps track of the **rated quality, credibility**, or some other desirable metric for each element in a set. The things being rated will typically be **websites, companies, products, or people**, but in theory anything can have a reputation that users may want to look up before taking action or doing business. The reputation metrics are typically collected from other users who have had dealings with the thing that is being rated. Each user would indicate whether he or she was satisfied or dissatisfied. In the simplest case, the reputation of something is the average rating received from all users who have interacted with it in the past.*

So are you looking out for your reputation?

Reputation Sites

Like many e-commerce innovations, Amazon.com seems to have been the first to trot out the dynamic, online reputation voting idea. Any reader can post an opinion—good or bad. And I don't mean whether they liked the book or not, I mean whether the review they wrote was worth the pixels they were printed with. So Amazon.com took a page from eBay's book.

eBay had a problem with unscrupulous sellers. There were some who would not deliver what was promised, overcharged their buyers, or had friends help jack up the price just before the bidding closed. What to do? Reputation management! eBay created a way for buyers to rate the sellers to acknowledge their integrity or to warn off potential buyers. Very well.

But not great from the seller's side of things. A vindictive buyer could ruin a seller's reputation. After all,

> **Who steals my purse steals trash; 'tis something, nothing;**
> **'Twas mine, 'tis his, and has been slave to thousands:**
> **But he that filches from me my good name**
> **Robs me of that which not enriches him**
> **And makes me poor indeed.**
> **(Othello, act 3, scene 3)**

eBay responded by turning the tables and letting the sellers post their opinions of the buyers. Do they pay on time? Do they pay at all? Do they return items after breaking them? Fair's fair.

So after receiving (and automatically posting) reviews that were not necessarily valuable, Amazon.com decided to let the people decide. Now, reviews are marked by the readers of the review for value. On October 25, 2001, Sarah Smith from Saratoga, California, said that my book, *World Wide Web Marketing, 3rd Edition*, was a "Great Book. . . This is one of the better books I've read on internet marketing. I really recommend this book for anyone who is getting into this web marketing arena." (Thank you, Sarah!) The review, like all of them, is followed by the question, "Was this review helpful to you?" a "Yes" button, and a "No" button.

Unfortunately, only "1 of 1 people," in Amazonian parlance, found the review help-ful. Why? Two reasons, I think. First, because it was the most recent review posted at the time and not that many people had seen it yet. Second, it's short—not a lot of infor-mation. But at least we're batting 1,000—everybody who voted was positive.

Not so with the next review by Andrew B. King from Ann Arbor, Michigan. Only ten out of eleven people found Andrew's review useful, and he was even more effusive and emphatically positive than Sarah. (Thank *you*, Mr. King!). He spent the time to write about the book and explain what people could find in it. Heck, he even copied the table of contents. That was useful.

Negative reviews can be useful as well. "A reader from United States" wrote a review of the first edition of *World Wide Web Marketing*, complaining that the first edi-tion of that book was, "Out of date!" and proceeded to bash it for being a waste of time. Considering that the book was published in 1995 (which means I wrote it in 1994) and he/she bought it in September 1998, I quickly posted a followup review warning people *not* to buy the book—that a new edition was available.

Amazon.com and eBay are the sites that got the whole thing started and then it blos-somed from there. Now we have a myriad of sites that do nothing but reputation man-agement. If you want to get twenty-three customer reviews of the Miele S 300 Series Vacuum Cleaner (Pros: Powerful, ergonomic, a pleasure to use. Cons: Expensive—if it were free, it would be perfect), Epinions.com is the place for you (see Figure 6.5). Epin-ions is a comparison shopping service that uses a reputation management system to gather high-quality, unbiased reviews from consumers. They even have reviews of online stores and local automobile mechanics.

Figure 6.5 Epinions, according to its Web site, "is the source for unbiased advice, personalized recommendations, and comparative shopping."

Is your company or product listed on Epinions? How about on any of the following sites:

Bizrate.com. "Compare prices and customer ratings of over 1,500 stores to always get the best deal!"

ConsumerReview.com. "Find products you're interested in, read reviews, participate in discussions about these products, and find places to buy them online."

Dooyoo.co.uk. "On dooyoo you can read trustworthy reviews of products and services, written by people who actually use them. You can even write your own—and we'll pay you for it."

Gamecritics.com. "Ratings, reviews, consumer advice, and more."

Gomez.com. "Gomez offers expert rankings, merchant rankings, and decision support tools to help consumers make informed decisions when choosing services or shopping online."

PlanetFeedback.com. "Ratings are report cards based on our users' opinions . . . derived from the opinions reported by PlanetFeedback users through the site's letter-writing utility."

OpenRatings.com. "Independent, unbiased e-commerce rating service designed to increase the level of trust, reliability, and brand recognition between buyer and seller."

RateItAll.com. "RateItAll helps other companies add consumer reviews to their Web sites. This site is the hub of our opinion-sharing network, where you can find and share opinions on thousands of topics."

Zagat Survey (www.zagat.com). "The world's premier provider of consumer survey-based dining, lodging and leisure information."

There are also the sites that are simply designed for complaints. Places like BitchAboutIt.com ("Online Complaint Department, gripes, complaining online, votes, opinions, consumer complaints, automotive complaints, telephone complaints . . . mad as hell and not going to take it anymore?"), Complaints.com ("Help other consumers avoid the same pitfalls. Post your complaints to the Complaints.com database. *The entire world can read your complaints!*"), ComputerGripes.com ("This web site is devoted to what stinks about computer products"), and FightBack.com (television's David Horowitz goes online).

Jakob Nielsen thinks reputation management is an important area to keep your eye on: "I see reputation managers as core to the success of the Web. As we get more sites, more content, and more services online, users need a way to learn what is credible and useful. Quality assessments must become an explicit component of most Web user interfaces. It is not sufficient to list millions of items for sale and leave it to the user to determine what they need. Everybody is *not* equal."

YourCompanySucks Sites

The poke in the corporate eye may not even be as blatant as www.chasebanksucks.com or www.homedepotsucks.com. Your company might simply be listed at www.sucks500.com

(see Figure 6.6) and you don't know it. The impact on your brand is obvious. The question is, how do you measure this outpouring of displeasure? Your job is to assign the task to somebody to review what's going on out there and report back.

How many sites have targeted your company? If that number is growing, you have a serious problem. If it's shrinking, you have a serious lawyer.

How many negative comments are posted to message boards? Total? New today? If you don't remember the Emulex story, you may be destined to repeat it:

Costa Mesa, Calif., August 25, 2000—Emulex Corporation (NASDAQ:EMLX), the world's largest supplier of fibre channel adapters, announced that unknown persons have published and circulated a fictitious press release this morning. Among the false statements in this fictitious Emulex press release were assertions that the company's CEO had resigned, that its recently reported fourth quarter results were to be restated, and that Emulex was under investigation by the Securities and Exchange Commission, all of which are untrue.

That press release from Emulex did not mention that their stock went from $113 to $45 in the next hour before trading was halted. Still think that reputation management isn't important?

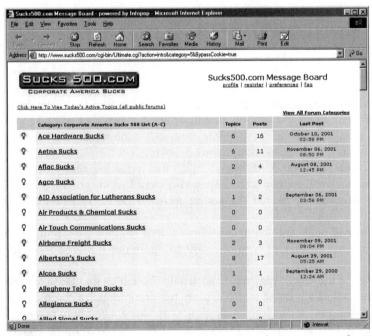

Figure 6.6 It's open season on complaints at Sucks 500.com, and your company could be in the gun sights.

You can get some help from companies like Intelliseek and their Corporate Intelligence Service (CIS). On their Web site (www.intelliseek.com), they describe their services like this:

Intelliseek's Corporate Intelligence Service (CIS) is a comprehensive, real-time, online monitoring service allowing corporations to get timely insights into consumer discussions and media coverage about their products or services, potentially damaging rumors and competitor activities. CIS is a secure, ASP service built on Intelliseek's ESS platform. It monitors tens of thousands of Usenet forums, message boards, online news, online publications and more.

CIS features patent-pending technology that converts information found in consumer postings and media coverage into actionable reports. In turn, these reports provide deep insights into consumer perceptions on specific attributes of a brand or company, competitive comparisons, as well as alerts on critical events or trends.

If your brand is strong and unsullied, then people will remember you and simply type in your URL. If you didn't register your domain name in the mid-1990s, if you need to distinguish your company with a URL like www.mcdonaldsdoors.co.uk, www.mcdonaldsrentacar.co.nz, or you simply don't have a billion-dollar budget for creating a global name for yourself, then you have to get visible online in other ways—and you'll need to measure that visibility.

Visibility

There are several ways to become visible, but there's no question that the first and foremost is through the search engines.

Search Engine

If you want to learn how to get ranked higher in search engine results, look elsewhere. There are more than enough people writing more than enough tips that will take you more than enough time to achieve questionable results. It's the results that are the question of the moment. What results should you be looking for?

You'll remember from Chapter 5, "Sawing Logs," that your log files remember which search engines are sending you traffic. They also record what terms were used to find you. So a WebTrends Top Search Phrases report (see Figure 6.7) is pretty standard fare.

That sort of report will help you determine which search engines are sending you traffic and how. You need a different type of report to figure out if there's room for improvement.

Since your standing in the search engines is mercurial at best, it's a good idea to keep track. Improving your standings in the search engines has become such a complex mix of branding, positioning, and technology wrangling that hiring some help is a good idea as well. A report like the one shown in Figure 6.8, from Web-Ignite (www.web-ignite.com), will give you up-to-the-minute results.

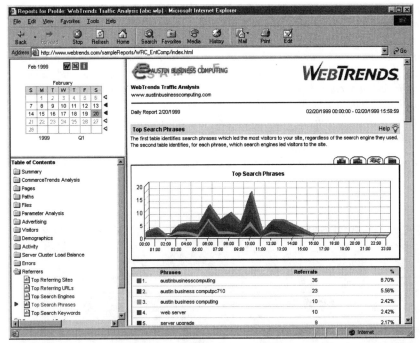

Figure 6.7   One of WebTrends standard reports shows which phrases are searched over time and by different search engines.

Measuring your search engine success is pretty straightforward. Measuring the cost of getting help from a search engine optimization and positioning (SEOP) company is a little more complex. Here's some advice from "MarketingSherpa's Buyer's Guide to Search Engine Optimization & Positioning Firms: Who should you hire & how much should you pay?" found at www.sherpastore.com:

Rough math to determine how much SEOP is worth to you:

1. *# of surfers searching under your terms at wordtracker.com.*

2. *Multiply total searches by 10% clickthrough rate.*

   (Case studies show 10% is achievable if you have a compellingly written listing ranked in the top three search results.)

3. *Multiply by average conversion % at your site.*

   (Conversion is the % of site visitors who convert by joining your email list, filling out an online form, or buying something.)

4. *Multiply by ultimate $ you make on average per conversion.*

So, if SEOP can make or break you online, why is it an afterthought for many marketers?

Simply put, until this year when everyone's bottom line began to really matter, SEOP wasn't sexy enough to get much mainstream attention. It doesn't cost millions. It doesn't feature exciting graphic design or Flash animation. It's rarely reported on in the major advertising media as must-read news the way other big campaigns are. Plus, it requires arcane and techy knowledge—the sort of thing many marketing creatives tend to shy away from. In fact, it's something a lot of marketers just leave to their webmaster or design firm. And that's a big mistake because most webmasters and design firms don't know or care about marketing like you do, and chances are they don't know SEOP as well as they think they do either.

While I always recommend outsourcing this effort, there are a couple of ways to do it yourself.

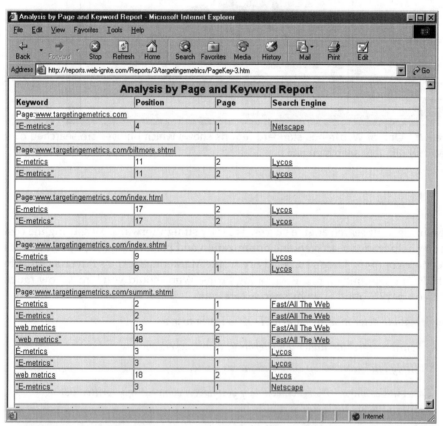

Figure 6.8   Web-Ignite lets me know where my TargetingEmetrics site shows up on which pages of which search engines.

PositionAgent

PositionAgent (www.positionagent.com) is a free service that allows you to enter a URL and a keyword phrase. It then submits the keyword to several major search engines and directories and searches the first five pages of results for your URL. A paid version of the service allows you to regularly monitor five similar keyword-URL combinations. Extensive, detailed reports can be viewed online or delivered via email.

WebPosition

WebPosition (www.webposition.com) is a software product that allows you to check page rankings from the desktop. You can enter different URL/keyword combinations, then send WebPosition on "missions" to report back on page position from a variety of major search engines. A trial version is available for evaluation and will check results from three search engines. The commercial versions support ten search engines.

Aside from knowing the URL and using search engines, people are going to find you in many different places online. One of the more interesting approaches is to quantify your visibility rating.

Overall Visibility Rating

Word of Net (www.wordofnet.com) decided to tackle the big picture:

Word of Net's Visibility Index automatically generates a comprehensive, quantitative analysis of a company's online visibility and that of competitors. Using proprietary research technologies, the Visibility Index scours the Internet for any items that drive traffic to a site, including mentions of a company's name, search engine keyword listings, directory listings, inbound links, and online advertisements. The resulting competitive intelligence and rankings let clients accurately gauge and enhance the performance of online marketing campaigns.

Online visibility consists of all the possible points of contact that can drive traffic to a site. These include online advertising (including banner ads, links from other Web sites, online news sources, mentions in discussion groups, search engine keywords and results mentions in chat rooms) and Internet directory and category listings mentions in news groups. The more of these points of contact that point a Web user to a site, the higher the likelihood that a customer will turn awareness into action.

The company's most comprehensive report, the Word of Net Visibility Analysis, provides clients with a detailed breakdown of the online presence of five URLs, including:

- *A raw visibility score*
- *Industry comparisons to show a client's Visibility Index in relation to key industry players*

- *Placement Visibility Analysis, detailing a site's search engine keywords and listings, inbound links from other Web sites, and category listings in online directories*

- *Media Visibility Analysis, detailing a company's impact from online advertisements, press releases, and news sources*

- *Competitive Visibility Analysis, providing an analysis of a client's online Visibility Index in relation to its competition and market space*

Now there are several companies that do the same sort of work. Cyveillance (www.cyveillance.com) suggests you manage your image, brands, and content online:

Cyveillance's technology enables companies to understand and manage their image, brands, and content online. It does this by pouring through all publicly available online sources and breaking down the HTML code on every page. It enables clients to quickly identify opportunities and threats related to their specific business goals and marketplace. Extremely flexible and capable of creating a unique model of the Internet for any business, this technology is the basis for all Cyveillance solutions.

Manipulating public opinion as best one can is a time-honored tradition. Listening to what others say about you is a must in the business world. Being seen in all the right places is de rigueur. But when we talk about driving traffic to a Web site, our attention seems to focus on the expenditure of cold, hard, cash—advertising. Evaluating the expense of driving traffic deserves its own chapter.

CHAPTER

7

How Good Are You at Buying Noise?

"There is an increased sensitivity for accountability and results orientation, especially on the Web, which has higher expectations and greater potential for tracking."

Tyler Schaeffer, senior vice president-director of Brand Media Planning, Foote, Cone & Belding

Time to fire up the spreadsheets; we're going to start counting things. We're going to count how much we pay to get people to show up and the value of each visit. We're going to count the cost of impressions, clicks, visitors, and the like. Let's keep this as simple as possible and divide the subject up into ads on Web sites and ads that go out via email.

Web Site Advertising

Creating powerful ads to display on Web sites is an art. But let's talk about the science part of it. I don't care if your ad wins awards, uses the latest technology, or causes a stir on Madison Avenue. I only care if the results cause a stir on Wall Street.

Starting from the top, you want your ad to be remembered. For those who remember the discussion in the previous chapter on branding, we start with the impression you leave with a surfer who has been exposed to your ad.

Awareness and Branding

Want instant gratification? Put up a banner that says, "Gifts for All Occasions. Click Here!"; and hope people will show up. But if you put up a banner that says "www.GIFTS.com for All Occasions," you've got a chance to get some traffic *and* make an impression—one that sticks.

Awareness and branding are eminently measurable, they're just soft numbers rather than hard numbers. You find out how people feel about you. You find out if people remember you. You hope they like what they remember.

For example, chances are excellent that if you were online for any appreciable amount of time in 2001, you were presented with a pop-under ad for the x10 cameras (see Figure 7.1).

Jupiter Media Metrix (www.jmm.com) reported in July 2001 that "while pop-under ad campaigns (which spawn a new browser that the user has to close manually) generate mass reach online, they fail to convert browsers to buyers. Media Metrix ratings data show that although x10.com reached 32.8 percent of the Web's entire audience between January 2001 and May 2001 with pop-under ads for wireless cameras, it also experienced a large traffic drop off, with 73 percent of unique visitors leaving the site or window before 20 seconds."

"Looking only at reach, it would appear that x10.com has deployed an incredibly successful campaign," said Marissa Gluck, senior analyst, Jupiter Media Metrix. "However, consumer behavior tells a different story. As advertisers become increasingly intrusive online, consumers react just as they do with their TV remote control—they eliminate advertising they don't find relevant or entertaining. That's what's happening with x10.com."

So let's start with *reach*.

Figure 7.1 Undoubtedly among the most annoying ads online at the time, everybody remembers the x10—but not fondly.

Reach

Time for the thesaurus. In this case we look first to the "IAB Glossary of Interactive Advertising Terms," on the Internet Advertising Bureau's Web site (see the link on this book's Web site: www.wiley.com/compbooks/sterne) for definitions of *reach*:

1. *Unique users that visited the site over the course of the reporting period, expressed as a percent of the universe for the demographic category; also called unduplicated audience.*

2. *The total number of unique users who will be served a given ad.*

I concur completely with definition 2; but when it comes to definition 1, they've been playing with their x10 cameras too long. The first definition involves have words like visitor, user, customer, and the like, and we'll get to those. For now, we have to stick with a definition we can agree with.

In our white paper, "E-Metrics, Business Metrics for the New Economy" (www .netgen.com/emetrics), Matt Cutler and I made the following point:

If you are trying to attract the attention of the 5 million buyers of 3-D rendering software tools for architects, you might place a banner ad on an architectural portal Web site. If that site draws 1 million distinct people a month who fit the description of a potential buyer, your reach on that site is 20 percent of the total universe of 5 million buyers.

Another aspect of reach is total site reach. Assume you decide to promote your software on the Expedia travel site. If Expedia attracts 25 million unique users per month and your ad was shown to 5 million unique users, then your reach to Expedia users was 20 percent for the month.

Some companies do not measure their reach until the potential buyer has clicked on the banner. They do not consider that prospect as "reached" until the message has been delivered, read, and acted on. Others call this step acquisition.

To be more blunt about it, there's the definition from *Advertising Management* (Batra, Myers, Aaker, Prentice-Hall, 1996):

The number of people or households that will be exposed to an advertising schedule at least once over a specified period of time.

That nails it down nicely.

Now, back to our x10 story. Because the x10 people inflicted pop-unders on us, the people at Jupiter Media Metrix counted them in an odd way. Jupiter counts site visits—people visiting sites. Because the ads served from the x10 servers are whole pages, they counted as *visits*. Wrongo.

Marissa Gluck was right on the money that people "eliminate advertising they don't find relevant or entertaining." But Jupiter missed the boat when they considered it significant that 73 percent of unique visitors left the site or window before 20 seconds. All we've learned from that is that 73 percent got rid of it as soon as possible. The rest merely ignored it longer.

Did x10 get their product into a lot of faces? Yep. Great reach. They paid for reach, they got reach, and they *know* they got reach because people had to click those aggravating windows closed. But reach only takes you so far.

"While pop-unders such as x10.com have achieved mass reach online, relevancy still matters more than format," Gluck said. "The ubiquity of the x10.com ads, and consumers' subsequent rejection of them, reinforces the notion that allowing consumers to exercise free will in their surfing and providing them with targeted, relevant offers are the keys to successful online marketing."

The advantage of annoying people with pop-ups or pop-unders is that you know how many people saw them *better* than with regular banners. Sure, a pop-up/-under may be served and never arrive; that can happen with a banner as well. But a pop-up/-under that *does* arrive must be closed. A banner can simply be scrolled off the screen. Or in the case of banners that rotate on a page (a single page showing multiple banners in rotation), they may be served to that portion of the screen that has been scrolled off the top of the window.

Pop-ups also have the advantage of duration.

Duration

If you're on a Train à Grande Vitesse (TGV) trip from Paris to Lyon and pass by a billboard at 200 miles an hour, you might have a little trouble reading it, much less looking up the words in your handy French-English dictionary. If, however, you are pulled up at a railroad crossing, you have a bit more time.

The length of the exposure can be critical. Netscape learned that lesson early on when they tried an experiment with banner ads inside frames (see Figure 7.2).

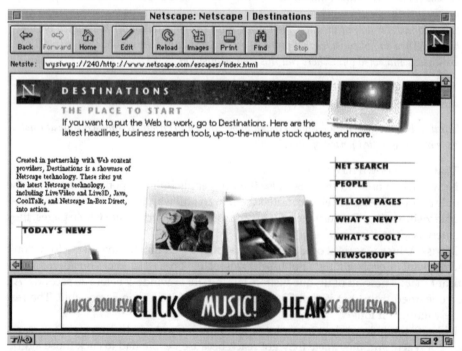

Figure 7.2 The surfer can navigate the site in the top frame, while being continually exposed to the banner ad in the bottom frame.

Just like pop-ups and -unders, people didn't like having the ads so forcefully fed to them, so Netscape dropped the practice.

One advertising approach that doesn't send surfers scurrying to another site is games. If you can get a surfer to play a game for 30 seconds or 30 minutes, it's going to have a strong impact on their awareness of and attitude toward your brand.

If you start to add up a little duration here and a little duration there, you can roll it all up into an overall amount of exposure. When it comes to branding, the duration on a Web site or in an online game can be a significant factor. For promotional purposes, most people simply assume the amount of exposure for surfers is the same each time and talk in terms of *frequency*.

Frequency

In their 1997 paper, "New Metrics for New Media" (http://www.w3j.com/5/s3.novak.html), Thomas Novak and Donna Hoffman defined frequency thusly: "The number of times that an individual is exposed to a particular advertising message in a given period of time."

Simple. But frequency by itself simply tells you what you paid, it doesn't tell you what you bought. For that, they defined *effective frequency*:

> The number of exposures needed for an ad to become "effective." In mass media models, effective frequency stipulates that a certain amount of exposure is necessary before it is effective and is used interchangeably with effective exposures. Research indicates that less than three exposures will not allow adequate recall. However, too many exposures are inefficient in that incremental recall after 7, 8, or 10 exposures during a purchase cycle is very small.

The rule of thumb online is that the efficacy of a banner peaks or plateaus at three to five exposures, but I promise you that your mileage will vary. Try it, measure it, tweak it (TIMITI)—again and again.

Before we get down to brass tacks about measuring the effectiveness of an ad, we should narrow down the parts of an ad that can be tweaked.

Ad Components

Let's say you run an ad and it gets a .04 percent response. Not bad. Not great. Now you want to change it a little and see if you can improve that response. Good idea. So you roll out another ad from a different agency and you get a .06 percent response. Progress! Terrific! Only one problem: What was the difference between the two that made the difference? Was it the color? The wording? The time of day? Here are a few of the ingredients that you'll have to keep an eye on in your measurement process— and why controlling them closely is the only way you're going to benefit from tracking the results.

The Offer

Discounts, two-for-ones, free shipping, custom engraving, a free armadillo with every purchase—there are lots of come-ons you can use to entice people. Some work better than others. Some are more tried-and-true and some work because they're so unusual.

Types of Ads

You must choose among many kinds of ads to promote yourself online:

Banner

Skyscraper

Dynamic HTML

Messaging plus unit

Pop-up

Pop-under

Superstitial

Streaming video

Email newsletter text ad

Email newsletter HTML ad

And six more that will be invented before you reach the end of this chapter.

The Placement

There are lots of places online to place an ad. But how do you compare them? First, you look to the NetRatings of the world (see *Who's Going Where?* in Chapter 4, "Web Measurement Standards"). They're the ones watching a panel of thousands of Internet users and extrapolating where the rest of us go on a daily basis.

Of course, you can always surf the Web yourself and pull together a list of the sites you think are most likely to attract the sort of people you want to see your ad. Or, you could get some help from SRDS.

What we used to call the Standard Rate and Data Service, which knew (and still does) all about where to advertise in print, is now called SRDS (www.srds.com) and also knows all about where to advertise online (see Figure 7.3).

SRDS also lost no time in Web-enabling their information offering. Here are the how-to instructions from their Web site:

Begin Your Search
The online version of the Interactive Advertising Source enables you to identify sites with the flexible search options you prefer to use. Search by SRDS market classification, keyword, or professionally audited sites.

SRDS Classification Search
This is a great way to quickly locate and analyze sites that reach a specific audience. Select from Business, Consumer, Geographic, Online Specialty, and Group Buy classifications. Market Classifications cover varying fields from architecture to welding and florists to robotics.

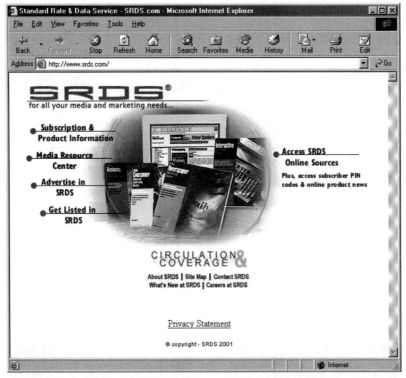

Figure 7.3 It didn't take SRDS long to realize that print advertisers were going to be online advertisers and need the same information on Web sites that they were publishing about magazines.

Keyword Search
Simply type in a keyword to begin a general search. You can narrow your search further by selecting Business, Consumer, Geographic, Online Specialty, or Group Buy sections. You'll uncover titles you may not have considered before!

Professionally Audited Search
Only interested in audited sites? Choose this option to select sites that are audited by ABC Interactive or BPA Interactive. You can narrow your search further by selecting Business, Consumer, Geographic, Online Specialty, or Group Buy sections.

View And Analyze Site Data
The Interactive Advertising Source saves you time by offering objective data, formatted consistently and updated continuously online. You'll find site profiles, rates, closing dates, usage, key contact information, and more without even making a phone call!

After setting the desired search criteria, all matching opportunities will appear in alphabetical order in the lower-left frame (Results Menu). You can choose to see an overview of all sites in the Results Menu or see details about specific sites.

View And Print Site Profiles
Click on the "View Site Profile" button to quickly scan the results of your search for top-line evaluation.

View And Print Detailed Listing Information
Complete specifications and rate information are found here and updated immediately as they are reported to SRDS. With ease, you'll find the facts you need to make comparisons and decisions about your buys.

SRDS lets you choose from 380 classifications, from advertising and marketing to woodworking, and the data they track on each site is sufficient to help you properly compare and contrast them.

Print and online listings include the following information:

- *Profile*
- *Personnel*
- *Office Locations*
- *Rep Firms/Ad Networks*
- *Audience Profile*
- *Advertising/Marketing Opportunities*
- *Advertising Rates*
- *Usage/Circulation Information*
- *Production Specifications*
- *Content Calendar and Deadlines*
- *Important Product and Service Details*
- *Site/Product Information*

Now that you know where to advertise on the Web and can compare one site to another, you still have to decide where to advertise *on each site* and compare the results of those decisions.

Do you advertise on the home page? Above the scroll line? On the right? In the center? Do you want your ad to run at certain times of day? Each will have an effect on response rates.

The Creative

Color, font, animation, language—there are a lot of tools in the creative toolbox. We've worked for years by trusting the twenty-something artistic genius in the black turtleneck to come up with killer creative. But we've also learned to bring in a test audience to give us feedback on television commercials before spending millions on 30-second spots for the Superbowl.

Before sending out half a million direct mail pieces, it's a good idea to send out a few thousand of different types to see which gets the best response. Postage isn't getting any cheaper either. But online, your test market can give you instant feedback—real time—as long as you're careful about making only incremental changes.

Test, test, and test some more. Once you've got the perfect banner working, design another one because sooner or later even the best banner runs out of steam. There comes a time when the same banner viewed by the same prospect over and over again suffers from fatigue.

Keep track of which banners seem to initiate the most clickthroughs. Some banners just seem to work better than others for no apparent reason. If you find one banner entices people to click on it more than others, use the successful one as your design base. But the most important thing to measure by far is which banner produces the most sales or registrations or survey responses—whatever your goal is. You'll often find that the banner that pulls the most clicks does not necessarily produce the most results.

The only way "try it, measure it, tweak it" is going to work is if you only change one thing at a time. It's much, *much* harder than it sounds. It takes somebody who is detail-oriented. Somebody like Ron Richards from ResultsLab (www.resultslab.com).

Ron Richards has been tweaking advertising since Hector was a pup. He's a fascinating combination of creativity and scientific analysis. Imagine a genetic blending of the DNA from David Ogilvy and Thomas Edison.

Richards is charming. He gets excited about ideas. He is gregarious. He's not nerdy in the least, but he is absolutely meticulous when it comes to the selection of every word and the precise layout of every graphic element in a printed promotion. He has worked on print ads, brochures, and direct mail promotions for years.

Creative? Oh, yes. But underneath, Richards is an experimenter and a statistician. He loves tabulation, calculation, and computation. His attention was seized by the prospects of online promotions in the middle of 1994 when he started focusing his intellectual microscope on the Web.

Richards has a great deal of experience fine-tuning new-media materials for his clients. But he demands complete control—and complete control is absolutely necessary. Given the many, many attributes even in a simple banner ad, it's very hard to keep from changing four or five things at the same time, sometimes without knowing it.

Richards very aggressively changes one and *only one* thing at a time and meticulously measures the results. Without complete control over all of the components of an ad, he won't take the job. He describes his approach as *persuasion engineering* and once you get him talking about measurement, engineering is exactly the right term.

As exacting as Richards is, he's very at ease in the land of storytelling as well. Over a Union Street lunch one day, just down the street from his ResultsLab office in San Francisco, Richards described his version of TIMITI in terms of a grasshopper looking for a better view:

"A grasshopper is down among the weeds and can't see much around him. But he's really good at telling the difference between how high he jumps and how long it takes to come back down. So he picks a direction, doesn't matter which, and jumps. If he lands a little higher than he was when he started, he jumps again in the same direction. If he ends up lower, then he changes direction until he finally finds which way will get him to the top of the hill."

"But Ron," says I, only too happy to wrestle a metaphor until it cries uncle, "that means the grasshopper can only find the top of the hill he's on at the moment. What if there's a really big hill right next door?"

It's obvious Ron's grappled with this particular metaphor before. "At some point, every direction he jumps is down. That's how he knows he's at the top. At this point, he has to get some additional information in order to make some tough decisions."

"What kind of information?"

"The grasshopper? Wind, smell, humidity, noises, the angle of the sun—how would I know? The advertiser? Market demographics, competitive information, historical campaign data, or maybe the wisdom of somebody who's been tweaking advertising since Hector was a pup."

Richards likes to take the task of A/B split testing (mailing multiple direct mail pieces to different people on the same list to see which draws the most response) to its logical conclusion and not just improve the response an ad gets, but double it, triple it, or more.

Memetrics (www.memetrics.com) is an Australian company dedicated to measuring the effect of subtle Web site changes. One of its clients, a health and vitamin site down under called Hilton Healthstream (www.lifestream.co.au) was doing well but wanted to do better (see Figure 7.4).

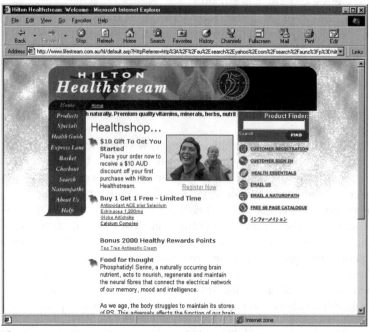

Figure 7.4 Memetrics recommended small changes to have this Healthstream site be more effective.

Is the picture of the couple on the beach best? Or should it go with a family portrait? Or should Memetrics replace it with a call to action that says, "Click here to talk to one of our naturopaths for free health advice"? Is the "$10 Gift to Get You Started" better than, say, "Save $10 on Your First Order"? What's better: "Buy One Get One Free— Limited Time" or "Check out our super savings!"?

We've all worked these sorts of promotions out in our heads. Oh, yes, you think, I'm sure the health-conscious public is more apt to respond to "Half Off" rather than "Save 50 Percent." But how do you *know*? You know by measuring, and that takes technology.

Memetrics created a Web server that can serve up multiple combinations of content to one visitor after the other and keep track of which was most effective. Its recommendations after running twenty different versions of the home page?

- Replace the picture with a button that says, "Click here for a complete list of this month's savings."

- Keep the "$10 Gift to Get You Started" (nothing else was as effective)

- Replace "Buy 1 Get 1 Free" with "Save up to 50 percent!"

Its results? Hilton Healthstream's whopping 13 percent conversion rate almost doubled to 25 percent. And after a 4-week test, guided home pages alterations boosted conversions by 78 percent.

In a February 22, 2001, article at Inside.com, Ellen Neuborne described companies tracking their clickthrough rates in near real time. The article says that Staples tracked the clickthrough rate of its online ads every hour. Sony went one step further:

Sony can report success from micromanaging its online ads. For the two weeks that the campaign ran, analysis was performed in real time, with daily updates to the ads, both text links and banners. The program was about 40 percent banner ads on such sites as AltaVista, Yahoo! and MSN. Targeted email went out via lists from companies like MyPoints.com. In the first few days, changing color schemes and converting the banners from static to looping (animation) boosted clickthrough rates by 25 percent, says Laura Berland, co-founder of ORB Inc., the digital marketing firm that executed the program for Sony. Overall, she said, of those who clicked on banners, 29.5 percent registered.

Text links, too, were massaged frequently. One on MSN honed in on the dollar amount of the sweepstakes prize, producing the best results. At the end of two weeks, Sony had amassed a database of 244,174 names, complete with permission to send further marketing messages. "It used to be you went out talking about marketing and real-time optimization, and everybody's eyes just glazed over. Too technical," says Berland. "Today, it's the first thing they want to know you can do for them."

The trick, then, is to change only one thing at a time, carefully note each of the changes you make, and track the results from each. The permutations quickly become overwhelming. Just take a look at Table 7.1, Ad Attributes.

Table 7.1   Ad Attributes

OFFER	TYPE OF AD	CREATIVE	PLACEMENT	RESPONSE MECHANISM	RESPONSE
2 for 1	Banner	Color	Yahoo!	Clickthrough	?
Free shipping	Rich media	Font	MSN	Email	?
10% off	Superstitial	Animation	Business 2.0	Phone number	?
No money down	Pop-under	Vocabulary	iVillage.com	SASE	?
Penguin with purchase*	AdSlap†	Flavor	The very last page‡	Canadian railway Signals§	?
Etc.	Etc.	Etc.	Etc.	Etc.	Etc.

* (Figure 7-5)
† www.clickz.com/mkt/emkt_strat/article.php/844581
‡ www.mythologic.net/end
§ http://railwayop.tripod.ca/Signals2/signal2a.html

You can see how quickly the permutations of all the different possibilities lead to brain strain, calculator battery failure, and spreadsheet paralysis. More important and more practically, they lead to budget fatigue.

The sad fact is that you cannot test everything, even though the good, empirical, scientific method says it's the only way to fly. Instead, you have to take your best guess at two, three, *maybe* four different permutations and test them against one another (see Figure 7.5).

Unless, of course, you're like one of my clients who grabbed the ball and ran with it.

Under nondisclosure, I can't tell you the name of the client and to protect their competitive edge, I can't tell you what industry they're in. But I can tell you that they started with specific category buys on Yahoo!, switched to keyword search terms, and ended up on Yahoo! remnant pages (the pages nobody else wanted to advertise on). Why remnants? Better return on investment.

This unnamed company bought millions of impressions a month. They tested colors, styles, offers, fonts, times of day, you name it—at tens of thousand of impressions each. This was TIMITI in action and on a serious scale. After several months, they narrowed down two best bets. The first got the most clicks, and the second turned up the most sales in the end.

What they learned about their target audience was valuable enough to pay for the whole test, valuable enough to alter their offline marketing, and valuable enough to protect with a nondisclosure agreement.

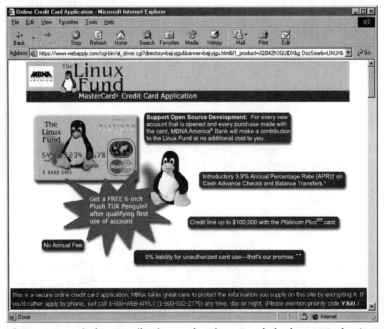

Figure 7.5 Is it the contribution to the Linux Fund, the low APR, the $100,000 line of credit, or the free penguin that pulls people in?

Ad Interactions

"Did they click?" is all we wanted to know at first. "Did they come to our site?" But these days, online ads do a great deal more than simply entice a clickthrough.

With Flash, Java, and other animation techniques, ads don't just sit there anymore. They wiggle, they scroll, they fly across the screen. You want to know what's going on in the surfer's mind while your ad is playing.

Mouseovers

Your ad may wiggle and wriggle and then do something different altogether when the surfer's mouse wanders over the top of it. Anything to get that click. So *did* the surfer mouseover your ad? More than once?

Intra-Ad Clicks

Your banner may include a clickable storyline, a form, or a game. How much clicking is going on inside your multipage, multimessage ad before the surfer turns into a visitor? Do surfers watch the whole animation before clicking through? Are they only playing half the game and then losing interest? Are they playing the whole game, but not rising to the bait and following you back to your Web site?

Recently, even Macromedia Flash movies have become measurable. Of course, you can record when a Flash movie is served. And, of course, you know when a clickthrough comes as the result of a Flash movie. But what about keeping track of what goes on while that movie is playing? That's where ActionScript comes in.

ActionScript is a scripting (programming-like) language that allows you to manipulate a Flash movie. While it's manipulating the movie, it can also send calls out to your server when a certain number of frames have been watched or clicked on a specific button.

Intra-Ad Purchases

It's simple math. If your ad can wriggle, giggle, and include a form, then it sure as shootin' can take an order. Did the customer want fries with that? We'll talk more about tracking the order taking process in Chapter 12, "Maximizing Customer Information: The Personalization Continuum."

Clickthroughs

Ahhh—finally—the simple clickthrough. Something we can all understand. Something that's so simple, it's just a matter of pressing that index finger down on the left mouse button and that surfer is whisked to your home page, ready, willing, and able to succumb to your persuasive powers.

If only it were that easy. Let's take a careful look at just what happens when an ad is served:

- A link to a new page is clicked.
- The request is received.
- The page is served.
- The server sends a request to the ad server to serve a banner.
- The banner ad is served.
- The banner reaches the clicker.
- The clicker sees the banner.
- The clicker clicks on the banner.
- The click is recorded as a request for the landing page by the ad server.
- The request is passed on to the server that hosts the landing page.
- The click is recorded as a request for the landing page by the page host.
- The landing page is served to the clicker.

At each and every one of these steps, the whole thing can come crashing down. Dropped data packets can cause time-outs. Server overloads can return error codes. The clicker can click the Stop button. The clicker can scroll the banner off the top of the window like a leaf snatched from the windshield of an accelerating car. And, of course, there's always the issue of the banner being displayed on a screen in an empty room.

To get the details of this click-and-serve process, take a look at the appendix, "How Interactive Ads Are Delivered and Measurement Implication," written by Dick Bennett of ABC Interactive (www.abcinteractiveaudits.com). So now you know why the reports that come from the sites that serve your banners, the reports from the sites that display your banners, and the reports from your own site showing how many people showed up are never in synch. That becomes very important when you start spending money. Time to turn our attention to where that money goes.

How Ads Are Purchased

In the beginning, Web sites were sponsored—literally brought to you by the seller of the goods. Banner ads came later, after those sellers realized they could put entice-ments up on other Web sites to drive traffic. The first method of purchasing that ban-ner as space was the same as in print—by the thousands of impressions.

CPM

When you think of reach, remember that the *impression* you are buying is actually an *opportunity to see*. A freeway billboard is sold based on impressions. Television ads are the same way. You pay on a CPM (cost per thousand) basis.

If you were to look up *reach* in "NetGenesis Glossary of Terms" (www.netgen.com/index.cfm?section=solutions&file=emetrics_glossary. or see the link on this book's Web site: www/wiley.com/compbooks/sterne), you would find this definition:

> *In the world of advertising, reach refers to the potential to gain the attention of your target audience. Used as a standard in the television industry, reach is the number of people (or households) who have the opportunity to see your message given a program's total active viewership. For instance, 180 million people might tune in to the Superbowl on any given year, so the reach of your ad that aired during the first timeout in the third quarter would be 180 million people. Of course, as an advertiser you have no guarantee that 7 million people did not change the channel, or that 15 million did not head to the refrigerator.*

You buy impressions in order to make an impression. If you're good, you end up with lots of clicks as well. In 1995, Procter & Gamble (P&G) figured they were a big enough player that they could find a creative way around the risk of paying for banners by the thousands from Yahoo! They were right.

Clickthroughs

P&G went to Yahoo! and said that the medium was too new and too risky and if this whole Internet advertising concept was so good, then Yahoo! should be willing to forgo the sale of banner ad space in deference to selling banner ad response—at least if they wanted P&G's money—and they did.

This method of buying advertising is great for the buyer but makes little sense from the seller's point of view. The sellers have no control over the creative, yet are on the hook for the response to that creative. If they are pure content sites (news, reviews, entertainment), that means they would be very motivated to skew their content to drive traffic to their customers' sites. Strange way to do business.

If you're buying ads and you can get them to sell you clickthroughs, do it! Then place a whole boatload of brand-building banners that will increase customer awareness, improve their opinion of your offerings, and get them to show up at your site in the next day or two. If they don't click, you pay nothing. An odd arrangement.

But as we have previously seen, measuring clickthroughs is technically difficult. It's also controversial. Whether it's called a CPC (cost per click) or a CPA (cost per action), make sure you understand exactly what you're buying in order to properly compare an ad buy on one site to an ad buy on another.

Mixing It Up

Another approach that's starting to see some play is the one-two combination. Pay a base rate for a base number of impressions with a CPC override, sort of like paying the performer a set fee plus a cut of the box office.

Alternately, you can pay on a cost per click basis, with an upper limit on the number of impressions. That way the publisher is protected from displaying too many banners that just say "Eat At Joe's" without any incentive to click.

But online advertisers and publishers are nothing if not inventive. The following is another approach from the front lines.

Sessions

In October 2001, the *New York Times* announced that it would start selling "surround sessions" on its Web site to change the approach of buying 5 million impressions and hoping they pop up in front of the right people at the right time. Instead, you identify the attributes of those most likely to be the right people and then tell the *Times* how many times you'd like that type of person to see your banner in one sitting.

So whether you want to think of this in terms of *duration* or *frequency* is up to you, the result is the same: a certain number of sightings per individual. If the visitor doesn't hang out long enough to have five ads delivered, you don't pay. If the visitor hangs out for an hour and looks at 100 pages, you only pay for that as a single session. The *New York Times* figures this will make buyers of television and radio media more comfortable, as they are used to buying in terms of gross ratings points that take into account reach and frequency.

Leads

The next step beyond clickthroughs is buying qualified leads. Defining a qualified lead is a matter of negotiation. A person who clicks on a banner may be well enough qualified to sign up for a contest to win a television set—whether that person signs up or not is the responsibility of the landing page. However, a clicker would have to fill out a financial application form to prove that she is a qualified lead for a home loan. So you get to calculate what constitutes a qualified lead:

- Looked at more than two pages on the site
- Searched the catalog for desired product
- Registered for the email newsletter
- Joined the discussion group and posted at least four messages
- Downloaded a white paper
- Ran a simulation
- Watched at least half of the animated presentation
- Scheduled a telephone interview

Sales are infinitely easier to determine. Did they actually buy something?

Sales: Show Me the Money

Amazon.com was the first to give this model a try and has been very successful at it. Whether you call it an associate's program or an affiliate's program doesn't matter. All that matters is that the link from the selling site to yours is appropriately coded so that your server can recognize which lead came from which site. We want to be able to appropriately compensate our partners.

Amazon takes it a step further. Even if the visitor doesn't buy the specifically offered product, the associate has a chance to earn anyway. Amazon describes it this way:

> *Amazon.com Associates earn up to 15% of the sale price on individually linked books that you feature on your site and 5% on anything else that is purchased through your links, including CDs, videos, DVDs, toys, consumer electronics, and more.*

Measuring the amount of sales made from various associates tells you who your friends are, but measuring the number of clicks per associate visitor and the number of sales per click can help you help your associates sell more.

Let's say you're running the Iranian Movies site (www.iranianmovies.com). You notice that Iran Kicks (www.irankicks.com) is outselling Iran Gift Shop (www.irangiftshop.com) and Debugger Techno International (www.techno-int.com) by orders of magnitude.

You may be getting more visitors from Iran Gift Shop, and they certainly have a nicer looking site, but if the visitors from Iran Kicks are buying more per capita, then you might be able to help Iran Gift Shop (and yourself) make more money by studying their fellow associates.

Commission Junction (www.cj.com) terms this per capita purchasing ratio as earnings per click (EPC) and uses it to help affiliates choose between associate programs they might wish to join. This is from their Open Marketplace FAQ (www.cj.com/downloads/ppfaq.asp):

> *EPC stands for "average earnings per one hundred clicks" and is a relative rating that shows effectiveness. It illustrates the ability to convert clicks into commissions. EPC is the primary metric being used in the Open Marketplace and will be published for each advertiser, publisher, and ad in the network. EPC metrics will be published in two forms, as a 7-day EPC and a 3-month EPC.*
>
> *The basic formula for calculating EPC is: Commissions earned (or commissions paid) divided by total number of clicks times 100.*
>
> *Advertiser and publisher 3-month EPC is calculated using commissions from the previous 3 months for which the commission payouts have stabilized (this can take up to two months, after which reversal and batch upload deadlines have passed). For example, in the month of July, the 3-month EPC will include revenue and clicks from February, March, and April.*
>
> *Seven-day EPC is designed to reflect recent performance. It is responsive to recent changes in the Open Marketplace, but lacks the stability of the 3-month figure. Seven-day EPC is calculated using data collected seven days leading up to the prior Monday. This time period will be used for one week (recalculated nightly for that same time period). On each Tuesday morning the time period will shift by 1 week.*
>
> *All advertisers and publishers are listed as "New" for their first three months in the network. In addition, all EPCs will be listed as N/A if they have less than 100 clicks.*

How Ads Are Valued

Getting more people to your Web site is good, but not all visitors represent value. If your only task—your only responsibility—is to get people to come to a specific landing page, then your company's conceptual grasp of "integrated marketing" is woefully short of the mark. As Matt Cutler points out, "It doesn't matter that 20 million 14-year-old girls came to your Web site because of your Ricky Martin/Britney Spears banner ad—they're *still* not going to buy your BMWs."

Let's start with measuring the cost of getting those eyeballs to your site.

Acquisition Cost

Reach and awareness have their place to build brands, but if you're selling anything that can't be sold on impulse in a single banner, you need to bring people to your site if you want to make the sale.

The cost of getting them there is the easiest to calculate. If you spend $5,000 on 1 million banner ads and get .05 percent clicks, you've wracked up 5,000 site visits at $1 each. If you place your banner in a spot that attracts people who are more attracted to your offer, or if you change your banner to increase the draw, you can have a direct impact on that clickthrough percentage.

As you busy yourself comparing one set of placement/creative combos to another, don't forget that clickthroughs are not the only way people come to your site. It's time to measure which combo is paying off the best.

Channel Preference

I've picked up a lot from Matt Cutler, including the calculation for channel preference. Sounds complicated, but like most of the ideas I've picked up from Matt, it's easy to understand. Simply give people three ways to respond, and see which they like best. Take the number of promotion responses you get via any specific channel, and divide by the total responses (see Table 7.2).

It's easy to assume the Web is the most cost-effective response channel. No call center, no email minders, no envelopes to open. If your only goal is raising awareness, you win. If you're interested in making sales, you'll have to wait for the discussion of conversion rates, which follows.

Until then, you need to look more closely at how online ads might be manipulated in real time and how to count the people who come to your sites because of them.

Table 7.2 Channel Preferences by Outbound Channel

OUTBOUND CHANNEL	MAIL RESPONSE	PHONE RESPONSE	WEB RESPONSE	EMAIL RESPONSE
Direct mail	36%	12%	45%	7%
Television ads	3%	54%	35%	8%
Banner ads	0%	4%	88%	8%
E-zine ads	0%	6%	78%	16%

Automating TIMITI

In my book *What Makes People Click: Advertising on the Web*, I took a long look into the future and wrote about the banner ad measurement/feedback loop.

It was the story of a woman wearing video goggles, datagloves, and headphones, who manipulated her online advertising efforts in real time. She grabbed virtual banner ads and tossed them onto a virtual grid, watching and listening to the click-throughs and sales until she had selected just the right combination of creative, audience, and offer. It was a fun piece to write and worth the price of the book.

Now, it seems as if my vision is starting on the road to instantiation with a little help from MOJO Optimizer. At least it seems that way, judging from the Mediaplex press release dated October 1, 2001:

> *SAN FRANCISCO, CA October 01, 2001—Mediaplex, Inc. (NASDAQ:MPLX), a leading advertising technology company for marketers and advertisers, today announced that it has launched MOJO Optimizer, a digital marketing tool developed to automatically update individual banner ad frequency based on real-time campaign performance and marketing goals. MOJO Optimizer works to improve campaign performance based on each client's predetermined settings. Throughout the duration of a campaign, successful banners are displayed more frequently while ineffective banners are displayed less.*
>
> *"With MOJO Optimizer, campaign analysts and traffickers are no longer required to review optimization reports and make manual adjustments," stated Andy Torgerson, vice president of product management for Mediaplex. "This saves the marketer or advertiser time and money while maximizing ROI."*
>
> *MOJO Optimizer allows advertisers and marketers to optimize on their most valued metrics like click-through rate, or campaign-specific ROI metrics such as dollars spent, registrations completed, or purchase confirmation. MOJO Optimizer can be applied across all advertising, particular campaigns, specific sites, or only designated placements.*
>
> *MOJO Optimizer results are aggregated into Mediaplex's real-time tracking and reporting system, MOJO Reports. MOJO Reports can be customized to analyze a client's specific business goals, including performance, monitoring, and conversion time. Mediaplex's reporting data can be integrated into a client's existing enterprise databases, thereby improving future targeting and optimization opportunities.*

As it becomes more and more possible to measure the immediate results of an ad campaign, we'll need auditing services less and less. But we'll always need them to help keep an eye on publishers, the vendors of advertising space.

Advertising Audit Services

You pay your money and you take your chances. You ask for half a million impressions from a major Web site and you wonder whether they are actually served. Your first stop: the Audit Bureau of Circulations (www.accessabc.com) or BPA International (www.bpai.com) (see Figure 7.6).

Figure 7.6 In the advertising auditing business for decades, ABC and BPA International are now auditing online ads as well.

The ABC is a nonprofit that has been keeping an eye on those who sell advertising since 1914. They conduct audits of how publishers publish ads and how they report their circulation figures. They are "responsible to advertisers, advertising agencies, and the media they use for the verification and dissemination of members' circulation, readership, and audience information."

These are the people that started life verifying whether a magazine really went out to the quantity and types of people the publisher claimed. That's a critical function because dollars are at stake: advertising dollars. In May 1996, the ABC established ABC Interactive (ABCi) to offer independent, third-party verification of online activity, "providing assurance to members of the advertising community that Web site traffic and ad delivery metrics are accurately reported. ABCi currently conducts audits for Web Sites, Search Engines, Email and Ad Delivery Systems, and Internet Broadcasters."

Along with ABCi, BPA International posts reports on their site. The reports are paid for by the publishers to prove that their claims are valid and therefore their pricing is competitive. As a result, you can easily find out that AuntMinnie.com typically gets more visitors on Thursday than any other day of the week, is busiest between two and three o'clock in the afternoon (Pacific time), and gets almost 900,000 visits per month who look at more than 1.8 million pages. AuntMinnie has more than 37,000 unique registered users who have visited at least once within the year. This might be very interesting to you if you sell bone densitometry or fluoroscopy equipment. AuntMinnie is a Web site for radiologists.

By the same token, reports at ABCi (see Figure 7.7) will tell you that, on average, AOL served up a daily average north of 1.6 billion ad impressions in June 2001 every day. You'll learn that Saturdays are their slowest day of the week and that they've grown from not quite 15 billion ad impressions per month in June 2000 to over 50 billion impressions in June 2001.

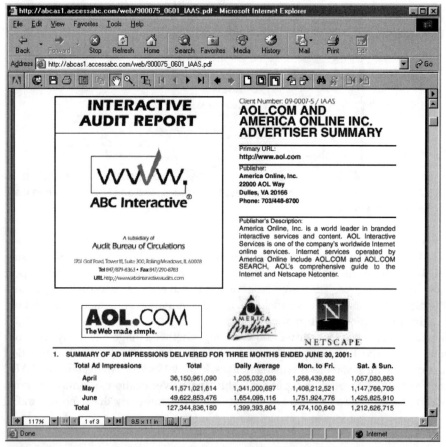

Figure 7.7 You can learn a lot about major Web sites like AOL, and some not-so-well-known sites, by reading reports at ABCi and BPA.

> **WHAT IS AN AUNTMINNIE?**
>
> The exact origins of the term *AuntMinnie* are a bit hazy, but it's believed to have been coined in the 1940s by Dr. Ben Felson, a radiologist at the University of Cincinnati. He used it to describe "a case with radiologic findings so specific and compelling that no realistic differential diagnosis exists." In other words, if it looks like your Aunt Minnie, then it's your Aunt Minnie.
> (From www.AuntMinnie.com)

The problem we face is the one addressed in Chapter 4, "Web Measurement Standards." If we don't have predetermined, standard methods of measurement, we'll never get anywhere.

Principals of Online Media Audience Measurement

FAST (Future of Advertising Stakeholders) and ARF (Advertising Research Foundation) published their "Principles of Online Media Audience Measurement" in January 2000. The entire document can be found at www.fastinfo.org/measurement/pages/index.cgi/audiencemeasurement. Here are the essential ethical and methodological principles:

PURPOSE
The purpose of this document is to further the quality and comparability of all online media audience measurement, through their subscription to a common set of principles.

THE ETHICAL PRINCIPLES

1. *Post and Practice Privacy Policies*
2. *Fully Disclose Methodology*
3. *Use Third-Party Measurement and Established Industry Audit Practices*
4. *Take Steps to Ensure That Data Are Used Responsibly*
5. *Support Global Harmonization*
6. *Encourage Methodological Experimentation*
7. *Participate in Industry Development of Best Practices Seeking Industry Consensus*

THE METHODOLOGICAL PRINCIPLES

1. *The Foundations for Measurement of Online Media Should Be Laid to Maximize Comparability to Other Existing Media*
2. *More Advanced Measurements that "Go Beyond the Basics" Should Reflect the Unique Capabilities of Online Media*
3. *All Measurement Systems Should Use Best Media Research Practices*
4. *All Measurement Systems Should Use Industry Standard Definitions*
5. *All Measurement Systems Should Use a Clearly Defined Universe*

6. *All Measurement Systems Should Accurately Measure the Behaviors They Claim to Measure*

7. *All Measurement Systems Should Employ Measurement That Is Non-Intrusive*

8. *All Measurements Must Be Comparable Across Measurement Systems*

Brand-New Standards

In January 2002, the Internet Advertising Bureau (www.iab.net) has released their Ad Measurement Guidelines. After months of tussling with potential descriptions, they've come up with the following definitions:

Ad Impression

A measurement of response from an ad delivery system to an ad request from the user's browser, which is filtered from robotic activity and is recorded at a point as late as possible in the process of delivery of the creative material to the user's browser—therefore closest to actual opportunity to see by the user (see specifics below).

Two methods are used to deliver ad content to the user— server-initiated and client-initiated. Server-initiated ad counting uses the site's Web content server for making requests, formatting, and redirecting content. Client-initiated ad counting relies on the user's browser to perform these activities.

For organizations that use a server-initiated ad counting method, counting should occur subsequent to the ad response at either the site's ad server or the Web content server or later in the process. For organizations using a client-initiated ad counting method, counting should occur at the publisher's ad server or third-party ad server, subsequent to the ad request, or later, in the process.

Click

There are three types of user reactions to the Internet content or advertising—click-through, in-unit click and mouse-over. All of these reactions are generally referred to as "clicks."

- *A click-through is the measurement of a user-initiated action of clicking on an ad element, causing a redirect to another Web location. Click-throughs are tracked and reported at the ad server, and generally include the user of a 302 redirect [one page that sends the visitor to another page].* The measurement is filtered for robotic activity.

- *In-unit clicks and mouse-overs (mouse-overs are a form of ad interaction) result in server log events and new content being served and are generally measured using 302s; however, they may not necessarily include a redirect to another Web location. Certain I-unit clicks and mouse-overs may be recorded in a batch mode and reported on a delayed basis. Organizations using a batch processing method should have proper controls over establishing cut-off measurement periods.*

- *Clicks can be reported in total; however, significant types of clicks should be presented with disaggregated detail. If, due to ad-counting software limitations, an organization cannot report the disaggregated detail of clicks, only click-throughs should be reported.*

It is important to note that clicks are not equivalent to Web-site referrals measured at the destination site. If the organization complies with the guidelines specified herein, there will still be measurement difference between originating-server measurement and the destination site (advertiser). The use of 302 redirects helps to mitigate this difference because of its easy and objective quantification; however, differences will remain from measurements taken at the destination site because of various issues such as latency, user aborts, etc.

Visit

One or more text and/or graphics downloads from a site qualifying as at least one page, without 30 consecutive minutes of inactivity, which can be reasonably attributed to a single browser for a single session. A browser must "pull" text or graphics content to be considered a visit. This measurement is filtered for robotic activity prior to reporting and is determined using one of two acceptable methods (presented in preferred order):

Unique Registration: *When access to a site is restricted solely to registered visitors (visitors who have completed a survey on the first visit to identify themselves and supply a user-id and password on subsequent visits), that site can determine visits using instances of unique registered visitors.*

Unique Cookie with a Heuristic *The site's Web server can store a small piece of information with a browser that uniquely identifies a browser for a single session. For browsers that accept cookies, visits can be approximated using the page and/or graphics downloads identifiable to a unique cookie (recognizing that this is not perfect because it merely measures unique "browsers"). For browsers that do not accept a cookie, a heuristic (decision rule) can be used to count visits using a unique IP address and user agent string, which would be added to the cookie-based counts. For these cases, using the full user agent string is recommended.*

Registration, cookies, and unique IP/User Agent String measurement methods can be used in combination.

Certain organizations rely on unique IP address and user agent string with a heuristic as a sole measurement technique for visits. This method should not be used solely because of inherent inaccuracies arising from dynamic IP addressing, which distorts these measures significantly.

"Unique" Measurements (Browsers, Visitors, and Users)

Unique users (and unique visitors)

The number of actual individual people, within a designated reporting timeframe, with activity consisting of one or more visits to a site or the delivery of pushed content. A unique user can include both:

- *an actual individual that accessed a site (referred to as a unique visitor).*

- *an actual individual that is pushed content and or ads such as email, newsletters, interstitials and pop-under ads. Each individual is counted only once in the unique user or visitor measures for the reporting period.*

The unique user and visitor measure are filtered for robotic activity prior to reporting and these measures are determined using one of two acceptable methods (presented in preferred order) or a combination of these methods:

■ *Resignation-Based Method: For sites that qualify for and use unique registration to determine visits (using a user-id and password in accordance with method 1 under "Visit" above) or recipients of pushed content, this information can be used as a basis to determine unique users across a reporting period. Best efforts should be made to avoid multiple counting of single users registered more than once as well as multiple users using the same registration.*

■ *Cookie-Based Method: For sites that utilize the unique cookie approach to determine visits (method 2 under "Visit" above) or recipients of pushed content, this information can be used to determine unique users across a reporting period. The use of persistent cookies is generally necessary for this measure. An algorithm is used to estimate the number of unique users on the basis of the number of unique cookies. The algorithm should adjust the unique cookie number therefore, accounting for multiple browser usage by individuals and multiple individuals using a single browser.*

Unique Browsers

For users using the cookie-based method for [determining] "uniques," if no adjustments are made to the unique cookie number of the site to adjust to actual people (adjusting to unique users from unique cookies), the number should be referred to as "Unique Browsers." The fact that no adjustment has been made to reflect unique users should be fully disclosed by the media company.

Other Guidance for "Unique" Measurements

For sites using cookie-based techniques, a method should be used to attribute unique user or visitor counts to those browsers that that do not accept cookies or those browsers accepting cookies that have "first use" or new cookies (essentially those that cannot [reasonably] be determined to be repeat visitors). A site can use either a census-based projection technique or a sampling method to estimate this activity. These methods are explained below. For census-based projection, the site uses its log to accumulate visits for browsers not accepting cookies and browsers with new cookies. Using this information, the site can:

■ *Assume no unique user activity from new cookies and cookie rejecting browsers, and then project unique user activity levels using a common measure (page impressions per visit, etc.) based on cookie-accepting repeat visitor activity.*

■ *Use a specific identification method (unique IP and user agent string) to assist in identifying the Unique Users represented in this group. Using the full user agent string is recommended.*

Census-based projection is generally preferred. However, for sites with unusually high volume (making census-based techniques infeasible) or other extenuating circumstances, a random sampling technique is acceptable.

For sample-based projection, the site log continues to be used; however, a sample of log data is used to build activity measures of non-cookied users with new cookies. The sampling method must be a known probability technique of adequate design and sample-size to provide estimates at the 95% [or greater] confidence level.

The burden of proof is on the measurement provider to establish the sufficiency of the sampling methods used.

Page Impressions

In addition to the metrics defined above, several organizations internally and/or externally report page impressions. For purposes of this document, page impression measurement needs further analysis to determine best practices and address certain industry issues. The IAB's Ad Campaign Measurement project included evaluation of page impression measurement, and the following is presented to provide a page-impression measurement definition:

> **Page Impression**: *A measurement of the responses from a Web server to page request from the user browser, which is filtered to remove robotic activity and error codes prior to reporting, and is recorded at a point as close as possible to opportunity to see the page by the user. Much of this activity is recorded at the content server level.*

Good filtration procedures are critical to page-impression measurement. Additionally, consistent handling of auto-refreshed pages and other pseudo-page content (surveys, pop-ups, etc.) in defining a "page" and establishing rules for the counting process is also critical. The page-like items should be counted as follows:

Pop-ups: *ad impressions*

Interstitials: *ad impressions*

Pop-unders: *ad impressions*

Surveys: *page impressions*

HTML Newsletters (if opened): *page impressions if not solely advertising content, otherwise ad impressions*

Auto-Refreshed Pages: *page impressions, unless the page is in background or minimized, therefore diminishing the opportunity to view. [If] the content-type is likely to be in background or minimized (for example, Internet radio) while in use and the organization cannot determine whether minimization has occurred, these auto-refreshed pages should not be counted.*

Frames: *page impressions; organizational rules should be developed for converting frame loads into page impressions and these rules should be disclosed. One acceptable method is to identify a frame which contains the majority of content and count a page impression only when this dominant frame is loaded.*

These items should be separately identified and quantified within page-impression totals. Significant disaggregated categories should be prominently displayed.

Ads not served by an ad-serving system (for example, ads embedded in page content) are generally counted by the same systems that derive page impressions or through the use of "beacon" technologies. In all cases, ads not served by ad-serving systems should be disaggregated for reporting purposes from other ad impressions.

Email Promotions

The old joke goes that if you took all the economists in the world and laid them out end to end, they'd all be pointing in different directions. The same can be said about marketing people when discussing the relative importance of the various components of a direct mail campaign.

In October 2001, David Cabrera of Aura Corporation (www.auracorp.co.uk) posted a reasonable model to the UK-Netmarketing list (www.chinwag.com/uk-netmarketing):

Targeting   600% difference between the best and worst lists

Incentives   400% difference between the best and worst incentives

Creative   35% difference between the best and worst creative

Response Device   15% difference between best and worst

Timing   10% difference between best and worst

In a classic TIMITI approach, you want to check out all of these elements. And when it comes to measuring email marketing, you want to check them at various stages in the email marketing life-cycle:

- Emails Sent
- Emails Opened
- Emails with Clickthrough Response
- Emails Bounced
- Emails Unsubscribed

Emails Sent

This one's easy. Either you have a database and you determine how many of your potential targets are going to be on the receiving end of your onslaught or you're renting lists from respectable email list managers who believe in opt-in-only email. So you know very well how many emails are supposed to go out.

When dealing with your own data managers and with third parties, make sure they provide you with reports showing how many actually went out. You may want to have the ISP that manages the mail servers provide a backup report.

The email promotion process starts getting more interesting, however, when you look at how many of your messages have been opened.

Emails Opened

You know how many direct mail pieces you mailed and you have a receipt for postage to prove it. You know how many went to bad addresses because you have the unopened envelopes unceremoniously returned to your desk. The same is true with bad email addresses—they bounce. And, of course, you know how many people responded to your offer because, well, they responded. But wouldn't it be nice if you knew how many people opened your envelope before tossing it in the wastebasket? With email, you can.

ReadNotify (www.readnotify.com) provides a service that makes use of the "return-receipt-requested" feature that requires the recipient to acknowledge the email. Not very elegant, but the information they provide in return is interesting: an activity report (see Figure 7.8) and a map (see Figure 7.9).

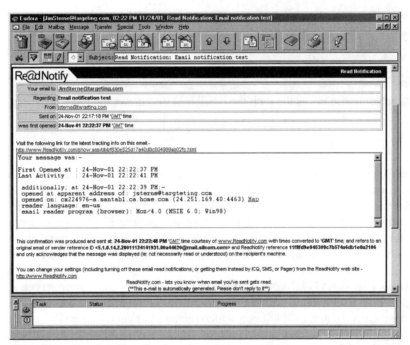

Figure 7.8 ReadNotify tells you when the message was opened, by whom, and at what IP address.

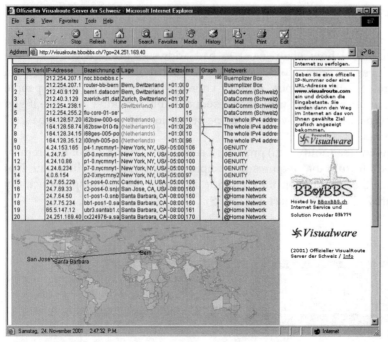

Figure 7.9   ReadNotify also traces the path the email took and draws the route on a map.

Much more elegant and much less intrusive is the single white pixel maneuver. It's a simple little trick, really, but it only works with email recipients who accept HTML messages. Most email clients come preconfigured to receive HTML, but due to personal preference (like when I'm in a foreign country and paying $3 per minute for a very slow hotel connection) and corporate firewalls, there is a significant percentage who want/need text-only messages. For the rest, a link to a single white pixel is the trigger.

Send messages out with HTML code that fetches the graphics from your server. A link to a single white pixel will tell you exactly when your email message was opened. If you code those links right, they'll tell you which recipient opened it as well:

```
www.company.com/email/LandingPage.html?mssg982359
```

So now you know how many messages went out and how many were opened. You'll also find out how many were misaddressed.

Emails Bounced

One of the nice things about email is that it automatically tells you when you've got the wrong address. Emails bounce. If you're sending out your own, those bounces will come right to you. If you're using a third party, make sure they provide the proper reports indicating how many bounces there were, to ensure you don't pay for faulting labeling.

There is one other negative bit of feedback you can expect and here, too, the fault might be shared: people who unsubscribe.

Emails Unsubscribed

If I directly sign up to get your email announcements or newsletter and I don't like what you send me, I'll sign off. That's an absolutely wonderful way to measure whether you're hitting the mark from a content perspective. When people like what they get, they tell their friends and your subscription rate goes up with every send. If they don't, they let you know in no uncertain terms.

If you rent (opt-in-only, please) email lists, then there's another layer of meaning when subscribers choose to no longer be subscribers:

- The email address collector may have collected the addresses under false pretenses.

- Your message may have been inartfully sent to the wrong list.

- Your content sucks.

Having content that sucks is more often than not a surprise. You think it's smashing content. Your subordinates all tell you you're right. Just count yourself lucky that you've learned something valuable at a small comparative expense. The other two problems, however, tell you a lot about the vendor you're dealing with.

Some email list database merchants collect names however and wherever they can. The worst collect them willy-nilly (which stands for will he or nil he—whether the address owner wants it or not). Any of your messages sent to this hodgepodge list will be met with a higher degree of disdain due to the lack of serious targeting.

But even the best email address accumulators may run afoul of the salesperson who is so intent on renting you tens of thousands of names he or she doesn't focus on which lists should and which should not be on the recipient list for your offer. Fortunately, this works against them.

At YesMail (www.yesmail.com), they are very careful to track which types of messages are of interest to which categories of subscribers. With more than 25 million people signed up, it's important to keep them all as happy as possible.

The novice sales consultant, calculating the commissions in advance, might think that a new chat software release might be of interest to all 3,936,384 subscribers to the Internet category and to all 2,958,777 subscribers to the Computer Software category. The sales consultant who's interested in keeping all of those subscribers will recommend sending the message to the 17,951 who signed up in the Chat category, a subset of the Internet group.

Tracking your own unsubscribes is critical when sending out your own corporate newsletter. Company branding, customer retention, and good old online relationship improvement all come to bear.

Emails with Clickthrough Response

As with online ads, the next phase in email marketing is measuring how many people respond with a click. Your server logs make this a very simple task if, again, you include a traceable link in every message. You then need to ensure that your server log analysis tools are up to the task of letting you slice and dice the results to show which email messages are bringing in the most/best people.

Before working with a third party, you'll want to take a close look at their reports to be sure they fill the bill. YesMail does a fairly good job at spelling out the results of a campaign, as well as the financial significance of those results (see Figures 7.10 to 12).

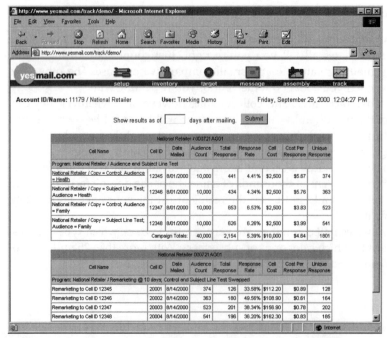

Figure 7.10   YesMail provides clear Cost Per Response reporting. . .

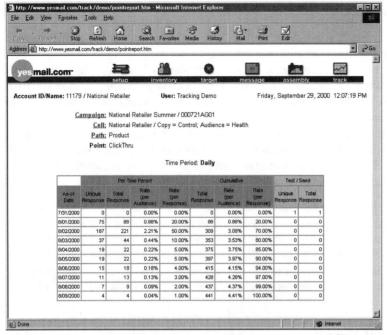

Figure 7.11 . . . a view of when responses came in. . .

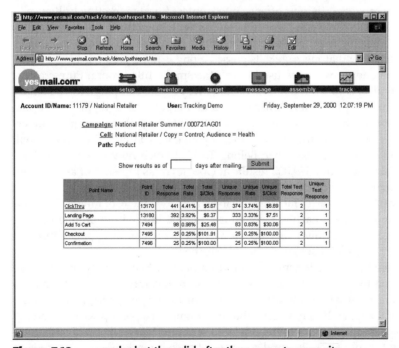

Figure 7.12 . . . and what they did after they came to your site.

Emails with Good Timing

When is the best time to send out an email come-on? Don't forget this little element when comparing the results of your marketing genius.

A newsletter that includes the deer-resistant plant of the month from www .mydeergarden.com is better received over the weekend than the "Corporate Trust Connection," the quarterly newsletter from U.S. Bank Corporate Trust Services (www.usbank.com).

Promotions, on the other hand, work well when timed together. ConsumerMarketingBiz (part of Anne Holland's MarketingSherpa.com empire) reported on Eric Welter's progress as the vice president of marketing at Geerlings & Wade, the online and offline wine merchant:

> Welter worked closely with his print broker, Ballantine Litho-Sales Inc., to time emails around his direct mail campaigns. He says, "We've been a direct mail company for 15 years, so we already knew the optimal time to send postal mail. It's the timing of the email around and in coordination with the mail schedule that makes a difference. You'll have a piece of mail in your postal mail box, then the next morning you'll get a similar promotion in your email reminding you that you're two clicks away from placing an order."

Tracking Viral Email

It's such a wonderful idea. You send out an email to a handful of people and they each forward it on to a handful of people and they forward it on, and before you know it, the whole world is abuzz with your offer/game/contest/viral marketing brilliance.

Only two problems. First, you have to come up with something so appealing, so compelling, so tantalizing that people actually *want* to forward it to friends and family. Second, measuring how that message gets passed along is not a piece of cake.

The first part is one for what we used to call the smoke-filled room. Pure creative genius coupled with absolute blind luck is the only way a viral campaign can be wildly successful. Oh, you can plan it, and schedule it, and budget it all right, just don't plan on spending the profits from your results. To say "results may vary" is a gross understatement. There's just no way to tell in advance if your shrewd marketing concept will be as widespread as All Your Base Are Belong To Us (which now produces 148,869 results on AltaVista and about 379,000 results at Google) or as unheard of as the thousands of intentional viral efforts that go nowhere every year.

Given an adequately powerful meme you can start an avalanche of interest by sending out just a few messages. Each one contains a unique link with a unique landing page. You can easily count how many people went to which landing pages, but you can't trace the viral network itself, only the source, the seed.

Let's say the seed message is sent to a hundred people. Even if only one of those people passes it on to a group of excitable viral communicators, you can still have a landslide of interest, but all you'll know is which of the original recipients was the Typhoid Mary of the gang. It may well be that the original recipient passed it along to somebody who passed it along to somebody who sent it to Mary.

The only way to truly track the viral progress of such a marketing campaign is to include some device that requires the identification of the previous sender. If, in order to register for the contest, join the discussion, get the discount, or download the game, participants must identify where they heard about the offer, they *might* be willing and able to give you a bit more information than you've been able to acquire to date—might.

If I got it from Larry, and he got it from Jerry, and Jerry got it from Mary, then I can't tell you that Mary was the one who makes the whole thing viable. I can only tell you about Larry—if I have a mind to.

The best viral marketing requires the least amount of effort for the propagator. Forwarding an email message is the easiest. If that message has a link that takes the recipient to a page where they have to fill out a form, you've thrown cold water on the whole process. Every time you add another hurdle, you add another viral vaccine.

Email Auditing

Just as there are companies to help track the veracity of online advertisers, we now have services from ABCi to track email. ABCi announced their new "effort to stamp out concerns over list accuracy and delivery validity—and perhaps help produce some standards along the way," according to an article by Christopher Saunders from November 1, 2001, on Internetnews.com (www.internetnews.com/IAR/article/0,,12_915291,00.html):

> For direct response service bureaus and email distribution companies, the Chicago-based ABC Interactive said it would study the systems used to create and deliver email campaigns—analyzing internal processes and reporting standards.
> Meanwhile, ABCi also said it would provide auditing services for list managers and marketers that would review the results of specific campaigns. ABCi said it would be able to verify the accuracy of lists' purported size and demographic makeup, their compliance with stated privacy rules, agreed-upon merge/purge activity, delivery and results.
> [The hope is to] help the email marketing industry by weeding out inaccurate procedures and players, and by making it easier for an apples-to-apples comparison of different vendors. Already, the group is working with associations like the Interactive Advertising Bureau to hammer out standards governing ad serving metrics and reporting, and it is huddling with the Advertising Research Foundation's Digital Media Measurement Council to create audience auditing standards. Now, it said, it plans to do the same for email.

Hope springs eternal.

Valuing Visitors

So here we are in the middle of Chapter 7 and all we've done so far is get people to come to our site. That's not bad, but so far all we know is how much it cost to get them there. We've just spent oodles of money renting buses to round up large numbers of people and bring them to the mall.

Will they enjoy the experience? Will they tell their friends? Will they buy? Just how valuable are these people anyway? Are they potential shopping junkies or are they merely looky-loos?

To get a handle on this area of analysis, let's define some terms. We need to be able to intelligently discuss the differences between the following:

- Visitor
- Unique visitor
- Return visitor
- Qualified visitor
- Stale visitor
- User
- Customer

Visitor

Somebody comes to your Web site. Pages have been served. Links have been clicked. You have a visitor. Buy why is that person there? No way to tell. At least you can calculate how costly it was to get the visitor there now that search engines like GoTo (now Overture.com) are selling placement:

Ameriquest Mortgage (www.ameriquestmortgage.com) knows exactly how much it costs to get a pair of eyeballs to its site from GoTo.com [see Figure 7.13]. It willingly paid $2.72 for each visitor. It now has a baseline. What would it cost to run a direct mail campaign to drive traffic to its site? If Ameriquest Mortgage sends 100,000 postcards, each costing 10¢ for paper and printing and 20¢ for postage, it would have to get an 11 percent response rate to get the same value.

On average, if you take the total cost of advertising in the home mortgage industry and divide it by the number of loan applications the mortgage companies receive for their trouble, it costs about $250 per application. Or, the companies could cut a deal with Sherri Neasham at FinanCenter.com for an order of magnitude less than that. You want a loan application sent to you electronically? That'll be $25, please.

The cost of acquisition has nothing to do with branding. We are not measuring whether people feel better about your company because of your animated banner ads and interstitial interruptions or if they feel worse. Cost of acquisition has nothing to do with sales . . . . We are measuring only the number of people who show up at your Web site. It is the cost of acquiring somebody's attention, the acquisition of their eyeballs.

You could stand on a street corner with fliers that say, "Come to our store and we'll hand you $5." What would happen? People would walk in, they'd get their $5, and some would spend it there. The next day, you hand out fliers that offer $2. The next day, $4. In time, you get a clear idea of what it costs to get people to show up. If you're good at tracking, you get an idea of how much it costs to get them to show up, look around, buy something—and come back and spend more another time.

What matters then is not how many people show up, but how many of the right people show up. Are they qualified leads? Are they serious potential buyers? Are they actual buyers? The surefire way to Web success is to track from that very first click all the way through to the sale and beyond. All in good time. Let's not get ahead of ourselves.

At the moment, you know that you've spent $X and got Y people to show up. At least you think you know. The site you buy banner ad space from says you got 2,082 clickthroughs yesterday. Your referrer logs show that you got only 1,765. What's wrong with this picture? Nothing — it's quite possible that both are correct. Your banner was clicked 2,082 times, but only 1,264 made it all the way to your landing page; 317 people clicked by mistake or waited too long for your page to load and hit the Back button. Happens all the time. From Sterne, World Wide Web Marketing, Third Edition, John Wiley & Sons, Inc., 1995

So you got somebody to the landing page—now what? Now it's time to determine if it's somebody you've seen before.

Unique Visitor

What makes this visitor different from that one? Your server logs show that two visitors came from two IP addresses. But if they come to you from the same AOL gateway, or the same corporate firewall opening, then they look identical to the server.

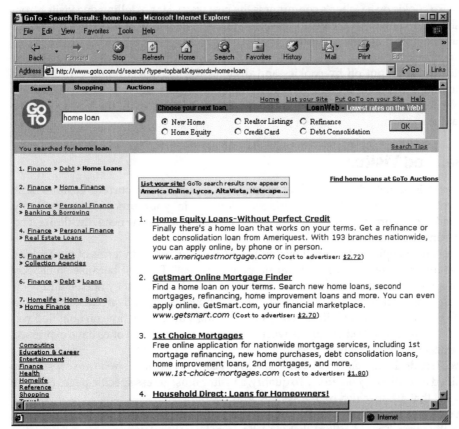

Figure 7.13 It used to cost $2.72 every time somebody clicked from Goto.com (now Overture.com: www.overture.com) to Ameriquest mortgage; now it costs the mortgage company $4.40.

When two visitors reach your home page from the same gateway, your log file tells you that the server sent the same page to the same IP address twice. Is this one visitor who hit the Refresh button? Maybe.

If they both click on the same link, perhaps the Products button, you still can't be sure. Then one clicks for Product A, and the other for Product B. Got 'em! Right? Not so fast. So far, we could have one person clicking the Refresh button on the home page, then the Product button, then the Product A button, and then the Back button before looking at Product B. Remember, your server doesn't tell you about the Back button unless you drop in a little Java code to watch for it.

In the end, without cookies, you'll never know if that's one person or two. You may try to design your site such that a visitor can only follow one path at a time, revealing a second visitor from the same gateway, but that won't account for a visitor right-clicking on a link and opening a new browser. Thus, one visitor can look like two, or four, or ten. The solution? Cookies.

Return Visitor

Placing a cookie on a visitor's computer is the best way so far of telling one visitor from another and knowing if the visitor has been to your site before. It identifies the visitor as coming from a unique computer.

Drawbacks? Two big ones. The first is that a small portion of the population is afraid/annoyed/put off by cookies and disables them. There's nothing you can do about that. The second is that a growing number of corporate network managers don't allow cookies to pass through the corporate firewall. Still, they're the best tool we've got at the moment.

Qualified Visitor

A *suspect* is somebody who shares characteristics with your current customers. A *prospect* is somebody who has expressed interest in your products—perhaps by responding to a promotion. A *qualified prospect* is one who has the need, the desire, and the means to make the buy.

Yes, some people buy things they don't need, so think of this in terms of psychology and emotion. "I really *need* that purple pair of pants!" But just because somebody needs a root canal, that doesn't mean they want it. Just because they need it and want it doesn't mean they can afford it. So all three components are really necessary for a visitor to be classified as a qualified prospect. Spending a little more time on qualified visitors than on unqualified visitors is worth it because the qualified ones have expressed some deeper interest than the rest.

WebTrends defines *qualified visits* this way: "Visits by customers who are considered qualified as revenue generators. To qualify, a visitor must access specific pages on your Web site that are specified by the system administrator."

A qualified visitor sees a certain number of pages or downloads the white paper or plays the game. That identifies that visitor as a potential customer.

Stale Visitor

Frequency is nice, but recency means everything online. Qualified visitors eventually lose their qualifications when they don't come back for a spell. How long? That depends on what you're selling. A car buyer is different from an office supplies purchasing agent, who is different from a refrigerator shopper, who is different from a chocolate consumer.

Just make sure that you have a designation in your database for those who previously expressed interest and haven't done so of late. The astute marketing maven will send out an inducement with a note that says "We miss you."

User

A visitor is a visitor. They come, they look, they may even become qualified if they stay long enough and dig deep enough. But a *user* comes to your site repeatedly and for a reason.

Be very careful when buying sponsorship space on sites and talking about how many users they have. One of the most amusing examples was Sixdegrees.com, which was built to help people find friends of friends. In the long run, they discovered that friends of friends of friends really didn't want to be found and the site folded up shop. But before they did, they were caught in a controversy of how many users they really had.

One press release claimed 3 million users. Their publicist stood by that number in an interview with *Silicon Alley*. But the marketing director, in a subsequent interview, said they only had about 750,000 active users. In this case, "active" meant that they were still receiving email from Sixdegrees.

Less than a month later, an email from Sixdegrees put the number at 462,000, while *PC Data*, which monitors Web traffic, estimated 340,000 unique visitors. That was only 11 percent of the Sixdegree's total registered users. Note the conflict between active and registered users.

Meanwhile, Media Metrix estimated 193,800 visitors and NetRating estimated 133,000. *Silicon Alley* reported that "the 3 million users cited did not indicate the number of daily, weekly, or even monthly users, as the release intimated. Instead, the number represents the aggregate of site browsers who, whether they ever returned or not, had once filled out the brief registration form and surfed the site in the three years since its launch."

The need for clarity is clear: A user is an identifiable individual (via cookie or logon) who meets certain criteria of frequency and sustained activity. Measuring whether that activity is sustained will help you keep your eye on your *churn rate*.

Churn

With goods in inventory, we refer to turnover. With users on a Web site, we talk in terms of *churn*. Visitors are too ghostly for this term to apply. They come, they go, and we don't know if they're new visitors or the same, loyal people coming back again and again.

In keeping track of your unique, identifiable users, you can calculate your churn rate. Why? So you'll know where to spend your time. Are you signing up more people than you're losing? Should you be spending more time on retention than acquisition?

Churn measures how much of your customer base rolls over during a given period of time. Divide the number of users who fail to return in a given time period by the total number of users at the end of the time period and you've got your baseline.

Christopher Knight provides a concise example of churn in his "Churning Out Marketing Ideas to Keep Customers" article that appeared in the September 1999 issue of *Boardwatch* magazine aimed at Internet service providers who wish to measure customer churn:

> *Say you have 2,000 subscribers on the first of the month. During the month you add 200 new subscribers. You also lose 50 subscribers. At the end of the month, you have 2,150 subscribers. Your churn rate is 50 divided by 2,150, which equals 2.3 percent, which is your churn ratio. Your growth rate for the month is 200 divided by 2,000, which equals a 10 percent growth rate. Annualized, this means (assuming you continue averaging the same performance each month) your ISP has a 27.6 percent churn rate and a 120 percent annual growth rate.*

Knight was looking at customers. Fortunately, customers are *much* easier to count than all the rest.

Customer

A customer is a visitor or a user who buys something.

The wonderful thing about customers is that you know so much about them. Name, address, and even credit card information are willingly offered up to your database. Simple.

Churn rates apply to customers as well, of course. How many people make the bounce from browser to buyer compared to the number of customers who don't come back? (Yes, I'm using *browser* in place of visitor or user. The difference? None at all. I just like the alliteration.)

We'll get serious about measuring conversion success in Chapter 11, "Calculating Conversion."But it's important to bring it up here, while we're talking about measuring the value of advertising your Web site and the value of those who are attracted to your site.

Acquisition Costs and Conversion Rates

The question of cost/benefit becomes very interesting very quickly. The first question is simple: Did we attract more flies with sugar than with vinegar? The next question revolves around the cost of the attraction materials. If there were fewer flies on the vinegar, but vinegar is cheaper than sugar, then we have to look at the relative cost per acquisition. Nothing new there.

Nothing new as well in the question of which method of attraction resulted in more profits at the end of the day. But what about tossing *brand* into the mix? Might the flies who noticed the sugar but didn't land be more likely to come back to the sugar than the vinegar later on?

Leo Sheiner is a member of the Online Ads email discussion list (www.o-a.com) and posted a thought-provoking message the day before Thanksgiving 2001:

```
Date: Wed, 21 Nov 2001 15:58:26 -0500
To: "Online Ads" <online-ads@>
From: Leo Sheiner <leo@managebid.com>
Subject: [online-ads] CPA CPM etc.
```

You know how it can be when you meet an old friend after a long absence.
Within minutes, it is like you have never been away. I have continued to
subscribe to online ads even though I have just been too busy to read
the posts let alone reply to any for the last year or so.
Well now that www.managebid.com is well under way I thought it time to
revisit an old friend and what do I find? The same subject of CPA versus
CPM and CPC being rehashed as if it hasn't been discussed to death.
I was long an advocate for CPC and CPA when CPM was the norm. I built a
very profitable network www.safe-audit.com on the strength of my belief
in charging advertising by results because so many publishers resisted
anything other than CPM. I argued then as now, that traffic on the net
will always far exceed the demand. In that situation the customer is
king unless you have some really unique demographic that can give you
special leverage. I see no reason to change my belief (that has served
me so well) that if you want to compete with offline advertising (whose
volumes make online look puny) you have to offer something more than
they do.
Take a look at these stats from Jupiter Metrix that showed ROI and
customer satisfaction from various sources of traffic [Table 7.3]
Paid inclusion is traffic from PPC SEs [search engines] and shows double
the ROI to CPM banners and 50% better ROI than CPC banners.
Interestingly Opt-in email is only a percentage point better ROI than
PPC SEs. Pay for placement is essentially affiliate deals and as most of
these are results based I would expect a higher ROI and customer
satisfaction, in fact I am surprised it isn't higher still at only five
percentage points better ROI than PPC SEs.

Table 7.3 Jupiter Media Metrix Survey of Marketers' Satisfaction With Promotional Methods

SOURCE OF TRAFFIC	ROI	OVERALL SATISFACTION
CPM Banners	19%	12%
CPC Banners	21%	16%
Paid Inclusion	31%	23%
Opt-In Email	33%	24%
Pay for Placement	41%	29%

I would like to focus on ROI since I have always maintained ROI is what it is all about. The rest is interesting for the people managing traffic, but for the guy writing the checks, only the bottom line counts. The really neat thing about advertising with PPC SEs is that you can modify your cost and volume of traffic from each source in realtime. As soon as you log in and reduce or increase your bid on any keyword in any SE you will have an immediate impact on both your costs and volumes of traffic from that source.

It follows from this, that if you can add an analysis of your ROI into the loop, you can increase or decrease costs and traffic volumes from any source according to how profitable or otherwise that source is (or would be).

Doing this manually, if you have perhaps a few thousand keywords and could be using ten different sources of traffic, is simply impossible. Even with smaller volumes it would be tedious at best, inaccurate and not a cost-effective use of time at worst. At www.managebid.com we have used clever tracking and some very sophisticated mathematics to solve this problem.

I have been in Internet advertising for six years now and I think Robo ROI is the most exciting development I have ever seen because it actually can guarantee the maximum ROI for any budget. We have just finished the latest report module for Robo ROI and frankly it is amazing. It shows each source of traffic with a breakdown of volumes, costs, and value generated. That is easy enough to do but still very useful. But here is the magic that comes from the maths: it shows the user where the bid started, where it is currently and projects the volumes, costs, and value generated for each position that it either did or could have bid for.

Of course you can sort this output in many different ways to provide different views that can gain you even more insight, but the essence is that not only is your budget being managed to achieve the maximum results for your money, but you are getting a comprehensive scientific analysis of all the alternatives to justify the decisions automatically made on your behalf. In my view that has never been done before and is a significant milestone reached for the advertising industry.

We have barely scratched the surface. But if we want to succeed we have to learn how to connect the value we give to the costs we charge in a way that offline advertising cannot replicate.

I was intrigued by Leo Sheiner's post and asked if I could reproduce it here. He replied:

I would be delighted if you do. The maths by the way is primarily Game theory with some damping algorithms and a little bit of AI thrown in. I had two PHDs in computational maths work on the problem.

The interesting thing is that in the real world people do not necessarily only want to get the most for their money. One large customer just told us that for the benefit of branding he would not want to be below position three in goto.

Fine we said, we would offer the additional facility to put in a stop to prevent bids from being ranked below a user defined position (which is a

```
kind of hybrid between auto-pilot and Robo ROI). But, we explained, if
he used that qualification/overide, it would mean that he would probably
be getting slightly less than optimal results in terms of the profit
generated. Go figure. It is an interesting world isn't it?
Of course our report will now actually tell him how much profit he has
foregone for his perceived benefit of branding.
```

Leo, it turns out, is focused on the bottom line, but in the most direct sort of way. The value of branding cannot be dismissed. I told Leo that he could codify the calculation for the value of that branding. It's based on asking people how they feel about the brand before and after exposure in a given venue.

You know how many people clicked through and how many people bought, but you don't know how many more people would have later gone to that site had they seen the site listed in the top three results in the search engine. You have to run studies to determine that figure, then rerun your end-results figures to tell you that a bird in the hand is worth 2.375 in the bush—maybe.

In Practice

Anne Holland's MarketingSherpa offers up the details on what it takes it track acquisition and sales well enough to realize a profit.

Seattle Lab Raises Sales 44% by Email Marketing to IT Professionals

CHALLENGE:

Like many high tech firms, Seattle Lab used to be run by engineers. Which meant that the Lab's marketing was pretty much non-existent. Still they did all right because they developed quality software products, and had a solid in-house sales team of five hardworking reps. But you can only grow so far without solid marketing behind you.

Two years ago, the Company was purchased by BVRP, a French software company with a marketing-centric corporate culture. So, the pressure was on for Seattle Lab to become marketing-centric as well. Last summer they hired an expensive VP Marketing and spent a bunch of money on everything from banners to print ads. But after six months of marketing spending, sales didn't seem to be growing as much as they should be.

Heather Fairchild, a direct marketing specialist, joined the Company in December 2000. Her job was to turn things around.

CAMPAIGN:

Fairchild says, "When I began, money was being spent on banners, newsletters, print, and whatever the company could throw money at. No tracking, no quantifying, no ROI analysis."

Almost immediately she stopped the marketing cash flow drain. She says, "There was a lot of pressure from the management team to continue marketing, but I didn't want to spend money to just spend it. I cut every single marketing activity and didn't do any at all for all of February 2001."

That month was filled with frantic preparation. With the support of sales support special- ist Sandreen, Fairchild accomplished the following five steps:

1. *Measurement of all past campaign results:*

   Fairchild says, "We found out, after quantifying, that we didn't have one single marketing activity that worked. Our banners only got a .01-.05% click-through rate and only 1-2% of those turned out to be good leads. Sales conversion rates were horrible."

2. *Market potential:*

   Were these lousy marketing numbers the product's fault? Fairchild examined both the total potential marketplace and the percent of product downloads from the com- pany's site that turned into sales. Both were high enough that she was sure her prod- ucts were worth investing marketing dollars in.

3. *An action plan:*

   So many things had to happen—media buying, offer creation, site development, database management, copywriting, reseller management, email newsletter creation, etc.—that Fairchild knew it would be easy to lose focus and end up not finishing any task successfully. So she set down a month-by-month set of steps and goals based on the company's sales targets and product launch schedule. Hence forward, every step was dictated by the plan.

4. *Customer and prospect database management:*

   Fairchild knew her best potential market were IT pros who had purchased Seattle Lab products in the past. However, getting the data into one, usable format wasn't easy. Fairchild says, "We had customer records over the last ten years spread across three databases—Excel sheets, Quickbooks and Act."

   With advice from Carney Direct, a list brokerage and database consultancy, she col- lected, cleaned, and deduped all the data into a single database and then negotiated with a vendor to house it for her.

5. *Email privacy policy:*

   Fairchild knew that email marketing would become an important part of her market- ing mix, so she set down company rules about how email could be used, and how opt-in permission would be gathered.

   Seattle Lab now only uses opt-in names and never opt-out names. In addition, unless personally requested, the only email customers receive is critical user-infor- mation (updates, patches to fix bugs, etc.) for products they have already purchased.

Next in March, Fairchild ran two outreach programs. The first was to the customer data- base. She explains, "The introductory email said, 'We haven't spoken to you in a while. We would like to communicate with you about updates and upgrades on the products you own.'"

Fairchild's second outreach program was to test the most targeted opt-in email lists avail- able on the rental market. Again working with Carney Direct, she tested groups of three- to-five lists at a time. She says, "I did mini-buys of 5,000 names." Each campaign included test cells to split out various title selections from the same lists, as well as two different subject lines with the same message body creative. She also tracked the results of text-only versus HTML messages.

By the end of March she'd learned which lists, title selections, and subject lines were worth investing in. So she was able to roll out much bigger campaigns without risking ROI. Initial campaigns were focused on making up the sales lost while the February-March prep work had been going on, so campaigns focused on promoting particular products, and often featured a time limited offer.

However, Fairchild had a greater vision beyond simply using email to generate direct sales. She wanted to use email to begin a long-term relationship with each IT professional that could result in much more profitable sales as they began to trust the Seattle Lab brand. Plus, while renting opt-in email lists is a lot less expensive than doing a direct mail campaign, it's still pricier than doing campaigns to your own in-house list.

Therefore, in June Fairchild began testing soft-offer campaigns that would help her grow her in-house prospect opt-in database, while starting long-term relationships with potential customers. She says, "The first time we talked to somebody, we wanted to add a lot of value to their experience. We didn't just want to hit them with a promotion. I wanted to start a dialog with them, let them know who we are."

She commissioned a white paper on content security from a third-party professional writer. Then she rolled out an email campaign to her best performing lists. She tested two different subject lines—"Free White Paper on Content Security" and "Free White Paper on How to Stop CyberCrime." Click-throughs landed on a special Web page that requested a small amount of information (name, state, and email.) In keeping with her privacy policy, Fairchild added a check box asking each visitor for permission to email them again. It read, "Do you wish to receive more information on products and services relating to security?" Although the white paper briefly mentioned Seattle Lab's products, it was not marketing focused. Fairchild explains the sales cycle from that point, "We give them time to read the white paper and then put opt-ins on a once-a-month schedule to receive further information. It's a longer qualifying cycle. We'll make them an offer probably six weeks later for our product." By which time presumably they are thoroughly impressed with Seattle Lab and are more likely to respond positively.

RESULTS:

Seattle Lab's sales figures for the month of July 2001 were 44% higher than its sales figures for the month of March 2001 when Fairchild's initial marketing tests began. The company's new product launch sales for 2001 are currently 20% higher than expected. Here are more results:

■ *Email list test results. Fairchild says, "Generally if I try five lists typically three will be around 1% response rate, one will always be around 2% and one will be around 3%. I go back and do a larger buy on the 3% list.*

"With the 2% list, it could be the list or the message, so I run another message to test offers and subject lines. If it does lackluster the second time, it doesn't matter how many times I change the offer or subject line, the list isn't right." She also notes that HTML almost always gets double the response rate that plain text does.

- *White paper test campaign. The results between the subject lines ("Free White Paper on Content Security" and "Free White Paper on How to Stop CyberCrime") tested were so close—2.9% CTR vs. 2.7% CTR—that Fairchild called it a tie.*

However, 52% of the clicks from the "Security" subject line actually downloaded the white paper, while a full 60% of the clicks from the "CyberCrime" subject line did. In both cases, about half of the visitors who downloaded the white papers also checked the box on the firm to opt-in to receive further information via email from Seattle Lab. Fairchild says, "We're very pleased with the results."

Reproduced with permission from www.MarketingSherpa.com, 08/21/2001

One other cost to keep in mind: the cost of the tools and services you're going to need to keep track of your campaigns. The prices range, of course, and the larger your campaigns, the larger the bill. When it comes to calculating the total return on investment for any given promotion, don't forget to add the calculator into the calculation.

You did a great job of raising awareness, getting people to remember your brand, getting people interested, and, finally, getting them to click. After all that, wouldn't it be a shame if they never made it all the way to your site? Time to measure whether your server is up to the task.

CHAPTER

8

Measuring Web Site Performance: The Need for Speed

"If it were done when 'tis done, then 'twere well
It were done quickly"
William Shakespeare
Macbeth, Act 1, Scene 7

Is your Web site fast enough? If you said "No," move to the head of the class.

I thought that as compression techniques improved and bandwidth grew, this issue would fade. My father proved me wrong. He called to ask if I thought he should install a cable modem and sign up for @Home. I said, "Absolutely. You'll love it. It's so much faster!" I was deeply annoyed that they were wiring his neighborhood before they wandered up the hill into my neck of the woods. It would be another 16 months before cable came to my humble abode, so I was all in favor of Dad getting broadbandedly wired.

A month later, he called to tell me that there were two men in his attic, one outside drilling a hole through the wall, and two underneath his desk arguing about protocols. Was I sure, he wanted to know, that this was a good idea? I said, "Absolutely! You're gonna love it! You'll be able to see videos and get music and not have to wait for Web sites anymore!" He said, "We have a television for videos."

Three days later, he called again to say that somebody was coming out again to try to config-ure the modem and he was going to bring a couple of spares along just in case and did I still think this was worth the pain and suffering I had encouraged him to bring into his home? I said, "Absolutely! Call me tomorrow."

He called the next day—ecstatic. "It's so fast! I'm watching the news on CNN. I'm get-ting pages to show up within seconds instead of minutes. This is great!" I breathed a very large sigh of relief.

I called him a couple of days later. "How's the new cable connection working out?"
"It's OK."

153

"Just OK?"
"Yeah."
"Isn't it faster? Can't you get a bunch more stuff without waiting?"
"Yeah. I guess."
"Isn't it way better than that 56K modem?"
"Yeah, I suppose." His voice clearly included phrases like, *"But it was a royal pain to install and isn't nearly as interesting as 'West Wing'."* I threw in the towel.
"Well," I said, *"for what you'll be paying per month, you might want to cancel it when the free period runs out and go back to the modem."*
"Oh, no! I'd never do that!"
And thus I learned that like computers themselves, there's no such thing as an Internet connection that's fast enough. If I have my own T1 line, it means only that I'll be waiting on the Web servers and the backbone traffic, instead of my dinky phone line. It will never be fast enough.
From Sterne, World Wide Web Marketing, Third Edition (Wiley, 2001)

For those of you interested in the deep, dark, technical side of this issue, proceed at once to Amazon.com or your favorite café-latte-serving hangout and pick up a copy of Patrick Killelea's technically detailed book *Web Performance Tuning* (O'Reilly & Associates, 1998). On the other hand, you may be satisfied to read his chapter entitled "Web Performance Measurement" at http://patrick.net/wpt/ch03.html.

If, however, you are on the business side of the house like me, you understand that when people leave your site because your pages load too slowly, it's your fault. It doesn't matter if your site pops up fine on your high-speed connection; if it looks slow to the guy on the 28.8 modem and he's a prospective customer, then it's your fault. You're not taking proper care of the online version of your brand.

As the business manager, it behooves you to understand Web site speed from a business perspective. Here, then, are the various things over which you should keep watch and for which somebody on the technical side should take responsibility.

Latency and Throughput

The World Wide Wait is the bane of surfers the world over because of latency and throughput.

Before getting into pings, bings, and traceroutes in *Web Performance Tuning*, Patrick Killelea is kind enough to describe latency and throughput better than I could ever hope to. Here are what he refers to as the three traditional examples:

1. *An overnight (24-hour) shipment of 1,000 different CDs holding 500 megabytes each has terrific throughput but lousy latency. The throughput is (500 x 2,201.05 x 8 x 1000) bits/(24 x 60 x 60) seconds = about 49 million bits/second, which is better than a T3's 45 million bits/second. The difference is that the overnight shipment bits are delayed for a day and then arrive all at once, but T3 bits begin to arrive immediately, so the T3 has much better latency, even though both methods have approximately the same throughput when considered over the interval of a day. We say that the overnight shipment is* bursty *traffic.*

2. *Supermarkets would like to achieve maximum throughput per checkout clerk because they can then get by with fewer of them. One way for them to do this is to increase*

your latency, that is, to make you wait in line, at least up to the limit of your toler-ance. In his book Configuration and Capacity Planning for Solaris Servers *(Prentice-Hall), Brian Wong phrased this dilemma well by saying that throughput is a measure of organizational productivity while latency is a measure of individual pro-ductivity. The supermarket may not want to waste your individual time, but it is even more interested in maximizing its own organizational productivity.*

3. *One woman has a throughput of one baby per 9 months, barring twins or triplets, etc. Nine women may be able to bear 9 babies in 9 months, giving the group a throughput of 1 baby per month, even though the latency cannot be decreased (i.e., even 9 women cannot produce 1 baby in 1 month). This mildly offensive but unfor-gettable example is from* The Mythical Man-Month, *by Frederick P. Brooks (Addi-son Wesley).*

Starting again from the customer's perspective (I do hope you're beginning to see a pattern here), the *first* slowness is experienced while waiting for your home page to appear at all. So what's the holdup? Assuming everything is hunky-dory on your end, the problem may lie in how your bits get out to the rest of the world.

A number of vendors have come forth to monitor the Internet stopwatch, vendors like Keynote Systems (www.keynote.com). On its site, Keynote shows off the speeds of the faster well-known sites on the Web (see Figure 8.1).

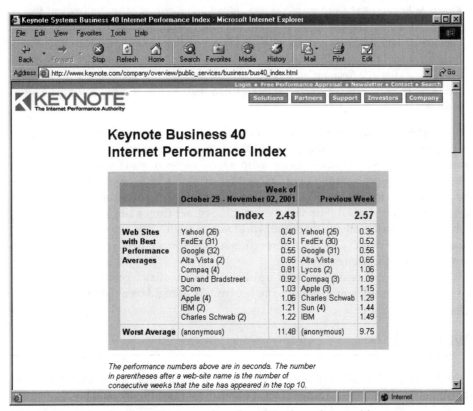

Figure 8.1   Yahoo! and FedEx are neck and neck in the subsecond home page response race, according to Keynote Systems.

Keynote measures your Web site from afar to make sure it's working to your liking. They will test your home page, your login pages, your email servers, your pagers, and then some. They will test all of the above from (last time I checked) as many as 106 locations/networks around the world. Keynote has a number of ways of looking at your site.

They measure the time it takes to grab and download a single picture or a whole page. They compare how long it takes to execute a multipage, interactive transaction. They monitor the quality of streaming content. They measure the time it takes to access and download pages over a 56-kilobyte modem, a DSL connection, or a cable connection.

If there's a problem, Keynote will email you a notification or page you. But, of course, it offers more than just throwing a red flag in your face. If you've got problems, Keynote has consultants who can help even if the problem isn't on your server. In the email Keynote sends when you first sign up, it assures you that you're not always to blame:

> *Please note that over 75% of all instances of site inaccessibility detected by Keynote Red Alert are NOT due to problems with the server, software, LAN, or ISP connection (though Keynote Red Alert detects these problems also). The vast majority of instances of site inaccessibility are due to problems with your "extended global connectivity", that is, problems with the Internet backbones to which you connect, their peering with other backbones, and the routes that are broadcast to direct traffic to your site.*
>
> *Expect to be surprised about problems you did not know existed. Also, understand that there IS something you can do about it, and that our staff can assist you in working with your bandwidth providers to zero in on and resolve these problems. Our customers include the world's largest ISPs and Internet backbone providers, because they know that monitoring your site from within its own network simply WILL NOT detect "extended connectivity" problems, which are THREE TIMES more prevalent than LAN and server problems.*

So what do you do if access to your site from different parts of the world is so slow it's scaring away business? You either duplicate your equipment and data in strategic places so that everybody has access to a more local server or you follow Oracle's lead.

Rene Bonvanie, vice president of Online Marketing at Oracle, worries about latency and throughput. He has to—all of his eggs are in one basket. "Whether you're in South Africa or China or the U.S.," he says, "everything comes from a single server." How do Web pages get to the other side of the world fast enough? "We have agreements with bandwidth providers." Oracle's approach is to pay for the bandwidth from here to there, wherever there might be.

If your site simply refuses to show up at all, it's not a latency problem or a throughput problem. Instead, you're going to be kept awake at night by availability anxiety.

Availability

"Our Web site is down" is not something a modern businessperson wants to hear, but unavailability does happen. Sometimes it's intentional (see Figure 8.2).

Figure 8.2   Imagine my surprise when Amazon.com refused to open the front door to its home page.

But often it's not. The server is overloaded. The server is confused. The server is offline for some reason or another. Just be sure somebody has the job of checking or has the tools to see if your server is serving. The next question is the big one: How fast is the server serving?

Web Site Performance

Assuming everything is hunky-dory *between* your site and your customer's computer, what about the server itself? There are several places to check its performance.

Pushing Pages

Just getting pages out the door in the morning is a struggle for some sites, and the possible problems are plentiful:

- Too many visitors
- Too many visitors wanting the same page

- Too much non-Web processing on the same machine
- Not enough memory
- Not enough disk storage
- Not enough CPUs to keep up with demand

The problem is usually pretty simple, but there are a lot of potential solutions. Make sure there are people on your team who can run them to ground efficiently.

Larry Bunyard at Tektronix uses site-monitoring tools to keep up on the competition: "I benchmark to make sure I'm beating Agilent. I believe in an information-based world where people are seeking information before they take action; speed is going to differentiate you. And when I took this thing over we were running at about—well, we were five times slower than Agilent's site. Now we are twice their speed."

Getting a single Web page out the door is only a part of the whole picture. When somebody comes to your site, they want more than just one page. That's how the phrase *customer experience* crept into the Web manager's lexicon.

Clickstream Scenario

The clickstream scenario is the simplest of customer-experience measurements, because it simply puts together a list of pages (a path) that customers are likely to traverse in search of whatever interests them at a particular site. Knowing that a visitor interested in your Malibu Prime Matter water-and-fire sculpture fountain has to go from your home page (www.orrstudio.com) to your selected projects page to /malibu .html is one thing. But measuring how long that takes, given the number of thumbnail graphics on the project page, is another.

BMC Software's (www.bmc.com) SiteAngel allows you to create a clickstream scenario by recording your mouse clicks, your passwords, and even your credit card number for testing an online purchase process from home page to final checkout.

Like Keynote, SiteAngel will test your site as often as you wish for as long as you wish and will email or page you if there are problems. It can verify that specified text was or was not found on the returned page as well as how long it took. Taken all together, you get graphs with high-level summaries of how all your critical paths compare to the operational goals you have set (see Figure 8.3).

Why does SiteAngel need to know your credit card number? Because it's not just the how fast the server spits out files or how fast those files make it across the Internet that have an effect on your customer's experience, it's also how fast their credit card is processed.

Application Processing

Keynote offers a Custom Perspective service for "inside-the-firewall performance measurements." How fast does your database server perform that search? How fast does your product configuration tool sort out the dependencies between various merchandise combinations? How fast does your personalization server find just the right up-sell and cross-sell offering?

The speed with which your server serves becomes even more important when you start adding new features to your site.

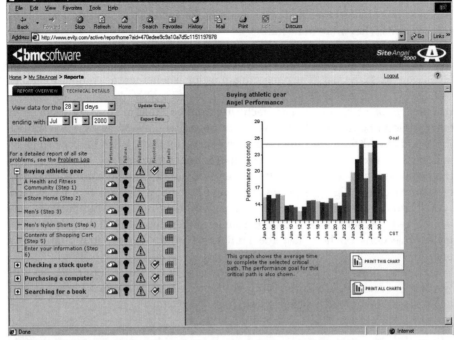

Figure 8.3   SiteAngel from BMC replays a recorded session to see how long it takes to click through your site.

Death by Success

Let's assume for a moment that you're a dynamite marketing person. You know all the public hot buttons. You have all the right co-op marketing connections. You have pull in places most others don't even know there *are* places. When it's time to put your mettle to the test, the clicks start rolling in. You knew it would happen and you made sure there were enough servers to dish out the pages. You even knew the orders would come in so you stress-tested the entire e-commerce infrastructure to ensure every customer's Submit Order click was met with an instant confirmation number and thanks rather than "Error 500; Internal Server Error."

You learned from Motley Fool's mistake of overlooking their growing need for disk space, which resulted in an inability to write orders. "You can imagine what the guys in ties were thinking when that happened," said Kevin Book, senior director of technology at www.fool.com (*Computerworld*, July 2, 2001).

So, you're certain you tested everything, aren't you? Aren't you?

A classic IBM television ad depicted a group of anxious dot-comers huddled over a computer terminal. With one keystroke, their e-commerce Web site went live. They watched with mounting joy as their site started racking up sales, two and three at a time, then ten and twelve at a time. Then their mood changed to wonder as sales came in a hundred at a time. Finally, they stood in shocked silence as the orders came in the thousands. It was obvious they had never planned for success and wouldn't be able to deliver the goods. They were done for.

Sure, the ad was televised in the excitement of the Internet bubble and looks naïve today. And, yes, the ad was produced by a company that wanted to show that the machines were up to the task. The remaining question is whether the company is up to the task.

One manager of a technology manufacturing company told me the tragic tale of an offer that couldn't be refused. "We gave a free book away. We thought it was a non-event. We had to withdraw the offer because we were flooded." What had been a great promotional idea turned into a prospect disappointment machine.

"They wanted it and they told . . . their friends about it. And we required that you register and we couldn't get the process fast enough to get it covered. So we collected your email and came back to you; tried to make you hold real quick while we recognized and fixed the problem. So we've had some conversations about how we'll try to do some projections on how fast the audience would respond if it's an online response."

It's not just whether your servers are up to the task; it's whether your company can survive being successful. Measuring your ability to ramp up logistics (shipping and receiving) is a time-honored problem. Good luck.

Speed Matters

The late Zona Research did a study in 2000 entitled "Economic Impact of Unacceptable Web Site Download Speeds." They tracked *bailout rates,* which are the percentage of those who hit the Back button or just surfed off in disgust after waiting too long for a page to show up.

They reported that more than half the people trying to download a page larger than 70 kilobytes would leave before the page finished loading. Thirty percent bailed out on pages that were 40 kilobytes, but that figure dropped to less than 7 percent for pages at or below the 34-kilobyte mark. Such a small amount of data drives a high percentage of people to distraction. Did they only ask 14.4-kilobyte-modem users? Doesn't matter.

Echoing my father's experience, columnist Jon Carroll complained about the very same problem in *Business 2.0* magazine (February 2001): "I'm sure the animated logo and the big picture of Claudia Schiffer holding your widget to her bosom and the dancing slogan 'We're the tomorrow people' looked just great when you all used some T-3 equivalent to look at in your home office, but with my modest DSL connection it times out or hangs or just sits there. And God forbid I should click on one of your links because that's another entire Schiffer-based nightmare. If I loved to spend hours shopping, I'd be down at the mall. You know?"

At this point you've got a lot of people coming to your site and you've got a site that can accommodate a lot of people. *Very* good. Now, how do you measure the value of the information they find there?

CHAPTER

9

Calculating the Caliber of Content

If you're selling boxes of stuff or downloaded data from your Web site, your focus is on driving traffic to your site, keeping people around long enough for them to make a purchase, and then getting them to come back and do it again. That's great. But let's say you sell complex technical products. And we're not talking about laptops here but stuff that isn't going to be put into a shopping cart. Something like a $500,000 medical imaging device. That changes things a little.

For those who are interested in sales and only sales, the rest of the book will be just your cup of tea. But spend a little time with this chapter first because, in the long run, your site is going to have to take content into account. Now's as good a time as any.

Content is that magical stuff that draws people to your site, helps them discover, learn, compare, and contrast, and finally pushes them over the threshold of inquiry and into the realm of action. Content delivers the information, raises the awareness, provides the education, and persuades the prospect.

I'm one of those who is forever saying that content is king. I'm also one of those who advise clients to make all of your information as findable as possible; two diametrically opposed goals.

Is there an optimal Web site size? If it's too small, it doesn't have the ability to produce the desired effect and isn't worth the expense. If it is too big, there's simply too much overhead and, again, it's not worth the expense. Lots of content means lots of people to manage it.

The vice president of corporate communications at a worldwide information services and technology company told me that benchmarking the right amount of people for the right amount of content was nearly impossible: "It's one of the hardest things that I think we're all facing. I can't tell you how hard it is to find out how many people are supporting Web sites at other companies. We're all going to our managers trying to get appropriate staffing, appropriate funding, yet you can't find that information anywhere. Companies will not give it out."

When you ask a company how much they spent on their Web site—working with external vendors, buying servers, buying software—some can tell you. But how many hours went into strategizing, designing, building, and maintaining it? No one has any idea.

In his report, "Web Site ROI and Scoring," Kurt Schlegel at the META Group (www.metagroup.com) identified content-oriented Web sites as typically hard to quantify in terms of benefits. Most large companies, the ones he calls the Global G2000, try to calculate the value of a given page based on the average amount of time a visitor is at that page and the value of the information consumed:

> Determining the value of information consumed requires data mining algorithms, which can associate subsequent actions (e.g., made purchase, joined user group) based on consuming a particular piece of content. High-end click-stream analysis vendors can track specific results after viewing a piece of content to create actionable metrics for content pages (e.g., 80% of viewers that read this page filled out this form). At times these assessments are made by aggregating offline and online data through the use of BI/OLAP [Business Intelligence/On-Line Analytical Processing] functionality, but most G2000 enterprises have not integrated their data sources at this level.

Basic corporate information will always be a conundrum. The head of corporate communications who holds sway over how the company is described online and how the CEO's bio is reproduced has a difficult time tying his expenditure to return. One such executive at a global manufacturer pondered the value he was providing:

> What is really the contribution of my unit to the bottom line? I'm an online publisher. I'm not selling anything. Every other business unit, whether they are selling things online or not, is also publishing, but how do I judge the value of the content and is it worth spending another $250,000 to put some more content up there or not is a huge question.

Multiple Content: Multiple Costs

Steve Robinson is responsible for the printer driver section of Xerox.com. When I talked to Steve, he reminded me that not all content is created by marketing people. Software, like printer drivers, is content as well: "So the business units themselves are the teams that manufacture the products and are responsible for maintaining the actual drivers that are out there on the site today. Each product team has a driver administrator who is responsible for doing the maintenance and loading when a new operating system gets released. We provide the rules, tools, and schools. That's kind of the framework we've been using."

I stopped him. I followed rules and tools. But schools?

"Training. It's training them on how to use the system, so that they are aware of how they handle the business processes. What we find is that the driver administration process is one that there's not really a job description [for]; it's something that somebody gets assigned from their business unit and they do it as 1 percent of their overall job responsibility. It's not their full thing, because the amount of time it takes to actually load and maintain a driver is very minimal.

"Plus turnover happens and it gets dropped and then all of a sudden you get a lot of emails coming to the Webmaster about 'how come there's not a driver out there for this product for this operating system?'"

So while you're calculating your content based on some of the following ideas, don't forget that people and training are important cost factors.

Computing Content Value

There are a number of ways to go about reckoning the worth of the content on your site. To start with, you have to figure out just how much content will serve your purpose. Otherwise, you could end up with an enormous Web site at enormous expense with nothing to show for it.

Too Much of a Good Thing?

In his book *Net Words: Creating High-Impact Online Copy* (McGraw-Hill, 2002), Nick Usborne describes Eric Lupton's efforts to figure out just how much text to put on his home page at Poolfence.com (see Figure 9.1):

If the customer is coming directly to your site, then up-front reassurances on the home page can go a long way towards making a new visitor feel comfortable. Remember, if your site isn't a household name, visitors will form a first impression based on what they see first. So be sure to get the relationship off on the right foot at your home page.

As an example, the main block of copy on the home page at Poolfence.com has been growing in length from its beginnings as a short, introductory block. It is now considerably longer, and very conversational in its tone.

Good afternoon!

Life Saver has been providing baby, child, and pet safety solutions for residential swimming pools and in homes for over a decade. Removable residential swimming pool fence has proven to be an effective drowning prevention aid for more than thirty-five years in the United States, and due to its commitment to saving lives, dedicated Life Saver Pool Fence Dealers can now be found from coast to coast in many larger cities.

Toddler driving you nuts at home?

Then this is the place for you! Practical child proofing tips that work in the real world for real families. Safety is kind of a boring subject, so we have written this do-it-yourselfer in-home guide for those that have a sense of humor. If you don't have a sense of humor, then you better get one fast if you're planning on raising normal children.

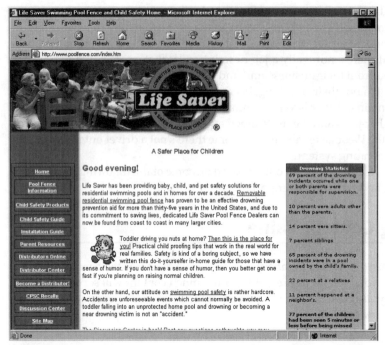

Figure 9.1 The Poolfence.com site home page takes a warm, personal approach to content style, and the longer the better.

On the other hand, our attitude on swimming pool safety is rather hardcore. Accidents are unforeseeable events which cannot normally be avoided. A toddler falling into an unprotected home pool and drowning or becoming a near drowning victim is not an "accident." The Discussion Center is back! Post any questions or thoughts you may have and get real parent answers. We'd like to use this space to thank as well as inform. We at Life Saver really appreciate you visiting our site and taking the time to learn about child safety and pool safety.

Like you, we're parents, and your love of your children is why we exist. So, when you're reading our child safety guide or about removable mesh pool fence, think about how you can apply the things you learn to your life.

We've learned so much writing this site for you and we learn more as we add and enhance it every day. We can always learn more. If you have a suggestion or idea, tell us.

Thank you for reading and enjoy the site.

Don't forget to save us as a favorite place. We're always changing.

There are experts by the barrelful who will tell you that this copy is far too long and won't be read by anyone. Not true, says Eric Lupton, the man behind the site and this very profitable business. Here's his reasoning behind the length and style of text that he uses.

"We started out with brief, precise copy on the home page and have slowly lengthened it. The longer it gets, the more people seem to connect with the site. Our product is one geared toward parents protecting their children, so you need to take that extra space to really let them know they can trust you. The more inviting and personable, the better. They have to know you are real."

"They know that you are real." That's a pretty good catchphrase to hold in your mind as you write your next email message or Web page. Let the people you connect with know you are real. When you do that, you have the beginning of a relationship based on trust.

I was intrigued by Nick's description of Eric's method. It showed a true sense of purpose and a surprising amount of patience. So I emailed Eric and asked him for more details. He replied:

```
The goal of our site is to gather leads of people interested in pool
fence. Here's what we noticed when we lengthened the copy:
    People moved on from the home page to our other pages more often.
    Our ratio of traffic to leads improved slightly. Nothing amazing, but
it was there.
    I received more e-mails directly from the home page.
    Inquiries seemed more informed.
I tracked this with WebTrends, the tracking reports my server provides,
and my own perception.
Though I have no hard evidence to support it, I believe the longer copy
increased referrals, too. I started hearing things like "I found your
Web site from my friend..." and "My mom sent me to your site to..." more
frequently.
Because we have no concrete sales taking place on the web, a lot of this
"tracking" is done by feel. Inquirers seemed like they explored the site
more when I presented longer copy. I heard my terms repeated back in
phone calls.
I'm yet to lengthen the copy until it drops off again. I'm still letting
this one run a bit.
I did with GoTo and Sprinks [search engines], though.
My copy in the bid-for-placement engines is tested every few weeks to
see what gets the most clicks with the same positioning. My Sprinks
clicks doubled when I shortened the copy and included a call to action.
Tell Nick hello for me. I think he's my hero. ;)
```

When it comes to paying attention and understanding the basics of measurement, I think Eric is my hero. And hello, Mr. Usborne.

Is It Good Content?

Does the content drive the traffic? Given two descriptions of hollow fiber microporous membranes, which one causes more people to head for the Purchase button and which causes more people to head for the door?

In an article on ClickZ ("Optimize Content to Maximize the Bottom Line"), Charlie Tarzian, chief strategy officer for Circle.com, recommended "describing the relationship of content to sales and relationships on the back end. The formulation of flexible data architecture that will mirror these relationships is critical. The reports and monitoring you do on a daily basis are crucial to site optimization. Things like content-read-to-leads-generated, to sales, to upsells, etc., all require predefinition and infrastructural commitment."

A case study on the Circle.com site describes a content-value program put into place by Symantec in their Small Business Resource Center (smallbiz.symantec.com) (see Figure 9.2), which calculates the value of their content.

According to Circle.com's case study (www.circle.com/casestudies/symantec.html), "The company's goal was to raise its visibility and position the company as a viable contender in the small business market sector. At the same time, it sought to establish brand equity and attract customers. Internally, the SBHO Internet investment had to be profitable and the site's performance had to be substantiated."

Circle developed and implemented a system that presented a constantly updated stream of objective content. "Six new articles appeared every two weeks to inform the target audience how to apply software to the solution of common business problems. This was intended to help business owners spend more time managing core responsibilities. Symantec validates content popularity based on traffic patterns, and adjusts editorial tactics accordingly."

Figure 9.2 Symantec knows if any given article is pulling its weight and helping make sales.

They take what they learn about which articles are the most popular, and use that to guide them in the creation of their monthly email newsletter and in the daily news feed that keeps the company top-of-mind.

Circle hosts the SBHO Web site and uses a suite of integrated tools to manage content delivery, e-mail distribution, and metrics reporting. With those Web-based e-metrics reporting tools, Symantec gauges user interest in Web content, product applications, trialware requests, and online sales. Among key results:

- *The number of visits to the client's Web site grows at an average quarterly rate of 15%, exclusive of online advertising.*

- *The number of product trialware downloads has increased at an average quarterly rate of over 50%—over three times faster than the growth in overall site traffic. In excess of 32% of free-trial users convert to a sale.*

- *Symantec's share in its competitive markets has more than doubled over the last year.*

It's always nice to be able to tie things back to the bottom line.

Payback Calculations: Savings versus Income

One of the simpler ways to calculate something's value is from the cost side of the equation. If you know what it costs, you know what it's worth, right? That may be true if you are a consumer, but not if you're a manufacturer.

So try like the dickens to figure out if the cost of creating, correcting, formatting, approving, hosting, and maintaining that content can be recouped.

Back in the mid-1990s, one of my large telecommunications clients was having a tough time convincing upper management that this whole Internet thing was a good idea. That, of course, led to anemic funding, which in turn made it harder to prove value. The solution? Focus on money saved rather than convincing them of potential dollars earned. The trick was to start simple.

"What does it cost to send out an annual report?" I asked.

"Well, it varies year to year, but this year, what with the cost of copywriting, graphics, layout, paper, ink, distribution, and postage, divided by the quantity that we print, we're looking at about $7 each."

"What does it cost to send an electronic version?"

"Well, we can't assume the same number of copies, so if we base it on one-tenth that number and use that to divide into the cost of repurposing the text and graphics and running the servers and doing the maintenance, it could run as high as 20 cents to 30 cents, but that's being very generous. It's probably more like 7 cents, and that number goes down with every copy that gets downloaded."

"For simplicity's sake, let's call it 25 cents just so it'll be easy to defend?"

"OK—then what?"

The "then what" turned out to be a chart, available on the intranet in real time to any manager who questioned the value of putting information online (see Table 9.1).

Table 9.1　The Value of Content as Expressed by Cost Reductions

	DOWNLOADED YTD	PRINT COST	ONLINE COST	TOTAL PRINTED COST	TOTAL ONLINE COST	SAVINGS
Annual Report	43,934	$ 7.00	$ 0.25	$ 307,538	$ 10,984	$296,555
Directors Bios	1,045	$ 1.00	$ 0.05	$ 1,045	$ 52	$ 993
SEC Filings	3,564	$ 1.25	$ 0.07	$ 4,455	$ 249	$ 4,206
Etc.						
					Total Savings	$301,753

You'll have to determine your own numbers for how many page views obviated the need for mailing an envelope with glossy paper inside and how many were viewed due to the ease of access to the information. Many people come to your Web site who would never have bothered calling you on the phone and requesting that you send them something.

In that case, it's time to come up with a way to measure the value of that interaction.

Let Content Interaction Be Your Guide

Measuring just how good good old-fashioned content really is ends up being a matter of whether people are looking at it, reading it, and using it. Turns out to be a tough nut to crack. The general manager of E-Commerce Development at one major airline explained to me just how hard it is:

> There are people who are going to continue to purchase our tickets either through our call centers or a travel agent or whatever. What we don't know and can't really measure that well. We believe they come to the site, we believe that they use the site—maybe they aren't buying the ticket, but they are using the site—and we can't show the connection between things. They're not logging in so we're not able to capture their [frequent flier] number. They're coming in and doing arrival/departure information. They're coming in and doing all sorts of things and getting value, but we're not able to tie it to that specific ticket that they have maybe sold or bought from another channel besides the Web site. So, if we could measure that we could make a really powerful argument for even increasing the investment we've got on the Web site.

So where do you start? You start with whether people even care about the content you put on your site. You start with *stickiness*.

Stickiness, the Roosevelt Reckoning

Stickiness was identified as a desirable trait in the early days of the portals. Yahoo!, Excite, and Lycos were desperately trying to get people to stay longer. That's why directories and search engines tacked on features like news, weather, and sports—and free email and auctions and shopping and address books and — well, you know. How do we get people to stay longer, look at more pages, and see more ads?

For commercial Web sites, the question became one of branding and persuasion. First, how can we get people to stay longer to bond with our brand? Coca-Cola offers screensavers, games, wish lists, and a tour of their bottling plant to drive the name and logo deep into the hearts and minds of consumers. It's a brand thing (see Figure 9.3).

Getting customers to commune with your brand is fine, as long as you're conducting those brand surveys that tell you whether your efforts are making the right impression. You may find that offering recipes from Grady Spears, the Cowboy in the Kitchen, on your site might be just the ticket for a cookware site. But Pepcid? (www.pepcidcomplete.com) (see Figure 9.4)

Figure 9.3 Coca-Cola doesn't expect to sell bottles of ice-cold Coke off its Web site for the holidays.

You can easily calculate stickiness by multiplying frequency (F) by duration (D) and reach (R) and come up with a benchmark for your content. You choose whether frequency is measured per day, per week, or per month. Duration can either be calculated in minutes or pages. If your visitors are playing games, minutes count. Reach is a percentage of your total potentially interested universe.

Let's say your average person comes 7 times in the given period and hangs out for 12 minutes. You've now got an FD of 84. Multiply that by the 8 percent of the target audience who actually showed up and you end up with an FDR, or stickiness, rating of 6.72.

Little consensus has emerged as to how to calculate stickiness, and many stickiness formulas are potentially valid, actionable, and consistent. Here is another stickiness formula that might work well for you that Matt Cutler and I published in our white paper, "E-Metrics, Business Metrics for the New Economy" (www.netgen.com/emetrics):

Your site has acquired a total of 200,000 unique users. Over the past month, 50,000 unique users went to your site. These 50,000 users accounted for a total of 250,000 visits (average frequency of 5 visits/unique user for the month), and during these visits the users spent a total of 1,000,000 minutes viewing pages on your site. Therefore:

$$\text{Monthly Stickiness} = \frac{250{,}000 \text{ Visits}}{50{,}000 \text{ Active Users}} \times \frac{1{,}000{,}000 \text{ Minutes}}{250{,}000 \text{ Visits}} \times \frac{50{,}000 \text{ Active Users}}{200{,}000 \text{ Total Users}}$$

Figure 9.4 In their never-ending battle for brand bonding, Johnson & Johnson-Merck Consumer Pharmaceuticals tries to boost sales of Pepcid by promoting heartburn.

Monthly Stickiness = 5 Minutes/User
This stickiness calculation can be applied to entire sites or sections of sites, and can also be used to compare trends between different customer segments. The mathematically inclined reader will recognize that the stickiness formula can be simplified as shown below, although this formulation gives less insight into the individual factors that affect stickiness.

$$\text{Stickiness} = \frac{\text{Total Amount of Time Spent Viewing All Pages}}{\text{Total Number of Unique Users}}$$

How does 6.72 rate on the grand scale of comparative stickiness? It doesn't. Just like hits, it only matters to your site from day to day and from section to section. One can only hope that the All About Heartburn page at Pepcidcomplete.com gets a much higher rating than their privacy policy. Yes, I'm all for the respect of privacy—

adamantly—but as a marketer I'd rather have people take a quick look at my policy and then dive back into the persuasion portion of my site.

Whether you're after branding or simply more time to make your point and make the sale, not all stickiness is good stickiness. Some pages are more valuable if they're slippery. We'll visit the measurement of slipperiness in Chapter 10, "Well-Marked Trails: Measuring Web Site Navigation," and Chapter 13, "Measuring the Value of Online Customer Service."

Number of Downloads

Have you got games and spreadsheets and software for people to download? Unless you're including some code that lets those downloadables talk to the mother ship, you aren't going to know how long people are bonding with your brand offline. But at least you can keep track of how many times your files get downloaded in a given time period.

When you put up a banner ad for your screensavers, calculators, plug-ins, demos, jingles, wallpaper, games, or icons, you may not be able to tell if more people have gotten the message, but you *will* know if more people have taken the desired action. Same goes for changes to the promotional devices on your own Web site and alterations to your navigation buttons.

And don't forget what we learned from Steve Robinson at Xerox: While keeping an eye on how many get downloaded, be sure you pay attention to how fast as well.

Comparative Popularity of Content

Knowing how sticky your content is provides a single datapoint. That's not very useful by itself. Compare that number to itself over time and now it turns into actionable information. You also want to compare it to stickiness and frequency numbers of other content on your site. What are people really looking at? What really interests them?

You may be promoting the bejeepers out of products A and B and not bothering with C yet. After all, C is just something the product development team has been toying with and because a product manager just got promoted from sales and doesn't know what he's doing. Meanwhile, there's a big push to get A's and B's numbers up to make it another stellar year so that everybody will get bonuses. You see where this is going, right?

Even after spending megabucks on ads, promotions, and interactive configurators for A and B, your site visitors are going to look at C by a wide margin. Is there anybody in your organization assigned to pay attention to that sort of thing?

As I noted in the third edition of my book *World Wide Web Marketing* (John Wiley & Sons, 2001):

> *National Semiconductor is all extranet, all the time. In March 1997 it knew the Net was the way to go. By the end of that year, it had customized customer service applications running for different customers. It was able to pass shipment requests of sample chips to the marketing team, so it could keep its finger on the pulse of leading-edge developers.*

Phil Gibson, director of interactive marketing, made sure the import of this data was understood. "There's a fairly common pattern in the development of sophisticated electronics. A design engineer orders a sample and hooks it up to a test bed. If it looks like it'll work, he orders a handful for prototyping. If it still looks good, he orders a couple of hundred for a test production run. At this point, our salespeople, and they may be several layers down the distribution channel, are well aware that a large order could pop out of this company the second they decide to go into a test market run. That's when we get real close to the customer so manufacturing can be ready the split second they turn on full-scale production. With the information from our extranet, marketing and sales can track the trends across multiple industries."

Phil keeps his eye on page views, .pdf downloads, sample requests, and email inquiries and can pretty much tell the production people when the orders are going to start coming in.

Fry Multimedia's Chief Customer Experience Officer Kara Heinrichs says:

If you look at people's visits to a product page as a percentage of times that that page has been viewed over visitors and you graph that against the number of conversions for that particular product, you expect to see that the things that people see more often they buy more often. They should add up in a nice diagonal.

But if they don't, if there are products that fall above or below that line into the top left or bottom right quadrant, you can say that there are opportunities within a product segment, where people are seeing it once and buying it immediately for some reason or they are seeing it eighteen times and still never buying it. There is a lost opportunity there. So we're trying to use what we see in the data that kind of points to how the merchandise is speaking or not speaking to customers and which buckets those tend to fall into.

That starts to get very interesting from a psychology perspective when I really want to buy the laptop with a 50-gigabyte drive and the DVD writer and I'm going to go drool over it five times, but I end up buying the cheaper one.

Most content on your site is there to get people to buy. But some of it is a means to get people to the content that will get people to buy.

Content as an Inter-Web Traffic Driver

I asked Kris Carpenter at Excite if they were able to move traffic from one side of their site to another in order to equalize their impression advertising versus clickthroughs.

"Well, it's both pieces," she told me. "If can you get your horoscope audience into other areas that are more valuable, that's one application. The majority of it is how to take specific offers that you're introducing within the health channel and getting a user to respond to that offer. The response may be, buy this particular type of headache medication online. Or it might be register to get information about a Breast Cancer event, sign up for the newsletter, or whatever.

"So the reality is that online today we're measured in lots of different ways and we're able to attribute how successful a particular area of the service is in terms of contributing to gross revenue and the ROI. It may cost us a ton to generate that revenue, or it may not cost us much at all. And is that visitor also generating revenue in this area and that area, or is it just this one event, once a month?

"Being able to effectively report on those types of statistics is incredibly complex, and what you don't want is to end up making a decision to eliminate a certain number of features or even a whole channel altogether without knowing what the network effect might be."

I asked, "So while you're looking at a content area as a revenue generator, you're also looking at is a traffic generator, which can then bolster other revenue areas?"

"Yes. Is it already feeding other areas so that if you removed that piece of content that particular audience is using would we also lose them from these three other areas?"

"You're beginning to sound like an environmentalist," I commented. "You're dealing with eco-culture here."

"That's absolutely the case. And you've got to figure out the value that each of those eyeballs represents in any given month and know what the explicit trade-offs are. This is one of the most difficult things for a really senior executive team to try to absorb because on one level they might look at the fixed, controllable costs. But it's the other types of trade-offs that you need to be able to model because, at the end of the day, that aggregate ROI might seem much better than a product that on the surface only takes two people to manage."

I asked Kris for an example of that kind of cross-traffic.

"A great example of that would probably be the personals category. Personals are interesting to advertisers with very specific types of offers. Things like real estate rentals—there are all kinds of offers that you can effectively overlay with that—but not as many as you might find for investing or health, the more traditional foundation categories. But the personals audience spends a lot of time on other parts of the service. You have a high concentration of eyeballs that come in to be amused or look for a date and so forth, but they also move through a high percentage of our applications and services. So that's an example of where you might say the *revenue* associated with that application isn't necessarily huge relative to other applications and services, but the reality is that audience represents a significant dollar amount per month."

One content question comes up frequently at my conferences and lectures, "Do I need to change my content every day?"

Freshness Factor

If your name is CNN.com or Yahoo!, then, yes, you need to change the content every day. Here's how Matt Cutler and I addressed the freshness factor in our E-Metrics white paper:

> It has long been believed that a Web site must change constantly to hold the interest of any given audience. While this makes sense for sites that depend on users returning daily (news, weather, and sports sites as well as portals like MSN), the constant creation of content is expensive and time consuming.
>
> The Freshness Factor (FF) measures the impact of dedicating resources to the job of continuous content publishing. The Freshness Factor is designed to measure how often

content is refreshed versus how frequently users visit the site. You will want to perform this calculation against individual customer segments since they will be interested in different site sections and will likely respond to fresh content in different ways.

$$\text{Freshness Factor} = \frac{\text{Average Content Area Refresh Rate}}{\text{Average Section Visit Frequency}}$$

Just as you weight the value of individual data elements collected about a specific customer, you must weight the value of content elements based on a number of factors. The most obvious is timeliness. If this data element is imported from a stock price reporting service or a news feed from a wire service, when does it expire? When should this news article be moved over into the archive section? If this content is part of a series of rotating elements, how recently has it been shown to this specific user? Different articles carry different weight based on their intended use. A white paper on choosing the right vendor may have a shelf-life of years, while updates on legislative issues are only interesting for a month or so.

If your Freshness Factor is less than 1, then—on average—your customers are visiting that section of your site more frequently than you are updating the content. Thus, they are seeing stale content and you can expect your stickiness numbers to decrease. On the other hand, if your Freshness Factor is greater than 1, then, again—on average—customers see new content each time they visit your site, and your stickiness numbers should improve. If your Freshness Factor goes above 1.5, then you are running the risk of wasting resources to create content that is not being viewed.

Be careful of multi-modal distributions. If half of your customers visit every hour, and the other half visit once every 9 hours, then your average frequency is 5 hours. This reveals the general necessity of segmenting your customers and your site and performing all calculations, including Freshness Factor, on customer segments rather than global site populations.

How much change is too much change? At what point are you spending money you don't need to spend because you're changing faster than you need to, and how do you measure that?

Rene Bonvanie, vice president of Online Marketing at Oracle, likes to go with the flow: "It's not because there is a routine that every 4 hours we change or every 24 hours we change. We look at the response numbers. We still have this idea that response and revenue are correlated. But with the visitors we deal with, which is also very important to understand, very few of those people are actually going to buy our stuff. They may recommend, they influence, they use it, but very few people actually buy our stuff. If I were Amazon, I would be in a different situation. But I want visitors to be impressed with how much our products and services can help them."

In an attempt to clarify the freshness factor in an online discussion list, Matt Cutler put it this way:

The intent of the Freshness Factor e-metric is to enable site managers to effectively and economically manage their content development resources. In other words, you might have four people dedicated to daily content updates in the Market Outlook section of the site. However, less than 2% of the user population visits on a daily basis (40% visit about once a week, 33% visit once a month, and 25% visit once but tend not to come back). In this case, you would be over-invested in the Market Outlook area based on your Freshness Factor calculations, so you could update the section only once a week, using just two people rather than four, with minimal impact on customer satisfaction.

With that said, "Average Content Area Refresh Rate" should capture how often pages in a given section are manually changed (as opposed to changed by a data feed such as stock ticker symbols, sports scores, or weather forecasts). Ideally, your content management system (such as Interwoven) will be configured to track this automatically. Depending on the nature of your content and your internal systems, you can create a simple system that tracks the last-modified-date of content files and calculated Refresh Rate on the fly. Of course, this won't work for everyone! Finally, you can also manually estimate your Refresh Rate.

Once you have your Refresh Rate, our NetGenesis 5 platform can calculate, report on, and provide analysis around your Freshness Factor by content section.

I wonder if the folks at NetGenesis measured the increased traffic to their site after Matt's post?

Cost of Content Creation and Correction

Content isn't simply a fixed-cost wholesale commodity. There's also a process involved. You're going to spend a fair amount on establishing and automating that process, and that becomes part of the fixed cost. But there's also the cost of generating, evaluating, approving, and fixing content on your site.

Every site will vary, but the question remains: How much do you spend on process, in order to save money on the back end making corrections? A bird in the hand? A penny saved? A stitch in time? Your mileage will vary.

It's not just a trade-off between effort spent now versus later. If that were the only criterion, then it would always be wise to invest in the ounce of prevention to avoid the pound of cure. But that prevention might have a negative impact on your opportunity cost.

If a new Web page must be examined and approved by the legal eagles, the corporate communications cabal, the usability specialists, and the Grand Master Web Council, it may take a while. In the meantime, your competitors have launched their version, the press has taken to running speculative articles on why your company is withholding information, and your prospective customers are taking their credit cards elsewhere. Not a pretty picture.

The Investor Relations Perspective on Content

Investor relations is all about publishing. There are some serious cost savings involved, but no profits. How, then, do you measure the return on investment of the content that you put up for investors? That's what I asked Kiko Suarez of DuPont:

"We are finding that we can measure the overall popularity and reach, which is the traditional traffic stuff. And that has to be in context of two things: One is overall traffic of the site. So you would say if I have all these people coming to DuPont.com, how many are interested in investor relations information and can be drawn to that section from the home page? Then there's the context of the audience that is specifically relevant to IR, like analysts and investors and institutional investors. Companies like Microsoft are really moving toward a more retail investor. We are more interested in institutional investors than retail.

"We want to measure the value of those visits. We don't want to just say the overall popularity of your section is 50 or 10 in the overall context of DuPont.com. That's great, but it doesn't tell me about why my people, the ones I am really interested in, go there.

"Everyone wants to know the overall thing, the big traffic. And it would be really weird to show some reports if they don't show this overall thing. How many people come to your site, that's fine. Now, from this perspective we go down to the detail, the next step. We see what works and what doesn't work in investor relations. What are the top sections that people use? What are the top downloads? This is especially relevant here because a lot of the information that we provide is information services. So we give access to the annual report and things like that. We want to be able to measure the amount of downloads that we get there.

"Ideally, we would like to match that with the specific, targeted audiences. We'd like very much to know that the two top ten institutional investors came to our site and what they downloaded. Once that match is made, that will generate actions—perhaps follow-up phone calls or outbound direct mail, even reorganizing the site.

"I have a few other things that I've been looking at recently. One we call a degree of compliance with disclosure requirements. As you know, with investors there are new disclosure regulations and we want to know to what degree DuPont is complying with that regulation. The only way of knowing that right now is whether we are getting more and more people attending the Web conferences and Webcasts and things like that. Of course, ideally we would like to get as many people as we can, but once again we would like to match that with our target audience."

But I wondered about measuring the bottom line on paying for that much content.

"If your sole goal is to get more investors to come to listen to the presentation of the annual report online," I asked Kiko, *"and you spend millions of dollars to promote it and you get hundreds of thousands of people to show up, wonderful, but what was the value?"*

He replied:

One of the investor relations strategies in this company is to get more retail investors. Then it will be a whole different world, because the Internet allows you to do that a lot easier than before. Companies like Microsoft or Volvo have that as one of their goals and if one of your goals is to get retail investors, then you can promote your Webcasts in places where you can get a guarantee that there are more investors coming and going. So right now we are more in the institutional investor area and that is kind of limited to institutional investors, maybe the top ten, and the analysts that follow you.

The real interest would be to measure what those specific people are doing. And, unfortunately, the dilemma here is registration. You know, how many opportunities you have to register people so you know who they are. We've added email alerts, and that is a way for us to know who is really interested. And to make sure that we gradually promote and foster this self-service culture because it will help us to have less and less resources if they can serve themselves. So we're also going to measure the success of our email alerts. How many of those that we want subscribed today to email alerts? If they do not subscribe, then we will have to do something to convince them to subscribe.

Right now subscriptions are the main measure of success for email alerts because we are starting with this. As soon as we have more people, we'll look at which new categories people choose the most and things like that. Right now it is more, Are we getting the right people? Just to give you an idea, we know that we are getting a lot of subscriptions from our own employees. That's not bad, but that can distort the whole thing—even if some of them are really investors.

Then the other thing that we are thinking about is in general, not just the investors section but the rest of the corporate information we provide. How many people have we helped? When you are thinking about a company like DuPont, that means probably how many people have downloaded technical specifications of our products.

When it comes to revenue generation, a site like DuPont.com can help increase the potential of our business unit Web site because a lot of people come to DuPont.com for the first time when they are trying to find their way through a big company like DuPont. So we try to measure the number of hand-offs or leads that we give to the business units.

We are trying to measure that from three places: from the internal search engine (how many people use the search engine to find and go to a business unit), the catalogue (how many people look at our products in the catalogue of all of the products in markets that DuPont serves), and from the public relations press releases. We are starting to provide the metrics of how many connections we provide to the e-business application that we call DuPont Direct. That e-business application is an order-entry system and is used only by regular customers. This is all contributing to the potential revenue going to the SBUs.

Content is king, indeed. But no matter how much content you have, or how good it is, the value goes to zero if people can't find it. That's where navigation comes in.

CHAPTER 10

Well-Marked Trails: Measuring Web Site Navigation

"Our interviewees spent from $100,000 to $1 million on their redesigns. While most tracked high-level business results, like revenue or customer satisfaction, few had any sense of which specific design changes paid off."
Get ROI from Design (June 2001), Forrester

"I want to know how people are navigating certain sections of the site. I think Web managers turn that capability on for everything and they get overwhelmed with the data and they don't end up using it. I think you need to target it for certain parts of the site. Given specific results, I would change my user interface design and it would lead to a better user experience. It might not be translated to more revenue, but if I could keep customers coming back from the consumer standpoint I think that's a big win."
Web Manager, Large Service Company

Keep them coming back and it *will* end up translating into more revenue.

What if you only had 3 minutes before boarding to look up alternative flights on a travel site you'd never been to before? Sound like one of those dreams where you're running as hard as possible to get to the final exam and you're not getting anywhere? Naked?

While your customers may not be under that sort of pressure, they still face the daunting task of understanding your Web site before their patience wears out. Just how frustrating is your Web site? How long does it take to accomplish something? How confusing is it? What helps and what gets in the way?

179

The problem, voiced by many and suffered by all, is that Web sites are designed by either software engineers, who are deeply entrenched in functional technology, or graphic artists, who are floating on the surface of eye appeal. Any thought to how easy it is to actually use the output from the former or the creations of the latter tend to fall by the wayside in a rush to market.

Many of us are creating and running Web sites with too few people, trying to accomplish too many things, with too little input from upper management or actual customers. Okay, *all* of us are in that boat, but only a few are taking the scientific approach to Web site navigation, and that approach is sorely needed.

The "Tangled Web 2001" survey conducted by Vividence (www.vividence.com) found that, of the sixty-nine Web sites accessed by the 13,000 users surveyed, 32 percent of the sites suffered from slow performance and 15 percent had problems with invasive registration. Everything else on the list related to navigation:

> *53% **had poorly organized search results***: *Common mistakes included erroneous results, items not ranked in order of fit to their search results, and too many results.*

> *32% **had poor information architecture***: *Many of the sites displayed poor information architecture through their product and content organization on their Web sites. Errors included poor grouping of information, inconsistent elements within a group, and random ordering of elements.*

> *27% **had cluttered home pages***: *Poor information architecture, a failure to communicate the value proposition, and failing to engage customers were common flaws found in cluttered home pages.*

> *25% **had problems with confusing labels***: *While navigating sites for the study, panelists often complained of confusing labels as a frequent mistake of Web sites. These included the use of marketing terminology and technology and industry jargon.*

> *13% **had difficulties with inconsistent navigation***: *Findings from the study also indicated inconsistent navigation was a problem area for Web sites. Unscalable designs, random links, and poor transitions between company divisions all contributed to the overall inconsistent navigation on the sites.*

> *From: www.vividence.com/public/news+and+events/press+releases/2001-06-07+web+design.htm*

Navigation on a Web site can make or break it. People have very little patience. If they can't find what they want, they won't stay. So how do you measure that?

The best place to start is with the first thing visitors see.

First Impressions

You only have one chance to make a first impression. If you're lucky, and people come back to your site again and again, that impression is made indelible. That may be good or bad, depending on how they respond to that first sighting of your site. What page do they see first? How does that page appear to them? What elements do they see on that first page and what do they miss?

Where Do They Land?

Think everybody sees your home page first? Think again. All log file analysis tools will show your site's top entry pages (see Figure 10.1).

Since it's likely that your home page is the first stop for more people than any other page, let's start there.

The Home Page

Navigation on the home page is going to set the tone for your whole site. Is your site well classified? If people are looking for a Palm PDA, will they find it in Computers, Electronics, or Office Gear? Where are people most likely to look for it?

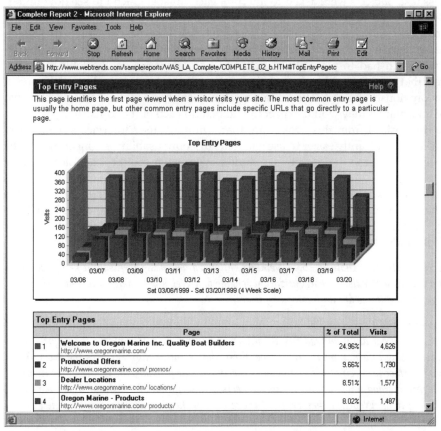

Figure 10.1 This Top Entry Page report from WebTrends shows that only one-quarter of the visitors to Oregon Marine arrive at the home page.

In their paper "SunWeb: User Interface Design for Sun Microsystems' Internal Web" (www.useit.com/papers/sunweb), Jakob Nielsen and Darrell Sano described four different usability studies to help them determine the navigational tools for the Sun Microsystems internal Web site:

1. Card sorting to discover categories

2. Icon intuitiveness testing

3. Card distribution to icons

4. Thinking aloud walk-through of page mock-up

The team wrote up fifty-one types of information that might be found on the internal Web site. They wrote each on note cards and scattered them across a table. The experiment subjects were asked to sort these cards into piles based on similarity. As a result, they created proper groupings for information categories for the home page.

The resulting categories required icons or pictograms to represent them on the home page. Once the first draft of these icons was created, it was submitted to the icon intuitiveness test. Subjects were asked to interpret each unlabeled icon to see how understandable it was. Most were good or excellent, but several had to be substantially altered.

The two tests were then combined. The new icons were printed and handed to subjects, who then had to place them in the proper categories on the table. This test ensured that users would associate the correct concepts with each of the general groups previously defined. The "thinking aloud" study simply asked subjects what sort of information they would expect to find behind each of the icons.

The conclusions from this project are that a uniform user interface structure can make a Web significantly easier to use and that "discount usability engineering" can be employed to base the design on user studies even when project schedules are very tight.

That was back in 1994 and it is still a valid method today. It's cheap, too. On the other hand, you could wander over to the National Institute of Standards and Technology Web site and get your hands on a WebCAT (http://zing.ncsl.nist.gov/WebTools/index.html). As the site describes:

The Web Category Analysis Tool (WebCAT) allows a web designer/usability engineer to test a proposed or existing categorization scheme of a Web site to determine how well the categories and items are understood by users.

Functions and Features
WebCAT is a variation on traditional card sorting techniques. Its process of categorizing and analyzing information is interactive. First, the usability engineer uses the WebCAT setup interface to specify the design of an experiment; she provides the names of the items, a category method, instructions for the subjects, a description of the study, and a variety of other options. WebCAT then creates the exercise for the user which is implemented as a Java applet that provides a satisfying interactive experience. The subject merely drags items from a list to one of several category bins. Items may be moved back and forth between bins until the subject is satisfied with his results, then enters his name, makes an optional comment, and presses "Done."

The usability engineer can view the collected data at any time using a new interface which implements a clustering algorithm.

It's a good idea to measure where your *visitors* think content should reside.

If you took the time to ask each visitor, you would find that almost every one cringes at being subjected to your all-singing, all-dancing, animated greetings on the pre-home page, also known as the splash page.

The Splash Page

What drives you crazy on a splash page? Could it be the spinning logo, talking CEO, and swirling graphics that tell you nothing and absorb your time? Upper management views the splash page as the "electronic cover of the electronic brochure." These people reign high enough in the organization that they have (a) decision-making power and (b) no clue about what properly belongs on a home page. Splash pages are intuitively a tool of the devil.

Gunkelmans Interior Design (www.gunkelmans.com) is as good an example as any of what a bad splash page is (see Figure 10.2).

Apparently, R. Thomas Gunkelman didn't listen when he was advised not to name his company eponymously. He also didn't hear when somebody told him that he shouldn't make his Web site an all-Flash extravaganza. On top of that, there's no way for R. Thomas to tell just how bad an idea this is. You have to *enter* and go to the next page before you find the "Skip Intro" button.

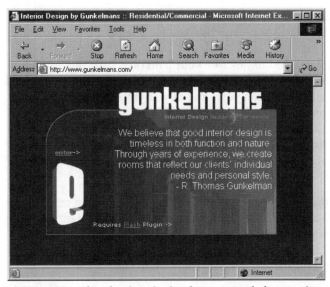

Figure 10.2 The classic spinning logo at Gunkelmans gives one pause about its interior design abilities.

Matt Cutler came up with the extremely well named *skip factor*. A quick search on Google recently found about 208,000 instances of the phrase "Skip Intro"—you're sure to come up with many more. How on earth can a company feel a Flash splash page is a good idea when they all know they have to add the Skip Intro button to it? Matt described the skip factor this way in an article in *Business 2.0* (May 15, 2001):

> *A Web site's design reinforces either the perception that a company has a solid e-strategy or that it doesn't know what it is doing. And when a company incorporates Flash graphics software into the design, well, it has arrived.*
>
> *But the story shouldn't end there. The impact of a Flash introduction diminishes over time. The presentation may wow visitors for the first few viewings, but it may forever annoy them after the tenth. The key is to show it only to folks who want to see it. To ensure that this occurs, measure the number of visitors who watch the Flash intro versus the number who click "Skip intro."*

$$\text{Skip Factor} = \frac{\text{No. of visitors who click "Skip intro"}}{\text{No. of visitors who view Flash intro}} \times (100)$$

> *A skip factor of less than 25 indicates visitors are watching the Flash intro, while a factor greater than 80 shows visitors are skipping it. A low skip factor is likely attributable to a high number of first-time visitors, while a high skip factor indicates that most visitors have already seen the Flash intro—and that they don't want to see it again.*
>
> *The skip factor should be recalculated separately for new and repeat visitors. If the factor is high for new visitors, the company might want to rethink its Flash design. If too many repeat visitors skip the intro, consider showing it only to first-timers. Then, when users return, they will automatically be routed to your home page.*

The skip factor can apply to other types of content as well, and managing the content on your site from the visitor's perspective is a lot like pain management in hospitals.

If you've ever had a nurse ask you to describe your pain on a scale of 1 to 10, you have my deepest sympathies. If you've ever given birth to a child, you know what a 10 feels like. If you've ever tried to find, compare, and buy anything online, you know how Web surfing easily becomes Web suffering.

But how do you know how painful your site is to visitors? For starters, keep an eye on whether people bother reading your pages. One worldwide information services and technology company does just that. In an interview, one of its Web managers shared some common sense:

> *Obviously if we see pages that are not being visited we either get rid of them or modify them. We learn things, such as people don't download .pdf files. We make it a part of our standards law. They can still put .pdf files in there, but part of our file guides say, "don't expect people to read these. The only reason for a .pdf file is if you really expect someone to print it off and read it on an airplane." They're not going to read it on the Web.*

The Landing Page

So you're watching the home page and you're limiting the Flash flood—good. Now, don't forget about those pages you have specifically designed to be welcome mats: the landing page.

Banners, promotional email, and even print and broadcast ads point to these pages. The advertising is vitally interested in these pages because they help identify whether people are actually clicking *through*, rather than simply clicking *to*. Do these people in fact *land* on your site?

But the same care and feeding that goes into your home page should be lavished on these side-door pages as well. So many things on a landing page will determine whether visitors leave, stay, dig deeper, stay longer, sign up, join in, leave an opinion, make an appointment, or yes, even buy something.

So take all of the following advice about navigation and apply it to your home page and your landing pages first. Don't think of these pages as the gateways to your site. They're the brick walls. They are the barrier between your customers and what they want. These pages are the firewall between your visitors and what you want them to do.

The Beam-Me-Up-Scotty Page

Search engines, favorites bookmarks, editorial links, and emailed URLs will allow your visitors to walk right through the walls of your fine establishment and end up you-know-not-where. Are you ready for them?

These are sometimes the most mysterious statistics of all. Why is there a spike in people going to the hose-and-couplings page of your hydraulics parts and service section?

Some answers are found in your referrer logs, but links that are sent from friends to friends or show up in an association handout at an annual meeting will remain mysteries. More than one marketing manager has told me that they get more traffic when their competitors fire up a big promotion. Their audience becomes interested in the offer—and the alternatives.

Understanding what drives traffic to strange pages deep in your Web site is less a matter of log files and more a matter of astrology, Ouija boards, and spirit channeling. The sticks-and-stones part of this issue is whether you're watching how people navigate from the nonobvious entry pages on your site as well as the obvious places. They are just as capable of being the first step in what will become your *customer experience*.

Customer experience is not the process and procedure you have in place, it's not the award-winning design your graphic artists have conjured up, and it's not the form you need filled out to satisfy the sales force automation tool, the customer support database, and those folks down in accounting. Customer experience is what an individual goes through while trying to accomplish a specific task. Accomplishing that task begins with what your site visitor actually sees.

What Does Their Browser Show?

The first step in tracking the navigation through your site is to see it through the users' eyes.

As Mark Gibbs put it in his interesting, useful, and downright avuncular *Network World Web Applications Newsletter* on October 8, 2001 (www.nwfusion.com/newsletters/web/2001/01047669.html): "One of the longest running and most pernicious problems in the world of Web apps is browser compatibility. The difficulty of creating cross-browser content is enormous, and short of running Windows, Macintosh, Linux and WebTV platforms with all versions of IE, Netscape, AOL, Opera and all the other HTML browsers, making sure that your content can be seen correctly no matter what the user is running is, well, tricky."

Indeed.

Fortunately, Mark was at the rescue with a solution: "Browser Photo from Net-Mechanic, which tests your Web site using fourteen different browsers." (see Figure 10.3)

One Fortune 500 utility company told me that they track "general statistics like which browser you are coming to our site with and what operating system and things like that. In the last month or two we looked at that and determined policy for development in the future. We found the development of the site was becoming very expensive because of the divergent technologies that you had to be able to build against. So, we're looking at trying to hit the majority of our customers. We're not going to test every possible combination."

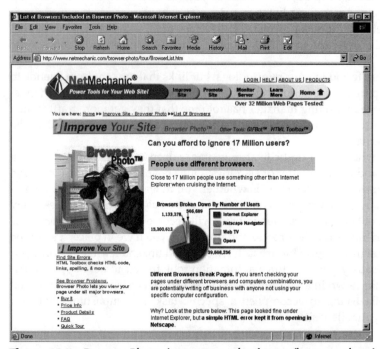

Figure 10.3   Browser Photo (www.netmechanic.com/browser-photo) is a good tool for your design team as well as a tracker of how many people use which browser.

The cost of building a site is high. If you *have* to build it twice, or even three times, there's serious cause for alarm. I wondered about their criteria. What were the thresholds? Is 11 percent of the population using older Netscape browsers enough to warrant multiple development tracks?

"We've agreed to review every 30 days and every 90 days to canonize the policy and bring that to the governance standard, so it's going to be always in flux. But right now we've agreed to hit at least 90 percent of the visitors, and in order to do that, we've determined that we would do the last two versions of the two most popular browsers.

"That boils down to a variance of IE5 and IE4 and a variance of Netscape 6 and Netscape 4 at the moment. We're not going to test every Netscape version before 4.77. If 4.31 doesn't work, we fix it for that, but we're not going to test it in advance. We're going to wait until we're notified of such a problem. We've found out that those are like 96 percent of the traffic we get right now. I don't know if that will always be the case, but right now it's pretty easy to keep that as the policy. And then we'll review every 90 days, and if that shifts, we'll change.

"We also don't just use PCs. Our site is also developed on the Mac. We do tests on the Mac and we do that primarily, even though that operating system is not 10 percent of our traffic. We do that primarily and, I mean, phrase this how you will, but somewhat out of fear because the group of people most likely to review this site is from the publishing part of the world and way more than 10 percent of them have Macs."

Now *that's* a tough calculation:

> **Cost of Mac Development for Multiple Browsers**
> **Cost of Bad Press for Not Being Mac Friendly**

What Do They Really See?

You've taken a hard look at the pages people see first. You've tested how those pages are rendered in different browsers. But have you—even for a moment—considered what people actually see? What do people actually look at on the screen? How do people perceive your site? Oh, and there's one more consideration.

How Much Do They Remember?

In October 2001, I received an impassioned email. At least it seemed that way at the time. In one of my books, I had espoused the well-known theory that humans can best remember a list of items as long as there are more than five and less than nine of them. Werner Lauwers, an information architect from Belgium, took umbrage:

```
From"Werner Lauwers" <wlauwers@pandora.be>
To: <jsterne@targeting.com>
Subject: seven items plus or minus two
Date: Thu, 18 Oct 2001 15:34:57 +0200
```

```
hello,
I'm reading your book 'world wide web marketing'. As an information
architect and marketing student I find your book very interesting. I've
just read chapter 3 and have a small remark about the part describing
the 7 items plus or minus 2 rule.
This study is old news and overwritten by a lot of more recent material.
http://www.internettg.org/newsletter/aug00/article_miller.html
Research data has only some value if you clearly describe the
environment of the testing and the limits for implementing it in the
real world. If the real world changes or the research topic changes, do
new research. A good example:
http://usupsy.psy.twsu.edu/surl/usability_news.html
```

The article Werner pointed me to offers a reasonable discreditation of George Miller's 1956 experiments with a list of numbers read aloud, complete with many citations. Fair enough. I hereby repudiate my statements in my previous writings and set the record straight. For those of you who are deeply interested, it's worth a look. Unfortunately, you will not find a conclusive number to replace 7 ± 2. Oh well.

But if you are interested in less general, more scientific studies of Web site design, Werner's pointer to the Wichita State University, Human-Computer Interaction Laboratory, Software Usability Research Laboratory *Usability News* newsletter is a satisfying find.

There you can read some formal research about topics such as the following:

A Comparison of Popular Online Fonts: Which Are Best and When?

What Is the Best Layout for Multiple-Column Web Pages?

Where Should You Put the Links? A Comparison of Four Locations

Satisfaction Survey by Web or by Paper? A Case Study at a Fortune 500 Company

And all of those are in just one issue.

Eye Tracking Studies

In order to know what people are seeing on your site, you need only gaze into their eyes—and not blink.

With two patents in the field of inferring mental state from patterns of eye movement, Greg Edwards founded a company that does just that. Eyetools, Inc. (www.eyetools.com) started with a head-mounted torture device that recorded eye movement (see Figure 10.4).

These days, Eyetools uses an infrared camera that watches the pupils to track precisely where on the screen a surfer is looking without the subject feeling like a brain donor in Dr. Frankenstein's lab.

Eyetools watches how people look in order to find design flaws and dead zones based on eye movement. In one amazing test, they altered the E*Trade home page. First they removed the text from the E*Trade Highlights, leaving just the bullet points to see if people would look at the choices for different lengths of time. Then they put the words back, scrambled, and only 5 percent of the test subjects even noticed that the words were garbled.

Figure 10.4 Eyetools' fancy headgear kept track of precisely where on the screen the surfer was looking.

Not only does Eyetools reveal site design flaws and dead zones, they also have patented software that analyzes the eyes' behavior to determine whether the surfer is reading, is confused, or is daydreaming. "The finest subtleties in layout and design can dramatically alter what a viewer actually looks at. You can measure how those changes guide a viewer's optical path further into your site—or drive them to your competition's," says Edwards.

Eyetools usually tests more than a dozen people. After that, no statistically significant new information is gathered. The data can point out the need for changes in layout, images, color, spacing, fonts, and animation, and then they can test the results of those changes.

But how long does it take people to understand what they see?

Cognitive Impact

How long it takes to buy something from your site is not just a matter of how many clicks but how long it takes to figure out where to click. How long does it take to choose between two alternatives? Not long. How about four options? A little longer. How about seven choices? A *lot* longer.

WebCriteria (www.webcriteria.com) has created a suite of tools that calculate how long it would take a human to read your pages, understand the choices, and make a decision. It's a systematic approach to letting you know if your site is suitable for human consumption. They assign duration values to each paragraph, each button, and the navigational difference from one page to the next. They even calculate the distance between a button on one page and the next button to be clicked on the next page to establish the time it will take to move the mouse.

They know people are not going to read every paragraph, but they also know that a page with six buttons takes less time to navigate than one with four buttons and six blocks of text.

WebCriteria looks at scroll factors, size-of-button influences, color contrast consequences, and more. The result is a tool that "reads" a set path through your site, from, say, home page to check out, and calculates how long it will take a human to worm his or her way through what you thought was a perfectly comprehensible process.

When these criteria are coupled with tools from Keynote Systems (see Chapter 8, "Measuring Web Site Performance: The Need for Speed"), you end up with a pretty good benchmark from which to start making improvements. You also end up with a benchmark you can use for competitive analysis. When introducing their Competitive Assessment services, WebCriteria describes it this way:

> WebCriteria's ability to model the time and effort required to navigate a Web site allows us to competitively assess that site without access to servers or log files. This means we can run our automated assessment on any website; as a result, we've amassed a wealth of data on hundreds of popular sites worldwide.

For example, Alaska Airlines is sitting right in the middle of its competitors for access/comprehension speed (see Figure 10.5).

As of June 27, 2001, TWA took twice as long to access and navigate as Southwest or Alaska Airlines. As of November 30, 2001, TWA stopped taking reservations (see Figure 10.6) and the brand was absorbed into AMR Corporation's other carrier, American.

United, are you paying attention to your WebCriteria scores?

The more esoteric measurements are fascinating, and more will arrive every day. But if your Web site budget doesn't reach into the octuple figures, there's a more direct way to take the measure of your navigational ingenuity: split testing.

Doing the Splits: Cookies Required

Remember Ron Richards and his love of A/B split tests for advertising? The same rules apply to navigation.

Fry Multimedia builds Web sites for large companies. They provide consulting, design, development, and managed services. Kara Heinrichs is the chief customer experience officer at Fry and knows a thing or two about testing.

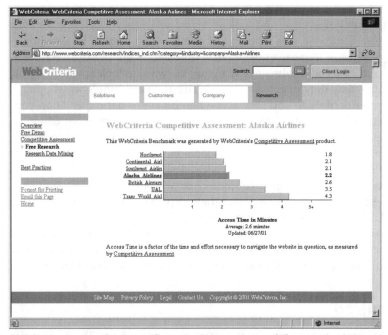

Figure 10.5   Northwest Airlines is sitting pretty, while TWA is sitting on its hands, in this WebCriteria comparison of airline competitors.

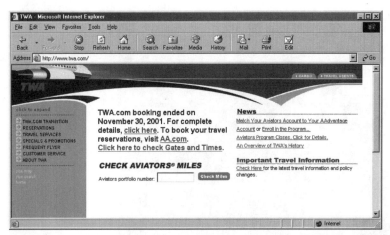

Figure 10.6   Poor Web design wasn't the only reason TWA was grounded. But it didn't help.

"We've done traditional cataloguing concepts like A/B splits where you can run one home page, run another home page, and look at its impact on buyer behavior or even non-buyer behavior. Visitor A sees homepage1.html, while visitor B sees homepage2.html. Cookies ensure that each visitor isn't confused by getting the wrong version next time around, and the results start piling up. We want to look at where people are going on the site—how they're getting around. This is a very simple way."

How deep do you double? Do you stop at the home page? That depends on your budget and how cumulative your test results are. Splits can be hosted anywhere on your site. Do people find solutions faster on customerservice1.html or customerservice2.html? Once again, we're faced with clearly defining "better" and "faster." More on that later in the chapter when we look at scenario design testing.

Once you discover that homepage1.html is a clear winner, don't leave it at that. Make records of what the differences were and their impact on how well people were able to get around. Those test results are interesting by themselves, but when properly harvested and made adequately accessible, they mount up to create institutional knowledge. In other words, once you've learned from your mistakes, figure out a way to keep others from having to make the same mistakes to learn the same lessons.

Cookies Required

Cookies are a matter of course when measuring more than page views. This book is not the place for the technical side of cookies. Cookie Central is the place for that (www.cookiecentral.com) (see Figure 10.7).

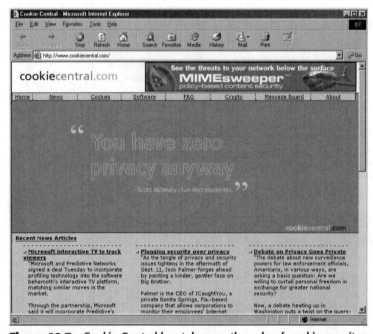

Figure 10.7   Cookie Central has taken on the role of cookie monitor.

You'll find articles, news, software, frequently asked questions, and more at Cookie Central, and it's geared to warm the cockles of technical types. For business types, the issue of cookies balances on only two points: Are enough people allowing them and are they okay from a privacy perspective?

Are cookies prevalent enough to make for a reasonable, statistical sample of visitors? Kiko Suarez from DuPont says yes. "We are finding less than 5 percent of our visitors have cookies turned off."

At Oracle, they cookie you before and after you register. Rene Bonvani explains: "In some cases it's enough for me to set an anonymous cookie. Like a press release. I don't want to make you register for the press release, but I still want to track you. I still want to count on that cookie. If some day I'm smart enough and I'm lucky enough that you register with me, I can track that traffic back to that one individual and see everything you did before you registered."

Rene worries about the privacy side of it as well: "There are some issues with anonymous cookies, not from a technology perspective, but people think it's sneaky. So what we've been doing is implementing some other log techniques. People, especially in Europe, are starting to turn off cookies. In some countries, like Germany, Austria, and Sweden, the government recommends that you turn off the cookie on your machine or at least be notified for each cookie. Every time a cookie is processed there is information being passed along and privacy is a big concern. What we've done is we also implement somewhat less invasive technologies like the single pixel you put in email. The content owner can selectively say I want to track this piece or I don't want to track this piece."

The best way around the privacy issue is full disclosure. National Semiconductor approached the problem by posting their cookies policy at www.national.com/webteam/cookies.html with a detailed description of how they use cookies and how they use the information they glean from that use.

Now you know where they're landing, what they're seeing, how they're interpreting what they see, and which alternative navigational design they tend to like best. You've even started using cookies to keep an eye on repeat visitors' habits. Now it's time to start encouraging them to go where you want them to.

Computing the Best Path

Yes, you can manipulate where people go, but only so much. You can only control the flow of traffic through your site if each page has only one link. Of course, that would dramatically limit the number of people flowing through your site. Not good.

People like having control. They like making their own choices. They want to be able to click at will. So before you try to finesse where they go on your site, it's time to *see* where they *actually* go.

Site Path Maps

Knowing which pages people see most often is good. That will tell you whether some products are more interesting to the public than others. It'll let you know that you have one very frequently asked question. All log analysis tools can show you that.

The question on the table at the moment is how people get from point A to point B. Most log analysis tools will show you which paths are most popular, such as this report from Sane Software's NetTracker (see Figure 10.8).

In larger sites, you want to look at this data from the perspective of a single page. How do most people get to that particular page? That's something WebTrends can provide (see Figure 10.9).

The first thing this report reveals is that nobody went directly to the contact page from the home page. Do people lack a need to contact the company until they have a question about their products? Or might it have something to do with the fact that there is no link from the Oregon Marine home page to the Contact Request page? Noticing that takes a sharp eye and a little insight; testing it is far simpler. Add a contact button to the home page and see what happens (Try It, Measure It, Tweak It—TIMITI).

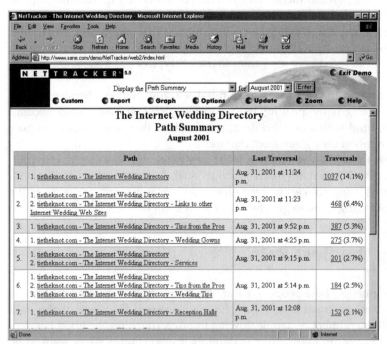

Figure 10.8 NetTracker displays the most popular paths through your site—the most common being a single visit to the home page.

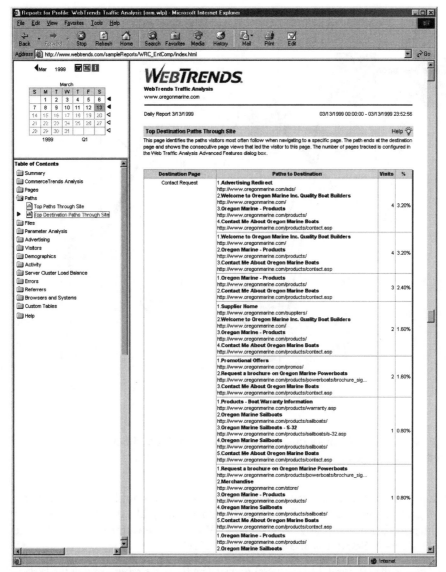

Figure 10.9   WebTrends shows how most people got to the contact request page.

Another helpful report would display the connections from page to page, with some of the most traveled links thicker than the rest. Such a visual representation (see Figure 10.10) would allow you to see where people were going at a glance.

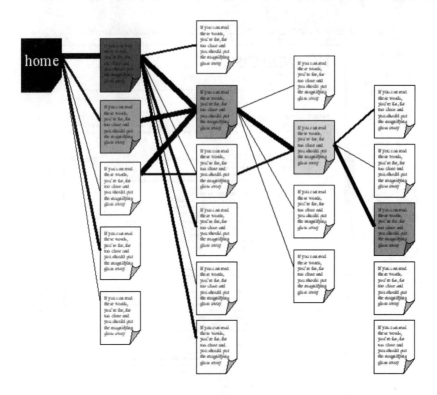

Figure 10.10   A report like this would make it obvious that there should be a faster way to get from the home page to that fifth layer.

Back in the mid-1990s I remember seeing some tools that would map out the wanderings of groups and individuals but I hadn't seen anything like it until I came across VisVip (http://zing.ncsl.nist.gov/WebTools/VisVIP/overview.html), created by the National Institute of Standards and Technology (NIST):

VisVIP allows the UE (usability engineer) to visualize the paths taken through the Web site by the subjects. This overview helps the UE to answer such questions as:

■ *Which parts of the Web site were used for the performance of a given task?*

■ *Which parts were* not *used?*

■ *How long did various subjects take to perform a task?*

■ *How long did they take when visiting individual pages?*

■ *How did subjects' paths compare with that of an expert?*

■ *What is the overall linkage structure of the Web site?*

■ *What patterns of navigational behavior did the subjects exhibit (e.g., re-visiting a home page, circling, etc.)?*

VisVIP presents a 3D visualization of subjects' navigational path data through the Web site. It automatically lays out a 2D graph of the Web site. Each node of the graph represents a Web page, and edges represent links between pages. Nodes are color-coded by type: blue for HTML, purple for directories, green for images, and so on. Because URLs tend to be long, a briefer nickname is generated for each page. The UE has several options to simplify the graph: nodes of a given type, or those not on or near a userpath, can be suppressed. Also, if a graph is highly interconnected, the UE can specify that the site be pictured as a tree emanating from a selected root node.

Once a satisfactory graph of the Web site has been obtained, the UE can select which userpaths to display. These paths are represented as spline curves, resting on the plane of the Web site graph [see Figure 10.11]. The time spent at each page is depicted as a dotted vertical line with its base at the appropriate node. Curvy vertical arrows into and out of the plane mark the beginning and end of each user path. Each user is assigned a unique color, so that several paths can be shown at once.

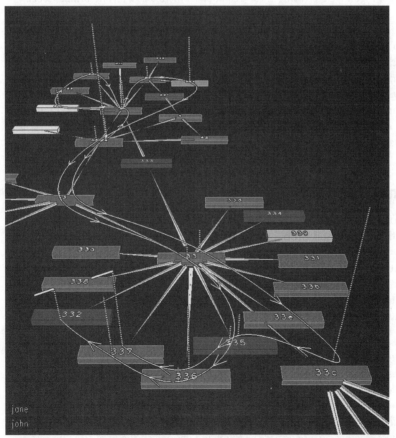

Figure 10.11 A VisVip plot gives the site developer visual insight about the type of wandering people do on a site.

Kris Carpenter at Excite speaks in terms of cow pathing:

It's basically how a user moves though the service [the site]—where they come in, what they do, how they actually move from application to application, and where they exit. They are not necessarily very deliberate. It's a little bit random, but you need to be able to trace and follow where the cows have been and be able to locate them and move them to a new field. This has been applied to the online space where you have users that are moving rapidly through very disparate subjects and you need to find where they've been, reach them where they are, and convince them to move in a new direction.

We can perform ad hoc queries of the clickstream on a regular basis instead of once a quarter or for a specific research purpose. We've made the investment to have that type of information available more broadly. This is now online analytical processing. Anybody can go over to their machine and put in a query about how people are getting from point A to point B.

Something that you might remember from a couple of years ago—everyone was using icons to represent different parts of the site. Everyone was convinced that that was something that you absolutely had to have in place. AOL had imprinted this on the consumer mind and therefore as the end-all-be-all. We had this incredible internal battle because the other dimension if you were creating these visual cues, there was a strong brand association that you also supported. The problem was that there are only so many visuals that you can create for certain types of activities. At a certain point, you're really stretching the paradigm a little bit and trying to make your navigation distinct and meaningful.

We made a very simple shift where we added a text link saying "mail" next to the mailbox icon and it had a dramatic impact. We saw usage more than triple for those navigational links in the matter of an hour. That was the kind of thing where it's absolutely obvious to people now, but there was a period of time when it was thought that the icon was sufficient and that you didn't have to have a text link that was clickable. We were allowed to test it and, lo and behold, it remains.

The Optimal Site Path

What's the one, best path through your site? No, not the fastest way to get from the home page to the check-out button, but the *best* path. The path that results in the most sales?

That's what Ford wanted to know, and J.G. Sandom from OgilvyInteractive described Ford's Web strategy in a July 1999 interview with the editors of *eMarketer* (www.emarketer.com), as described in our "E-Metrics: Business Metrics for the New Economy" white paper:

Ford found that there were a number of alternative optimal site paths to reach Ford's goal of users asking a dealer for a quote on a vehicle. Ford is not selling cars online, but trying to increase the number of people who ask for a formal price quote and make contact with the retail outlet—the car dealership. Customers who viewed the vehicle pages, configured the options to their liking, and selected the audio system and paint color of their choice did not necessarily ask for a dealer quote. The people who were the most likely to ask for a quote were those who had also reviewed the financing options on the Ford site.

Once Ford had identified this as a critical step in the optimal site path, they were able to consider ways to encourage people to take this step. Financial calculation tools, expanded financing options, and email and Web-based reminders were put into place to increase the number of users who traversed the optimal site path.

An Optimal Site Path (OSP) can reveal where in the life cycle pipeline each customer resides. It does not matter if that path requires 10 minutes or 10 weeks to traverse. The OSP reveals the viewing habits of real buyers and makes it easier to classify those who have not yet purchased. If those who actually became customers typically looked at the product specifications, the warranty, the success stories, the price, and then the licensing, it is likely that other prospects should have the same experience on their way to becoming customers. This sort of data suggests where you should focus your promotional efforts. If customers are much more interested in one set of specifications over another, then those are the specs that belong in the catalog, in the direct mail piece, or on the banner ad.

If you know where the best visitors go, you can encourage others to follow suit. Just don't think that getting them to look at a lot of pages or to hang around for a long time are good things in and of themselves.

Pogo-Sticking

Pogo-sticking is a term User Interface Engineering (www.uie.com) came up with to explain why people have trouble shopping online. It refers to people jumping from a list of products to a product page and back again, over and over and over. Why?

In a white paper called "Are the Product Lists on Your Site Reducing Sales?" (http://world.std.com/~uieweb/whitepaper.htm), User Interface Engineering wrote, "Shoppers pogo-sticked when they did not find enough information in the product lists. On the other hand, shoppers bought more and had more satisfying experiences when they encountered product lists that provided sufficient product information so that they could make a product selection right from the list without pogo-sticking."

How much more? "When users comparison-shopped using pogo-sticking techniques, they purchased 11% of the time. When they used product lists to evaluate products, they purchased 55% of the time."

Slipperiness

Stickiness is good if you're selling ad space or time. But *slipperiness* is also a virtue.

Some areas of your site are significantly better if they have very low stickiness or high slipperiness. Let's start with some simple categorization.

Navigation Page

This is the one you want to be as slippery as possible. The only reason people come to a navigation page is if they're trying to get somewhere else.

Data Entry Page

This could be a form for registration or a transaction page. Common sense says that the fewer clicks, pages, questions—hurdles—between the registrant/buyer/visitor, and the goal, the higher the likelihood that the transaction will complete. How many browsers do not become buyers if you place additional clicks in their way? Your mileage will vary. But clearly, making your data entry pages as slippery as possible is a good idea.

Content Page

This is the pot of gold at the end of the rainbow. These are the pages that you want people to spend their time with, the pages you want to persuade them with, the pages you want to represent your brand. Here: sticky good—slippery bad.

Participation Page

Before you say, "Sticky, sticky, sticky!" remember that more often than not, "It depends."

If people are participating in a game, then sticky wins the day. If the participation is an online chat discussion, then you want people to stay, but you want the intrapage elements to be as slippery as possible. This page should be as fast to use as possible.

If the participation page is in, say, the customer service or technical support area, you want the interaction to be as slippery as can be, *provided the outcome is positive.* You don't want customers to get lost looking at dozens of pages in your customer service section. You want them to find what they need and get the heck out of there. You don't want the interaction to just be short; you want it to be short and sweet. This is a classic call center problem that we'll look at in more detail in Chapter 13, "Measuring the Value of Online Customer Service."

Shopping basket blues are caused by a lack of slipperiness. Every additional click is another opportunity for the prospect to change his or her mind and back out. Given the three factors of stickiness, a slippery section is one where visits are short, visit frequencies are low, or users are few—or some combination.

Migration Rate

What about slipperiness between sections? Kris Carpenter from Excite talked about watching traffic flow from one part of a site to another in Chapter 6, "How Good Are You at Making Noise?" Matt Cutler has a few words on the subject as well, as first published in *Business 2.0* (April 17, 2001):

> *Do your Web pages act as turnstiles or black holes? Turnstiles direct customers further into your site. Black holes, on the other hand, are areas where your customers just seem to disappear. In fact, they have left your site. To determine if your site is holding on to visitors or sucking them into oblivion, calculate:*

$$\text{Migration rate} = \frac{\text{Average number of exits from content area}}{\text{Average number of visits to content area}} \times (100)$$

Turnstiles are characterized by few exits from a site and can be identified by a migration rate of less than 20. As you approach 100, you are entering a black hole, which always has as many site exits as it has total visitors.

The "content area" can be defined as a network of content properties, a stand-alone site, a content section, a specific browser-based application, or even a specific page. Of course, migration rates across an entire site are generally useful only in identifying the exit door, as every user who enters a site must eventually leave. Thus, when you calculate the migration rate of an entire closed system, it will always equal 100.

The migration-rate e-metric is a useful tool for information architects and site designers as they struggle to identify the major gateways and hidden back alleys on their site or site network. Migration rates can reveal prime areas for targeted promotions, affiliate recommendations, and—perhaps more importantly—where visitors are accidentally encouraged to leave.

Focus

Next, Matt tackled how much attention people are paying to your pages:

Focus is another concept related to page visit behavior within a section of the site. Suppose there are 15 pages in a section. A focused visit may touch 2 or 3 of these, a less focused visit might touch 5 or 6 of them, and an unfocused visit might touch 8 or 10 of them. Therefore:

$$\text{Focus} = \frac{\textbf{Average number of pages visited in a given section}}{\textbf{Total number of pages in the section}}$$

If the average user views 3 pages in a section out of 15, then the user's focus in that content section is 0.20. Smaller values for focus are referred to as narrow focus while larger values are termed wide focus.

Is wide or narrow focus better? The answers depend on the type of section and on the user behavior viewed as desirable for that section. A sticky area of content is likely a good sign, but a sticky checkout area at an e-commerce site may signal an unnecessarily complex checkout process. Narrow focus is good at a customer service area of a site, but perhaps not at an online auction section of a site.

[The] table [Table 10.1] shows stickiness and focus in combination for a given section of the site.

Since certain combinations are open to multiple interpretations, optimal site path analysis will help shed more light on what is really happening. But the combination of the **stickiness** *and* **focus** *e-metrics for a whole site or a specific section can often be more powerful than stickiness alone.*

In the long run, an optimal site path is a pipe dream. You can't please all the people all the time. But you should at least try to please the most people you can for as long as possible. Your job is to measure just how well you're helping people get around on your site.

For a more definitive answer, we need to leave the realm of the server logs and enter the world of humans. It's time to watch our surfers in action.

Table 10.1   Focus and Stickiness Compared

HIGH STICKINESS	LOW STICKINESS
Narrow focus	Wide focus
Either consuming interest on the part of users, or users are stuck. Further investigation required.	Enjoyable browsing indicates a site "magnet area."
Either quick satisfaction or perhaps disinterest in this section.	Attempting to locate the correct information.

Usability Studies

A usability lab is a disconcerting place. It's a place where every word, every keystroke, every frown, every mutter, and every twitch is recorded, noted, categorized, analyzed, or as Arlo Guthrie might say, "injected, inspected, detected, infected, neglected, and selected." It's enough to make a fella nervous.

In a typical usability lab, you'll find bright lights, three video cameras (keyboard, screen, and face), a keystroke recorder, a human monitor in a white lab coat with a clipboard, and a one-way mirror with who knows *how* many people behind it, and the first thing they say is, "Okay now, just relax."

The Sun Microsystems Usability Lab (see Figure 10.12) includes:

> *22' x 24' lab with observation/control room,* with three analog cameras, scan converter, and two-way audio; five output videotapes include composite (quad) image.

> *14' x 18' lab with observation/control room,* with two digital cameras, scan converter, and two-way audio plus battery-operated headset; three output videotapes include picture-in-a-picture image.

> *11' x 19' lab with observation/control room,* with three analog cameras, scan converter, and two-way audio; five output videotapes include composite (quad) image.

> *Recent-model Sun SPARC systems and Intel-based PCs.*

> *Non-linear video editing* with CD, Betacam, SVHS, VHS, or Sony digital output.

For all the complex gear, the goal is simple: Watch you like a hawk.

Typically, they'll give you a task: Fill out a form, find a database entry, submit a report, and then they'll watch you to see how easy it is to get the job done. They want to see how useful their offering is. They'll ask questions about your user satisfaction.

They'll finish up by taking plaster tire tracks, footprints, and dog-smelling prints. They'll write reports from here till Tuesday with charts, graphs, trends, and twenty-seven eight-by-ten color glossy photographs with circles and arrows and a paragraph on the back of each one explaining what each one is.

Alternatively, you could round up five guys off the street and hand them the mouse for 15 minutes.

Figure 10.12   Sun Microsystems has been doing usability evaluations for decades.

Jakob Nielsen

As personal brands go, Jakob Nielsen has done a wonderful job of placing himself at the center of Web site usability. He's earned his ranking, starting on Web site usability at Sun Microsystems in 1994, and writing ten books on the subject. If you ever get the chance to see him on stage (something he does a lot), you might discover that he also does a wonderful imitation of a browsing giraffe. You can find him and his output at www.useit.com.

The Jakob Nielsen approach to Web site usability is very straightforward and very reliable: Ask a handful of nonemployees, who may know something about your industry but nothing about your Web site, to sit down and try and accomplish something. Something specific. Take notes. Jakob suggests that running just five people through this process is sufficient to bring to light more than enough problems to solve.

I watched Jakob perform this sort of usability test on stage at a conference where we both gave presentations. He asked for two volunteers: one who was willing to have his or her site reviewed and one to be the testing guinea pig. Jakob told us all in advance that the one rule we all had to abide by was simple in theory, but difficult in practice: Shut up.

That was it—the platinum rule. Do not vocalize, point, drop hints, hum, clap, or whistle. Turned out to be whoppingly hard to do.

The guinea pig, who we all assumed had at least a normal amount of intelligence, was asked to find the cost of shipping a specific item to Florida. We in the audience could see the "Free Shipping" button in the main button bar. We couldn't help but see the "Free Shipping" sign on the side of the delivery van that animatedly drove across the bottom of the screen every 5 seconds. It was all we could do to keep from jumping up on stage as a group and snatching the mouse out of the hands of the miscreant whom we had assumed knew how to tie his own shoes.

It became obvious that somebody looking for the shipping charges was looking in a great many places *other* than where the designer thought he would. Jakob's point was well made. No matter how easy you think it is to find something on your site, you'll never know without the help of a guinea pig or two.

Clearly, Jakob knows a thing or two about usability and how to measure it. So I went directly to the source and found his *Alertbox* newsletter for January 21, 2001, entitled "Usability Metrics"(www.useit.com/alertbox/20010121.html):

> *Usability can be measured, but it rarely is. The reason? Metrics are expensive and are a poor use of typically scarce usability resources.*
>
> *Most companies still under-invest in usability. With a small budget, you're far better off passing on quantitative measures and reaching for the low-hanging fruit of qualitative methods, which provide a much better return on investment. Generally, to improve a design, insight is better than numbers.*
>
> *However, the tide might be turning on usability funding. I've recently worked on several projects to establish formal usability metrics in different companies. As organizations increase their usability investments, collecting actual measurements is a natural next step and does provide benefits. In general, usability metrics let you:*
>
> > ***Track progress between releases.*** *You cannot fine-tune your methodology unless you know how well you're doing.*
> >
> > ***Assess your competitive position.*** *Are you better or worse than other companies? Where are you better or worse?*
> >
> > ***Make a Stop/Go decision before launch.*** *Is the design good enough to release to an unsuspecting world?*
> >
> > ***Create bonus plans for design managers and higher-level executives.*** *For example, you can determine bonus amounts for development project leaders based on how many customer-support calls or emails their products generated during the year.*
>
> *How to Measure*
>
> *It is easy to specify usability metrics but hard to collect them. Typically, usability is measured relative to users' performance on a given set of test tasks. The most basic measures are:*
>
> - *the time a task requires*
> - *the error rate*
> - *users' subjective satisfaction*

It is also possible to collect more specific metrics, such as the percentage of time that users follow an optimal navigation path or the number of times they need to backtrack.

You can collect usability metrics for both novice users and experienced users (see www.useit.com/alertbox/20000206.html). Few Web sites have truly expert users, since people rarely spend enough time on any given site to learn it in great detail. Given this, most Web sites benefit most from studying novice users. Exceptions are sites like Yahoo! and Amazon, which have highly committed and loyal users and can benefit from studying expert users.

Intranets, extranets, and weblications are similar to traditional software design and will hopefully have skilled users; studying experienced users is thus more important than working with the novice users who typically dominate public Web sites.

With qualitative user testing, it is enough to test three to five users (see www.useit .com/alertbox/20000319.html). After the fifth user tests, you have all the insight you are likely to get and your best bet is to go back to the drawing board and improve the design so that you can test it again. Testing more than five users wastes resources, reducing the number of design iterations and compromising the final design quality.

*Unfortunately, when you're collecting usability metrics, you must test with more than five users. In order to get a reasonably tight confidence interval on the results, I usually recommend **testing 20 users** for each design. Thus, conducting quantitative usability studies is approximately four times as expensive as conducting qualitative ones. Considering that you can learn more from the simpler studies, I usually recommend against metrics unless the project is very well funded.*

Comparing Two Designs

To illustrate quantitative results, we can look at those recently posted by Macromedia from its usability study of a Flash site (see www.macromedia.com/software/flash/ productinfo/usability/usability_test), aimed at showing that Flash is not necessarily bad. Basically, Macromedia took a design, redesigned it according to a set of usability guidelines, and tested both versions with a group of users. Here are the results (Table 10.2):

Table 10.2   Macromedia Redesign Test Results

	ORIGINAL DESIGN	REDESIGN
Task 1	12 sec.	6 sec.
Task 2	75 sec.	15 sec.
Task 3	9 sec.	8 sec.
Task 4	140 sec.	40 sec.
Satisfaction score*	44.75	74.50

*Measured on a scale ranging from 12 (unsatisfactory on all counts) to 84 (excellent on all counts).

It is very rare for usability studies to employ tasks that are so simple that users can perform them in a few seconds. Usually, it is better to have the users perform more goal-directed tasks that will take several minutes. In a project I'm working on now, the tasks often take more than half an hour (admittedly, it's a site that needs much improvement). Given that the redesign scored better than the original design on all measures, there is no doubt that the new design is better than the old one. The only sensible move is to go with the new design and launch it as quickly as possible. However, in many cases, results will not be so clear cut. In those cases, it's important to look in more detail at how much the design has improved.

Measuring Success

There are two ways of looking at the time-to-task measures in our example case:

■ *Adding the time for all four tasks produces a single number that indicates "how long it takes users to do stuff" with each design. You can then easily compute the improvement. With the original design, the set of tasks took 236 seconds. With the new design, the set of tasks took 69 seconds. The improvement is thus 242%. This approach is reasonable if site visitors typically perform all four tasks in sequence; in other words, when the test tasks are really subtasks of a single, bigger task that is the unit of interest to users.*

■ *Even though it is simpler to add up the task times, doing so can be misleading if the tasks are not performed equally often. If, for example, users commonly perform Task 3 but rarely perform the other tasks, the new design would be only slightly better than the old one; task throughput would be nowhere near 242% higher. When tasks are unevenly performed, you should compute the improvement separately for each of the tasks:*

   ■ *Task 1: Relative score 200% (improvement of 100%)*

   ■ *Task 2: Relative score 500% (improvement of 400%)*

   ■ *Task 3: Relative score 113% (improvement of 13%)*

   ■ *Task 4: Relative score 350% (improvement of 250%)*

You can then take the geometric mean of these four scores, which leads to an overall improvement in task time of 150%.

*Why do I recommend using the **geometric mean** rather than the more common arithmetic mean? Two reasons: First, you don't want a single big number to skew the result. Second, the geometric mean accounts fairly for cases in which some of the metrics are negative (for example, the second design scores less than 100% of the first design).*

Consider a simple example containing two metrics: one in which the new design doubles usability and one in which the new design has half the usability of the old. If you take the arithmetic average of the two scores (200% and 50%), you would conclude that the new design scored 125%. In other words, the new design would be 25% better than the old design. Obviously, this is not a reasonable conclusion.

The geometric mean provides a better answer. In general, the geometric mean of N numbers is the Nth root of the product of the numbers. In our sample case, you would multiply 2.0 by 0.5, take the square root, and arrive at 1.0 (or 100%), indicating that the new design has the same usability as the baseline.

Although it is possible to assign different weights to the different tasks when computing the geometric mean, absent any knowledge as to the relative frequency or importance of the tasks, I've assumed equal weights here.

Summarizing Results

Once you've gathered the metrics, you can use the numbers to formulate an overall conclusion about your design's usability. However, you should first examine the relative importance of performance versus satisfaction. In the Macromedia example, users' subjective satisfaction with the new design was 66% higher than the old design. For a business-oriented Web site or a Web site that is intended for frequent use (say, stock quotes), performance might be weighted higher than preference. For an entertainment site or a site that will only be used once, preference may get the higher weight. Before making a general conclusion, I would also prefer to have error rates and perhaps a few additional usability attributes, but, all else being equal, I typically give the same weight to all the usability metrics. Thus, in the Macromedia example, the geometric mean averages the set of scores as: sqrt(2.50*1.66)=2.04. In other words, the new design scores 204% compared with the baseline score of 100% for the control condition (the old design).

The new design thus has 104% higher usability than the old one. This result does not surprise me: It is common for usability to double as a result of a redesign. In fact, whenever you redesign a Web site that was created without a systematic usability process, you can often improve measured usability even more. However, the first numbers you should focus on are those in your budget. Only when those figures are sufficiently large should you make metrics a part of your usability improvement strategy.

If you have the budget, how much do you allocate to usability?

The Usefulness of Usability Studies

According to DialogDesign's own Web site (www.dialogdesign.dk), "DialogDesign is a small Danish usability consultancy that offers a range of usability consultancy services to help you research, design and evaluate your interactive products." The reason you should know about them is a study they did on usability studies.

DialogDesign tested the testers. They charged eight different usability teams with spotting the problems with one Web site. They go into great detail (all downloadable) on how they went about running this study. The results were most revealing.

These eight teams came up with some 300 usability problems that needed fixing. Sounds helpful. But there were some disturbing results: No single problem was reported by all teams, and only one team reported as many as seventy-five problems. Were they using different definitions? No. Were they given different tasks to perform? No. They were all human beings, using their non-superhuman powers to detect faults, failings, and fumbles.

The lesson? Don't ever think that you can cross usability testing off your list. You need to keep at it. The other lesson? Testing and tweaking your site forever would be a great idea, if it weren't for limited resources.

So what do you do? You can't depend on eight evaluation teams to agree on anything, and you can't spend like there's no tomorrow. Your job is to figure out the most important things to focus on and stick to your guns. What's important? Test from your customers' point of view.

Scenario Design Testing

The whole point of scenario design testing is helping people complete their tasks. What, then, are people trying to accomplish on your site? Where are they trying to go?

Jakob Nielsen's desire to measure success was amplified in his February 18, 2001, *Alertbox* entitled, "Success Rate: The Simplest Usability Metric." Here's an excerpt:.

> *To collect metrics, I recommend using a very simple usability measure: the user success rate. I define this rate as the **percentage of tasks that users complete correctly.** This is an admittedly coarse metric; it says nothing about* why *users fail or* how well *they perform the tasks they did complete.*
>
> *Nonetheless, I like success rates because they are easy to collect and a very telling statistic. After all, if users can't accomplish their target task, all else is irrelevant. User success is the bottom line of usability.*
>
> *Success rates are easy to measure, with one major exception: How do we account for cases of partial success? If users can accomplish part of a task, but fail other parts, how should we score them?*
>
> *Let's say, for example, that the users' task is to order twelve yellow roses to be delivered to their mothers on their birthday. True task success would mean just that: Mom receives a dozen roses on her birthday. If a test user leaves the site in a state where this will occur, we can certainly score the task as a success. If the user fails to place any order, we can just as easily determine the task a failure.*
>
> *But there are other possibilities as well. For example, a user might:*
>
> - *Order twelve yellow tulips, twenty-four yellow roses, or some other deviant bouquet*
>
> - *Fail to specify a shipping address, and thus have the flowers delivered to their own billing address*
>
> - *Specify the correct address, but the wrong date*
>
> - *Do everything perfectly except forget to specify a gift message to enclose with the shipment, so that Mom gets the flowers but has no idea who they are from*
>
> *Each of these cases constitutes some degree of failure (though if in the first instance the user openly states a desire to send, say, tulips rather than roses, you could count this as a success).*
>
> *If a user does not perform a task as specified, you could be strict and score it as a failure. It's certainly a simple model: Users either do everything correctly or they fail. No middle ground. Success is success, without qualification.*
>
> *However, I often **grant partial credit** for a partially successful task. To me, it seems unreasonable to give the same score (zero) to both users who did nothing and those who successfully completed much of the task. How to score partial success depends on the magnitude of user error.*

In the flower example, we might give 80% credit for placing a correct order but omitting the gift message; 50% credit for (unintentionally) ordering the wrong flowers or having them delivered on the wrong date; and only 25% credit for having the wrong delivery address. Of course, the precise numbers would depend on a domain analysis.

There is no firm rule for assigning credit for partial success. Partial scores are only esti-mates, but they still provide a more realistic impression of design quality than an absolute approach to success and failure.

Case Study

Table 10.3 shows task success data from a study I recently completed. In it, we tested a fairly big content site, asking four users to perform six tasks.

In total, we observed twenty-four attempts to perform the tasks. Of those attempts, nine were successful and four were partially successful. For this particular site, we gave each partial success half a point. In general, 50% credit works well if you have no compelling reasons to give different types of errors especially high or low scores.

In this example, the success rate was (9+(4*0.5))/24 = 46%.

Simplified success rates are best used to provide a general picture of how your site sup-ports users and how much improvement is needed to make the site really work. You should not get too hung up on the details of such numbers, especially if you're dealing with a small number of observations and a rough estimate of partial success scores. For example, if your site scored 46% but another site scored 47%, it's not necessarily a better site.

*That a 46% success rate is not at all uncommon might provide some cold comfort. In fact, most Web sites score less than 50%. Given this, the **average Internet user's experience is one of failure.** When users try to do something on the Web for the first time, they typ-ically fail.*

Although using metrics alone will not solve this dilemma, it can give us a way to measure our progress toward better, more usable designs. But don't expect better navigation to solve all your problems. Some of your visitors don't like to click links anyway.

Table 10.3   Task Success Data

	TASK 1	TASK 2	TASK 3	TASK 4	TASK 5	TASK 6
User 1	F	F	S	F	F	S
User 2	F	F	P	F	P	F
User 3	S	F	S	S	P	S
User 4	S	F	S	F	P	S

Note: S=Success, F=Failure, P=Partial success

Deciphering Searches

Measuring how well people can find you online through the directories and search engines is important. So is measuring how well people can find what they want on your site through your own search engine. You'll learn how to improve your navigation and how to improve your communication with the outside world.

Search as a Measure of Navigation

David Thompson, manager of Information Products and Services in the Information, Planning and Program Management Branch of Industry Canada (yes, that all fits on his card in both English *and* French), talked with me about Web navigation at a recent Internet World conference.

David said that their navigational improvements were important, but only about one-third of the visitors to the Canadian government's Industry Canada (www.ic.gc.ca) site bothered clicking on regular navigational links. One-third went straight for the Links By Alphabetical Order and the final third went straight for the search engine.

How effective is the search tool on your site? How well does it help people find what they want?

The director of Internet Business at a large technology company found that "in the engineering community, about 50 percent of the navigation from the start is through the search engine. We were missing that totally. We started tuning the navigation buttons, and now we're getting about 25 percent of our traffic directed by the search engine."

Lowering the need for the search engine by having better navigation is good. Making the search engine easy to find is also good. Jakob Nielsen found out how good on his own site: "When I changed the useit.com home page to include a search box instead of a link, search engine use increased by 91 percent. Small change, big effect (as is often the outcome when implementing usability guidelines). In his article about on-site search engines (www.useit.com/alertbox/20010513.html), Jakob revealed that people aren't very good searchers:

Typical users are very poor at query reformulation: If they don't get good results on the first try, later search attempts rarely succeed. In fact, they often give up. We recently studied a large group of people as they shopped on various e-commerce sites. Their search success rate was:

   First query: 51%

   Second query: 32%

   Third query: 18%

You might want to use cookies and navigational tracking to create a *seek-to-find ratio*. This ratio would keep tabs on whether the tweaks you make to your search engine are working in your favor.

A *seek* is tallied every time a visitor enters some text and hits the Search button. How you identify a *find* is a bit trickier. A *find* can occur in a number of ways, and your server log is not going to tell you how it was done. Instead, you're going to have to go back to the scenario testing lab and watch people use your search engine.

Lure some real-live customers into your parlor and ask them to find something specific on your site. Customers are required because they know the subject matter at hand. Asking a nine-year-old girl to find and compare the main and magnification view timebases on your digital sampling oscilloscopes will be about as informative as asking an electronics design engineer to find out how many of what size batteries go in a Barbie "Dance with Me" Talking Boombox. My bet's on the nine-year-old.

Measuring the effectiveness of your search engine is useful, but examining what phrases people type in the search box may be more interesting.

Search as a Measure of Promotion

If all your banner ads show pictures of and use the words "suri alpaca," how many people come to your Web site and search for llamas? Are you out of step with your audience? Are you promoting bison while your potential customers are looking for buffalo? If people keep coming to your site and searching for Katahdins, maybe that banner ad that just says "sheep" isn't performing as well as it might.

Track the changes to search terms people use over time and see if the competition is sending traffic your way. You'll know when people stop searching for the buzzwords you're promoting (dyestuff for textiles) and start searching for the buzzwords that appear in your competitor's ads (reactive dyes).

Search as a Measure of Temperament

The reverse works as well: Keep an eye on the search terms people use in order to determine what words should show up in your advertising. If you're pushing "Tastes Great" and people are searching for "Less Filling," you now have a momentary insight into the consumer's mind.

That director of Internet Business at that large technology company I mentioned earlier in the chapter reviews the terms that people use as a matter of course. "We make the association back to content. When we see terms appear that we are uncertain of sometimes, we investigate and then we start making associations back to our product. So we're constantly tuning the search engine now. We're teaching the marketing departments in the business units to do that. So we're working our way out of being the experts on search engines and we're starting to migrate that into the businesses. We're encouraging them to pay attention to vocabulary development around the search tool."

In the End, Everything Is a Compromise

Scott Berkun is a design and usability training manager at Microsoft. He also posts essays at www.uiweb.com. His September 2001 article caught my eye because after he has designed or managed the development of many IE UI features, including explorer bars, autocomplete, favorites, history, search, and lots of other things, he understands one significant truth about Web site navigation systems and all software interfaces: Perfection in design is not possible.

> *No matter how much is known about a given business, user group or technology, you cannot simultaneously satisfy all possible objectives. . . . An optimal design, in the broadest sense, is a mythical idea.*
>
> *Whether you are designing an intranet Web site or a microwave oven, you have at least three sets of overlapping criteria to deal with: Business objectives, user experience objectives, and resource limitations. These aspects create lines of both synergy and tension. If you focus on any one of them, it will pull or push against at least one of the others. For example, if your Web site is forced to ship on a certain schedule, you will have to reduce the depth to which you can satisfy business or user experience goals. It's a zero sum game: Choices that benefit one attribute are often at the expense of another. To call something optimal, it has to be the most desirable outcome of a specific set of restrictions.*
>
> *The real secret ingredient is synergy, and mastery of trade-offs, not an isolated brilliance in any singular domain. It's not about finding a specific measurement or applying a singular technique: It's having a rationale and strategy for combining disciplines and methods that may naturally overlap, or conflict, with each other. There is no single metric for this in any industry or philosophy and, in part, this is why the idea of an optimal design is so strange.*
>
> *From www.uiweb.com/issues/issue17.htm*

Different Strokes for Different Folks

Scott Berkun mentioned one more critical and painful factor in his article:

> *The last straw is that your users are not homogeneous: They have conflicting needs and opinions about the stuff you make. With a user base of a reasonable size, you will always find contradictions in their needs, desires, and performance in the usability lab. The same feature that one segment of users has difficulty with will sometimes be the exact same feature another group of advanced users can't live without.*

What's a designer to do? Personalize!

CHAPTER

11

Calculating Conversion

"Business.com's marketing team runs tests on more than 10 different sites and networks. We analyze the results by looking at back-end data rather than click-through rates. This allows us to optimize and leverage for efficient buys. We have learned that click-through rates are often the smallest factor in determining the success of a campaign."

Chris Hylen, senior vice president of Business Development,
Sales and Marketing at Business.com,
as quoted by eMarketing Magazine (www.eMarketingmag.com)

What's the surest measurement in determining the success of a campaign? When people give you their money. Yes, there are other ways to tell if you're on the right track, but the right track is that one that leads to people giving you their money.

Qualification Process

There are several steps on the road to making a sale. You target your promotions at *suspects*. They're the ones that have the same attributes as people who have purchased from you in the past. As mentioned in Chapter 7, a *prospect* is somebody who has expressed interest in your products by responding to a promotion or showing up at your site unannounced. A *qualified prospect* is one who has the need, the desire, and the means to make the buy.

Anybody who's been in sales for more than 10 minutes can describe a sales pipeline to you. It's the numbers game side of selling that is so daunting to those who hate cold calling and prefer that their efforts not be measured at all.

It takes so many cold calls to get somebody on the phone. It takes so many conversations to find even an unqualified prospect. It takes so many unqualified prospects to find a qualified one. It takes so many qualified prospects to find one that you can turn into a customer.

Sales managers want to see how many calls the salespeople are making to determine if they're on the right track, the track that leads to the money. If a sales rep isn't making the cold calls, there's no way he or she will make the grade. If the rep has lots of qualified prospects and no sales, then training that rep on closing the deal is the obvious next step.

Identifying the qualification process on your Web site is the surest way to figure out how to increase your conversion rate. What are the steps a visitor makes on his or her way to buying your goods or services?

If you do not sell directly, that's okay. When I say *buy* or *conversion*, I want you to think of whatever moment of commitment happens on your site. *Conversion* might mean:

Registering for a seminar

Subscribing to a newsletter

Participating in a discussion

Downloading a white paper

Buying a product

Your qualification process will probably include a combination of factors, all leading up to the conversion event on the preceding list. Think in terms of an optimal site path, but think beyond mere navigation. The qualification process might include an email exchange, a prerequisite number of repeat visits, or a willingness to share personal information. Each Web site has its own set of stipulations that separate the wheat from the chaff.

Conversion Benchmarks

In terms of pure sales, you can become seriously depressed or maniacally happy looking at some of the conversion figures periodically reported. Do you measure up?

An article posted at the Wharton School Web site (http://knowledge.wharton.upenn.edu) laments how low online conversion rates really are:

According to Forrester Research, a consulting firm in Boston, more than 70% of Internet retailers in 1999 had a conversion rate of less than 2%, which is to say that of every 100 visits to a retail Web site, only two resulted in purchases. Industry experts suggest that market leaders such as Amazon.com have conversion rates no higher than 15% to 20%.

Iconocast (see Figure 11.1) reported on a Nielsen//NetRatings report from May 2001, which disclosed conversion rates across several industries.

Video merchants were experiencing a conversion rate of 18 percent. Travel services beat them out at 19 percent. Clothing and apparel converted 23 percent of their shoppers, while bookstores enjoyed a 27 percent rate. Auctions were on top at 28 percent. Of course, numbers like these are always confusing. While the June 14, 2001, issue of *Iconocast* was reporting that 28 percent number, a Nielsen//NetRatings press release in May 2001 announced different conversion rates at different auction sites, none of which reached 28 percent (see Table 11.1)

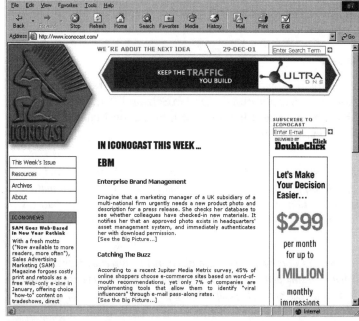

Figure 11.1   *Iconocast* is an excellent source of information about online advertising and marketing.

In November 2000, the Yankee Group reported a range of conversion rates for online retailers running from 4 percent for furniture and lighting site Bellacor.com to 20.5 percent for beauty and bath site Sephora.com.

As always, your mileage may vary. What matters is not what gets reported, but what you experience on your own site. Your conversion rate is X, and you want to make it better.

Table 11.1   Top Auction Sites Ranked by Revenue Share, May 2001 (U.S.)

AUCTION SITE*	REVENUE SHARE	SATISFACTION RATE	CONVERSION RATE
eBay.com†	64.3%	8.42	22.5%
uBid.com	14.7%	7.87	11.0%
Egghead.com (Onsale.com)	4.0%	7.75	8.0%
Yahoo! Auctions	2.4%	7.84	4.4%
Amazon Auctions	2.0%	7.64	6.5%

Source: Nielsen//NetRatings & Harris Interactive eCommercePulse, May 2001
*Auction sites do not include travel related sites.
†Figures for eBay.com do not include figures for Half.com.

The goal is to find those measurable items that are the most likely to have an impact on conversion, measure them, tweak them, and measure the results. Where do you look? Along the path to qualification.

Transaction Phases

In their paper "Web Assessment: A Model for the Evaluation and the Assessment of Successful Electronic Commerce Applications," Dorian Selz and Petra Schubert from the University of St. Gallen, Switzerland Institute for Information Management, outline three *transaction phases* on a Web site:

Information Phase

In the information phase customers collect information on potential products and services. They look for possible suppliers, asking for prices and conditions. The information phase covers the initial satisfaction of a consumer's need for information to conciliate his demand for a product or service with the offer.

Agreement Phase

Negotiations between suppliers and customers take place in the agreement phase. The phase serves to establish a firm link between supplier and buyer that will eventually lead to a contract, fixing details such as product specifications, payment, delivery, etc.

Settlement Phase

The last of the conventional steps is called the settlement phase. The (physical/virtual) delivery of the product ordered will take place during this phase. Also possible after-sales interactions like guarantee claims or help desk services occur.

We're interested in how those steps through the information phase and the agreement phase can impact the first part of the settlement phase, where the order is placed.

Call it transaction phase, call it sales cycle stage, or call it the customer life cycle funnel, it's still a numbers game. One of my favorite diagrams from the white paper I wrote with Matt Cutler, "E-Metrics: Business Metrics for the New Economy," is the Customer Life Cycle Funnel (see Figure 11.2) .

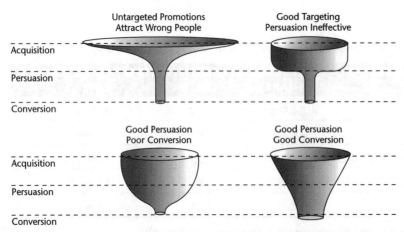

Figure 11.2 The Customer Life Cycle Funnel quickly identifies roadblocks and bottlenecks in your qualification process.

Does your Customer Life Cycle Funnel resemble a martini glass? Then you're attracting a lot of people to your site, but they're the wrong people. Banner ads that attract 14-year-old girls to your BMW site are not helping you. Those girls come to the home page and leave upon arrival. It's time to check your advertising and see why you're not pulling in serious leads.

Does your funnel look like a margarita glass? You have the right people showing up, but they lose interest. You have a problem with navigation or persuasion. They're certainly interested, but they came, they saw, and they got confused or bored and they bolted.

Does your funnel resemble a wineglass? You've got the right people and they like what they see, but they just don't seem to be able to seal the deal at the end of the process. People are abandoning their shopping carts. Time to review your sales order process and make it easier to use. Show the shipping charges up front. Let them find out how much the tax is *before* they have to enter their life story.

You say your funnel looks like a shot glass? Congratulations! You've got the right people, they're interested, they've followed the optimal site path you've designed, and they end up making a purchase. Well done.

Upper management at Oracle is very interested in the shape of their funnel. Rene Bonvanie, vice president of Online Marketing, admits they are interested in revenue as well, but they're more focused on the pipeline.

"To some extent revenues is kind of a result rather than a cause, so what we look at is pipeline. And pipeline is determined by positive response to marketing campaigns and conversion through a qualification cycle, which means that the marketing system has to communicate very well with the sales system in which qualification happens."

Okay, the pipeline is where all good things happen. What factors go into moving visitors from one phase of the relationship to the next?

Navigation and Search Impact Conversion

I don't wish to belabor the point, but if they can't find it, they ain't gonna buy it.

The sooner they find it, the sooner they buy it, so take note of the exact number of clicks required to make a purchase. Start from your home page and do your best to minimize these.

Of course, visitors to your site are like visitors to Paris. There's a straight path from the Louvre to the Eiffel Tower, but there are a lot of other interesting things between the two. They are very likely going to wander about on their own without any regard whatsoever to how much you want them to head straight for the shopping cart.

Keep count of the actual number of clicks-to-purchase, and compare those to the minimum requirement to buy something. This will give you valuable information about the clarity of your navigation. Reducing the *first purchase momentum* will increase sales.

$$\text{First purchase momentum} = \frac{\text{Required clicks to first purchase}}{\text{Actual clicks to first purchase}}$$

In their white paper, "What Causes Customers to Buy on Impulse?" User Interface Engineering (UIE) identified navigation as being counterintuitively more important than sales prices and promotions. Not only counterintuitive but counter to some Yankee Group findings that claimed people make impulse purchases because of special sales prices, free shipping, and holiday or seasonal promotions.

"In reality," said the UIE paper, "very few impulse purchases resulted from promotions. The impulse buys were spread across 41% of the sites in our study. These included everything from pet stores to apparel stores to computer accessory stores. All the impulse purchases were for different items, none of which were special promotions or products on sale. Instead, they were all just items that the shoppers thought of while shopping for other items.

"In analyzing our observational data, we found that a major driver of impulse purchases is the use of the category links on the site. Certain designs led shoppers to find products through category links rather than the sites' search engines. When shoppers used these categories, they were far more likely to make impulse purchases than when they used the search engines."

UIE identified that 87 percent of the dollars spent on impulse purchases came from visitors using links while only 13 percent of the money was spent after using the sites' search engines. In addition, customers were three times more likely to continue browsing for more items once they found the item they originally were looking for than the shoppers who used the site's search engine.

Some people are going to use your on-site search engine no matter what, so there's another feature that deserves your attention when trying to improve your conversion rate.

An article in the *Industry Standard* (March 6, 2000) reported that adding one new navigational feature made a significant impact on Tower Records' conversion rate. People looking for artists or song titles do not always type the exact name, so Tower implemented a search engine that finds similar items, rather than only finding exact matches. Tower doubled their conversion rate. And that's not uncommon.

An article published at *InternetWeek* (www.internetweek.com/story/INW20011128S0004) reported that Macys.com "more than doubled the rate at which it converts site visitors into buyers." They implemented a search engine that "finds a specific product even when a shopper types in keywords that don't match the terms Macy's uses to index the item."

How much more than double?" Although Federated wouldn't disclose Macys.com's actual conversion rate, it said the rate had increased 150 percent since summer." Apparently, Mercado Software's IntuiFind 4 search technology (www.mercado.com) is getting a great deal of the credit.

But it's not just how they move around your site that could be indicative of their proclivity to purchase. There are a number of other factors at work. For instance, how long do they stay?

Duration

Duration came up briefly in Chapter 9, "Calculating the Caliber of Content." As with the vast majority of these numbers, how you calculate them depends on what you're trying to accomplish.

Selling Stuff

If your goal is consumer sales, then your records will tell you whether a longer duration is good for business or bad for slowing down your server. It's a lot like a physical retail store. Having people stay in the store might be a great thing—if they buy more.

Sticking around is not good in a restaurant, where customers would hog tables and limit the number of customers you can serve. It's not good in a shoe store, where you have a limited number of salespeople to fetch and carry the right size and color for each prospect.

Amazon.com probably loves having people wander from page to page dropping things into their shopping carts. Disney counts their blessings in terms of brand bonding. Yahoo! sells more ads with every page view, so the more time on the site, the better.

But if your duration rate is high and your conversion rate is low, you may be putting too many hoops between the prospect and the purchase. It's time to streamline. How much value does Nike get out of kids designing their shoes without buying? Does the brand bonding generate enough offline sales to maintain the servers and the software?

Complex Explanations

If you sell complex equipment or sophisticated services, a longer duration may mean your prospects are finding out what they need to know without taking up a lot of sales rep telephone time. On the other hand, it might also mean they haven't been quickly persuaded to download the white paper, sign up for a seminar, or schedule a meeting.

There is no ideal duration on the Web. There is no ideal duration for your Web site. There is no ideal duration for one of your products. There is no ideal duration for an individual portion of your site. There is only the duration that seems to lead to more sales.

Your database can tell you that, of all the people who bought things, they spent more than X minutes and less than Y minutes in various sections of your site. Your job is to:

1. Find out if you can encourage others to spend more than X and less than Y minutes.

2. Determine whether that change actually has a positive impact on sales.

Depth

Right after *how long*? comes *how deep*? How many pages did they look at?

Huston Smith has written several books on comparative religion. He likes to talk about how interesting it is delving into the world's many religions to see how they're alike and how they're different. But he cautions his readers not to spread themselves too thin. Digging one 80-foot well is much more likely to yield results when digging eight 10-foot wells will not.

You may be delighted that your visitors are spending hours on your site, but if they're looking at everything in general and nothing in specific, they won't be spending their dollars. General Electric has so many divisions and departments, that you can wander their Web site for days without finding anything of interest (see Figure 11.3).

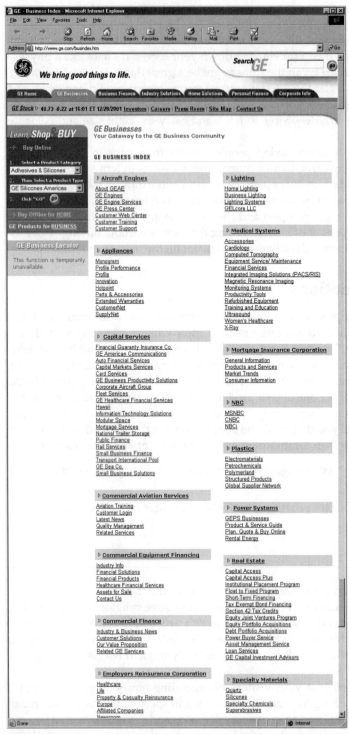

Figure 11.3 GE doesn't derive any value by having you bounce around their site without focus.

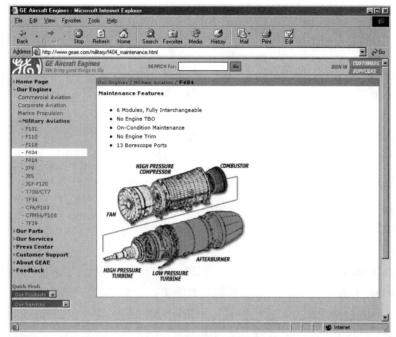

Figure 11.4 Visitors rooting around at this level of the GE site are serious prospects.

If you bounce from Healthcare Financial Services to Specialty Chemicals to Mortgage Insurance Products and Services to Aviation Training to National Trailer Storage, the time you spend is wasted. But if you drill down to read up on the maintenance features of a military F404 engine (see Figure 11.4), chances are pretty good that you're getting value from the visit and that GE will as well.

Doing the Math

For the spreadsheet-inclined, we have already generated a healthy number of variables to play with. In a retail environment, we might work with these numbers:

T   Time, or duration in minutes

P   Page views

D   Depth, or level of detail

PV Purchases per visit

IP Items per purchase

$P Dollar value per purchase

Our fictitious Web site for this example is the Middling Magic Market, operated by Martin Middling. Middling has been meddling with mathematics since he was a mite.

Here's what Martin has come up with as the average visit to his Web site by an average customer:

Buyers spend 6 minutes on the site	$T = 6$
They look at 12 pages	$P = 12$
They drill down 3 levels	$D = 3$
They purchase once every 10 visits	$PV = 10$ percent
They usually buy 3.5 items	$IP = 3.5$
They usually spend \$20	$\$P = \$20$

Martin then looks at the same numbers for his *best* customers:

Best buyers spend 8 minutes	$T = 8$
They look at 15 pages	$P = 15$
They drill down 6 levels	$D = 6$
They purchase once every 5 visits	$PV = 20$ percent
They usually buy 4 items	$IP = 4$
They usually spend \$30	$\$P = \$30$

Because Martin is a visually oriented spreadsheet kind of guy, he creates a radar chart to compare the two groups (see Figure 11.5).

The amount of time spent on the site (T) isn't a great deal different. Page views are even less different. But the best customers are those who go deep, rather than wander around. These are people who know what they want. They're buyers on a mission.

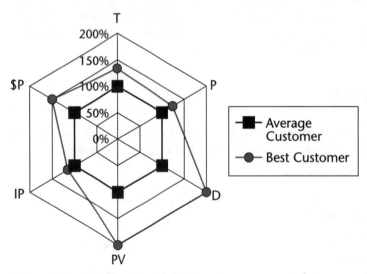

Figure 11.5 Middling Magic's best customers seem to buy more often and click deeper than the average customer.

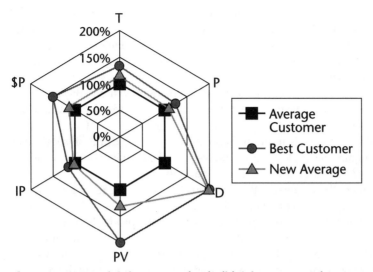

Figure 11.6   Martin's impact on depth didn't improve purchases per visit.

So Martin Middling is left in a muddle. Can he turn browsers into buyers by drawing them deeper? He decides to give it a try. He adds links that promise more pictures and more detail. He alters the wording on his pages to include promises of more revealing information, just a click away. Martin successfully draws his browsers deeper into his site. But he doesn't notice much of an increase in sales, so he goes back to his radar chart for another look (see Figure 11.6).

Yep, old Martin succeeded at getting people to click deeper. As a magician, he was well versed in drawing people's attention where he wanted them to look. And the results were impressive. They stayed 17 percent longer. They looked at thirteen pages instead of twelve. They dug down to six levels, just the same as his best customers. But the increases in purchases per visit and dollars per purchase were pretty small.

Martin knew he was on the right track, but he felt he was missing something, and he was right. He forgot to look at visits over time.

Recency and Frequency

Not all buyers are first-time visitors, and not all first-time visitors are buyers. What's the relationship? What is the pattern of visits for an individual?

That's something that's caught the attention of Peter Fader, associate professor of Marketing at the University of Pennsylvania's Wharton School, and Bruce Hardie, assistant professor of Marketing at London Business School. Fader gets excited about this stuff quickly.

"Okay, let me tell you about recency and frequency," he tells me over the phone and I can almost see him rubbing his hands together, warming to his subject. "One of my partners in crime, Bruce Hardie, and I do a lot of work together. He has a dissertation student working right now on duration in both ways and trying to link together duration of visits with frequency of visits.

"Nielsen//NetRatings will say that the heaviest visitors who visited eBay spent 500 visits there for the month. The question is whether that's five hundred 1-minute visits or two 250-minute visits.

"Where is the real variability? Is it on the frequency side or the duration side? So as a company, if we are going to deploy our resources to make the site stickier, which of those two should it be? You can't analyze them separately."

You also can't analyze them generically. Let's say I'm shopping for a new laptop. Over a period of days, my pattern of visits looks like Table 11.2.

My visit on the first day showed some passing interest in the products. The next day, I came back and looked at a wider variety of products but didn't get serious about the specifications until day 3. That day, I showed up on two different occasions (sessions are usually ended after 30 minutes of inactivity) and dug down six layers deep.

If that weren't enough of an indication of interest and intent, I came back again on days 4 and 5 looking at more, deep pages and then at fewer deep pages. What was I thinking? I was hunting around for the best model or configuration of the laptop I wanted. By day 6, I had narrowed it down to two different models and I came back *twice* to look them over.

I wasn't wandering around like a browser. I was on a mission. I wanted to look at those four particular pages located seven layers deep in the Web site. Then something happened. I stopped coming. Why?

Table 11.2 Jim Goes Shopping

DAY	VISITS	PAGES	DEPTH
1	1	5	2
2	1	10	3
3	2	30	6
4	3	25	7
5	3	15	7
6	2	4	7
7	0	0	0
8	0	0	0
9	0	0	0

Three possible choices: (1) I was placing an order on those four pages on day 6, (2) I decided not to buy a laptop at all, or, worst-case scenario, (3) I bought from your competitor.

Recency, then, has a huge impact on how you use your frequency numbers. It's great that I showed up a lot and looked at a lot of pages. But if I haven't been back for months. . . .

Matt Cutler came up with a metric for his June 26, 2000, article in *Business 2.0* magazine he called the *deactivation threshold*:

> Most Web sites place visitors into one of two categories: new visitor or repeat visitor. But not all repeat visitors are the same. Web surfers who visit a site once a week are loyal; those who visit twice a year are fickle. And when it comes down to it, fickle users have to be offered the same incentives and interactions as newbies. Users who haven't come around for some time should be treated as new ones.
>
> The tough part is determining when to downgrade a repeat visitor to a nonuser. To do this, calculate the deactivation threshold, which is the last time a user visited your site divided by the average length of time a user remains loyal to a site.

$$\text{Deactivation threshold} = \frac{\text{Recency}}{\text{Average user loyalty}}$$

> If the average online user is loyal for 90 days, a user who visited the site three days ago—thus earning a recency score of 3—would have a deactivation threshold of 0.03. Users with deactivation thresholds close to 0 are likely to remain loyal. As users' deactivation thresholds approach 1, however, loyalty may well be waning. Once thresholds rise beyond 2, users should be "deactivated" and treated as new visitors.
>
> The greatest challenge with this formulation is determining average user loyalty. For many traditional businesses, this number is measured in years. For many Net businesses, the number is measured in weeks or months.

Which visits lead to purchases? That is, in fact, the title of a paper by Wendy Moe, assistant professor of marketing at the University of Texas at Austin, and Pete Fader, professor of marketing at the Wharton School of the University of Pennsylvania, written in February 2001. In it, they discuss the proper allocation of marketing resources in the effort to improve conversion rates:

> Many e-commerce sites hold the philosophy that every visit is a buying opportunity and therefore try to induce purchases with promotions and discounts. However, offering promotions and discounts for all visits is inefficient. Many purchasers are likely to initiate a transaction without the added incentive of a promotion; offering these shoppers a promotion would be a poor use of resources. A more efficient option is to limit promotional offerings to those who were unlikely to buy rather than to extend an offer to all shoppers and reducing margins for the likely buyers.
>
> The key in both of these applications is the ability to predict purchasing probabilities for a given visit. Those visits that are likely to result in a purchase need to be identified and the visitors possibly redirected to a server that will provide a better shopping experience and increase the visitors' likelihood of buying. Those visits that are less likely to result in a purchase, without any added incentive, may be identified as targets for promotion.

With these (and other) resource allocation decisions in mind, we develop a model of conversion behavior that predicts each customer's probability of purchasing at a given visit based on that individual's observed history of visits and purchases. We offer an individual-level probability model that allows for customer heterogeneity in a very flexible way. We discuss and allow for the fact that visits may play very different roles in the purchasing process. For example, some visits are motivated by planned purchases while others are simply browsing visits. The Conversion Model developed in this paper has the flexibility to accommodate a variety of visit-to-purchase relationships. Finally, customers' shopping behavior may evolve over time as a function of past experiences. Thus, the Conversion Model also allows for nonstationarity in behavior.

The Moe/Fader Conversion Model is based on four components:

1. **Baseline probability of purchasing.** *For each individual, there is a baseline probability of purchase at each visit. This baseline reflects the extent to which visits are purchase-directed and likely to result in purchasing regardless of any effects from past visits or purchases.*

2. **Positive visit effect on purchasing.** *Each visit has its own stochastic impact (assumed to be non-negative), and as the effects of these visits accumulate, the probability of purchase increases over time. In other words, as a shopper makes more visits, she will be increasingly likely to purchase in subsequent visits, depending on the magnitude of these visit effects on purchasing. If and when a purchase occurs, this "bank" of visit effects is reset to zero, and visit effects begin to build up again upon the next visit opportunity. However, incremental visit effects may also be zero. In this case, there is no accumulated visit effect, and purchasing is driven primarily by the baseline effect.*

3. **Negative purchasing threshold effect.** *Purchasing propensity is negatively affected by an individual's level of purchase-related anxiety toward a given retailer. For example, shoppers new to a site may be risk averse and reluctant to provide personal information, such as credit card numbers, home addresses, etc., to an unknown vendor as part of the transaction process. In effect, shoppers have a threshold that must be overcome before a purchase will occur. Therefore, as a shopper visits a store, the associated visit effects are measured against a purchasing threshold construct which varies across individuals. When the accumulated effect of visits becomes high relative to this threshold, purchase occurs.*

4. **Evolving effects over time.** *The expected magnitudes of both visit effects and purchasing threshold may evolve over time, as the customer gains experience with the shopping environment. For example, subsequent visits to a Web site may have smaller effects on purchasing as the shopper gets used to the environmental stimuli and becomes less persuaded by content that has been seen repeatedly in the past. Therefore, our Conversion Model will allow for and provide a measure to characterize the trends that may be affected by past visiting. Additionally, purchasing thresholds may also evolve as a function of past purchasing experiences. For example, as shoppers make repeated purchases, the original reluctance to purchase from an unknown site may decrease, making future purchasing more likely. Many*

> *researchers have found that customers are less resistant to purchase from a particular store in the future if they have already purchased from them in the past.*

The paper immediately dives down into some serious math—the type that reminds me why I was an English major, specializing in Shakespeare. Needless to say, that math is there to validate the conversion model and compare it to several others. If you were *not* a Shakespeare major, you might like to download the whole paper from www.marketing.wharton.edu/people/faculty/fader.html.

It's all a matter of applying the right numbers to the right situation. If you run a portal, like Excite, your perspective is different. Kris Carpenter tells me they apply this type of data in a couple of ways:

> *The first is in understanding what sort of feature sets to prioritize, and it varies by application. There are certain daily usage applications, and we pay attention to the types of features that meet the needs of the user within that context. So if it's horoscopes, it's usually a quick information grab, sort of an entertainment-leisure kind of activity. If it's investing and it's a daily routine, there's activity associated with it, whether it be trading or portfolio analysis, and there're other dimensions to that activity that really need to be catered to or you lose the daily usage. So that's one dimension.*
>
> *The second dimension is understanding the demand on the advertising side for this particular type of user. In some cases the daily user is very much in demand by the advertising community. In other cases, the daily user is interesting, but isn't necessarily the premiere target demographic slice . . . that an advertiser might want to reach. So, we often will measure the quality of the usage as well as frequency.*

That stops me. I have to know: "How do you quantify quality?"
Kris doesn't miss a beat:

> *Quality has two primary dimensions to it. The first is just the fact that the user is engaged in a type of activity that signals a purchase intent. We may not know a ton about the users themselves, but if we know that they are engaged in researching or comparing two automobiles, there's a high probability that either they themselves are in a purchase process for an automobile or they're helping someone with that purchase process and can be an influencer in their purchasing decision.*
>
> *It's an example of a quality activity that doesn't have a very high frequency but shouldn't be discounted because it's very valuable from an advertiser perspective.*
>
> *The second dimension of that is a little bit harder to quantify but is one where when you say, okay, we have this body of users coming in the front door of our service. Now there's a large subset of those users navigating through the service in a particular pattern. So they're not just going into email, but they are going into investing and weather and sports and some other applications, whatever they may be. You have a user that has a certain pattern of behavior that is pretty regular, pretty consistent, and is something that an advertiser is pretty interested in.*
>
> *You can have a similar body of users with very similar demographics, but maybe they're going to personals, or an application where you have to be a little bit more creative with the type of campaign you run, and the advertising community is not quite as broad in their interests in meeting that particular audience.*

Several minutes later, I have Rene Bonvanie, vice president of Online Marketing for Oracle, on the phone, and recency/frequency is still on my mind. But, of course, Oracle has very different goals than Excite and the conversation bears that out.

Rene has assured me that they use their own tools in very sophisticated ways while analyzing the Oracle site. He's appropriately circumspect about revealing any competitive advantage information, so I ask him questions in hypothetical terms. "If you were to put in a system that could measure how quickly people move through the qualification process, and you could figure out a way to tweak things so that they could move through the qualification process faster, it doesn't necessarily mean they are more qualified, does it?"

"No," says Rene. "They are just more curious. It just means that you figured out a way to get them to specific pages faster. This is the learning curve that we are in right now. Is there a difference between someone taking a day or a week to go through the five or six or seven steps of the flow and someone who goes through it in five minutes? That's what we are trying to find out right now by looking into opportunities created against those profiles."

What's the progression through your qualification process look like? Have you mapped it out? A map of your qualification process (see Figure 11.7) will help determine roles and responsibilities, and it will be a guide to tracking your Web site visitors' momentum through your site.

Helping people move through that process is the positive side. But you also need to keep an eye on the negative side. You know about leakage—those pages where people just drift away—but there's also that frustrating moment when prospective buyers are on the cusp of placing the order and then back away.

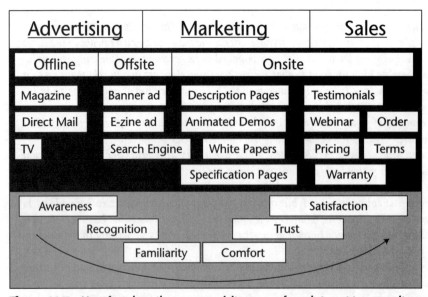

Figure 11.7 How fast does the average visitor move from interest to commitment on your site?

Abandonment

Matt Cutler and I tackled the issue of *abandonment* this way:

One of the curious characteristics of online sales is the shopping cart abandonment factor. In the bricks and mortar world, it is relatively rare for a shopper to fill a cart and then leave it and all of its contents without going through the checkout line. Yet this is a very common occurrence on Web sites. The reasons are many, with studies pointing to causes including poor site navigation and usability. How can a shopper be encouraged to become a buyer? By tracking, measurement, and management.

Online stores are taking action based on:

- *The ratio of abandoned carts to completed purchases per day*
- *The number of items per abandoned cart vs. completed transactions*
- *The profile of items abandoned versus purchased*
- *The profile of a shopper versus a buyer*

When a shopper with a profile resembling that of an abandoner begins placing items in a cart, or the list of items is very similar to those in carts abandoned in the past, a dynamic Web site can take action by offering special incentives or displaying messages regarding the ease of completing the purchase. The goal is to turn more shoppers into buyers. Watching shopping behavior for signs of trouble can prove profitable.

Suppose that shoppers at a business telephony Web site tend to buy two or three items at a time. When a shopping cart begins to fill with ten or twelve items, the activity might set off a trigger to include persuasive content on the next screen. The site might offer to open a business account for the shopper, or offer a chat session with an online service representative to discuss the shopper's needs.

Abandonment does not apply strictly to electronic shopping carts in online stores selling packaged goods. Any multi-step buying process may suffer from abandonment. An online brokerage wants to make sure that its users do not merely trade, but also add more funds to their portfolios. If a steadily trading client makes no deposits over a given period of time, the site might offer specialized consulting, education, or access to additional investment research.

Between clicking on a banner ad and making a purchase, there are many points where a prospective customer may fall out of the life cycle. The overall abandonment rate is the number of people who commence but do not complete the buying process. If the reason is a lack of qualification, you will need to adjust the mechanisms that attract people to your site. If the problem is poor site navigation, a new site design may be in order.

From "E-Metrics: Business Metrics for the New Economy"

So what can you learn by looking into a shopping cart? Kara Heinrichs, chief user experience officer at Fry Multimedia, is consumed with curiosity. She wants "to see what people thought was cool enough to consider, but not good enough to buy. But most people have no intention of buying; they use the cart to fill another information gap, like the need for shipping charges and so on.

"Often you can see that if they take it far enough, there is that huge desire, but there is either not enough product information or not enough sales information or persuasion that's done on the product page or on the details product page to push them over the edge to make that commitment."

Kara knows whereof she speaks. In a white paper called "Abandonment and Conversion" (April 30, 2001), Kara and Chris Grant, senior data analyst at Fry, made a very interesting point about the fitting room in department stores:

> *Shoppers also use carts to bridge information gaps—to keep running totals and uncover tax and shipping charges, for example. If we have to draw a parallel to a physical store, a Web site shopping cart functions more like a fitting room than a cart—it's the place to put things while you decide whether to buy. You walk away from those items for a lot of reasons but at that point the store design is unlikely to be a factor (though the checkout line might).*

I hadn't seen anything in Paco Underhill's *Why We Buy: The Science of Shopping* (Touchstone Books, 2000) about sifting through the things left behind in the fitting rooms. What a great missed opportunity, something that you can more easily do online than off. Kara continues:

> *We don't want to go so far as to say abandoned shopping carts are good, but we've learned from our own data and experience that they're not singularly bad, either. To an e-tailer, shopping carts (abandoned or otherwise) should be a measure of consumer interest. Rather than focusing solely on what percentage of carts are abandoned (consumer disinterest), e-tailers should recast the question and focus on what proportion of their visitors are interested enough to start a cart in the first place. Back-systems tell e-tailers what consumers purchase, but "abandoned" shopping carts reveal what they wanted to buy but didn't, which is infinitely more intriguing. (Imagine the cross-sell, personalization, and promotional possibilities there!) Abandoned carts are a huge source of valuable, but largely unmined, data.*
>
> *Data from our sites show that customers rarely buy on their first visit to an online store. They buy on their third through seventh visit, often 20 to 30 days after their first visit. The parallel to a physical store is easy to see. Unless you walk into a mall knowing exactly what you want and from where, you tend to window shop, compare products, perhaps try things on, maybe stop for a latté, and eventually decide to buy (or not); you may even leave and come back another day to complete the purchase.*

And so we come back to the Middling Magic Market and find Martin tracking his radar diagram over time (see Figure 11.8)

He's detecting the fact that people are staying or leaving, but he's only a bit closer to figuring out why. When Martin starts wiring up his e-commerce tracking system to his lava lamp for a full three-dimensional, interactive, real-time display of his Web site, that's the point where we leave him to his own devices. If a certain amount of abandonment is to be expected, what's reasonable?

The Atlas Institute (www.atlasdmt.com) is the research and education arm of Atlas DMT, a provider of digital marketing management systems and an operating unit of Avenue A, Inc. The Atlas Institute analyzed drop-off data from twenty-six advertisers in four 1-month periods in 2000, to determine when a prospective customer leaves, or "drops off," a Web site prior to completing a purchase or registration:

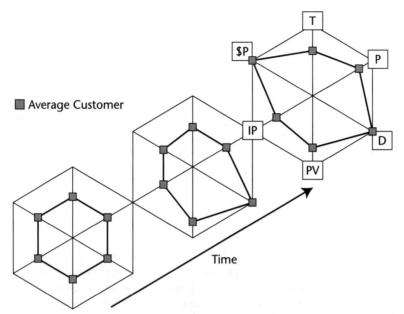

Figure 11.8 Martin Middling realizes that the increase in revenues will happen, but it's a matter of time.

Web sites within high consideration industries (finance and computer electronics) [>$500] exhibited the highest drop-off rates of all industry categories (generally greater than 80%), whereas Web sites within low consideration industries (health and beauty, recreation, and food) [<$100] displayed the lowest rates (generally lower than 40%). Drop-off rates by business model revealed that e-commerce had the highest drop-off rate followed by e-content and mixed model sites.

Atlas is then kind enough to offer the sort of advice you'd expect: Measure and compare your site's drop-off rates to benchmarks for your industry, and if your drop-off rates are significantly higher, take steps to find and fix the problem. But they stop short of telling us where such industry numbers can be found.

As of this writing, Vividence (www.vividence.com) hasn't broken down their abandonment numbers by industry, but they do give us an interesting look at the top reasons for cart abandonment in a press release issued on November 5, 2001. They evaluated the experiences of 719 consumers as they used shopping carts on e-commerce sites, and they came up with this list:

- High shipping prices (72%)
- Comparison shopping or browsing (61%)
- Changed mind (56%)
- Saving items for later purchase (51%)
- Total cost of items is too high (43%)
- Checkout process is too long (41%)

- Checkout requires too much personal information (35%)
- Site requires registration before purchase (34%)
- Site is unstable or unreliable (31%)
- Checkout process is confusing (27%)

That's why companies like NetGenesis create tools like CartSmarts, which, in their own words, "creates a set of over 40 automated reports, such as Purchase Path Conversion, Shopping Cart Activity, Purchase Frequency & Recency, and Acquisition Source, that enable e-commerce companies to better understand online visitor behavior patterns within the context of the online shopping cart environment." Bingo.

Conversion

So much for the abandonment side of the coin. Let's turn that coin over and look at the positive side: When people really do make a purchase. Your qualification map can include a lot of checkpoints, all available for factoring into a most-likely-to-become-a-customer number. The variety of elements companies use to track their Web sites is directly proportional to the number of Web site managers I spoke with.

Do people show up at all? That's a necessity. But then what? Do they just look around? Or do they get involved?

Participation

When Matt Cutler and I put out the e-metrics white paper, we asked for feedback. We wanted to show we had at least read *The Cluetrain Manifesto* (Locke, et al., Perseus Books, 2001). We understood that "markets are conversations," and we were trying to start one. It worked.

Right off the bat, we got a message from Elizabeth Van Couvering, a senior interactive strategist at Organic (www.organic.com), in the company's London office.

> *Rather than looking at the customer life-cycle funnel, which ends with conversion, you need to focus on loyalty metrics, which you touch on in section 12 of the paper. [And we do again in this book, in Chapter 12, "Maximizing Customer Information: The Personalization Continuum"].*
>
> *Your aim with these customers is retention and the creation of advocacy (possibly also upsell). You go on two principles: increased contact increases retention and increased positive interaction increases advocacy.*
>
> *I would therefore add a final layer to your funnel, called "Dialogue," which begins when your customer has their first post-purchase interaction with you. I would define a key site metric, call it "Engagement," as the number of "interactive" contacts divided by the number of "passive" contacts. What do you reckon?*

We reckoned that we were actually dealing with an hourglass, rather than a funnel. We also realized that the participation measurement of the hourglass could come both before *and* after the conversion (see Figure 11.9).

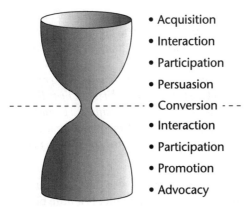

- Acquisition
- Interaction
- Participation
- Persuasion
- Conversion - - -
- Interaction
- Participation
- Promotion
- Advocacy

Figure 11.9 Tracking interaction and participation can be indicative of buying propensity and loyalty.

How often do they run the product configurator? The color selector? The financing calculations? Keeping track of what people do as well as what they look at can provide vital clues to their behavior.

Registration

Do you run a transactional site? According to Brian Ferry, group president of Strategy, Products and Technology for Monster.com, everything is a transaction. Brian doesn't worry about whether people buy gloves with their sweaters. He doesn't pay close attention to whether they buy more if the picture of the product is a little bigger or a little smaller. That's because his site doesn't sell stuff; it sells sell information and match-making services.

"User interaction, whether they like the site enough to create an account and put their resumé online, is one of the metrics we use. That's the success of the site, that's not really Web traffic-related. It's more functions and features on the site." Monster.com tries to match employers with employees. They focus on improving the search capabilities and the browse capabilities so that people are more likely to find a good match, and so that paying advertisers are likelier to come back.

"The bottom line,"says Brian, "is applications. I track how many people view a job that has been posted, and how many apply for a job."

Brian's got a virtuous cycle to feed. The more people who look at jobs, the more will apply. The more that apply, the happier the advertiser. The happier the advertiser, the more they pay to advertise more jobs.

We have a resumé acquisition cost which is based on a percentage of marketing costs versus number of resumés required. We know currently it costs us x dollars to get a resumé, so if I was to spend $250,000 on a new feature to help people create resumés, I'd know right away if it was worthwhile. We monitor if there is any increase in effectiveness because we tell our salespeople to tell their clients how to get better throughput or better conversion.

We also want to know how our clients are using their job posting inventory. They might buy a hundred job pack, and we want to track how they are actually using that inventory to put into revenue forecast models. Are clients using them up right away or are they going to use it up over 3 months?

We have more customers and jobs than any other niche site, and we need to be able to reinforce that with our salespeople. Like tech jobs—IT jobs—there are some sites out there that claim to have more, but that's not the case. We have ten times more traffic of IT professionals than anyone else. So we need to keep track of how clients and applicants are using the site and then follow the traffic by industry and segment, and obviously all the revenue reporting and cost reporting.

Do you worry about whether people buy gloves with their sweaters? Do you pay close attention to whether they buy more if the picture of the product is a little bigger or a little smaller? Does your site sell stuff?

Merchandizing

According to Forrester Research in their August 2001, "The ROI of Selling Online" report, it's possible to boost shopping basket sizes with bare-bones merchandising. "It doesn't take much for consumers picking up replenishment items to toss additional items into their shopping carts to justify shipping costs. Replenishers like DuaneReade.com will find that even one-size-fits-all merchandising—no personalized anything—works just as well as the end caps in their stores—and can generate 18% of cROI [companywide ROI]."

Remember what Kara Heinrichs of Fry Multimedia said about A/B split testing in Chapter 10? They put up two different pages and watch to see which helps people navigate the site better.

Kara turns that approach toward sales: "If you put merchandise on a home page, the more expensive the merchandise, within reason, the higher the average order size. We think it's aspirational. If you put the great stuff out there, people may not buy the great stuff, and they often don't—we didn't actually see a bump in that particular merchandise being purchased—but more people bought more stuff."

The Hammacher Schlemmer catalogue always has their most expensive items on the cover of their catalog. Turns out it works online as well.

Merchandizing is all about showing the right product at the right time. With the advent of dynamic content servers, we can engage in a three-step process of calculating when to cross-sell and up-sell and which offers are best by guessing, testing, and letting the computer figure it out.

The Smoke-Filled Room

"Look," says Sandy, "everybody needs to buy a new blouse or shirt when they pick up a sweater. It's one of those unwritten laws of shopping."

"Uhm," hesitates Harry. "I'm sure you're right, but only 12 percent of our shoppers buy a blouse or shirt when they buy a sweater."

"That's because they don't see the blouses! Put a picture of a color-coordinated blouse on every page that has a sweater and you'll see sales go up. No question. Case closed."

"Well, uh . . . okay."

Will it work? Probably. Is it a repeatable process?

In 1993, the Software Engineering Institute at Carnegie Mellon University (www.sei.cmu.edu) came up with a Maturity Model for software engineering. (You are keeping in mind that a Web site is a software application, right?) This model consists of five stages: initial, repeatable, defined, managed, and optimizing.

They describe these stages as follows:

1. **Initial.** *The software process is characterized as ad hoc, and occasionally even chaotic. Few processes are defined, and success depends on individual effort.*

2. **Repeatable.** *Basic project management processes are established to track cost, schedule, and functionality. The necessary process discipline is in place to repeat earlier successes on projects with similar applications.*

3. **Defined.** *The software process for both management and engineering activities is documented, standardized, and integrated into a standard software process for the organization. All projects use an approved, tailored version of the organization's standard software process for developing and maintaining software.*

4. **Managed.** *Detailed measures of the software process and product quality are collected. Both the software process and products are quantitatively understood and controlled.*

5. **Optimizing.** *Continuous process improvement is enabled by quantitative feedback from the process and from piloting innovative ideas and technologies.*

It would seem that Sandy and Harry are caught in stage 1. Yes, their brilliant ideas might produce more sales, but they don't have a method. You can't just put your direct reports in a room and say, "Be brilliant!" Eventually, they're going to run out of good ideas. You won't know when they do until you get serious about moving from guessing to trying, and that gets expensive.

Sandy is smug (as usual) when Harry reads the following week's reports. "Sales of blouses purchased with sweaters are up 6 percent."

"See? It's a natural. Now, here's my next idea. . . ."

Trial and Error

My parents spent a few days with us at Christmas. It was wonderful—one of those times with your family that was pleasant, relaxed, and everybody seemed to enjoy themselves. It was perfect— except for the toaster.

Why our Sunbeam Model 3802 Toast Logic gave up the ghost while my father was trying to acclimate himself to a strange kitchen first thing in the morning is a mystery for the ages, but as this was the worst speed bump of our holiday gathering, I was only too happy to accept it as fate.

In my zeal to get a great deal on a replacement during the post-Christmas sale-a-thons, I wandered over to macys.com and found a perfectly serviceable Hamilton Beach IntelliToast 2-Slice Toaster for under 20 bucks (see Figure 11.10).

The right column contained a couple of other items "you might also like," such as a Circulon Hard Anodized Nonstick 11-Piece Set of cooking pots and an Anolon Professional Masher.

I was intrigued by the choice. After all, I was interested in a toaster. Wouldn't this be a prime opportunity to offer me a toaster cover? Or perhaps a tray to set underneath to capture the crumbs that inevitably escape in the course of toast making? Why cookware and a masher?

That's when I realized that macys.com was probably just throwing spaghetti at the wall.

"Ever since Sandy and Harry ran out of ideas, we'll just let the computer come up with random suggestions" is the sound reasoning I imagined behind this approach.

I hit the Refresh button and was told I might also like an Anolon Professional Open Stir Fry Pan, 12" or a Circulon Solid Spoon (see Figure 11.11).

Figure 11.10   macys.com was happy to sell me a toaster, but also offered some things "you might also like."

Figure 11.11   macys.com was doing its best to find something, anything, I might also like.

In subsequent refreshed displays, it was suggested that I might also like:

Calphalon Commercial Anodized Stirfry Pan, 10"

Circulon Ladle

Emerilware 7-Piece Set

OXO Good Grips Tools

All-Clad Stainless Fry Pan, 10"

KitchenAid High Density 12" Grill Pan

Anolon Professional Solid Spoon

All-Clad 2.5-Quart Casserole Plus Julia Child Cookbook

Anolon Professional Strainer Spoon

Anolon Professional Turner

. . . and a George Foreman "The Champ" Grill, before the suggested items started to randomly repeat.

I asked macys.com Vice President of Marketing Kara Parsons how those items were selected, and she replied that they are "strategic merchandising tools that fluctuate based on the different promotional times of the year. They're not based on overstock positions."

Then I asked how well this cross-selling effort was working and she replied, "We aren't able to track the cross-selling clicks to purchase." So I don't have to feel guilty about there being too many George Foreman Grills in the back room. The people at macys.com are not alone in their inability to keep track. This is tough stuff.

As Dave Chambers, director of customer relationship management at Kmart's Blue-Light.com, put it in a *Reuters* article (March 11, 2000): "There has been a lot of buzz about personalization and one-to-one marketing, but the reality is we've got a long way to go. Everything that is being reported is well ahead of the actual reality." The article said that most online stores admit they don't have three-dimensional, head-to-toe profiles of customers just by tracking their mouse clicks. "It's kind of like saying it is easy to solve world hunger because you know how to plant food," said Chambers.

Keeping track of all the permutations and which ones might be more successful than others is an enormous task. You'd need a *computer* to manage that much information. Lucky for us we've got computers, eh?

Calculated Commerce

What if you could combine a dynamic content server with a system that would keep track of each successful sale and create a statistical model of how to induce more of the same?

There's a company in Newburyport, Massachusetts, called Genalytics (www.genalytics. com) that offers up some compelling technology. Here's how they describe it:

Proprietary and patent-pending evolutionary algorithms are the power behind the Genalytics technology. Evolutionary algorithms allow our applications to automatically generate superior predictive models and provide intelligent e-marketing solutions. Benefits include:

  Real-time customer behavior predictions

  Scoring and model generation scalability

  Dynamically adaptive predictive models

  High-volume customer data analyses

  Online and offline data evaluation

Genalytics utilizes Java and CORBA technology to ensure portability and completely distributed applications. Our applications are compatible with Sun's Java2 ORB and Inprise's VisiBroker for Java, and they run on any Java-enabled platform.

Here's how I describe it: Start with the end result you're after, let's say sales. You want to make more sales online. That's a reasonable goal. Take all of the information you have (and the more the merrier) and drop it all into one happy data set.

You've got technographics, and demographics, and clickstream data, and preferences, and implicit information, and explicit information, and sales data, and then some. You hand all of this data over to Genalytics and they ask a simple question: Of all the people who did what we wanted them to do (buy something), what traits do they have in common that separate them from the rest of the herd? Now that's a pretty straightforward question, but it's fundamentally important to what they do next, so let me clarify.

One hundred people walk into the showroom and twenty-five of them buy a car. (It was a very good day.) What do the buyers have in common?

- *They had looked at other cars already.*
- *They were preapproved for financing.*
- *They'd done research for their car online.*
- *They came in the morning instead of the afternoon.*
- *They came in pairs (couples).*
- *They were between 35 and 55 years old.*
- *They drove up in a late-model vehicle.*
- *They asked for a salesperson rather than waiting for one to notice them.*

If you knew this much about the people walking onto your car lot, you'd know right away which ones were the most likely to buy and, therefore, which to spend your time with. But if you ask everybody all of these questions, you're not saving any time at all. The trick is to figure out the fewest of the traits listed above that are indicative of automobile buyers.

Some of these attributes, although shared by the buyers, were also found in those who came, looked, and split. So we create a statistical model that says that the only information we have about all the people who came in is recorded in numbers 1, 2, and 3. How good an indicator is that of their propensity to buy? Let's say the answer is 6. Is 6 good? Doesn't matter. What matters is that we do it again.

What if all we know about all the people who came in is 1, 2, 4, and 7. How good an indicator is that of their propensity to buy? 4. Hmmm. How about 1, 3, 4 and 7? 12. Ahhhh, now we're getting somewhere. It doesn't matter what the answers are, as long as we can compare them to see which is going to give us the best results. Which attributes best predict the desired outcome?

It might be that number 3 is all you need to know. If they've done their research online before coming into the showroom, then you know there is a sale waiting to be made. The problem is that building these statistical models is a bear. It takes a well-educated mathematician more than a while to put one together, much less all of the permutations of eight possible attributes. That's where Genalytics comes in.

When they say evolutionary algorithms, they mean that the software creates statistical models and then mutates them on the fly. So they can "automatically generate superior predictive models." Their software generates something like 200 models every second and compares them all to determine the most clairvoyant attributes.

In a nutshell, they take all of your data, crunch it down to the nth degree and tell you that the people who come to your Web site before lunch, using Internet Explorer, who click on the Products button and then the Specifications button, are statistically more likely to buy your product if you show them the Limited Time Offer banner on the home page. Nifty.

From World Wide Web Marketing, Third Edition *(John Wiley & Sons, 2001)*

Seducible Moments

If you're not in a position to make use of the latest and greatest in patent-pending evolutionary algorithms, you can still make the most of your site by keeping an eye on the seduction factor.

Julie Khaslavsky and Nathan Shedroff wrote how "seduction is an aspect of the growing field of captology, the study of how technologies persuade" in their article "Understanding the Seductive Experience" (Communications of the ACM, May 1999). They pointed out the three phases of seduction—enticement, relationship, and fulfillment—which are closely related to advertising, marketing, and sales.

The relationship phase works if the customer experiences growth. "As long as the user is growing emotionally or intellectually in some way due to the experience, the product or experience will be viewed as valuable, even if the experience is essentially unchanged during the lifetime of the product." So how do you recognize a seduction in process? How do you know your Web site is properly seducing your visitors? Khaslavsky and Shedroff wrote about software (we *are* remembering that a Web site is a software application, right?), and they suggested asking yourself whether your software (site):

- Entices you by diverting your attention
- Surprises you with something novel
- Goes beyond obvious needs and expectations
- Creates an instinctive emotional response
- Espouses values or connects to personal goals
- Makes inherent promises to fulfill these goals
- Leads you to discover something deeper than what you expected
- Fulfills small promises related to your values and aspirations

To be measurable, you have to narrow down the seduction process to specific transactions. The e-metrics white paper describes seducible moments as "those junctures where a prospect is exceptionally susceptible to an offer."

It may be the rapid purchase button next to a desired product—or an up-sell offer at the moment a customer is deciding between two service choices. A seducible moment does not have to be product-related—it may be the point where a user must decide to join a discussion group or subscribe to a newsletter. The right encouragement or the right graphic might just do the trick—seducible moments will be different on every site.

Rough patches, on the other hand, diminish the momentum or the speed at which a browser becomes a buyer. Rough patches often appear as those places where the shape of the customer life-cycle funnel suddenly gets narrower because many users are abandoning the process.

Reviewing the profiles of the members of a given market segment reveals different attributes of those slow to decide and those quick to buy. Skewing your promotional efforts toward those with a higher velocity rating can have a direct effect on bottom line sales,

*while altering your persuasion techniques to those who are slow and need more assurance
may bring in buyers who have previously been considered unacquirable.*

First, get people to the site. Next, entice them into placing items in their shopping
carts. The roughest patch on most commerce sites is the checkout line. Getting people
to hit the Place Order button is a neat trick, and we can discuss abandonment all day
long. But what you can learn from measuring the behavior of buyers can be directly
applied to making more sales.

The Checkout Line

Grocery stores have been tracking what's in your cart since the day they installed
checkout scanners. Retail stores have mastered the art of cross-sell and up-sell by training their sales representatives to review the items you bring to the register and make
suggestions. A Web site gets to see what you look at, what you put in your cart, what
you take out of your cart, what you end up buying, and what you return. All the while,
it can make suggestions and recommendations on how well this tie will go with that
shirt, how well this toolbox will hold that wrench set, and how well this passport
holder will match that wallet.

So what can you learn from tracking a few numbers and how can that impact conversion?

What is the ratio of browsers to shoppers? (Shoppers, in this case, are people who
actually put things in the cart.) Forget benchmarks—your site is unique. Just focus on
improving the numbers you record day to day and month to month.

What is the ratio of shoppers to buyers? It's great that you got more people to put
things in carts, but are you hurting or helping the shop-to-purchase ratio?

How many page views are there and how much time does it take for the average
browser to make a selection and place an item in the cart? Can you shorten either of
those?

What items do people examine most but add to their carts least? In other words,
which items get the most page views but the least sales? What is it that's enticing people to look but fails to get them to seriously consider a purchase?

Which items are most frequently placed in the shopping basket and then removed?

What does the shopping cart of a real buyer usually contain? What about the average abandoner?

What is the ratio of shoppers to buyers?

Is it all worthwhile? Kara Heinrichs at Fry Multimedia thinks so. "If I can tell you
where in the checkout process somebody drops out and what percentage of users actually get through it successfully, that totally tells you what you can do on your site to fix
it."

Obviously, the numbers you derive from plumbing the depths of shopping carts can
also tell you a great deal about merchandise trends. What are people interested in
today? Which services are getting more attention? Which colors seem more popular?
Which add-on components are the most desirable?

Cost of Conversions

Since "cost of sales" is a formal, generally accepted accounting principal type of measurement, let's talk in terms of Cost Per Conversion. Here's how we described it in the e-metrics white paper:

> *If you spent $25,000 on marketing programs, acquired 5,000 users for your efforts, and 5% of these prospects converted—resulting in 250 new paying customers—the cost per conversion was $100. This is good if you are selling real estate to high-income professionals but not sustainable if you are selling stationery to students. The cost per conversion is the number that marketing people use to determine the best investment of their promotional budget. Spending $2 million on a Super Bowl ad campaign may seem like a large check to write. But if the resulting traffic and sales produce an acquisition and conversion cost below alternative means, the cost may not be so alarming.*

$$\text{Cost Per Conversion} = \frac{\text{Advertising and Promotional Costs}}{\text{Number of Sales}}$$

Net yield *determines the effectiveness of a multi-step process where incremental costs are not available, such as creative/banner testing or the comparison of two paths leading to the same goal.*

Here are two examples to help illustrate how net yield calculations can help in your decision-making processes:

Banner A had a high click rate, but a low conversion to sale. Banner B had a low click rate, but a high conversion to sale. By comparing the net yield calculations for Banner A against Banner B, you can quickly identify the better-performing banner.

For a Web-based contest, some users might receive an intermediate jump page before the registration page, while others might land on the entry form immediately. To determine the optimal path in terms of conversion, the net yield would be calculated by dividing the total number of contest entries by the total entry page visits. This lets you determine if the interstitial jump page helps users understand the contest and makes form completion more likely, or if it gets in the way and causes abandonment before the form is filled out.

$$\text{Net Yield} = \frac{\text{Total Promotion Cost}}{\text{Total Promotion Results}}$$

Keep in mind that conversion does not always mean sales. The director of e-business at a large energy company told me they measure success by how many people pay their bills online:

> *We are more interested in how many transactions we're accomplishing on the Web site. The goal of the Web site is to provide an alternate payment channel, and so the metric we focus on is how many we drove off the phone and into the Web site. And so we have probably 10, 15, or 20 different metrics around those transactions. We measure whether you turn your service on, you pay your bills, you make a credit arrangement, you find out more about some of our products. So we believe that if you're doing it on the Web site, that's more important to us than if you just read some information about it and then call.*

Cost per Revenue

In a white paper called "Evolution of Online Advertising Metrics" (DMT's Atlas Institute, www.atlasdmt.com/media/pdfs/insights/AIDMICostRevenueMetric.pdf), Erik Snowberg, senior marketing analyst, came up with a cost per revenue (CPR) that "takes into account the actual revenue generated from particular sites and channels, allowing advertisers to consider both the number of transactions *and* the dollar size of the transactions.

"CPR measures how much it costs an advertiser to generate a dollar of revenue from a particular site or channel. For example, if a given site on a media buy generated a CPR of 0.2, it means that it cost $0.20 for every dollar the site produced in revenue."

The Atlas Institute did a study examining the correlation between cost per revenue and cost per sale for BestBuy.com and learned that all sales are *not* created equal:

> *Some site populations efficiently produce a high number of sales, but with low average order sizes. Conversely, we see cases of sites that produced few sales but resulted in high total sales revenue.*
>
> *This relationship showed that optimizing based on cost per revenue can produce better financial results than optimizing solely on cost per sale. Thirty percent of the [advertising] sites that Best Buy and their Avenue A team decided to retain in the media plan based on cost per revenue would have been dropped had they optimized on cost per sale alone. Optimization resulted in a 36% decrease in cost per revenue across their media plan."*

So don't just count on getting people to come to your site. Don't just count on getting people to buy things. Measure your cost per revenue to build advertising campaigns that more accurately deliver on their business goals.

VALUING EACH PROMOTION

Ashley Friedlein, CEO of e-consultancy (www.e-consultancy.com) and author of *Web Project Management: Delivering Successful Commercial Web Sites* **(Morgan Kaufmann Publishers, 2000) occasionally posts to the UK Net Marketing email list (www.chinwag.com/uk-netmarketing). In November 2001, Ashley posted the results of a few advertising campaigns he ran:**

"I absolutely believe that Web analytics is worth its return on investment salt—if done properly. As others have pointed out, you need people who know what they are doing to make it work. Just one area where I have seen significant impact is in measuring the value of inbound traffic resulting from advertising spending to optimize ROI. Case study below:

In order to promote www.e-consultancy.com, a number of text adverts were placed in third-party newsletters. The target market is UK e-business professionals so we could be fairly precise. Here are the actual results from three different newsletters (site names not given for obvious reasons):

Continues

VALUING EACH PROMOTION (CONTINUED)

Site: A
E-mails sent: 2,750
Cost: £45
No. of clickthroughs: 204
No. of resulting conversions: 56
View/conversion rate: 2.04%
Average Customer Acquisition Cost: £0.80

Site: B
E-mails sent: 41,000
Cost: £900
No. of clickthroughs: 48
No. of resulting conversions: 16
View/conversion rate: 0.04%
Average Customer Acquisition Cost: £56.25

Site: C
E-mails sent: 6,000
Cost: £350
No. of clickthroughs: 80
No. of resulting conversions: 18
View/conversion rate: 0.3%
Average Customer Acquisition Cost: £19.44

Let us discount for the moment the effect that the creative, timing of the campaign, etc. had—we used pretty much the same approach for each. The points about Web analytics are more the following:

1. You need to know what you are trying to achieve. Your strategy should form the basis for defining appropriate targets, metrics, and benchmarks. E-consultancy.com [is] interested primarily in UK e-business professionals at CEO, Director, or Consultant level. There is a target customer acquisition cost of <£10.

2. You need to then craft your analytic capabilities to answer your commercial needs.

In the above example, we were able to track response and conversion rates to work out the average customer acquisition cost. What the results don't show, however, is that we also tracked *who* the resulting registrants from each campaign were. This means that we could also gauge the quality and value of registrant each site delivered against our target profile.

"Show me the money" . . . As you might guess, we're still enjoying a good relationship with site A. We negotiated a free campaign out of site C based on the fact that we had to pay twice our target customer acquisition cost first time round. And site B agreed that we needn't pay them anything at all unless they could do a whole lot better.

Clearly the scale involved in this case was small but the principles are the same. You cannot manage what you cannot measure and you cannot measure what you cannot define. Any e-business that is not seriously interested in Web analytics should think again."

Profits above All

The final measurement, of course, is whether you're driving sales of more profitable products. The following lesson was not learned from a Web site but is unquestionably applicable.

I gave a full-day seminar in Sao Paulo at a business conference and then had to walk a mile in my students' shoes the next day as I listened to a series of presenters via simultaneous translation. Most conferences are tedious anyway (which is why I work so hard at giving presentations), but this was actually painful—except for one presentation.

The data mining manager from a Brazilian grocery store told the story of a marketing program gone wrong. They came up with a plan to get more people in the store with a contest. The more often you shop, the more chances you had to win. The contest lived up to the goal brilliantly.

More sales were made in the next 2 months than they had ever made before. Store traffic was sky-high. Everybody was pleased and they decided to run the contest again, until the CFO pulled the plug. It turns out that, during those 2 months, the chain store recorded the lowest profitability ever. There would be no advertising of anything other than the standard promotions for the next 3 months to make up for it.

The head of marketing was fit to be tied. What happened? They met their goals. He worked with the data mining technicians until the light dawned.

1. The prizes were toasters, coffeemakers, and boom boxes—things that would appeal to the vast majority of their customers.

2. They had offered a new chance to win each time a customer went through the checkout line, so people went through the lines two and three times rather than once. That increased the time it took to serve them, raising the overhead in personnel time and the cost of printing receipts and bagging the food.

3. The vast majority of their customers are very low income and purchased only the lowest margin food items.

The solution was to create a new contest, limit the chances to win to one per day, and offer different prizes. This time they offered a Rolls-Royce, a diamond necklace, and a world cruise. The new contest caused a very small increase in store traffic, but dramatically raised profits for the month. The 3 percent of their customers who could afford the finer things in life (champagne and imported delicacies) came to the store more often and bought more high-margin items.

EBAGS CASE STUDY: EBAGS RAISES SALES CONVERSION RATES 150 PERCENT WITH HIGHLY FOCUSED TESTS

Peter Cobb, eBags cofounder and vice president of marketing, is always one of the most popular speakers at marketing events because (a) he's not a vendor trying to sell something and (b) he gives great presentations packed with numbers, useful tips, and hands-on revelations. So we were pleased when he agreed to be interviewed for the following case study.

Continues

EBAGS CASE STUDY: EBAGS RAISES SALES CONVERSION RATES 150 PERCENT WITH HIGHLY FOCUSED TESTS (CONTINUED)

Challenge:

Like many e-commerce companies, eBags has had to tighten its belt and focus on profitability recently. The marketing department cut its PR budget and ceased all offline and much online advertising that cost money. Peter Cobb, vice president of marketing, says, "It's all about really buckling down."

His official goals as of January 1, 2001, were to increase site traffic, build the prospect database and improve conversion rates . . . while spending less money.

Campaign:

eBags got very targeted, very fast. Cobb set up three key committees, each including both marketing and IT staffers who were focused on finding a data-driven answer to improving marketing. Cobb says, "These are SWAT teams."

Each committee meets for an intensive hour once a week, during which time they review the data from the past week's tests and hammer out plans for the next week's tests.

1. The committee to increase traffic at lowest (or no) cost, while growing the company's prospect database has tested:

   - Sweepstakes offers to encourage people to opt-in to the email program

   - Pop-up boxes versus offers incorporated into the regular screen

   - Placing sweepstakes pop-ups on third-party Web sites who allow them to run the campaign for free in exchange for a co-registration button on the box

2. The committee to improve effectiveness of the email marketing programs that are sent to the database has tested:

   - Offers including percents off versus dollars off, free shipping, and free airmiles

   - "Cutesy versus inviting" subject lines

   - Size, number, and layout of photographs on screen

   - Text versus html

   - Special offer emails versus quick travel tips versus newsy informational newsletters

3. The committee to grow sales conversion through effective site and shopping cart process design has tested:

   - Using graphics for navigation on the home page versus a "Yahoo!-style" text directory

   - Site load time

   - The colors and shape of the site's navigation tabs

   - Layout of landing pages when people click through from email offers

Continues

EBAGS CASE STUDY: EBAGS RAISES SALES CONVERSION RATES 150 PERCENT WITH HIGHLY FOCUSED TESTS (CONTINUED)

- Size and placement of photographs on pages
- Adding a box for shoppers to enter their zip code into so they can tell when their order will arrive
- Every (and we mean every!) possible detail during the purchasing process that might decrease shopping cart abandonment

eBags runs all campaigns using in-house technology, including 12 servers, so it's fairly easy for the company to split out test cells. For example, if the site committee wants to test photographs appearing on the left versus right side of the page, they can split the site's traffic into two streams, and serve a different version of the page to each. Cobb says you need a test cell of about 10,000 visitors (or emails) to get statistically reliable results.

Results:

Back when eBags launched in 1998, the site's conversion rate of traffic to buyers was about 1%—which is a respectable figure in e-retail land. Now eBags converts an average of 2.5-3% of all visitors to buyers—which is highly impressive.

Cobb says, "It's the beauty of the Internet. I can put something up and within five minutes I can change the price or the photo, or if it's sold out I can remove it completely. When a print catalog goes out, you can't do that."

Here are some specific test results:

- ◆ Out of all the site design tests, the most significant factor by far was load time (the speed at which a page appears on a visitor's screen). Cobb says, "Conversion rates are 10-20% better on faster pages. It doesn't sound like much, but in our business you look for slight increases."

    So, the team wound up going with a Yahoo!-style home page directory because it loaded much more quickly.

- ◆ eBags has been able to reduce its shopping cart abandonment rate by 20% by tweaking each one of the five pages in the purchasing process. Cobb says, "Keep it simple. Show people exactly what they're buying, what they're saving, and where they are in the process." The zip code entry box, which helps people find out when their purchases will arrive, has also helped by "absolutely" cutting down on in-bound customer service calls.

- ◆ Although testing pop-up boxes for the sweepstakes opt-in offer was initially controversial amongst eBags staffers, the test proved so successful that the company has implemented pop-ups on an ongoing basis.

- ◆ When the pop-up sweeps offers appear as a co-branded offer on third-party sites, an average of 8% of visitors sign up, 75% of whom specifically choose to be added to eBags' list or on both the host site's list and eBags' list.

Continues

EBAGS CASE STUDY: EBAGS RAISES SALES CONVERSION RATES 150 PERCENT WITH HIGHLY FOCUSED TESTS (CONTINUED)

♦ These sweeps entrants immediately receive a "thank you" email from eBags. The offer that works the best is a 20% off coupon. Seven percent of "thank you" email recipients click through to the store, and of these a total of 5% convert to buyers. So the conversion rate for these email campaigns is about double the site's average conversion rate!

♦ eBags' other regular email campaigns to opt-ins and customers generate an average 8% click-through rate. These campaigns are responsible for 90% of all repeat purchases!

The special offer messages tend to work the best, but the newsletter style messages also have their fans and enhance the site's credibility. The "cutesy" subject lines were definitely *not* winners though. Bigger pictures tend to work better than smaller ones, but this must be juggled versus download time concerns.

eBags' buyer follow-up campaign, whereby buyers get an email 30 days after their purchase that solicits testimonials and product ratings (and incidentally also includes a 20% off coupon), has been so successful that the company just instituted an annual campaign as well. Now buyers get an email a full year later, also soliciting product feedback (plus offering the coupon). Note: Cobb is interested in partnering with other consumer sites to grow his sweeps pop-up campaign. You'll get a co-branded pop-up for your home page that will help you grow your own opt-in database. Interested? Contact him at peter@ebags.com

Reproduced with permission from www.MarketingSherpa.com, 05/04/2001

So while you're patting yourself on the back for counting more than page views, don't forget to track those sales all the way to the bottom line.

Sales Rep Sales

For those of you who sell directly to large, corporate clients using field sales representatives, the Web has been a channel challenge from the beginning. By now, I hope, you've figured out ways to avoid having the Web cannibalize sales from the commissioned sales team and you've turned it into a lead generation machine for them. That's the first step to determining whether the Web is working for you or against you and your sales reps.

Lead Generation for the Sales Team

A corporate communications executive for a Fortune 500 company that earns a living from selling systems integration and technology support services told me his site doesn't do much in the way of e-commerce aside from some consumable supplies sales.

Most of his contracts are with large companies and are in the multiple millions of dollars:

There are things like continuing or upgrading a warranty, stuff like that. And, if you consider customer support e-commerce, we have that but it's not actually paying for stuff over the Web. Our goals are pretty simple. Our main goal is to generate leads.

We have ways that prospects can contact various people. People tend to like to contact someone in their own vicinity, so we have contact names and numbers and email addresses for people around the world. It's all consultative types of selling. No one comes to us and sees the site and says "Oh, I want one of those" or "I need a complete billing solution. I think I'll buy one."

I don't think we've ever had a sale that was really less than a 6- to 10-week process. So our intent is purely to generate leads, so we try to motivate calls to action whenever possible, get information from people as they traverse the site, invite them to seminars and online presentations, and yada, yada, yada.

I ask if they're tracking their promotions-to-leads ratios and if they measure the quality of their leads. He replies:

Generally, the leads end up in our call centers where they are further qualified. We have a plan in place to do more of that on the Web. So by asking more and more in-depth questions, we'll get them to self-qualify. It's a hell of a lot cheaper to do on the Web.

It's a big project to get people to think through the process so that they can self-qualify, because we cater to so many diverse industries and types of clients that one size certainly doesn't fit all. One size rarely fits two. What we watch is people drilling down the click paths to where we can tell that they are serious. And we relate that back to the method of promotion. You know, when we ran a radio ad, it had no effect, but when we run ads in Computerworld, it works for us. We put up special pages for individual promotional activities so it's easy to track, whether it's a trade show handout or an ad in a magazine. We recently had a recruiting effort going on where we stuck the URL on the side of a van and drove it around the parking lots of competitors that are having struggles and laying people off. It was a perfect opportunity and real cheap way to get a lot of good leads.

I'm curious about the calculations. I want to know if there's a dollar figure attached to acquiring a lead, and then passing it along to the sales team.

"We can rarely trace a single lead to a single sale. We can track an increase in people visiting our Web site based on a certain type of ad or a promotion, but we are not very good as yet at tracking that lead through the entire process to a sale. A lead costs about a dollar if a pure sale comes through the Web, about $25 through a call center, and it's about $500 to $750 depending on the country for a live sales call. But it's always going to wind up as a live sales call anyway; it's just how many of them, how qualified are they, and how many prospects can one hit with live people?"

A large test and measurement technology company I spoke with calls it demand creation. Their Internet director spells out the sequence "demand creation creates leads which creates opportunities which creates a funnel opportunity which creates a quote which creates an order.

"So," he continues, "we're setting that whole process up to have traceablity. We finally figured out how to get from funnel opportunity to a quote, because that was from our sales force system across to order processing. We finally figured out how to make it so it is an advantage to the sales guy to do it the way we want, which then makes the association. We decreased the amount of [data entry] keying he had to do and set up an administrative support process that says feed your quote request to these people; they'll create a quote. When you feed the quote request you have to feed your funnel number, and we gave them a little tool on their laptop that says you have a funnel number with an order, enter it here, and we will automatically download it [the] next cycle you sync, and therefore your opportunity has exactly what the quote has."

I asked him to back up the leads and walk me through that area. He replied:

When we buy a list we do a projection of how many responses we should get. So we are classic in that sense. We know that we should yield 10 percent. Are we getting back a thousand or are we getting back a hundred? Are we getting a hundred hits? When programs fail they do the analysis to understand why we were under. When we get something over, we try to understand why we got a better hit response. What was clear in the messaging or in the targeting? So, we're getting pretty disciplined about that.

We're in the final stages of a program called retention marketing, but it's really the full spectrum of it. If I touch [contact] you, where do I touch you? Where's the value? What's the value? How many times do I have to touch you? What kind of methods? We're trying to get that so we can proceduralize it.

I asked him if they were correlating leads with the calls that the salespeople make.

Not yet. That's the next step. We're doing it within the buckets in the chain, but we're not doing it across boundaries in the chain. That's the next step we're doing. That's why we have to get the traceability through the chain, because we want to know where we fall out and where the failure rate is, what the abandonment rate is and what cost is the failure. Sometimes those are restarts that can happen fairly quickly because the [advertising message] is wrong.

It's starting to sound familiar. There's a real gap between the online and offline worlds. How do you close the loop? How do you bring all those together technically? I could tell he was making a wish list in his head as he thought through the process.

"Well, that's why I start with a lead process. I can tie a lead to an offer to a campaign. I've got a tie to the marketing process; that's where we start and make the allocations on what we plan to spend. We tie that back into marketing programs. So a lead then converts into a site visit, it then goes into an opportunity. I then know the relationship from tactic to lead to opportunity. Then if it goes to a funnel entry, I know that the salesperson scored the opportunity. If he doesn't, I know there's something wrong with it. I force every lead to be scored by the salesperson. So I can take all the hits and all the misses and I can take those back upstream against the tactics."

Then reality sunk in.

"I haven't spent a lot of time with the marketing guys to figure out how are they doing that yet. The capability is getting there so you can almost see the total picture."

I've only come across one company that directly sells large orders which has really integrated the browsing, shopping, information-gathering side of their systems with the sales side. It's a business-to-business technology firm that has understood how to get the most out of the Web from the beginning: National Semiconductor.

National Semiconductor: Connecting the Dots

Phil Gibson, vice president, Web Business & Sales Automation, has been at National Semiconductor for 15 years. In fact, he's been in the same building in Sunnyvale, California, for 15 years. In 2002, he's breaking that trend by moving into the brand-new corporate headquarters building—directly across the street from his current quarters. He promises me they let him out for lunch and to go home in the evening.

He resides in a sea of cubicles that has come to define corporate life. Manuals, calendars, clipped magazine articles, and world maps surround him along with an abundance of family photos (see Figure 11.12).

But the list of Viking Laws seems to stand out.

- Be Brave and Aggressive
- Be direct
- Grab all opportunities
- Use varying methods of attack
- Be versatile and agile
- Attack one target at a time
- Don't plan everything in detail
- Use top-quality weapons

Figure 11.12 Phil Gibson has made National Semiconductor a Web leader since 1995.

Phil Gibson (or Son of Gib in Vikingspeak), doesn't appear to be Viking by stature nor complexion, but get him talking about what's possible and what National Semi-conductor has already achieved online and a somewhat Norse appetite for conquest gleams in his eyes. You begin to understand that National Semi's Internet victories are due greatly to Gibson's ability to follow those Viking Laws.

Gibson is a marketing guy in a sales organization. Brand and image and market share are on his mind, but he lives and breathes the numbers; specifically—the fore-cast. "The products we sell go in and out of favor from one day to the next. Some are constant and some are impossible to guess. Heat and light sensors were the top of the heap for a while, and now wireless anything is all the rage. And everything needs a power supply, so that's *almost* predictable," says Gibson, with his back turned so he can peer into his monitor more often than not.

His fingers dance over the keys and the screen shifts through a wide variety of logs, reports, and forecasts. He finally settles on the Interactive Weekly Marketing Sum-mary. This report enjoys wide distribution at National because it contains information of interest to the production team, the sales staff, managers, and executives. And it's all about the sales process. "We track everything from a sales cycle perspective—by opportunity."

The first bucket holds Qualified Business. Those are potential sales that are identi-fied and that the sales team feels are probable enough to put in the hopper for poten-tial bonuses. "We have financial incentives for early forecasting," Gibson explains. "If you get a contract that's not in the forecast, the commission isn't as high as if you spot-ted it coming. That's the best way to get the sales department to communicate market-place direction to the rest of the company. We give the direct sales force bonuses for meeting milestones by a specified time, and there's nothing like putting money on the table to help hone a salesperson's ability to recognize business while it's still on the hoof."

But they don't stop with the internal sales force. "The distributor channel is incen-tivized with a 'registration' commission for registering first contact with a customer on a product design. This allows them to sell the part at a discount when the customer comes to place an order."

The next category is the Active Selling bucket. That means the customer is in a for-mal process of choosing the right products and has committed to making a purchase. After that comes the Selected bin, which is where they place customers who have made their choice of product and are now working out the contract, the schedule, and the pricing. It's all about negotiations at this point.

The Design Win category contains the business that is essentially booked in advance. The customer tried a number of National Semi's components in the testing phase and bought a passel of them for the prototype stage. That's where they make a test batch to work out the manufacturing and assembly kinks. Then the customer ships samples off to *his* customers for testing. The Design Win category is where the cus-tomer has given their internal project the green light and given the go-ahead to start buying products from National in bulk.

Each estimate is entered by the field sales force and calculated based on an algo-rithm that takes into account the historical run rate for each given product and the sales teams' estimate of the likelihood of the sale to each specific customer.

A separate report is generated for each division of the company with these five categories broken out by region around the world. Each number for each category is drillable on the National intranet down to the specific customers that make up those estimates, the contacts for each customer, and the next action item planned for each customer.

Finally, there's a classification for National's distributors who are also incentivized to register potential sales for the Weekly Summary.

At this point, I have to stop Gibson and remind him of his title and my purpose. "This all sounds like sales force automation to me," I warn.

"Yes," he responds guilelessly, "it's all part of the same system."

"So, where do the Web metrics fit into the picture?"

Gibson smiles and scrolls the report just a bit more to the right. There, for each part number, after the Trend column with a Down, Same, or Up designation and the links to their respective graphs; after the regional totals, are Product Folder Requests, Datasheets Downloads, Sample Order Requests, and Distributor Order Referrals.

I'm beginning to believe National may have bridged the Web/Selling gap.

A folder request relates to an individual product home page. How many times was general information about the product accessed? A datasheet download can be either a viewing or a printing of the specifications on a given part number. When an engineer is sufficiently interested in a part, he or she may ask for a sample, something to bring into the lab in order to poke, prod, and ponder in an up close and personal way. Distributor referrals reflect the Web traffic that came from a distributor's Web site.

This mix of sales estimates, page views, and customer requests is a more holistic view of the customer that gives the National sales force a leg up on the competition. The sales force knows what questions their customers may have, what issues they've been investigating, and what information they've been ruminating over. They are prepared to be useful.

A quick search of the Web reveals a few more Viking Laws that Gibson doesn't have posted in his office:

- Be a Good Merchant in and out of what the market needs
- Don't promise what you can't keep
- Don't demand overpayment
- Arrange things so that you can return

It seems National has been following these rules well, even without seeing them every day.

Channel Metrics

For as hard as it is to get your own Web site to talk to your own contact management system, imagine what it's like for people who sell through third parties.

One of the new business models made possible by the Internet is the *exchange*. It's one thing to sell to people coming to your site, but how do you keep track of what's going on behind the screen of a Web site that's set up to bring buyers and sellers together and you're not running the show? VARStreet has an answer.

VAR is an industry term for value-added reseller. You may buy a large printer directly from Hewlett-Packard, or you may buy it from a local vendor who will deliver it, install it, hook it up to your network, and sell you ongoing service and supplies. Tracking your online sales gets tricky when third parties are part of the value chain.

VARStreet (www.varstreet.com) is an e-commerce exchange (see Figure 11.13). Rad Sundar, cofounder and chairman of VARStreet describes it this way: "We are an e-business network and we provide a hosted service to all the constituents in the supply chain. That means we connect with distributors, we work with IT manufacturers, and we also work with the IT resellers. Since we are a business network, we are actually getting all these participants into one place where they can not only look for information, they can exchange data and conduct business."

Sundar has a keen sense of purpose, value, and what buyers, sellers, distributors, and manufacturers can get out of VARStreet: "If you look at the world from the point of view of a reseller, how many extranets can a reseller visit? Ten extranets? Twenty extranets? And they deal with multiple manufacturers, so we have to be able to do their work from one place. Our focus has been putting the resellers at the center of this network and [we] currently have about 2,000 resellers signed onto our service [as of the middle of 2001]."

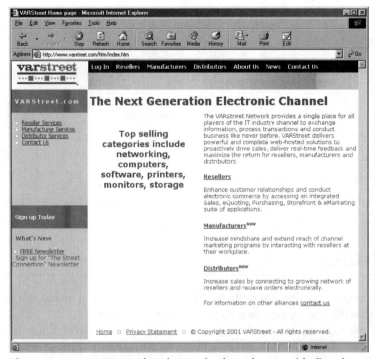

Figure 11.13 VARStreet bends over backward to provide live data to the buyers, sellers, and manufacturers who conduct business here.

Resellers can use a quoting application powered by an aggregated catalogue, which includes information from multiple distributors like Ingram, Tech Data, Cinex, and others. When resellers are putting their bids together, they see live price and availability information.

"We offer two things to the reseller," says Sundar. "One is an e-business workplace, which deals with managing their price lists, marketing, sales, customers, and purchasing. The second aspect is the e-commerce storefronts, where we allow them to set up customer-specific storefronts."

With 600 e-commerce storefronts set up by the resellers and about $50 million worth of quoting activity taking place on a monthly basis, this is a site that not only helps make business easier to conduct but has a unique perspective on one corner of the business world.

Sundar warms to his topic: "When you go back to an IT manufacturer, the question comes up, 'Why should I participate in this network? I have my own PRM [partner relationship management] application.' And our story to them is that there is just not enough value in their application to the majority of resellers because resellers can't go to *all* the manufacturers' sites. It's not a viable option. So we tell them to go ahead with their PRM efforts; we are not trying to substitute that, but we will complement that. We can tell you a lot more about what your resellers are working on—we created something we call the Channel Performance Scorecard.

"Our scorecard shows the population of the resellers who are signed on to our network. We show a report card for each manufacturer." Sundar displays a report for a specific client that we'll call Acme. "We count all of the categories of products that Acme carries. We update this everyday, end of day. Now, the VarStreet network sold 2,180 printers and plotters for a total of $940,000. $886,000 were Acme products, sold by twenty-eight Acme resellers. They were bought by 195 customers."

That's wonderful channel conversion information, but VARStreet doesn't stop there and Sundar is quick to explain: "We created a ten parameter scorecard. The first parameter is market share, which is easy to understand—Acme market share is 88 percent. Their month-to-date rank is number one.

"The second parameter, we call reseller loyalty. Of those resellers who sold Acme products, how many printers and plotters did they sell across all manufacturers? Next comes reseller coverage. Thirty-eight resellers sold Acme products. Overall there are forty-one resellers that account for the $940,000 in sales. So this is Acme's market share of resellers.

"Then this next one is a very exotic thing, which is a reseller customer fan out ratio. We are talking about the channels, right? And a reseller connects Acme to X number of customers, right? So we see that thirty-eight resellers sold Acme products to 225 customers. The customer fan out ratio is 5.92. So that's the fan out that you are getting—each reseller is giving Acme access to about six customers.

"Just like we have reseller loyalty, we have customer loyalty, then comes repeat customers, average price, daily units sold, e-commerce pull ratio—that's customers buying right off the site, versus products sold the traditional way, which is through a sales rep quoting the customer and then closing the deal.

"So what this indicates is that there are $3,200 of printers and plotters sold on the site to customers that came in and bought printers of their own accord.

"If reseller loyalty is very low or reseller coverage is very low, it means that they have not got the mind share of the resellers. If the reseller coverage is good but they are not having good loyalty, that means they need to work differently. And the interesting thing in this is that you can get the scorecard on an ongoing basis. It's real time. So everyday you can see if your things are moving up. Are you doing better on coverage now? Are you getting better on customer loyalty? So how are you performing? How is your channel looking overall?"

When Sundar starts showing me graphic reports, I lament that they have manufacturer names all over them so I can't publish them. "We call this a bubble graph. If you just scroll down a little bit, you will see a competitive landscape for printers and plotters. The average price and the number of units sold are the x- and y-axis and then the size of the dot is the quantity. So this tells you which part of the market you are playing in. And it's active. It is real-time."

"We can go down to a consummate level of detail on many dimensions, and you can analyze your reseller behavior at a priority detail level. We are finding that this is too much information for most people. They have never had anywhere close to this kind of information, and we need to give them advice about how to interpret it."

Of course, that's just the manufacturers' side of the site. Resellers and distributors are also learning more and more on a real-time basis.

The Customer Buy-Cycle: A View from the Other Side

If you've read any of my other books, magazine articles, or my email newsletter, you'll know that I am seriously focused on the customer. I admonish clients to "wear customer-colored glasses." That's very important when creating a Web site strategy, when designing a site, and no less important when trying to grasp conversion metrics.

Fry Multimedia's chief customer experience officer Kara Heinrichs likes to keep customers in mind as well:

> I think sometimes there's a real tendency in the data analytics industry to talk about the customer life cycle in terms of the seller side of the arrangement so that it is attract-acquire-convert-develop-retain.
>
> That sort of approach, which is accurate, doesn't really get inside the shopper's mind. It doesn't help you craft questions in regard to the data that will help you influence that shopper. While the seller's engaged in the process, the buyer is as well. And the buyer's decision-making process is what takes them from awareness and consideration to preference and commitment. And if you can talk businesspeople into thinking from the consumer's viewpoint instead of the seller's, that is really where you can focus your analytical questions.
>
> It's the same funnel, but it's looking at it from the other side. If you can't get somebody out the end of the funnel to the commitment piece, then you can see blockages in the way of registration or checkout or whatever it is that you are trying to convert people to. But if you are doing well there, then you have to look further, to the preference and consideration phases, and then design things within the environment that contribute to those. Gift finders, search engines, all those are about how people form preference.

Depth of product information is about how they continue to form that preference. When our customers only look at it from the point of view of attract-acquire-convert and compress that entire transaction into just convert or not convert; they lose sensitivity to the fact that there is a whole relationship that happens before somebody buys.

Are you considering all of those pre-shopping-cart phases? Are you measuring the impact an email newsletter might have on conversion?

Are you using the computer behind the Web site to keep track of individuals so you can make their shopping experience better? How would you measure the effectiveness of implementing a Web-based personalization system? Good question—and one that deserves its own chapter.

Maximizing Customer Information: The Personalization Continuum

"Wall Street says you're driven by financial measurements so you organize around P and L, but customer intimacy dictates that you organize around the customer, which means completely different structures and paradigms and measurements."

Gary Bird, Vice President, e-Business, Honeywell

This is the subject that captured my attention from the very first. Oh sure, it was great that you can see some company's brochure from anywhere in the world in an instant. It's terrific that you can compare thirty-two kinds of stereo amplifiers before you buff up your home sound system. It's astonishing that the reach and immediacy of the Web allows for new, unheard of business models. Cool enough.

But what really got my eyes to do that wide-eyed stare you see on 3-year-old kids watching a man make animals out of balloons was personalization.

We started with the general store of the Old West, where they know how much flour and sugar you're going to need because you've got family coming to visit. Or the local butcher shop where they not only know how you like your meat cut, but that you need one big bone and one little bone to take home to your dogs. We ended up with mass production and mass distribution, which called for mass communication—also known as mass advertising. The seller and the buyer relationship went the way of the buggy whip.

But now, superefficient disk drives can remember everything there is to know about each and every customer. Sophisticated algorithms can suss out just the right offer to make at just the right time to delight the customer and fill the company coffers. Those were the dancing sugarplum visions that made my eyes go buggy in 1994.

Fast-forward to the twenty-first century and we have a whole industry of analytics companies that claim their software can slice and dice data sets better, faster, and cheaper than the rest. The question remains: Can they slice and dice quickly, efficiently, and most importantly, cheaply enough to make them worthwhile?

Frank Petrilli, COO of the online financial services firm TD Waterhouse, tunes the question a little tighter: "We need research for three main purposes: to convert leads into customers, to retain existing customers, and to get a larger share of our customer's wallet and wealth. We do research to come up with ways to make it easy for customers to give us their money."

If I walked into your office, I could get your eyes to turn to saucers with promises of happy customers, lower costs, and skyrocketing revenues. "Look," I'd say, "I've got this great idea to keep track of how people come in and personalize the Web site. We are going to track the ways that they are personalizing in order to segment them into finer and finer marketplaces so that we can do one-to-one marketing. Oh, by the way, it is going to cost $6 to $8 million worth of hardware and software."

Is there some business method of determining how much information really is *not* worth getting? Certainly, it's called return on investment, or ROI, and before we delve into the various ways you can measure the effectiveness of an ever-expanding panoply of personalization applications, let's revisit ROI for just a moment.

ROI Redux

One of the reasons I love going to Internet World (aside from the fact that I get an absolutely enormous ego boost from being their top-rated speaker 8 years in a row) is the people I meet.

I invariably get emails from people who are going to be in New York, Los Angeles, London, and so on for the conference asking if I could take a few moments to meet with them. Always a pleasure.

At Internet World, Fall 2001, in New York, I had a drink with Jim Lenskold, president of the Lenskold Marketing Group (www.lenskold.com) and a long-time marketing strategist and ROI champion. His company offers strategic planning, marketing, and ROI consulting and workshops for corporate and emerging businesses.

Lenskold is also the author of the reminder that subtracting expense from income to derive return on investment is not as easy as it seems as explained in his "Seven Common Errors in ROI Measurements," below.

SEVEN COMMON ERRORS IN ROI MEASUREMENTS

In today's economy, the pressure is on for the marketing department to improve upon results with a scaled back budget. If you are not already using ROI measurements to guide your marketing investments, now is the time to do so—but make sure you avoid these common errors that can lead to poor decision-making. Many of these errors are made by well-respected, leading marketing companies and consultants, so check your own internal measurements carefully.

The basic ROI equation is:

$$ROI = \frac{(\text{Net present value of profits \& expenses}) - \text{Investment}}{\text{Investment}}$$

Error #1: Revenue is used in place of return

In the English language, "return" could be construed to mean everything gained back from an investment, but in the financial language, return is equal to the net profit minus the original investment. It is the amount that goes to the bottom line, not the top line. Most corporate measurement processes have this correct, but beware of the worksheets on Web sites that are trying to convince you to use their email or direct marketing services where revenue is often used in place of profits. If you are going to make a marketing investment, you need to know what profit it will generate for your company. If you are going to make many marketing investments, you need to have an accurate view of ROI to establish the correct priority.

Error #2: The investment is overstated with cost of sales

You will have marketing expenses to get business and then expenses associated with delivering that new business. The Investment portion of the equation represents only the marketing expenses that are put *at risk*. The easiest way to clarify what counts as an investment is to determine what expenses will be lost if the marketing program generates no sales at all. In addition to the cost of materials and media, this could include development costs and system costs that are incurred specifically for the marketing campaign being measured.

Error #3: Only immediate profit is counted, neglecting future value

The return generated by marketing programs is sometimes restricted to the profit from an immediate sale without taking into account the future value of that customer. This may be based on limited data, the need to make decisions promptly in order to replicate the performance of a marketing program, or a priority on short-term profits over long term value. The extra effort to capture the future value of a customer and appropriately discount the future value into a net present value can alter marketing decisions in such a way that increases the profits generated with the same marketing budget or less.

Error #4: The total customer lifetime value is counted in place of incremental profits

Here we have the opposite problem where too much value is counted instead of too little. It is important that all of the profits generated immediately and in the future that result directly from this investment are captured—no more, no less. Some companies identify the total lifetime value of a customer and use that as the value of each new customer. However, typically the amount of profit a customer is expected to generate over the course of their lifetime with the company is dependent on additional marketing investments. The customer value should be measured as if no additional investments were to be made. A portion of customers will continue to do business with the company, while others will not contribute additional profit without additional marketing investment.

(continues)

SEVEN COMMON ERRORS IN ROI MEASUREMENTS *(Continued)*

Error #5: The ROI analysis is not aligned with the decision to be made

The ROI analysis should be different when measuring past performance or future investments. Expenses already incurred are not important when choosing between possible marketing investments; however, these expenses are very important when measuring the performance of a marketing program as a benchmark for future decisions or measuring the performance of decision-makers for rewards and recognition.

Error #6: Overriding ROI analyses because of "strategic" value

It is sometimes claimed that certain "strategic" business objectives must override the financial analysis that would guide marketing investments toward the greatest profit. Strategic decisions could include customer satisfaction, employee satisfaction, or service quality. However, since businesses exist for the purpose of generating profits, there is typically some financial benefit that is expected to be derived in the future from these strategic decisions. Developing assumptions as to the incremental value of these decisions, or running an ROI analysis to determine the results necessary to justify the strategic decisions, will lead to better, fact-based investments from the marketing budget.

Error #7: A total ROI is calculated in place of an incremental ROI

Using the power of ROI as a planning tool for marketing leads to a better understanding of the expected value for each investment so the budget can be effectively allocated to maximize the total return. Each investment decision should be made comparing the incremental investment to the incremental return. When comparing a marketing campaign with and without an offer, it is common practice to compare the total ROI for each marketing program and choose the higher ROI. However, the ROI for the incremental investment into the offer should be run separately from the ROI for the base campaign. The incremental return generated from that incremental investment must be compared to alternative investments. It is possible that the ROI for the offer itself is positive, but lower than other investment opportunities.

The key to successfully using ROI in marketing is establishing a standard formula that:

1. Is accurate
2. Aligns with strategic decisions
3. Can be used consistently throughout a company for a fair comparison to guide investments.

Every company has a budget committee that wants, really *wants* to believe that there is some magic software application out there that will boost profits, raise shareholder value, and increase the size of their annual bonus by raking up all of the customer data that falls from company transactions like autumn leaves, then slicing and dicing them into a rich compost of fecund, fertile information. The list of possible trees grows longer every day, and the forest can be classified as *customer relationship management* (CRM). CRM encompasses the following areas:

- Advertising campaign management
- Business intelligence
- Channel partner relationship management
- Contact management
- Customer intelligence management
- Customer interaction management
- Customer retention management
- Customer service and support
- Data mining
- Knowledge management
- Marketing automation
- Marketing information systems
- Sales force automation
- Web analytics
- Web content management
- Web personalization
- Web usage analysis

Lynne Harvey, senior consultant/analyst from the Patricia Seybold Group (www.psgroup.com) wrote an article called "The Future Use of Analytic Applications" (November 2, 2000) in which she nails the three key capabilities provided by all of the areas in the preceding list:

1 *The Ability to Quantify the Value of the Customer Interaction. The analytic applications' reporting solutions help quantify the value of the customer interaction. The metrics tracked and reported can help guide e-businesses with their CI and CRM strategies. For example, call center managers, sales managers, and marketing managers can determine the number of customers that interact and purchase at particular touchpoints. They can also determine which touchpoint is best suited for doing business with customers (e.g., whether John Smith responds better to an e-mail campaign or Mary Jones prefers telemarketing).*

2. *The Ability to Set Thresholds to Trigger Rules and Events. The results of the calculations that analytic applications provide can be used to set thresholds that can trigger business rules and events, which in turn automate the delivery of specific content (such as personalized offers and product recommendations). The analytic application can then be used as the "brain" to help facilitate real-time interaction and personalization. For example, I spent $500 buying books on line at books.com one week, and the site's analytic application calculates the average order size on a weekly basis. The analytic application could then compare my purchases against the average purchase rate metric and, if it's greater than the average, could trigger a special discount or coupon for future use.*

3. ***The Ability to Help Qualify Customer Information.*** *Analytic applications can also be used in tandem with CI and CRM solutions to help sort out and qualify customer information, thereby enriching a company's customer intelligence data-gathering activities. When James Weston calls the customer service department to find out when the video that he purchased online will arrive at his house, the customer service department can then ask him what kind of delivery service he typically prefers. The information about the call can be entered into a CRM system, and analytic applications can help determine how Jim's delivery preferences affect the company's current delivery services model. In this example, analytic applications could help the company determine if Jim's delivery service preference is profitable for the company.*

Each of these capabilities fits into the gather, analyze, strategize, and act framework for delivering customer intelligence and ultimately fostering the development of a deeper, mutually beneficial relationship between the customer and the company. This is, after all, the main goal of CRM.

CRM is such a large conglomeration of tools and techniques, we should break it down and tackle it one step at a time: segmentation, customization, personalization, retention/attrition, loyalty, and lifetime value.

Segmentation

The human mind loves to categorize things: kingdom, phylum, class, order, family, genus, species. It makes us feel better. It helps us understand the world around us, so we can respond to things appropriately.

Is it larger than you? Able to move quickly? Has large, sharp teeth? Seems to be interested in you as a lunchtime snack? It doesn't matter if you know what it is or not, you have enough information to respond in an appropriate manner: Run!

So the first thing we do when it comes to Web site visitors is segment them. First by way of immediate observation, and then by way of long-term memory or database.

By Technographic

This is the information you get for free from your server logs. Do people who use Macintosh computers buy more when offered free shipping than those who use Netscape on a Windows machine? Are you more likely to up-sell a visitor using a newer version of the browser? How important is it that they are Java-enabled?

By Interest

What are they looking at?

All the qualification process metrics covered in the previous chapter apply—duration, depth, recency, and frequency—but mostly we're interested in their interests at this point. You can segment site visitors by the level of attention they pay to specific sets of pages on your site.

Cliff Allen is president of Coravue, publisher of a line of Web personalization and content management system software. He's also coauthor of *One-to-One Web Marketing: Build a Relationship Marketing Strategy One Customer at a Time, Second Edition* (John Wiley & Sons, 2001).

I ran into Allen at a DCI CRM conference in Los Angeles, and he described a couple of illustrative Coravue reports for me. The example results are real, even if the Web site (SureToFind.com) is mostly a test/development site for the tool.

"The Interest Profile (see Figure 12.1) pulls together data from the user profile database, the content database, and the Web access database," Allen explained, "and shows which type of users are visiting various pages. The report shows that several pages are visited by clusters of users, indicating that people with those interests visit those pages more than they visit other pages."

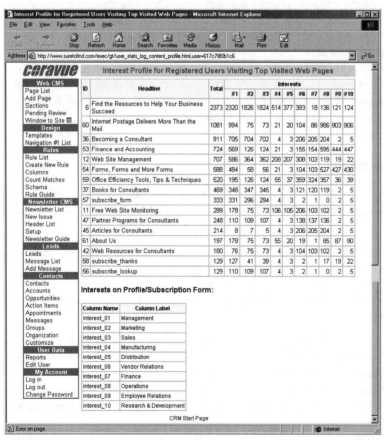

Figure 12.1 Interest Profile from Coravue for registered users visiting top visited Web pages.

The ID is the content identification, and the Total is the number of people who looked at that content, so right off the bat, you can tell which content is the most popular. Then, by categorizing the content itself, you can see that people who are interested in Manufacturing (#4) don't care about Becoming a Consultant, Books for Consultants, or anything else that has to do with consultants. They have a great deal in common with those interested in distribution.

The Customer Status Profile report (see Figure 12.2) relates the same content pages to Customer Status; indicating whether the visitor is registered on the site, a newsletter subscriber, a qualified lead, a prospect, or an actual customer.

The Registered and the Newsletter Subscriber columns are automatically set, while the Qualified Lead, Prospect, and Customer columns are set from the sales automation application by the representative assigned to handle the contact. Somebody who looks at About Us is very unlikely to become a customer and those looking at Office Efficiency Tools, Tips & Techniques are the most likely.

In an article he wrote back in 1999 (www.allen.com/1999-07-20.html), Allen describes how visitor segmentation leads to collaborative filtering:

> So what can we actually learn by segmenting our audience?
>
> Perhaps the easiest thing to learn is which products are purchased by the same people. Web sites that use collaborative filtering are helping marketers and consumers answer this question. You've probably seen sites that say, "People who bought this product also purchased these other products."
>
> For instance, if a group of customers buys what appear to be unrelated products, try cross-promoting the two products and see if other customers buy that combination, too. By using market segmentation tools and techniques, unique groups of people can be identified and marketing programs created to take advantage of this opportunity.

By Demographic

Even without expensive collaborative filtering tools, you can learn a lot about your customers just by grouping them into logical clusters, writes Allen:

> For example, how does the geographic distribution of your customers compare to the country as a whole? California has 12 percent of the U.S. population, so if less than 12 percent of your U.S. customers are from California, that segment might not respond to the same marketing messages as other regions. By targeting a different email message to that market segment, you might find results are higher than sending the same email newsletter to everyone.

You might also find results are higher by dynamically serving specialized content to them. At the very least, you can keep track of who's coming to your site in order to have the right type of content waiting for the majority of your visitors.

Financial institutions mostly segment their audiences based on income and investment approach (risk takers or avoiders), but they also look at something as simple as age (see Table 12.1).

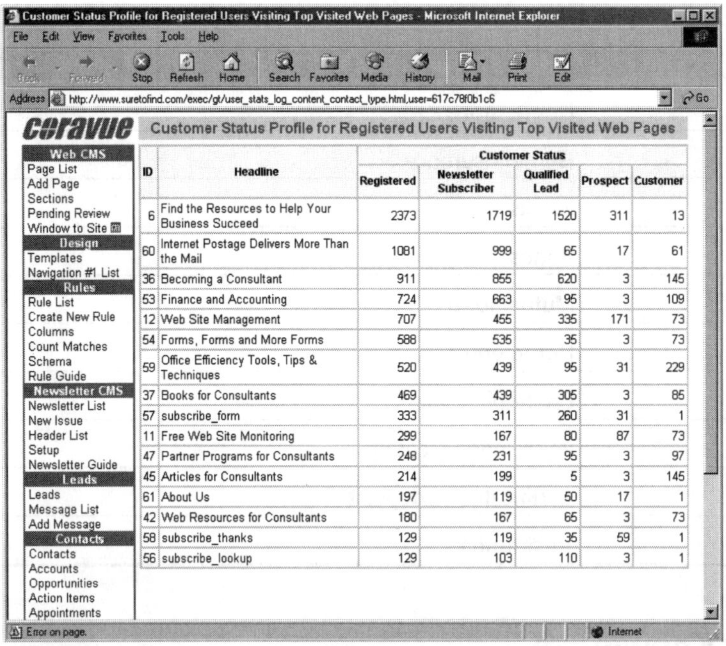

ID	Headline	Customer Status				
		Registered	Newsletter Subscriber	Qualified Lead	Prospect	Customer
6	Find the Resources to Help Your Business Succeed	2373	1719	1520	311	13
60	Internet Postage Delivers More Than the Mail	1081	999	65	17	61
36	Becoming a Consultant	911	855	620	3	145
53	Finance and Accounting	724	663	95	3	109
12	Web Site Management	707	455	335	171	73
54	Forms, Forms and More Forms	588	535	35	3	73
59	Office Efficiency Tools, Tips & Techniques	520	439	95	31	229
37	Books for Consultants	469	439	305	3	85
57	subscribe_form	333	311	260	31	1
11	Free Web Site Monitoring	299	167	80	87	73
47	Partner Programs for Consultants	248	231	95	3	97
45	Articles for Consultants	214	199	5	3	145
61	About Us	197	119	50	17	1
42	Web Resources for Consultants	180	167	65	3	73
58	subscribe_thanks	129	119	35	59	1
56	subscribe_lookup	129	103	110	3	1

Figure 12.2 Customer Status Profile from Coravue for registered users visiting top visited Web pages.

At Oracle, the product managers and program managers review real-time dashboards where they can view registration demographics. Knowing that 20 percent of your audience are IT managers and 40 percent are software developers helps put the right message where the right person is likely to find it. Then, an interest profile report will tell you if you've made the right changes to your content.

Table 12.1 Investment Interest Segmentation by Age

AGE	INVESTMENT INTERESTS
0-17	Savings account
18-24	Checking account with ATM
25-34	Car insurance
	Car loan
	Credit cards
	Life insurance
	College savings plans

Table 12.1 *Continued*

AGE	INVESTMENT INTERESTS
35-44	Home mortgage
	Home insurance
	Stocks
	Bonds
	Mutual funds
45-54	Home equity loan
	Estate planning
	Retirement accounts
55-64	Certificates of deposit
65 +	Trust funds

By Customer Knowledge

Once you start using cookies, you can keep track of people on a repeat visit basis. That means you can grow your profile of the individual and cater to him or her better.

Terry Lund at Kodak describes their approach like this: "We put you in a bucket of high-end amateurs based on prior knowledge and next time you come you're going to get something we've tailored to high-end amateurs. We won't be making decisions about Jim Sterne as an individual. That's a privacy issue. How far can we actually go when we know it's Jim Sterne who just arrived?

"Most sites seem to be able to get away with 'Hi Jim, welcome back,' and we're not getting too much push back on that. We could say 'Gee, you haven't been here in 3 weeks and here are some new sections. And the last time you were here, you stopped your visit looking at this section.'"

This sort of personalization works if you adopt a strict opt-in approach. You tell visitors all of the great stuff that you can do, and invite them to sign up for level A, B, or C. They're pleased as punch because they show up at a Web site that knows who they are and can cater to their needs.

By Industry and Job Function

Got a headache? Go to www.excedrin.com. Want to color your hair? Go to www.clairol.com. Those are the brands you know and love. It probably didn't occur to you to head over to www.bms.com.

That's where you'll find Bristol-Myers Squibb, a $20 billion company doing business worldwide. But they have nowhere near the brand-name connection between need and solution that their products have. Why is that? Branding. What to do? Create multiple Web sites, of course.

I recently spoke to a company that writes software for the Department of Defense. Their client list includes customers like the Ballistic Missile Defense Organization. On the other hand, they sell agricultural accounting and information management software. Clearly, the guys building missiles and the guys driving tractors not only have nothing in common, they don't feel comfortable buying from somebody who consorts with the other. Solution? Two Web sites.

But then they had a little problem. They have a project-estimating tool that's great for anybody and everybody. This is a product Uncle Sam can make use of just as well as Farmer John. What to do? Create a third Web site? Maybe, maybe not.

Sometimes different markets call for a different look and feel for the same product. That software package, dressed up in olive drab, will appeal to the DoD a lot faster than if it's clothed in a plain blue suit. The same goes for draping it in denim coveralls. Tractor drivers will cotton to it faster in that style than they will if it's wearing wing tips.

Create multiple Web sites for each vertical? When the verticals are that far apart, yes. But we're not done yet. In time, the right choice will be to subdivide the brand by job responsibility within a given company, within a given market segment.

Different people within each company have different needs and respond to different offers, different language, and different branding. For those of you who missed the now out of print *"Strategic Selling: The Unique Sales System Proven Successful by America's Best Companies,"* it may be worth looking for it in the used bin (Robert Miller and Stephen Heiman, Warner Books, 1986). Maybe *"The New Conceptual Selling"* by one of the same authors (Stephen E. Heiman, Warner Books, 1999) will fill the bill.

The original book divided prospective customers into four areas of interest: the product user, the economic buyer, the advisor, and the manager. Each of these individuals is motivated by different things in order to achieve different goals. Does your Web site recognize these divergent needs and offer up a different brand to each?

Is your product easy to use? Will it save money? Is it used successfully by others? Will it make a company more productive? The answer should be yes to all of these questions and presented to different Web visitors in these different lights.

So now you have a Web site for a given vertical and a brand for buyer types within each vertical. While we're at it, let's add another layer: the size of the prospective customer's business. That's how many verticals multiplied by four types of buyers across four or five business size classifications. How much is all this going to cost? Wait! Don't answer yet. Because we're not done slicing and dicing yet.

How is your brand presented to John G. Smith who lives at 123 Main Street, Anytown, USA? Mr. Smith is an interesting mixture. He works for a manufacturing company in the textiles industry. His responsibilities revolve around facilities management and shop floor control. He's more interested in quality than cost savings. He doesn't eat meat. He has a flexible budget, but no ability to hire more people.

Does your site brand your product to cater to Mr. Smith's hopes and fears and sway him with persuasion that is geared to his psyche? It will.

The same sort of tools being used to match up banner ads with Web surfers based on their clicks and their search terms—used to put the right message in front of the right person at the right time—can be used on your site to match up the right benefit statement to the prospect and deliver the right brand at the right time.

And then it gets interesting.

By Personality

If you can get your site visitors to reveal how much they like variety, theories, outrageous people and things, and whether they like to make things and follow the latest trends and fashions—a total of forty questions—you can pigeonhole them into VALS categories.

VALS was created in 1978 by SRI International and is currently run by SRI Consulting Business Intelligence (SRIC-BI; http://www.sric-bi.com/VALS). It's a consumer-segmentation system that goes beyond demographics and geographics, and focuses on the psychographic factors (a combination of psychology and demographics) that motivate consumer buying behavior. The categories include such designations as Fulfilleds, Believers, and Strivers (see Figure 12.3).

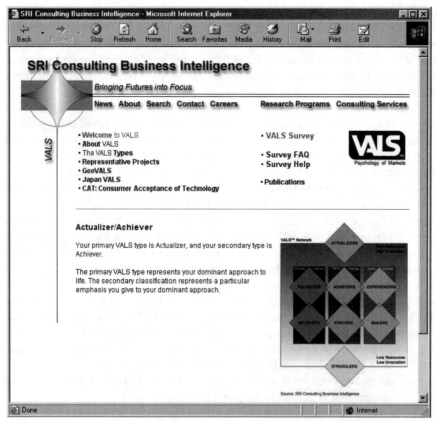

Figure 12.3 My VALS survey results claim I am primarily an Actualizer with Achiever tendencies.

Source: SRI Consulting Business Intelligence

A VALS result of Actualizer/Achiever is interesting, but only if you know how to make the most use of that information. That's why VALS works closely with its clients and provides them with in-depth descriptions and product and media purchase data for each of the VALS types. Common uses of the VALS system include product creation, target identification, and product positioning and advertising.

One of the marketing segments Web sites have been toying with is matching the customer experience on the site with the mood/mode the customer is in at the moment.

By Surfing Mode

Why did those visitors come to your site and how do they feel about it? They might be there to do the following:

- Browse
- Hunt
- Research
- Compare
- Locate
- Acquire
- Complain

In April 2001, Booz Allen Hamilton and Nielsen//NetRatings put out a press release identifying seven types of Web users:

Study of Online Consumer Segmentation Uncovers "Occasionalization" as Next Step to Reviving Marketing and Retailing on the Web

NEW YORK, April 2, 2001—To increase the effectiveness of their online marketing, advertisers and retailers must study how users actually use the Web, according to Booz Allen Hamilton, the elite management and technology consulting firm, and NetRatings, Inc. (Nasdaq: NTRT), a provider of the Nielsen//NetRatings Internet audience measurement service. Web usage patterns fall into seven categories of online behavior, according to Booz Allen and Nielsen//NetRatings, and while in some categories consumers are more likely to buy, in others they are nearly immune to traditional online marketing pleas.

These findings are part of Booz Allen and NetRatings' co-branded study, Seize the Occasion—Usage-based Segmentation for Internet Marketers, which was released today. This marks the second in a series of studies from Booz Allen and NetRatings' Digital Customer Project, which examines facts about online behavior to improve the ways that business interacts with its customers via the Internet and other new technologies.

According to the study, focusing on how people actually use the Internet—exploiting Internet technology's ability to track behavior—is superior to marketers' current reliance on "best-guess" demographic and other user-based segmentations. The findings are based on analysis of proprietary click-stream data collected from nearly 2,500 users between July and December 2000.

Market Segmentation Based on Behavior

Focusing on the wide behavioral variations exhibited by online consumers and the opportunities that these variations can provide for marketers, the study introduces "occasionalization," a new form of Internet market segmentation that identifies consumer segments based on online usage occasions rather than on user-based characteristics, such as demographics or attitudinal data.

By exploring users' session characteristics—how long a user stayed online, how much time the user spent on each page, site familiarity and the category concentration of sites visited—the study uncovered seven types of sessions, and found that three—Information, Please; Loitering; and Surfing—are more likely to involve shopping than others. These sessions are the lengthiest, ranging from 33 to 70 minutes, and page views are 1 to 2 minutes, so users are likely to linger on a page and be exposed to different messages.

[The seven categories are as follows:]

Quickies: *Typically short (1-minute) sessions that center around visits to two or fewer familiar sites. Users spend about 15 seconds per page extracting specific bits of information or sending email. Users in Quickie sessions may not notice any type of message as they scoop up the needed information and log off.*

Just the Facts: *Users seeking specific pieces of information from known sites. At 9 minutes, these sessions are longer than Quickies but share the aspect of rapid page views. These occasions are less likely to involve sites best enjoyed at leisure, such as entertainment. Users in Just the Facts sessions have a low propensity to buy.*

Single Mission: *Users want to complete a certain task or gather specific information, then leave the Internet. During these visits, generally lasting 10 minutes, users venture into unfamiliar sites to find what they need, while concentrating on sites within a single category. Users in Single Mission sessions are only open to messages related to the purpose of the session, but a well-targeted banner ad may provide a good return.*

Do It Again: *These sessions are 14 minutes in length and are notable for lingering page views: 2 minutes, tied with Loitering for the longest of the seven types of sessions. Ninety-five percent of the time is spent at sites the user has visited at least four times in the past. Users in Do It Again sessions may be willing to click through banner ads that are strategically placed on their favorite sites or react to site sponsorships that bring real content directly to the consumer.*

Loitering: *At 33 minutes in length, with 2-minute page views, Loitering sessions are similar to Do It Agains: leisurely visits to familiar "sticky" sites, such as news, games, telecommunications/ISP, and entertainment sites. A company undertaking a brand positioning campaign would focus on Loitering sessions, where the consumer spends more time on each page and is more likely to absorb the marketer's message and develop the necessary brand associations.*

Information, Please: *These sessions average 37 minutes in length and are used to build in-depth knowledge of a topic, perhaps for a research report. They differ from Single Missions because users gather broad information from a range of sites. Users in Information, Please sessions are mostly going to familiar sites, but are willing to cross categories and linger on a page that piques their interest, giving marketers an opportunity to expose them to different messages.*

Surfing: Surfing sessions are the longest, averaging 70 minutes, with few stops at familiar sites, as users hit nearly 45 sites in a typical session. Time per page is a minute or more, suggesting wide, but not deep, explorations. Surfers usually spend time on sites with lots of content, giving marketers opportunities to build branding awareness, since during these occasions users will be exposed to messages for a relatively long time. Sponsorships of content are another good approach, encouraging users to associate their favorite content with a specific brand name.

Lessons for e-Tailers

The Booz Allen and Nielsen//NetRatings study indicates that a successful e-tailing site is likely to evolve from a "one size fits all" approach into a series of parallel sites targeted to appeal to multiple usage occasions. The challenge for e-tailers is to use available technology to detect which occasion a user coming into the site may be in, and to use that information to trigger an interface geared to that occasion. For example, users engaged in Quickie or Single Mission sessions can get a rapid, no-frills self-serve experience marked by text-only pages and no pop-up ads, while users in Loitering and Information, Please sessions can be steered toward the full-service option, with video pop-ups and personal shoppers.

As you might expect, there are many ways to categorize Web visitors. Another study, this one performed by Dr. William R. Swinyard and fellow Brigham Young University professor Scott M. Smith at the BYU Marriott School of Management in July 2001 (www.byu.edu/news/releases/archive01/Jul/internetshoppingstudy.htm), looked at 4,000 Web users to determine which types of surfers would respond to marketing efforts (see Figure 12.4).

The BYU study found the following eight categories:

- *With 11.1 percent of the market share, Shopping Lovers enjoy buying online and do so frequently. They are competent computer users and will likely continue their shopping habits. They also spread the word to others about joys of online shopping whenever they have the opportunity. They represent an ideal target for retailers.*

- *Adventurous Explorers (8.9 percent) are a small segment that presents a large opportunity. They require little special attention by Internet vendors because they believe online shopping is fun. They are likely the opinion leaders for all things online. Retailers should nurture and cultivate them to be online community builders and shopping advocates.*

- *Suspicious Learners (9.6 percent) comprise another small segment with growth potential. Their reluctance to purchase online more often hinges on their lack of computer training, but they are open to new ways of doing things. In contrast to more fearful segments, they don't have a problem giving a computer their credit card number. Further guidance and training would help coax them into online buying.*

- *Among the most computer literate, Business Users (12.4 percent) use the Internet primarily for business purposes. They take a serious interest in what it can do for their professional life. They don't view online shopping as novel and aren't usually champions of the practice.*

■ *Fearful Browsers (10.7 percent) are on the cusp of buying online. They are capable Internet and computer users, spending a good deal of time "window shopping." They could become a significant buying group if their fears about credit card security, shipping charges, and buying products sight unseen were overcome.*

■ *Shopping Avoiders (15.6 percent) have an appealing income level, but their values make them a poor target for online retailers. They don't like to wait for products to be shipped to them, and they like seeing merchandise in person before buying. They have online shopping issues that retailers will not easily be able to overcome.*

■ *Technology Muddlers (19.6 percent) face large computer literacy hurdles. They spend less time than any other segment online and show little excitement about increasing their online comfort level. They are not an attractive market for online retailers.*

■ *Fun Seekers (12.1 percent) are the least wealthy and least educated market segment. They see entertainment value in the Internet, but buying things online frightens them. Although security and privacy issues might be overcome, the spending power of the segment suggests that only a marginal long-term payback would be possible.*

Then, of course, there are those people who simply want to *buy something*. Robin Edwards of the UK Web consultancy and design shop Clockworx (www.clockworx.com) likes to segment people who have and have not purchased.

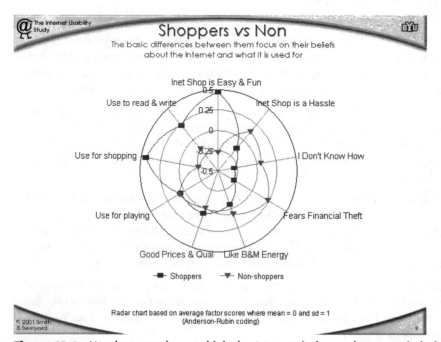

Figure 12.4 Nonshoppers do not think the Internet is fun and are worried about the sanctity of their credit cards.

We are counting unique session ID cookies, as counting IP addresses (like so many stats packages do) is kind of pointless in these days of proxy servers and corporate/education access. This gives us a daily total of the number of people who were on the site and thus the overall conversion rate. The next step is to break the conversion rate down further by looking at historical data for each person so we can work out the following:

- *Conversion rate for first time visitors becoming customers*
- *Conversion rate for repeat visitors becoming customers*
- *Conversion rate for repeat customers placing an order rather than just browsing*

Each stat will tell us something different about the way the site works and how it can be improved further. For example, if we don't get a high conversion rate for the latter type of visitor, then we need to seriously look at our CRM systems.

If your company is in the entertainment business or your brand depends on being entertaining, then catering to those who show up just to play games, hear music, or watch videos might be important. These people might be more willing to register and return, giving you the opportunity to do a lot of cross-referencing between visits, game plays, duration, and purchases.

Understand that individuals can and do operate in different moods/modes at different points in time, so segmentation only goes so far. At some point, you have to get down to the individual, and that calls for Web site customization.

Customization

On the path of the great continuum from segmentation to full-on CRM (see Figure 12.5), we make a brief stop at Customization/Profiles.

Customization/Profiling lets visitors modify your Web site to their taste. They can add and subtract menus, change colors, and as Yahoo! has shown us for the past several years, add the news, weather, business, and sports that they want to see.

This is a slightly different kettle of fish because the visitors are actively segmenting themselves. Road Runner Sports (www.roadrunnersports.com) encourages you to take advantage of Shoe Dog, who will help you find just the right pair of shoes (see Figure 12.6).

To get Shoe Dog to fetch, you must divulge a Great Dane's worth of information or this dog just won't hunt:

- Gender
- U.S. Shoe Size
- Shoe Width
- Weight
- Do you use orthotics?
- Arch Type: Unknown, Flat, Average, High
- Running Mechanics: Unknown, Over-Pronator, Neutral, Under-Pronator
- # of days per week you run

- Miles per week
- Have you been running less than a year?
- Do you wear thick or padded socks?
- What is your average training pace per mile?
- What is your primary running surface?
- Have you had an injury in the past 6 months?
    - If Yes, what type of injury?
- Search for Shoes in the Following Brands. . .

Road Runner Sports matches up those answers with spending habits and serves up more articles and special discounts to those who have let their personal information off the leash. VIP members, who get even more special offers as well as special "VIP sale days," have a 15 to 20 percent higher overall lifetime value than other shoppers.

Depending on how you answered the question about injuries (the options being Achilles Tendonitis, Plantar Fasciitis, Shin Splints, Iliotibial Band Syndrome (IT Band), Runner's Knee, or Excessive Ankle Sprains), you might get unique content offers on physical therapies or special products made to compensate for your malady.

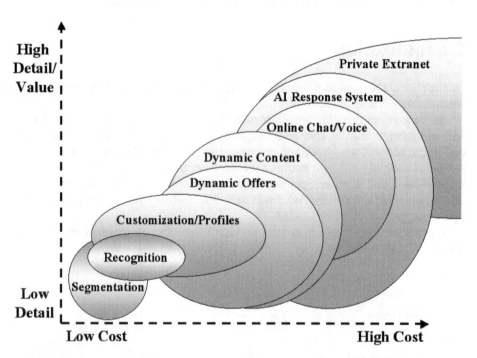

Figure 12.5 The Personalization Continuum identifies the range of possibilities.

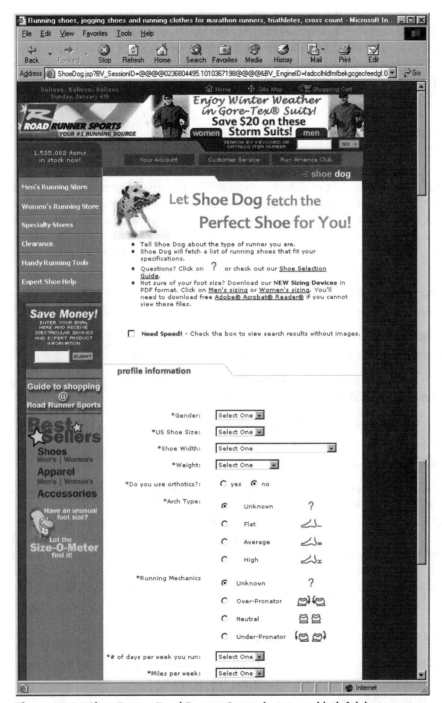

Figure 12.6   Shoe Dog at Road Runner Sports is cute and helpful, but nosey.

Road Runner Shoes measures the value of their BroadVision (www.broadvision.com) software implementation in terms of dollars per sale. Their average order has gone up by $5 to $7 per customer and they've doubled their conversion rate. (Not to mention the fact that Shoe Dog only recommended one pair of shoes to me that was under $100, but not by much!)

Personalization

As the relationship changes from casual browser to interested prospect and then to active buyer, your Web site can collect a whole host of personal preferences, plans, penchants, and peccadilloes. You need merely ask. Coupling that information with offline data from surveys and commercial databases, you now have a chance to build a fully realized portrait of each customer. Just how balanced is your portrait?

In the end, you have to decide what granularity of identification will suit you best. Is it enough to know the following about a certain type of visitor?:

- Interested in product A
- Works in industry B
- At a company that's size C
- Is moving through the qualification process at a rate of D

Or, in order to sell more, faster, at a higher margin, does it add significantly to the bottom line if you also know the following about her?:

- A shopping type E (adventurous explorer)
- Reviews the F section with a frequency rating of G
- Wears size H shoes

After all, just how valuable *is* it that you know which customers like green marshmallow moons in their Rice Chex? (see Figure 12.7)

While the sheer quantity of data elements is the most significant factor in your personal profile depth scoring, each element must be weighted according to its value. A customer identification number has no weight at all because one is indistinguishable from the next. The usual information collected about a customer (name, address, phone number) is critical but carries a low weight because it is not actionable.

Types of Customer Information

Actionable information pertains to a customer's predilections, purchasing history, and declared interests. Be sure you properly weigh implicit, explicit, and factual information:

Implicit: He looked at those pages so he must be interested in these items.

Explicit: He filled out a survey and told us he was interested in these items.

Fact: He looked at those pages and bought these items.

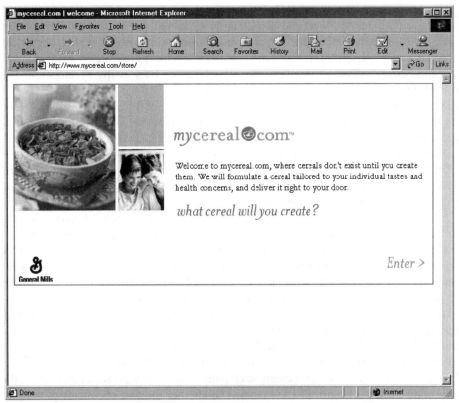

Figure 12.7   General Mills experiments with letting customers choose their own cereal configurations.

Web site visitors tell you explicit information, and you derive implicit information. For instance, a customer can say he likes reading biographies and wants Amazon.com to email notifications about famous figures in European history. But if he buys books about dogs, Amazon knows what to put on his recommendation list. Watching what customers actually do is far more revealing than reading what they say. And it's revealing in ways that don't necessarily make sense.

Suppose the database shows that visitors who are shopping for electric razors are also buying personal CD players, or that visitors who read the detailed specifications of the surface mining and construction equipment are seldom interested in extended warranty information. Are these the sorts of correlations marketing mavens are going to come up with in brainstorming meetings? No. They don't make any sense, but they're true. So now the marketing mavens have a new datapoint to work with, and the systems behind the scenes have the ability to act on the information in real time.

Besides weighing data elements based on whether they are declared or derived, their value must take into account freshness and results. Knowing the correlation between electric razors and personal CD players is the first step, using that information is the second, and measuring the results of that use is the most important.

Data Cleansing

Living up to customer relationship management means ensuring that the information used by the marketing systems and the customer service representatives is fresh, current, and accurate. That means bringing data together from many systems and *that* means figuring out how to get all that data to look alike.

Data normalization has typically applied to the format of information that is entered into a system. Does the middle initial carry a period? Does the phone number include parentheses or dashes? Is the zip code five digits or nine? Is there a hyphen in the middle? But in these days of CRM, data cleansing goes far beyond punctuation.

Let's assume you have a sales contact management system, an invoicing system, and a customer care database in each of four divisions. Let's say John Smith sends you an email from JohnSmith@Yahoo.com. Which John Smith is this?

You'll need multiple points of comparison. Maybe JohnSmith@Yahoo.com let slip that he was having trouble with your product while he was in California for the first time. You can then eliminate all of the John Smiths who live in California. Possibly he mentioned which product or service of yours he was using. Perhaps he includes his phone number in his email signature file. That could be the clue you need to identify this John Smith from the twenty-seven others in your database.

Data cleansing focuses on the verification and validation of the information. If all your John Smiths are formatted the same, you're off to a good start. If none of your John Smith records have been verified for more than 6 months, their value deteriorates.

I'm trying to clearly depict a set of problems that are neither easy nor quick to solve. If it's going to cost so much and create such pain, how do you go about measuring the value of all these possibilities? The question is whether the cost of collecting and processing the information is worth the value you derive from having the information, less the pain you cause your customers in its collection.

Personalization Quotient

Dr. Kamran Parsaye, president of Intelligence Ware, Inc. and author of *Intelligent Database Tools and Applications* (John Wiley & Sons, 1993) wrote a white paper called "PQ: The Personalization Quotient of a Website." At the moment, the paper can be found online (www.kellen.net/ect586/personalization_parsaye.pdf), even though the company Parsaye worked at when he wrote it (NovuWeb) cannot.

In his paper, Parsaye made a valiant attempt to create "a framework and a theory to measure how personalized a system is in terms of the Personalization Quotient (PQ) and illustrate how the theory can be used to improve e-service." The concept of the *personalization quotient* is then used to measure how personalized a system really is.

In this paper, Dr. Parsaye differentiates between an impersonal system, which treats everyone the same way, and a fully personalized system, which adjusts its behavior to specific users. An impersonal system has a PQ of zero, since it provides the same static response to all users regardless of their characteristics.

Personalization comes about as a reaction to individual information, and Dr. Parsaye divides personalization into three areas—customization, individualization and group-characterization. Customization is the oldest and at times the easiest to address. It allows you to set specific preferences, e.g., the stocks you want to track, the type of news you want to see, the colors you want set on your screen, etc. Individualization goes beyond this fixed setting and uses patterns of your own behavior (and not any other user's) to deliver specific content to you. [For instance,] if you have clicked a lot on finance-related items but not on sports, it will show you more financial news rather than sports news, without your asking for it. In group-characterization you receive a recommendation based on the preferences of people "like" you, e.g., books may be recommended to you based on books ordered by people with similar interests. Approaches based on collaborative filtering, case-based reasoning, etc. focus on the group-characterization measure.

> *PQ: The Personalization Quotient takes all three of these issues into account. It has three specific components, PQ1, PQ2 and PQ3, where:*
>
> > *PQ1   measures the system's ability to customize items.*
> >
> > *PQ2   measures the system's ability to use individual preferences.*
> >
> > *PQ3   measures the system's ability to deal with group-based preferences.*

We then measure PQ as the average of these two elements, i.e.:
PQ = (PQ1 + PQ2 + PQ3)/3
Here each PQ1, PQ2 and PQ3 will be a number between 0 and 100. A system with a PQ of 100 is totally personalized, while a system with a PQ of zero is totally impersonal.

Dr. Parsaye then describes creating an ultimate profile of your site visitor:

One way to represent and measure similarity of users and customers is in terms of DNA strings or attribute vectors.
A DNA string for a Web user is a set string of integers between 0 and 9, e.g., the string 1309735183291. Each integer here shows the relative value of some trait, e.g., scoring an 8 or a 9 on the "sportspage" indicator means that you view many sports-related pages, while a 0 means that you never see such pages at all. Similarly, other integers on the string can tell us how you visit the site and how you click through on banner advertising—all in relative terms.
Similarly, we can define a DNA string for a Web page by considering the components that comprise it. For instance, the number of banners and the type of banners.

He concludes by suggesting "An interesting direction for enhancements will be that of measuring the comparative PQ of two systems."

He then wanders off into a world where only mathematicians dare to tread by slipping into some serious formulae such as: $PQ3(U, P) = 100 / \text{maximum}((\delta U / \delta P), (\delta P / \delta U))$.

But how do we factor in the pain caused to the site visitor who is followed around from page to page by a cookie and asked for an opinion about whether a woman's life is fulfilled only if she can provide a happy home for her family? That's where the *personalization index* comes in.

Personalization Index

The universe of profile elements is virtually unbounded, covering familiar items such as last name and business address, technical concepts such as IP address and connection speed, and domain-specific attributes from pore size (for cosmetics) to lifestyle risk profile (for insurance). By adding incremental profile information, e-business managers are able to move prospects and customers through the four stages of e-customer understanding (see Figure 12.8), transforming category 1 anonymous users into the distinct, real-world category 4 individuals.

Collecting information is one thing. Using it in a judicious way is another. The *personalization index* (PI) distinguishes just how well you are using the data you are gathering. The index is a measure of how effectively an e-business is leveraging this customer data.

$$\text{Personalization index} = \frac{\text{Total number of profile elements used in customer interaction}}{\text{Total number of customer profile elements collected}}$$

If your PI is above 0.75, then you are making the most of the information you are collecting. That means your efforts are not wasted, nor are those of your customers who are providing the raw material.

The preceding assumes that you are using a significant number of elements to make a personalized Web experience. If you are only collecting two elements and using them both, your PI score may be 1.00, but here it means you are only going so far as market segmentation rather than personalization—you're only grouping your prospects and customers into broad categories. While useful, broad categories aren't as powerful as true personalization based on dozens of attributes.

When you collect more and more elements, you can classify users into more and more clusters, and broad segmentation moves toward personalization. This is where you start to foster a customer relationship and turn it into a loyalty relationship, significantly raising the cost for your customer to switch to another vendor.

If your PI is less than 0.30, then you are collecting more information than you are using. The good news is that you have a huge untapped reservoir of actionable data about your customers. The bad news is that the data is lying fallow and probably getting stale fast. You need to either start using the data you have more effectively or cut down on how much explicit data you are trying to collect. Most likely, the correct answer is both. You are spinning your wheels collecting that information, but you are not using it to benefit your customers, which adversely affects your customers' experience.

That's the greatest downside to a low personalization quotient. All that time and effort that you force your customers to invest in giving you information is a waste. They get nothing out of it. Even when the process is simple, such as scanning a key chain fob at the grocery store, there's still no real value to the customer. Why bother? Why are they being bothered?

At this point, we have finally attracted, navigated, persuaded, and converted that unknown prospect into a known customer. Can we get that customer to come back?

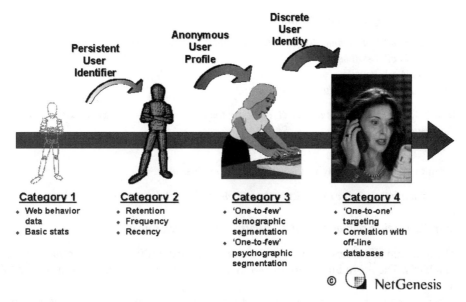

Stages of Customer Understanding

Persistent User Identifier

Anonymous User Profile

Discrete User Identity

Category 1
- Web behavior data
- Basic stats

Category 2
- Retention
- Frequency
- Recency

Category 3
- 'One-to-few' demographic segmentation
- 'One-to-few' psychographic segmentation

Category 4
- 'One-to-one' targeting
- Correlation with off-line databases

© NetGenesis

Figure 12.8 This Four Stages of Customer Understanding graphic was developed by NetGenesis, now part of SPSS.

Retention/Attrition

It costs (fill-in-the-blank) times less to sell something to a current customer, than it does to go out and find a new one. Try and fill in that blank and you'll have a lot of fun coming up with a common figure. Here are a few samples from various companies:

It costs three times more to acquire new clients than to introduce a new product to your existent.
High Tech Marketing
http://www.hitechmarketinginc.com/statistics.htm

It costs five times more to attract a new customer than to retain an existing one.
Southern California Chapter of the International Customer Service Association
http://www.icsa-socal.com/membership.html

The Coalition of Brand Equity estimates that it costs six times more money to win over a new client than to keep a current one.
Adbusters
http://www.adbusters.org/magazine/21/branding.html

It costs 10 times more to attract and acquire a customer than to retain one.
Microsoft Business
http://www.microsoft.com/business/crm/crmsupport.asp

Did you know that it costs eleven times more to attract a new customer than it does to retain an existing customer?
Cybeer
http://www.cybeer.co.uk/loyalty.htm

Since it costs 12 times more to get a customer than to keep one, no business can afford to neglect this vital skill set.
Coreplus Workshops
http://www.coremap.com/ws-selling.htm

It costs twenty times more to attract a new customer than it does to keep an existing one.
Basic Success
(http://www.basicsuccess.com/aboutus.php)

I think I'm going to go with Cisco Systems' assessment:

It costs many times more to attract a new customer [than] it does to retain an existing one.
Cisco
(http://www.cisco.com/warp/public/3/be/discover/customer_care.htm)

The question about how many times more it costs can only be answered on an individual basis. The more important question is this: Are you measuring your ability to retain customers?

When a would-be buyer surfs away from your site before finishing the buying process, that's called *abandonment*. *Attrition* is when that would-be buyer never returns. The opposite of abandonment is a sale. The opposite of attrition is retention. Hook 'em and keep 'em.

At some specific point in time, a potential customer becomes aware of your offerings. You have reached her. At some point, she shows up at your site. You have acquired her. She becomes more and more qualified, until, at a specific point, she turns into a customer. From then on, continued selling becomes a matter of retention (see Figure 12.9). It's a question of product cycle, lifestyle, and persuasion engineering.

Attrition, then, is the percentage of existing, converted customers who have ceased buying from you and have gone elsewhere after a specific period of time. It can apply to purchases, and it can apply to game players, email newsletter subscribers, and periodic online discussion sessions.

My brother Doug buys a new car every 2 or 3 years. I buy a new car every 10 or 12 years. We've both done well financially, it's a matter of style. My wife, the attorney, goes through ink-jet printer cartridges on a weekly basis. It takes me several months to work through one laser printer toner cartridge.

The Web site that sells cars and the Web site that sells printer cartridges cannot rate my brother, my wife, and myself on the sale scale. When, then, does attrition occur? Four weeks? Four months? Three years? Fifteen years? It boils down to the law of averages and some personal database machinations. We'll save that for the next chapter. In the meantime, you'll need to identify some broad thresholds and a few business rules for dealing with customers who are just about to take that one step beyond. A retention program is a must.

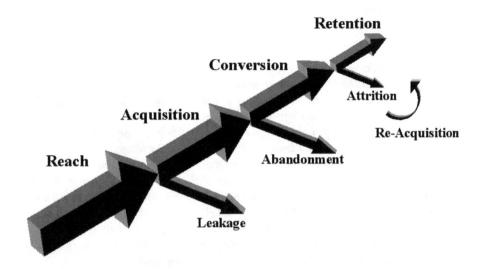

Figure 12.9 Customer retention, whether measured by frequency, participation, or purchases, must be watched.

Churn

Churn is the ratio of retention to attrition. It's great that your site is managing to get 5,000 new people a day to sign up, but if only 1,000 stick around for an appreciable period of time, you have an 80 percent churn rate and you're wasting a great deal of time and money on your promotions. You're spending more and more to get more and more water into that bucket with a very large hole in the bottom.

My own, mostly monthly *Full Sterne Ahead* newsletter goes out to about 5,000 people. If the issue is not very interesting, is too long, or is just not what people want to read, I can lose as many as half a percent of my subscribers in a single day. But if the newsletter is good, I can pick up twice that many in a day, as people forward it to their friends and colleagues. That, coupled with a steady, daily rise in subscriptions, keeps my active subscription numbers growing steadily.

If they have purchased, and they haven't attrited, at what point can they be counted as a loyal customer?

Loyalty

The Merriam-Webster site (www.m-w.com) defines *loyal* as "unswerving in allegiance." People are unswervingly loyal to their utility companies due to lack of choice. People are unswervingly loyal to their life insurance companies through a lack of interaction. But there are very few industries where absolute, unswerving loyalty can be hoped for.

Matt Cutler and I took a hard look at loyalty in our white paper "E-Metrics: Business Metrics for the New Economy" "and found ourselves revisiting recency and frequency, and finally getting around to monetary value:

The customers with the greatest lifetime value are generally those who are not only loyal to your products, but also loyal to your company. They are the ones who are willing to promote your firm and act as references to other prospects. They run user groups and fan clubs. They tattoo your company logo on their bodies.

You know you have a strong brand when a significant portion of your customer base tattoos your logo on their chests and forearms. Just ask Harley Davidson.

On the Web, loyalty also refers to site visits over time. People who visit your site more than once a week may be more valuable than those who visit once a month. Prospects who are considering the purchase of an automobile are more likely to buy if they show up on a daily basis for a month. But there is no expectation they will return month after month. Once the buying decision has been made, they usually will stop visiting car sites altogether.

"Loyalty to me is repeat customers—who's visiting our Web site the most, who is actually purchasing product, data, or whatever. . ." (Technology company)

Loyalty, then, means very different things to different sites. Those selling advertising space to generate income are completely dedicated to increasing the number of site visits and page views. Yahoo!, AltaVista, MSN, and other portal sites are constantly looking for ways to get people to come back more often and stay longer.

"We're starting to look at defining loyalty in terms of our promotions. Are our customers loyal because of coupons or are they loyal because of the brand?" (Retail company)

Loyal customers come back frequently, buy often, recommend your company to others, and readily try out new things. They may even come looking for products or services that you do not offer. Perhaps a customer is a regular buyer at BarnesandNoble.com, but does she also buy at Amazon.com? What if BarnesandNoble.com started selling travel? How quickly would she start buying travel from them? She might be a loyal book buyer, but will she be a loyal CD buyer as well? Will she be devoted and buy just about everything she can from Barnes & Noble? Will she recommend Barnes & Noble to her friends?

Recency, Frequency, and Monetary Value (RFM) analysis helps to answer the most fundamental question in database marketing: Who are my best customers? Using past transactions, each customer is viewed simultaneously in three different dimensions:

>   *Recency. Has the customer made a purchase—or visited your site—recently?*

>   *Frequency. How often has the customer placed orders—or visited your site—historically?*

>   *Monetary value. What is the customer's total spending and profitability?*

Each dimension provides a unique insight about a customer's purchasing behavior:

>   *Recency. Decades of statistical analysis have shown that customers who have made a purchase recently are more likely to purchase again in the near future.*

>   *Frequency. Frequent purchasers are likely to repeat purchasing into the future.*

> *Monetary value.* Customers with high spending in the past might spend again in the near future. This dimension is different from frequency in that it identifies customers who place infrequent but high value orders and, therefore, could be highly profitable.

> Dividing customers into a number of segments using RFM-based clustering methods helps identify and profile customer segments that are not intuitively obvious or visible from reports, yet represent significant opportunities.

Recency

When was the last time a particular visitor came to your site. Does that have a bearing on their loyalty? Oh, yes.

From the e-metrics white paper:

> *Recency is a core measure that describes how long it has been since your Web site recorded a customer event (e.g., visited the site, purchased a product, etc.). Recency is generally considered to be the strongest indicator of future behavior. According to RFM, the most likely users to purchase tomorrow can be readily calculated from past experience. A loyal luggage buyer may buy a suitcase once every three years. Milk, bread, and egg buyers tend to shop weekly. When browser-based cookies first came on the scene, they were used to welcome people back and let them know how the site had changed since their last visit. More than just a parlor trick and more than just a convenient way of keeping people up to date, knowing when somebody was last at your site is an important part of user profiling. As recency diminishes—as the time since the last activity or event increases—the potential for future purchases decreases. Eventually, a predetermined amount of time lapses and the user has officially attrited. In an attempt to reactivate customers, different offers might be targeted to different users as recency fades. If you have shopped at Amazon.com with any regularity, you may have received a "we miss you" gift certificate. The Amazon system notes the consistency of your visits and purchases and sends off an email enticement should you fall outside of your normal purchasing pattern.*

Frequency

From the white paper:

> *Users may visit hourly, daily, weekly, monthly, or less. Here are three scenarios where frequency means different things to different sites.*

> **The Retail Experience**
> *A user who only comes to a florist Web site four times a year may be considered a very loyal customer. A wedding anniversary, Valentine's Day, a spouse's birthday, and Mother's Day are the major flower-giving occasions. A one-time-only user can be encouraged to come back for another holiday as can the user who only comes twice a year. But the*

user who comes four times needs special enticement to increase his or her frequency. A dollars-off coupon, a bouquet-of-the-month club, or a "buy ten, get one free" offer may all appeal. Offers can be tested on each level of frequency to increase response rates.

The Considered Purchase

Deciding on the acquisition of an expensive item creates a decidedly different rhythm of site visits. The occasional click-through at the start of the process gives way to a steadily increasing number of visits up to the moment of purchase. If these traffic patterns are properly modeled, they can lead to a clear indication of when the sale may occur. With this knowledge—and some clever data mining techniques— a company can build predictive models to be more proactive, launch opt-in email campaigns, dynamically alter the site, or have a salesperson call on the prospect. Manufacturers can use information about the frequency of visits to notify their distribution chain about potential sales. Service organizations can watch customer activity to determine the right moment to up-sell and cross-sell. Training departments can track frequency to decide when to offer additional courses.

The Business-to-Business Bond

Frequency becomes even more important when the relationship between parties is long-standing. When extranets are used in the place of electronic data interchange (EDI), the pattern of visits and orders can be very telling as Web site traffic becomes the pulse of the buyer/seller relationship. If a steady customer with a predictable pattern of visits changes her browsing and buying habits, it is a good sign that human intervention can increase the spending potential. Frequency information can yield insight into a customer's displeasure, expose a shift in customer personnel, or signal the possibility of increased business.

Monetary Value

From the white paper:

The monetary value of a Web site user can only be estimated until a purchase is made. The user who comes once a day for a week is assigned a much higher probability of purchasing than one who comes once every three months. As soon as a user becomes a customer, actual monetary value can be derived from spend and profit margin data. Over time, how much does the customer buy per month? How profitable are those sales? What are the characteristics of a high spender versus a low spender?

Figure 12.10 shows a three-dimensional representation of 125 customer segments stratified by recency, frequency, and monetary value scores. How might you market to, sell to, and support customers differently in segment 555 versus 111? What about segments 515 and 254?

Clearly, different Web sites will have different indexes for purchase probability and profitability. But historical ratings of actual customers are of great value when spread across the users of a single site. These are the figures that help sites recognize which users are most likely to become profitable buyers.

Later in the white paper, we discussed how the measurement of these factors would be different, depending on whether you were running a site aimed at a quick purchase, a lengthy, considered purchase, or a business-to-business long-term relationship.

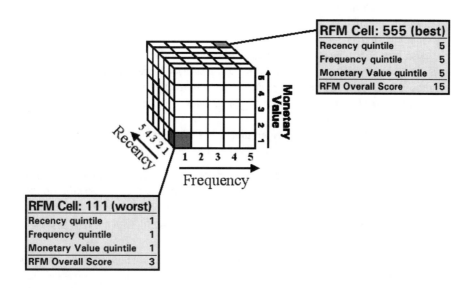

Figure 12.10 Visualization of 125 RFM segments.

The Retail Experience

Customer loyalty here is measured in purchases. How much do they buy? How often do they buy? Are they a profitable customer? The formula for loyalty will include the following variables:

- *Visit frequency. Scored based on number of visits per month.*

- *Visit duration. Scored based on number of minutes per visit.*

- *Visit depth. Scored based on number of page views per visit.*

- *Purchases per visit.*

- *Number of items purchased per visit.*

- *Total revenue of purchases per visit.*

- *Profitability of purchases per month.*

If additional marketing programs are implemented, the customer might be evaluated on factors such as:

- *Number of referrals per month: Did the customer refer others?*

- *Value of referrals per month: Did those referrals buy? How much?*

- *Questionnaire propensity: How willing is the customer to answer survey questions?*

- *Contest participation: How willing is the customer to participate in contests?*

- *Reward points program: How willing is the customer to participate in affinity programs?*

The Considered Purchase

Loyalty can be measured on a short-term basis to try to clinch the sale. It can also be measured on a much longer-term time scale.

If the customer is buying a refrigerator, chances are excellent that she will not need another one for years. You can keep her in your database for those years while waiting for the right opportunity to remind her of your quality and value. Insurance companies keep information on newborns in their database for decades in order to offer additional auto insurance in fifteen-and-a-half years.

Most loyalty calculations will revolve around how the user browses your site. Here we begin with the same variables as above in the Retail Experience, but with a twist:

- *Visit frequency. This is scored based on visits per decision period and mapped to a decision-making curve. Buyers of one type of product will visit a certain number of times in the first period, a certain amount in the middle of the process, and signal that a buying decision is actively being made when they increase (or decrease) to a different number of visits in a set time span.*

- *Visit duration. Scored per session. This is another indication of how close to a decision the user may be.*

- *Visit depth. Page views per visit are as revealing as frequency and duration.*

To this list, we add the important analysis of how the user traverses the site:

- *Site path. How well is the user following an optimal site path?*

- *Contact. How often does the user send email, engage in a chat session, or fill in a form on the site? What sort of questions does the user ask?*

- *Product configurator. How many times does the user run the configurator and which features are selected?*

The Business-to-Business Bond

The metrics change again when it comes to extranets. In the business-to-business environment, the emphasis on selling is replaced with a focus on service. Taking orders and solving problems are paramount, while a less aggressive eye is kept open for up-selling and cross-selling. Loyalty comes in many shapes and sizes, and hence loyalty metrics naturally tend to differ greatly between different sites with different business models.

Visit frequency. *In this environment, the watchword is consistency. Is the user coming to the site at set intervals and doing what is expected?*

Visit duration. *Are there any changes in the amount of time it takes the user to place the order?*

Visit depth. *Is the user looking at products above and beyond his or her norm?*

Visit tenure. *Time elapsed since first visit.*

Purchase tenure. *Time elapsed since first purchase.*

Purchase frequency. *Number of purchases per quarter (or month).*

Total lifetime spending. *Total spending since first visit.*

Visit recency. *Time elapsed since most recent visit.*

Purchase recency. *Time elapsed since most recent purchase.*

Required clicks to first purchase. *Minimum number of clicks required to complete the first purchase in a visit. The first purchase may require more clicks than repeat purchases.*

Required clicks to repeat purchase. *Minimum number of clicks required to make a repeat purchase.*

Actual clicks to first purchase. *Actual number of clicks until the first purchase was made.*

Actual clicks to purchase. *Number of clicks until a repeat purchase.*

Tracking where they went is part of the loyalty factor; the other part is tracking what they do.

Participation Analysis

There's a very large psychological barrier between watching and participating. Any wallflower at a high-school dance can tell you that and the same holds true on a Web site.

It costs nothing (emotionally) to go to a Web site and click around. But provide an email address in return for downloading a white paper? Fill out a survey in exchange for a screen saver? Cough up personal contact information for a chance at winning a contest? Those require a decision and a commitment.

Gregg Dixon is vice president of Internet services at Binney & Smith, named after Edwin Binney and C. Harold Smith, who produced the very first box of eight Crayola crayons in 1903. Dixon knows there's a direct tie between participation and revenue; he just can't quantify it:

Besides the financial sort of things, what we care most about is consumer acquisition and consumer retention. One of the most important performance metrics at Crayola.com is the number of consumer relationships acquired.

At the very end of the day we look at everything as money over time. How many relationships? You can tie everything to that. How many consumer relationships have you actually been able to acquire online? How often do you talk to them? How often are the consumers interacting with the brand?

I really care about how often they come back to the site and how much time they spend immersed in the brand. I'm less interested in whether they view ten pages of stuff—that's great. But certain consumers may only view five pages, and view each of those pages for three minutes and be totally immersed in it. That's the equation that you have to constantly balance. If you've got great quality content, a consumer may only view one page.

Dixon is delighted if a child only looks at one page, as long as it's the right page:

I'll give you a solid example. Part of our site has activity pages for kids to print out. We've got thousands of them. And a child will go there or parents will go there and print things up for them to do; we track how many of those pages they print. You can make a safe assumption given that we pretty much own the market for markers and crayons and pencils for kids, they're probably going to be using our products to engage in those activities. And if they're printing out two million pages per month, we know that they are using our products more.

What we hope to do is make it very easy for them, make it something that they do on a fairly frequent basis and then try to measure the incremental effect. And how many more pages are they printing than before?

Dixon is also able to keep his eye on what activities, themes, and media people prefer because they get to choose (see Figure 12.11).

What do they want to do? They can choose from activities such as these:

- From the Crayola Factory
- Gifts to Make
- Group Activity
- Homework Helpers
- Just for Kids
- Kitchen Table Crafts
- On the Go/Travel
- Outdoor Art
- Party Fun
- Rainy Day/ Everyday Art
- Recycled Art
- Simple Fun for Kids

Then they get to pick a theme:

- Alphabet
- Animals
- Architecture
- Artists' Lives & Work
- Autumn/Fall
- Awards & Honors
- Being Your Best
- Birthdays & Birthday Parties
- Boats & Ships
- Books: Read & Respond

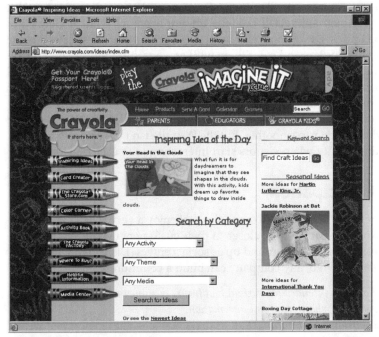

Figure 12.11   By offering fledgling artists a myriad of choices, Crayola is able to capture the shifting trends in their interests.

And that's only up to the B's. There are close to a hundred choices here. Finally, they get to choose just the right medium to express themselves:

- Chalk
- Color Wonder
- Colored Pencils
- Crayola Dough
- Crayola Clay
- Crayons
- Gel Pens
- Glitter Glue
- Glue
- Glue Sticks

Again, the list goes on and on. Simply by watching what kids want to play with, Dixon can tell what products are gaining favor and which are losing ground.

Granted, if you're running a site like WomenSpirit at www.womenspirit.com ("We design and create vestments especially for the unique needs of women clergy"), it might be hard to get priests, ministers, and acolytes to print out their style choices of robes, chasubles, and scapulars and color them with crayons, but there are other ways of measuring interactivity.

I occasionally have this image of a Web as a massive machine, steam operated, with people running around looking at dials and gauges, altering valve settings here, adding a little bit of oil there, watching and listening to it hum, increasing the speed and making the whole thing run smoother. But the Web site isn't the only moving part. It gets tricky tracking loyalty when visitors start interacting with each other.

Community Participation

Socializing has previously belonged to companies that enjoy a very strong brand affinity (Harley-Davidson and Saturn), are closer to their customers (Mary Kay and Tupperware), or are designed from the ground up as social centers (Disneyland and Chuck E. Cheese). Thanks to the Web, any company can build a community:

> *This Discussion Forum is intended for current and future customers of Dragon Systems products to discuss issues, share ideas and information.*
> *www.dragonsys.com/support/webforum.html*

> *Discussion forums are another rich source of information regarding Kodak products and services. Discussions include Digital Photography, Professional Photography, Graphic Arts & Publishing, and Wish List.*
> *www.kodak.com/US/en/corp/forums/index.shtm*

> *One of the best ways to find answers to your questions is to speak with other Parallax customers. Parallax maintains automated email lists to provide a discussion forum.*
> *www.parallaxinc.com/html_files/tech_support/discussion_lists.htm*

Some have learned how to make the most of attracting a group of like-minded individuals.

HOW MARTHASTEWART.COM GROWS PRODUCT SALES WITH ONLINE COMMUNITY

Everyone knows female Web surfers love community. It's genetic. Women are far more likely than men to enjoy writing, sharing information, and reaching out a helping hand. Sites with predominantly female traffic have taken advantage of this from day one of the Web.

But once you have lots of women (and ok, unusually communicative men) visiting your site's community section, how exactly do you make money from it?

Challenge:

When the Web team at Martha Stewart Living Omnimedia (MSLO) decided to add community to their MarthaStewart.com site, Martha herself got involved. Michael Gutkowski, VP Marketing & Business Development MSLO, says, "She really wanted to have it sound distinctive." So, instead of just naming the site area "Community" like every other site, the MSLO gang named it, "Meeting Place."

Gutkowski was in charge of making sure MSLO's investment in this new Meeting Place wasn't wasted.

Campaign:

Realizing that almost everyone who comes to MarthaStewart.com dreams of having a personal interaction with Martha herself, or a Martha-blessed expert, the MSLO online team tried to make the Meeting Place fulfill as many visitor hopes as possible.

First they met with Martha and top company editorial experts to determine which topics and subtopics the site included message boards for—such as Gardening: Seed Swap.

Then they worked deals with related professional associations, such as the National Gardening Association, so professional members would be identified with a "blue ribbon" when posting to the Meeting Place. This meant even though Martha couldn't be everywhere, at least certified professionals could pitch in and give the boards visible credibility.

Gutkowski also hired Blue Barn Interactive, a firm specializing in providing trained staff to manage online community. Blue Barn's job is to make sure that every board is 'touched' at least twice a day. Josh Sinel, CEO of Blue Barn says, "Our approach is subtle. A customer's level of trust in the brand, feeling like they're cared for, will increase exponentially their ability or impulse to buy."

So the Blue Barn team trains MarthaStewart.com Meeting Place reps carefully. These reps read the latest MSLO magazines, watch the TV shows, and know how to drop a non-salesy mention about one of MSLO's 5,000 products available online when the time is right. But as Sinel puts it, "That's not why community is there. If you've outraged people, you've done it too soon." Subtlety versus salesmanship is the order of the day.

Blue Barn keeps its community reps fresh and effective by keeping their hours short. Sinel says, "We allow 2-3 hour shifts for active boards. It varies to intermittent contact in the morning, afternoon, and evening for message boards." In the meantime, the on-site marketing team, led by Gutkowski, maximizes community involvement to sales in three ways (beyond the occasional product mentions tossed in by Blue Barn's folks):

1. **Gathering Mailing Lists:** Before you can post at MarthaStewart.com or explore Q&A transcripts on topics such as "'Weddings," you must become a registered member. The community content itself is a powerful draw to get millions of visitors to sign up. MSLO then uses the information gathered to promote to these highly qualified lists via snail mail and email. In the past few months, Gotkowski's team has been testing more personalized questions (not required) in the regular membership sign-up area. The answers are used to determine if a subscriber should get a particular newsletter, such as Gardening, which contains related content and MSLO product ads.

2. **Following Up with New Members:** When new Meeting Place members sign up, their "Member Confirmation" page and corresponding email features

(continues)

**HOW MARTHASTEWART.COM GROWS PRODUCT SALES
WITH ONLINE COMMUNITY *(Continued)***

a special offer for a 10% off discount at the Martha Stewart By Mail Web site in the next 14 days. They receive a personal source code to input to get their discount so sales can be tracked.

3. Running Special Offers on the Boards: As Meeting Place members visit, they're presented with very tasteful, color photographs of a "Featured Product" at the upper left area of each main category and subcategory page. Featured products simply reveal a pic, price and name—no overt sales copy until one clicks to learn more.

These classy, hotlinked photos add more to the Meeting Place than they take away in terms of crass commercialism. We can't imagine that many visitors actively dislike them. Price points range between $15-$300. Gutkowski says, "In a perfect world we'd sell lots of $500 things, but our visitors want lots of different things."

Results:

James Follo, CFO of MSLO, says, "One of the things we're most pleased about is we've gotten to a point where more than half of commerce revenues are coming via the Internet site. There really are long-term economic, fulfillment and CSR cost benefits from that!"

More interesting numbers from Follo:

♦ MarthaStewart.com's registered users, the vast majority of whom joined to get access to the community features of the site, have now surpassed the 2 million mark. About 100,000 new visitors register at the site each month.

♦ MSLO's total direct buyer files (including online and print catalog buyers) have "increased in excess of 60% over the last 12 months," with an average order size of $74.

♦ More than 50% of MSLO's direct buyer sales are made online—NOT including the sales made by Kmart's Bluelight.com, which are counted separately on the earnings statement under "royalties."

♦ According to Gutkowski, the snail mail addresses captured during the online registration process have a "very high value" and print catalog mailings are "extremely effective" to them. So community is a great way to gather solid direct postal mail lists.

BTW: When Gutkowski talks about the MSLO upcoming site upgrades (and he can't resist slipping in a mention every other minute), he makes little kids excited about Christmas look like nonchalant slackers. In the late fall, the MarthaStewart.com site will apparently be upgraded in many, almost-too-wonderful-to-believe ways. Plus, the company's lucky marketers will able to access a whole new line of back-end reports integrating results from all media — online and off. We promise to bring you an update on this next year. In the meantime, be jealous.

From ConsumerMarketingBiz.com 08/10/2001

That's great. But how do you measure the value of implementing the software, paying the moderator, and making sure your legal retainers are up to date?

PeopleLink (www.peoplelink.com) provides software and services to companies that want to build online communities with chat, discussion groups, instant messaging, online events, and something pretty nifty called Plink Light that lets you discuss the Web page you're looking at with your online friends. In an effort to prove the value of online communities, PeopleLink commissioned the management consulting firm McKinsey & Company (www.mckinsey.com) to conduct a study which evaluated 300 million user sessions across 50,000 unique users between January 2000 and June 2000.

They found that community members are more likely to be buyers. At first, that's sort of like saying people who like to talk about cars are more likely to buy a car. No great discovery there, but it's nice to have the numbers to back up the common sense (see Figure 12.12).

Community contributors visited up to nine times as frequently and purchased nearly twice as often. "Overall, the investigating team found that eCommunity features—specifically message boards and chat rooms—increased both visit frequency and the number of page views. The study also showed that eCommunity features increase retention on media and entertainment-focused Web sites."

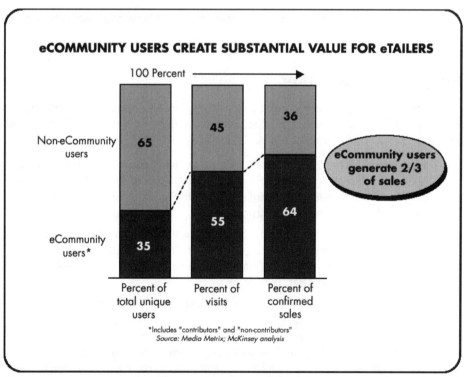

Figure 12.12 The PeopleLink study shows that community members may not be in the majority of visitors, but they are certainly in the majority of online buyers.

The study also came up with the following tidbits:

- Frequent eCommunity users viewed more than two times as many non-eCommunity pages and stayed almost twice as long on non-eCommunity pages.

- eCommunity features add substantial value in cost savings on sales and support web sites.

- Product development costs can be reduced by up to 30 percent.

- Product development cycle time can be reduced by up to 60 percent.

The PeopleLink/McKinsey study was not a lone voice in the wilderness. Jupiter Media Metrix (www.jmm.com) was the first research firm to cover the Internet economy and has been studying, measuring, and reporting on the Internet since 1986. Here's their take on online communities:

High-tech companies should leverage collaborative services. Tools by Betasphere, Quiq, Orbital, and Centerwheel allow businesses to deploy a community for the expressed purpose of allowing customers to collaborate with others to find answers to their queries. These tools are most applicable to high-tech businesses, where engaged clients have a high level of domain expertise. Beyond the potential cost savings that customer-to-customer service can represent, businesses deploying these tools are able to identify those clients that are highly engaged and loyal to the brand. Businesses such as Compaq, National Instruments, and ViewPoint have realized such benefits.
"Understanding Customer Loyalty," Jupiter Media Metrix, 2001

So it turns out that all that touchy-feely stuff that sounds so good, actually *is* good. What a relief.

Bringing It All Together

In order to really get your arms around measuring loyalty, Jupiter says you've got to amass a portfolio of data from four different domains: transactional, marketing, feedback, and channel (see Figure 12.13):

> *Transactional data.* These provide information on spending and transactional habits. Feeding off commerce, site-analysis, and financial applications, transactional data detail customers' overall spending, profitability, visits, clickstream, and merchandise and content category preferences.

> *Marketing data.* Pulling from across channels, these data should identify the source and cost of customer acquisition as well as statistics that detail how involved the customer was in the campaign. Data points include open rate, click-through rate (i.e., response rate), and pass-along rate.

> *Feedback data.* Surveys and community tools that invite participation and feedback provide insight into customers' engagement and levels of satisfaction. Satisfaction is the point at which customers move from passive to active involvement in a brand's development, suggesting that as customers become more satisfied, they are more actively involved with that brand and therefore more likely to tout its advantages to

others. (Overall, the more highly satisfied or dissatisfied customers are, the more likely they are to pass along positive or negative information about the brand.) Feedback mechanisms are further incorporated into the customer valuation and segmentation process.

Channel data. *Incorporating many different businesses units, these data introduce customer service information from a contact center, off-line customer data from retail locations, and field sales and service data. Depending on the complexity of the business and its customers, companies could insert a variety of channel and third-party data here, such as demographic information. Advanced analysis also includes predictive analysis tools that can identify trends and automate companies' reactions to such trends.*

"Understanding Customer Loyalty," Jupiter Media Metrix, 2001

Then, of course, there's all of the other data you collect about customers besides what you glean off your Web site.

In the Q2 2001 issue of *The Journal of Customer Loyalty*, Frank Capek, vice president, eLoyalty (www.eloyalty.com), a company that provides customer loyalty services and software, wrote an article called "The Customer Loyalty Mirror." Capek describes numerous ways a company can improve customer loyalty. He also offers up a chart (see Figure 12.14) to help the reader understand just what we're talking about: personal attitudes.

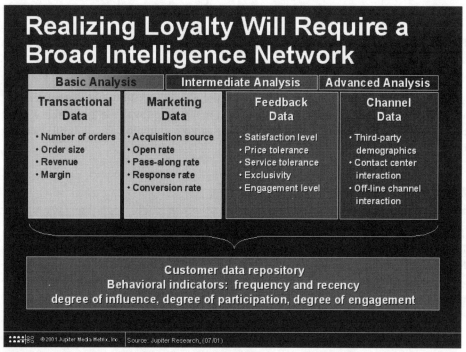

Figure 12.13   Jupiter knows a lot goes into building a loyalty profile.

Loyalty Threshold

Purchase Exclusivity	Open The customer openly tries alternative brands; purchases are distributed over several brands	Favored The customer makes a consistent choice between two comparable and equally convenient brands	Committed The customer makes a conscious decision to concentrate purchases with a single brand	Exclusive The customer refuses to consider or actively resists buying another brand
Willing Inconvenience	Convenience The customer does not seek this brand and buys only when it is convenient	Preferred The customer looks for this brand but generally buys only when it is convenient	Sought The customer looks for and buys this brand over other more convenient alternatives	Pursued The customer willingly goes (way) out of his/her way to purchase this brand
Price Premium	Par Strong demand-price elasticity. Not able to charge a premium over comparable brands without sacrificing share	Premium Pricing is incrementally higher but may be due to market inefficiencies	Insensitive The customer is consciously willing to pay more for this brand than competitive alternatives	Identity The customer identifies with paying more for this brand
Active Promotion	Passive The customer does not demonstrate a point of view about the brand	Willing When asked, the customer is willing to provide a positive recommendation to others	Proactive The customer proactively promotes the brand to others	Enthusiastic The customer enthusiastically and deliberately influences others to purchase the brand

Figure 12.14 Frank Capek shows how to differentiate various degrees of loyalty in customers.

Since you've worked so hard to convince the all-powerful budget committee that Web-based communities are a good thing and measuring loyalty in general is a good thing, convincing them to keep track of *lifetime value* is going to be easy. Implementing it, on the other hand, will not.

Lifetime Value

Tom Peters loves to tell his audiences to fire their customers. Don Peppers and Martha Rogers of One to One Marketing fame love it too. Get rid of those customers who buy low margin products and soak up your customer service time.

The lifetime value (LTV) of a customer is based on the premise that the most expensive part of the relationship is starting it in the first place. Field sales reps in the business-to-business world, advertising in the consumer marketplace, direct mail, print and broadcast advertising all around—it adds up. It can cost hundreds to thousands of dollars to find a suspect, qualify her as a prospect, and close her as a customer.

I asked the director of Internet strategy at a large communications and embedded electronic company what information she was you hoping for, that she'd like to get her hands on, that she's not getting at the moment. She replied: "Calculating the LTV is pretty difficult. And I think that is one of the ones I would really like to get at over time. It's a different kind of business because phones are not bought every month, but we are getting into the application market of downloading applications and accessories, which is opening up the door for more valuable lifetime value analysis."

I then asked: "Have you mapped out the sort of optimal customer experience as far as what they've purchased? We want to start them off buying this and then they buy all the accessories and then they upgrade to that and then we cross-sell them to this other pager, etcetera."

Then the finance manager chimed in: "I've only talked to one company in the past that I thought really did the LTV thing well and that was Harrah's. I've benchmarked with a lot of companies and I haven't found any others than them that really take it to an economic level as well as them."

I had remembered seeing a wonderful article about Harrah's in *Darwin* magazine (May 2001; see Figure 12.15).

Harrah's was able to move customers from property to property once they assured those customers they'd receive the same treatment in Atlantic City as they did in Las Vegas. Then all Harrah's had to do was convince the individual property owners that they weren't giving up the keys to the kingdom by sharing information companywide.

The concept was a good one. After launching a loyalty card program, the 13 percent of customers willing to try out a new location in 1997 rose to 23 percent in 1999. The fact that customers were spending more during each visit didn't hurt either. The fact that Harrah's profits more than doubled since the introduction of the loyalty program didn't hurt at all.

So how do you tell which customers are worth creating special programs? Which are worth the effort of implementing new features on your Web site?

Measuring LTV

The first step in measuring the lifetime value of your customers is thinking of your customers as assets. Just as you would want to spend more of your energy on building maintenance rather than buying a new one every year, you want to focus on customer relationships as something of value to be preserved. You want to calculate the net present value of the profit a single customer will generate over time. This is the sort of thinking that allows stores to sell loss leaders. If they can get the customer into the shop and show them what a nice store they have, that customer will become a loyal customer.

Figure 12.15 Harrah's customers are willing to identify themselves at every slot machine. Harrah's knows who you are.

The questions that need numerical answers are easy to ask but not easy to answer. Some creative accounting may be in order to give you some idea of the LTV of your customers:

- New customers per year (or month, or quarter)
- Customer loss per year (for churn)
- Revenue per customer per year (for static value)
- Cost per new customer per year (acquisition)
- Cost of service per customer per year (service)
- Cost of general overhead and administration per customer per year (G&A)

A net present value (NPV) calculation is thrown in as a discount you apply based on the time value of money and a rate you apply for risk. If 2 percent of your receivables end up as bad debt, that needs to be part of the equation.

In an ideal spreadsheet, the numbers apply to a specific market segment. If it costs three times as much to sell something to a teenager in the Northeast who is five times more likely to leave the fold within months, then advertising on MTV.com is not your best move.

You're going to use the resulting LTV to give you a compass. Should you spend more on customer retention such as a frequent buyers program? More on up-selling and cross-selling? Changes in customer-complaint management systems?

Be sure to consider all the elements that go into valuing a customer, some of which are depicted in Figure 12.16 from Mark Turchan and Paul Marushka's article, "Developing a methodology for measuring customer value" in the Fall 2000 issue of the *Journal of Customer Loyalty*.

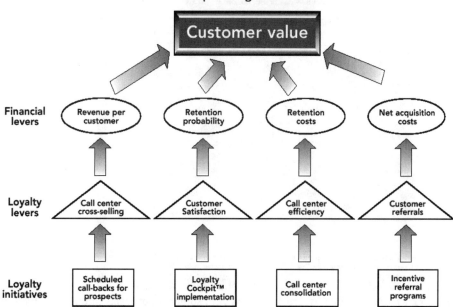

Figure 12.16 Loyalty initiatives, loyalty levers, and financial levers are all part of the customer value mix according to Mark Turchan, senior vice president, and Paul Marushka, vice president, of eLoyalty (www.eloyalty.com).

Clearly, customer value is made up of a lot of different components. If you're serious about LTV, Arthur Hughes of M\S Database Marketing (www.msdbm.com), the author of *The Complete Database Marketer* (McGraw-Hill, 1996) and the article at http://www.dbmarketing.com/articles/Art174.htm, is a good place to start (see Figure 12.17).

Now it's time to bring the discussion back to the Internet and back to the beginning for a moment, and consider how you might recognize a potentially high value visitor on your site.

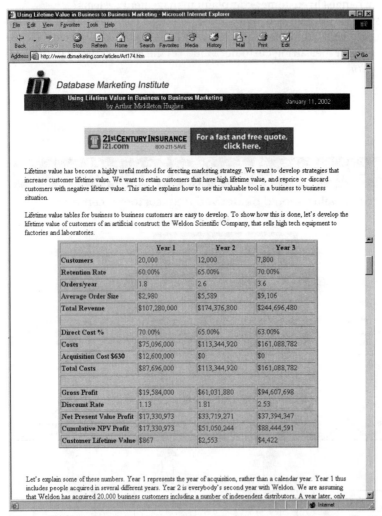

Figure 12.17 Arthur Hughes' article is filled with spreadsheet walks through the math of calculating the lifetime value of your customers.

Buying Power Index (BPI)

The Internet has given us lots of new things to measure, but every now and then, somebody comes up with some new twist on how to calibrate people, actions, or values. That's good—it keeps us all on our toes.

NetScore (www.netscoreonline.com) has combined a couple of old standbys with one of those new twists. Here's how they describe themselves:

netScore is a unique online traffic measurement service designed to provide more accurate indicators of online business performance for both e-commerce and content sites in three ways.

First, netScore utilizes a massive panel of over 1.5 million people, allowing for more accurate results as well as a significant representation of all key audience segments: Home, Work, College & University, and Non-U.S.

Second, netScore uses a revolutionary, patent-pending technology to capture both surfing and buying behavior. In fact, netScore includes the ability to rank sites according to their visitors' online purchasing behavior using its proprietary Buying Power Index (BPI).

And finally, netScore uses a measurement methodology designed to more closely match the way Web log files are created, providing results that are more consistent with a site's actual Web logs.

Assembling panels of people and watching what they do is a time-honored tradition and nothing new. Generating statistics from Web logs or even ways that "more closely match" Web logs is nothing to write home about. But the Buying Power Index is a twist. Here's how netScore defines BPI:

To set the basis for comparison, netScore calculates the average Internet expenditures across all visitors. Specifically, the average dollars spent by all Internet users is calculated by taking total Internet dollars spent divided by all Internet visitors over the analysis period. This number becomes the denominator in the BPI calculation and represents what the "average" Internet visitor is spending. While it is indeed the "true average" of Internet spending, keep in mind that by definition we are therefore including even those very marginal Internet users who have not yet become committed or regular Internet users or buyers.

This number is then compared to the total Internet dollars spent by visitors to a given site or site category. Specifically, we create the numerator for the BPI by summing all the dollars spent across the entire Internet by visitors to a specific site and dividing that number by the number of site unique visitors. Thus, we have the average level of total Internet spending by visitors to the site. The ratio of these two numbers (average Internet $ spent by visitors to site X/average Internet $ spent by all Internet visitors) yields the BPI.

For November 2001, netScore found that all of the top ten BPI sites were travel related (see Table 12.2). I suppose only the well-heeled can afford to travel.

Table 12.2 BPI™ Top 10 November 2001

SITE	BPI
itn.net	659
continental.com	637
united.com	566
delta.com	563
nwa.com	562
hoteldiscounts.com	554
travelnow.com	550
southwest.com	500
hotwire.com	499
aa.com	498

Lucky for those of us who are not in the travel industry, netScore tracks major shopping sites (see Table 12.3), and the top fifty online properties as well.

There's another type of value your customers can provide and it's a little harder to measure: influence over others.

Table 12.3 Total U.S. Unique Visitors (000)—Major Shopping Sites

VS. OCTOBER	NOVEMBER 2001	CHANGE	PERCENT CHANGE
amazon.com	44,212	4,980	13%
Walmart.com	6,612	2,892	77%
Bestbuy.com	7,241	2,506	53%
compaq.com	4,979	2,258	83%
target.com	4,505	1,956	77%
Overstock.com	5,000	1,625	48%
Sears.com	4,698	1,290	38%
Bluelight.com	4,437	733	20%

Viral Value

In the offline world, we call it pass-along for print and word-of-mouth for, well, word of mouth. A customer tells a friend or acquaintance that they had a good experience and that influences the recipient of the news. Online, we've taken to calling it *viral marketing*:

> *A Jupiter Consumer Survey found that viral, or word-of-mouth, marketing has a significant influence on consumers' site selection [see Figure 12.18]; 45 percent of respondents said they frequently select sites based on recommendations from others. The Internet allows businesses to measure such socio-behavioral traits of their online customers, which is nearly impossible to do in the off-line world. Yet, in a Jupiter Executive Survey, 26 percent of respondents said they do not track viral marketing behavior, such as the passing along of email, choosing instead to focus on typical response-rate metrics of email campaign performance. As such, Web sites are missing the opportunity to identify and measure the effects of customers who promote the sites they frequent to people in their sphere of influence—users Jupiter refers to as "viral influencers." The survey also found that only 7 percent of Web sites track measurable viral marketing activities, such as email pass-along rate. Only 10 percent of respondents said they would invest in systems to track viral behavior.*
> *Understanding Customer Loyalty, Jupiter Media Metrix, 2001*

Fig. 2 Sites' Measurement of Viral Behavior

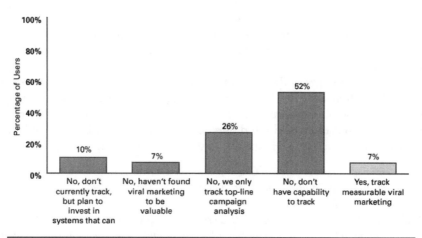

Source: Jupiter Executive Survey (3/01), n = 31 (US only)
© 2001 Jupiter Media Metrix, Inc.

Figure 12.18 A paltry 7 percent of those interviewed by Jupiter Media Metrix were actively valuing the impact of viral marketing.

Yes, we all know the story of Hotmail: free email accounts and every message you send invites the recipient to get their own account. It spread like wildfire. As I said in Chapter 7, "How Good Are You at Buying Noise?," You can't count on a viral marketing campaign. But you *can* count customers, and recalibrate their worth to the company, if you track their viral value.

If customer John Smith recommends entering your contest to a friend, that's great. If Smith recommends the contest to ten friends, that's much better. But if Smith recommends your contest to ten friends who *also* recommend it to ten others—ten whom you have no way of reaching in the first place—then Smith is a very valuable viral node.

A *viral node* is a person, place, or event where the message gets spread. It used to be referred to as the "water cooler" at large corporations before the advent of email. It can also be applied to memes on a global scale as in, "Hong Kong is one of the first viral nodes for Japanese pop trends, along with Taiwan and to some extent, Korea, before those trends metastasize to the rest of Asia and the world." (*Asia Internet Report No. 6,* June 2001, www.asiainternetreport.com/AIR_0106.html.)

When the product announcement budget is limited, those customers who seem to be the most connected become the most valuable. When you're dicing your customers into various slices of revenue potential, don't forget their viral potential. Television, telephone, tell-a-Smith.

CRM

I've tried to avoid moving too far away from the Internet in this chapter, and that's why I haven't tackled customer relationship management head on. Fortunately, others have.

CRM is generally described as mixing all of the customer data you can get your hands on with the fastest computers, the most elegant algorithms, the wisest business rules, and last but not least, a complete change in the philosophical disposition of your corporation. Effortless.

I'm intrigued (and grateful) when others more attuned than I to this area of corporate transformation are able to deconstruct large globs of ideas into manageable chunks. Case in point: John Strabley, Internet consultant at Peppers and Rogers Group. Strabley was asked to explain the difference between analytical CRM, collaborative CRM, and operational CRM. His answer (from www.1to1.com):

> In order to maximize the value of CRM, it must be an enterprise-wide initiative. To that end, analytical, collaborative, and operational describe the three main components in an enterprise-wide CRM initiative.
>
> Analytical CRM refers to utilizing data warehouses, customer and product datamarts in conjunction with tools such as epiphany, SPSS, SAS and NetPerceptions (just to name a few) to drive CRM-focused marketing and campaign management.
>
> Operational CRM refers to CRM implementation in the back office (transaction, order and fulfillment management) components of the enterprise.
>
> Collaborative CRM refers to implementing CRM in customer interaction channels such as call centers, web and email. A few examples of tools/platforms that enable Collaborative CRM are eGain, AskIt and AskJeeves.

While implementing a CRM approach in either of these areas can make a positive impact on the enterprise's bottom line, tying all three around the customer can provide the firm with a 360-degree view, making the initiative more successful and strengthening the firm's competitive advantage.

Silvon Software (www.silvon.com) is a business performance management analytics company. One of their white papers ("Customer Relationship Analytics") included the following tables (see Tables 12.4 to 12.6) outlining what sort of information is collected, how it's analyzed, and what the goals are for doing so.

As you can see, CRM is a huge undertaking, referred in, yet still outside the scope of, a book on Web metrics.

Table 12.4   What Customer Analytics Measure

GETTING CUSTOMERS	KEEPING CUSTOMERS	REWARDING CUSTOMERS
Advertising	Call Center Interaction	Buyer Bonuses
Campaign management	Customer service	Customer incentives
Customer profiling	Privacy support	Discount policies
Merchandising	Product quality	Loyalty programs
Sales analyses	Service quality	Problem resolution
User segmentation	Shipping and fulfillment	Return policies

Source: Zona Research, 2001

Table 12.5   What Is Analyzed

LIFETIME REVENUE CONTRIBUTION	DISCOUNT IMPACT
Net profitability	Performance by month
Channel profitability	Trending
RFM ranking	Propensity to buy
Opportunity analysis	Campaign effectiveness
Return patterns	Return impact on revenue
Return reason ranking	Order fill rate
Order line fill rate	Order shipment rate
Backorder duration	Problem severity ranking
CSR performance	Problem impact on sales

Source: Silvon Software

Table 12.6 What Is Achieved

MARKETING	SALES	SERVICE
Campaign effectiveness	Pipeline improvement	Improved support planning
Visitor experience	Qualification	Reputation improvement
Predictive modeling	Interaction performance	Support plan implementation
Backlog reduction	Lower cost of sales	Delivery performance
Consumption maximization	A/R closure	Fulfillment performance
Production improvement	Distribution effectiveness	Response performance
Churn reduction	Usage improvement	Satisfaction improvement

Source: META Group

CRM ROI

If you're going to follow the path of CRM ROI to its logical conclusion, you can always pick up a copy of Glen S. Petersen's *Customer Relationship Management Systems: ROI and Results Measurement* (Strategic Sales Performance, Inc. 1999).

And, of course, searching for "CRM ROI" in any search engine will keep you busy for weeks.

What are the most important things to remember about measuring the value of personalization on your site?

Divide up your customer base by their needs—the things that interest them. Then rank them by value, remembering that value takes the future into account, as well as those attributes that lead to indirect profits.

Pay attention to what they're doing on a day-by-day basis. Once you have visitors nicely pigeonholed, you have to allow for changes in their needs. Plus, they're going to be after different information or interactions at different times. Treat the shopper differently from the buyer and the merely inquisitive differently from the emphatically engaged.

Pay attention to how visitors fix up your site to their liking. There's a great opportunity for outreach based on their choices and through collaborative filtering.

Use the information you collect and only collect information you can use. As Bruce Kasanoff, author of *Making It Personal: How to Profit from Personalization without Invading Privacy* (Perseus Books, 2001), likes to say: collect information for people, not about them.

Whatever method you use to calculate loyalty, make sure you get enough agreement across your whole company so that year-on-year and department-to-department comparisons are valid.

And finally, don't forget that customer retention has a lot to do with how well you treat them. So much so that customer service deserves its own chapter.

Measuring the Value of Online Customer Service

Customer service seems to get worse and worse. Why, in *my* day, there was such a thing as respect for the customer instead of just respect for the customer's wallet.

Those words could have been spoken yesterday or yesteryear. Sort of like the comment about teenagers not respecting their parents, which is so often attributed to Plato.

The feeling that customer service is bad is pervasive and borne out in study after study. Jupiter Media Metrix (www.jmm.com) surveyed 250 Web sites in December 2001 and found that only 30 percent of the retail sites they sent email or Web forms to responded within 6 hours. It took 18 percent of them between 6 to 24 hours, and another 18 percent took 1 to 3 days. A full third took longer than that, if they responded at all.

Keeping up with the deluge of customer questions is only going to get worse. Dr. Jon Anton of Purdue University says that customer contacts were estimated to have been 15 billion in 2000, apportioned as follows:

- 85 percent by telephone
- 5 percent face-to-face
- 3 percent by email
- 2 percent by Web site
- 5 percent by all other means

By 2005, Anton says the number of contacts will double to 30 billion and look like this:

- 45 percent by telephone
- 25 percent by Web site
- 20 percent by email
- 5 percent face-to-face
- 5 percent by all other means

No, the phone's not going to go away, but the Web and email are becoming more and more a part of daily business.

Having been through the calculations on customer loyalty, we know that good customer service means happier customers, which means more revenues from those happy customers. The trick is quantifying that in order to know how much to invest in customer service that delights rather than disappoints.

Customer Satisfaction *Does* Relate to Revenue

The University of Michigan Business School's National Quality Research Center (www.bus.umich.edu/research/nqrc), the American Society for Quality (www.asq.org), and the CFI Group (www.cfigroup.com) ganged up to create the American Customer Satisfaction Index (ACSI). The ACSI was designed to be a national economic indicator of customer satisfaction with the quality of goods and services available to household consumers in the United States.

It has the distinction of being the only cross-industry national indicator that links customer satisfaction to financial returns. According to the National Quality Research Center:

ACSI's predictive power comes from use of an econometric model that ties customers' evaluations of quality and value to satisfaction; and then explains the effects of satisfaction on customer complaints and customer loyalty. The model also estimates the percent of customers who will use each company again on the next purchase occasion.

Faculty research at the University of Michigan Business School shows that Market Value Added (MVA), stock price, and return on investment are highly related to ACSI. For example, in the most recent year for which ACSI and MVA data are available, firms with the top 50% of ACSI scores generated an average $24 billion in shareholder wealth while firms with the bottom 50% of scores created only $14 billion. Since 1994, changes in ACSI have correlated with changes in the Dow Jones Industrial average. The ACSI model [see Figure 13.1] is a set of causal equations that link customer expectations, perceived quality, and perceived value to customer satisfaction (ACSI). ACSI is linked, in turn, to its consequences in terms of customer complaints and customer loyalty (measured by price tolerance and customer retention). For most companies, repeat customers are major contributors to profit. Thus, customer retention (estimated as repurchase probability) is a major indicator of financial performance. By translating that estimate into dollar amounts, the ACSI is able to calculate the net present value of a company's customer base as an asset over time.

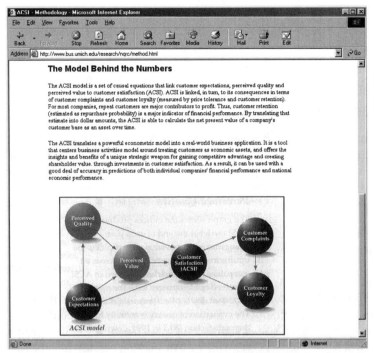

Figure 13.1 The ACSI can be used with a good deal of accuracy in predictions of both individual companies' financial performance and national economic performance.

So there's a benchmark out there, keeping track of how customer delight is or is not turning into increased revenues.

For our current purposes, it's enough to know that there are ways to measure *online* customer service to see if it's helping or hindering our efforts to increase profits.

Online Customer Service Checklist

Online customer service is the greatest thing since sliced bread. Is it saving you time? Check. Is it saving your customers time? Check. Is it saving you money? Check. Is it increasing customer satisfaction? Check. But just how good is it? How much time and money is it saving? How much happier are your customers? It's time to check.

The following handy-dandy Online Customer Service Checklist can be torn out of this book and posted to your wall. Please purchase the book first. And I personally recommend using a copy machine. Once ensconced on the cushy felt paneling of your cubicle, it will remind you to take a look at how you're doing every now and then, instead of spending all of your time just getting it done.

This checklist is only three questions, but they're recursive. Once you've addressed the issues, it's time to readdress the issues. You're never finished asking these questions, and trying to improve on the answers you get:

1. How many people are using your online customer services?

2. How much does that decrease the need for other, more expensive forms of support?

3. How well does online customer service improve customer satisfaction?

How Many People Use It?

How many people are using your Web-based customer service tools? Is it a lot? Is it a little? Is there an industry standard? No. There are no typical answers. There are only your own internal benchmarks and comparisons. The benchmarks include the number of people on your site today versus yesterday and the day before. The comparisons are the number of people using other, more expensive means of getting help from your company.

In the beginning, there were zero people using your Web site for customer service. Slowly, more and more people discovered its value. If the Web really is saving you time and money, then getting more people to use it is a worthy goal. Step 1, count them. Step 2, increase their number.

Getting more people to the customer service portion of your site takes the same skills as getting them there in the first place. You'll need to promote your online customer services just as you would any other significant product feature. Remind people to use your Web site when they contact you in other ways. Playing music while the customer is on hold is nice, but a gentle reminder that they can go to your Web site is nice, too. Give them specific hints. If they pressed the number 3 for order status, the very next message-on-hold should describe where to go on your site for that information, instead of waiting for the next operator. Don't forget to include the cost of educating your customers in that great ROI spreadsheet you're preparing.

How Much Does It Help?

Just how well your Web-based customer care efforts are helping the company depends on how you define your charter. What does your customer service department do? What is its charter? What specific services does it provide? What tasks does it perform to deliver those services? Here're a couple of quick examples (your mileage may vary):

Example 1:

What does your customer service department do?

   Helps customers install and implement our products

What specific services does it provide?

   Telephone support

What tasks does it perform to deliver those services?

   Receive calls

   Respond to calls

   Log calls

   Follow up on installations via phone

Example 2:

What does your customer service department do?

Answers questions about deliveries

What specific services does it provide?

Telephone, fax, and email correspondence

What tasks does it perform to deliver those services?

Receive calls, faxes, emails

Investigate shipments

Respond with anticipated delivery dates

Resolve customer schedule problems

Given a list of the particular tasks your department performs in its daily chores, you can start measuring how much your Web site has improved things for your customers. You can start to track the number of calls and email messages you receive. You can measure the number of problems that come in and the speed with which they are resolved. You can produce a formula to calculate how many calls you deferred due to customers electronically getting answers for themselves.

While you're increasing site traffic, don't forget to record benchmarks for those other means of communication. If call center activity is down, you'll want to correlate that to the increase in Web utilization. If the flow of email slows, you'll want to see if it's related to additional traffic to the new knowledge base. With these numbers in hand, you can begin the ROI calculations that upper management likes so well.

As for whether your Web-based self-help systems improve customer satisfaction, that will have to wait until closer to the end of this chapter. Until then, let's try to populate that spreadsheet with the amount of money we're going to save by having customers answer their own questions and solve their own problems.

Cost Avoidance

What do you do for your customers that costs you money? If you can get them to do it themselves, the first-year gains can be significant.

Niagara Mohawk Power provides electricity to more than 1.5 million in upstate New York. Pam Ingersoll is Niagara Mohawk's director of Digital Marketing and she knows her goals: "I have to do a specific number of online meter readings in 2 months to claim success. We know how much it saves us every time we don't have to make a house call, and we targeted a 20 percent growth rate in savings and did the math. My target is very clear."

At BellSouth, the issue is billing suppressions. Every customer they can get to view their bill online instead of mailing it to them is a monetary win for the company. Getting that up and running might have been the cause of more than one Maalox Moment, but they had a brainstorm that created a perfect testing ground.

Elyse Hammett, manager of Internal Communications, described it to me this way: "We realized that one of the greatest groups that we could immediately impact with this bill suppression campaign that we are currently running was our own employees.

We have 100,000 BellSouth employees, so we created a campaign that we sent out to them to say, 'We need you to suppress your bill.' And we offered them a $5 gift certificate to do that through our BellSouth store for buying things with the BellSouth logo on [them] that they can use personally. The impact of 100,000 employees suppressing their bill and then getting that bill to their email address here at work or at home has saved the company hundreds of thousands of dollars."

At one major airline, they started out just measuring the ticket sales. But then they realized there were savings along with the revenues. Their e-commerce development manager told me, "We don't end up creating a [travel] booking on the site every visit, but the planning features still alleviate call volume and call time spent. We look at all those things with the business unit in mind, and then we come up with some collective measurements. That's especially important with frequent flier award travel because, at the end of the day, award travel is basically free."

"We have three broad levels we look at—migration of communication activities, migration of distribution activities, and migration of service activities—with goals around each of those. Distribution is kind of product delivery or the purchase of an airline ticket. So when we look at migration of distribution activities, that would be migration of customers purchasing from offline channels to purchasing on our site. 'Service' is all the activities that support the primary delivery of our product. So it might be your ability to check on your flight arrival and departure information online."

Not everybody is swallowing the money-savings panacea without thinking. Alan Sacco is the performance manager for e-business at another utility company, First Energy (www.firstenergycorp.com). On the phone with Alan, I divulged my qualms about one of the assumptions I had made and passed along to many a convention audience. I had said that one of the best things about customers doing their own data entry is that they seldom misspell their names. In 1994, that sounded pretty good. Unfortunately, it's not true. People *do* misspell their names.

Sacco jumped on that comment because he's lived with it: "You are then forced to remedy those situations, and if it ends up costing you more than it did the original way; then you gain nothing. In fact, you've lost something. So, you know, it's nice that I've got 100 percent of my customers doing bill paying online except for 15 percent of them make errors. Maybe it was better to do it the original way. Nothing is a slam-dunk."

But there is a wealth of wonderful numbers out there. Hewlett-Packard emails product support alerts instead of using the mail or waiting by the phone and claims the number of calls to the call center have dropped to the tune of $150,000 per month.

IBM claims to have eliminated 99 million calls to help desks by providing online support, which they chalk up as $2 billion in savings.

Just by automating the process of setting up a new password and sending it out 75 percent of the time, SunTrust, the nation's ninth largest commercial banking association, expects to save $2 million every year.

In 1999 Polaroid calculated that support for its digital cameras ran to $4.50 per unit. In 2000, after putting up a self-service Web site (see Figure 13.2), their costs went down to $1.50 per camera.

Figure 13.2 Polaroid initially figured they saved $3.9 million in support costs by having this site available.

But there were those at Polaroid who weren't pleased with the math. Yes, they had 700,000 visitor sessions and only about 5 percent sent in email questions after each session. But general manager Yale Cohen wasn't going for it. Instead, Polaroid ran customer surveys and determined that only about half of the sessions were successful and estimated that 250,000 sessions precluded the need for a phone call. Since they peg their customer support calls at $8, that still represents $2 million in savings. Not bad.

Cost Comparison

Remember my comment about how much more it costs to get a new customer than to sell something to a current customer? Remember how the multiple varied from three times to twenty times? The variance in the difference between providing customer service offline and online is almost as dramatic.

Table 13.1 shows a round-up of costs for supporting customers, taken from white papers, advertisements, magazine articles, industry studies, convention presentations, and interviews during 2001. Your mileage *will* vary.

Table 13.1   Single-Incident Customer Support Costs

TYPE OF ORGANIZATION/TRANSACTION	OFFLINE	ONLINE
Financial	$8	$.38
Hotel booking	$9	$3
Password reset	$30	$.03
Stock transaction	$45	$5.25
Membership registrations	$4.73	$.04
Phone	$5.50	n/a
Web chat	n/a	$7
Email	n/a	$5
Email	n/a	$2.50 - $10
Web self-service	$.35	n/a

You shouldn't spend all your time thinking about making money, but you also shouldn't spend all your time thinking about saving money. There's also the problem of potentially missing out on future income.

Opportunity Cost

First Energy's Alan Sacco put it well: "When you design an effective portal for customers to allow them to pay online, it gives you the ability to track a lot of things. Number one, it gives you return email capabilities. You can respond to most customers who go to your Web site and pay electronically, and solicit them for additional services. You can provide them a portal environment where they can monitor their usage, you can read their meter, and perhaps remotely install software. There are just a thousand and one doors it opens up."

If you avoid those opportunities, you're leaving money on the table. If online bill presentment and online bill payment don't offer up an immediate return on investment, they might open some of those doors Alan alluded to.

Pain Avoidance

Making money is good. Saving money is too. But making your customers happy is critical. Your Web site can offer you a few additional clues to your visitors' well-being, in order to make their experience as pleasant as possible.

Call Center Complaints as a Navigational Barometer

I remember my first call to a phone number on a Web site. It was 1995 and I called the 800 number on the Panasonic site. I wanted to know if their brand-new all-in-one fax/copier/printer would work on a Mac and I ask if they had posted any detailed specifications on their Web site. I had looked but couldn't find anything.

"Any specifications on our what?"

"On your Web site."

"I don't know that we have a product by that name."

"Yes, I know. I'm trying to find out about your new multifunction fax machine."

"Yes! I can help you with that."

"And I was wondering if you had any additional information about it on your Web site."

"Oh, you mean that Internet stuff? Oh, heck, darlin', I don't know anything about that stuff."

"Ahh."

I asked some serious customer service people (Cisco Systems) about their call center experiences; I had heard about how customers are getting smarter because of the Web and how customer service has changed at that company.

"Our customers are better informed, and are asking a higher tier of question when they do write or call in," says Peter Corless, content manager for Cisco Systems' Web site (www.cisco.com).

As a result, customer service reps have to be better informed and better connected to the systems and people who have the answers. "The Cisco channel and support representatives have to step back from controlling—or bottlenecking—customer transactions, says Corless. "Instead, they must become facilitators and escalation points. They need education on the mechanism the customer is using to obtain self-service. They need to learn it inside and out from the customer's point-of-view rather than the finer details of how the machine operates under the hood. They do not need to be breathing encyclopedia volumes, but rather reference librarians."

So keep a sharp eye on the types of questions your call center is getting. If the number of questions about finding information on a particular product starts climbing, you might have a really popular product on your hands. Or, you may have a Web site that is actively keeping people away from the information they want.

Kio Suarez from DuPont translated call center calls to a new site design and directly back to savings. "We have saved around $100,000 in processing unsolicited inquiries for our 800 number since we launched the new site, because with the old site people were not able to find their way. With the new site they can. So we have registered 600 to 800 less phone calls a month after we launched the new site.

"And also the number of complaints about the usability of the site that we get by other means, like email, are declining. So it's not just the 800 number. We've saving on all the other ways of getting that feedback."

The Most Frequently Asked Questions

One of the more interesting pieces of information you can dig out of your server logs is this: Which frequently asked question is the *most* frequently asked? This will highlight a subject that requires immediate attention. If there is one question that gets far more attention than any others, you'll want to use all haste in getting that question answered before others have to ask.

Chances are excellent that there is some root cause for this question being asked so often. Is it a question people have because of a misconception about your goods and services? Did your advertising give them the wrong impression? Did your competitor start promoting a new feature or service and suddenly people are looking to see what you have to say about that feature on your product?

The FAQ has come a long way since it was a text list of questions and answers. As new types of customer self-service tools become available, new types of metrics come with them.

The single.html Q&A page went out in 1995. Today, at the very least, your FAQ should be made up of a list of questions that link to the appropriate answer pages. That way, your logs can tell you what's on people's minds simply by reporting the questions they click on.

Troubleshooting Guide

A troubleshooting guide takes your site visitors by the hand and leads them gently down whatever path best describes their troubles.

Following the path leads, hopefully, to a resolution. Following the paths your visitors follow leads to insight about where they're having trouble. The implementation is simple and the insights can be significant.

At the Automotive Information Center's AutoSite (see Figure 13.3) (www.autosite. com), it's a simple matter of deciding whether your car looks bad, feels bad, sounds bad, or smells bad.

If strange noises are emanating from your vehicle, you have to identify the type of noise you're hearing:

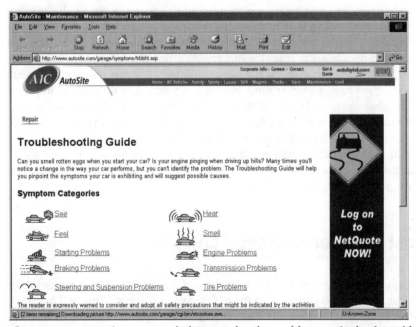

Figure 13.3   AutoSite wants to help you solve the problem you're having with your car.

- Thumping and Clunking
- Grinding, Squealing, Scraping, and Growling
- Popping, Clicking, and Knocking
- Hissing, Whirring, and Buzzing
- Radio or Horn Not Working
- Too Loud
- Rattling

Follow the grinding, squealing, scraping, and growling path and you may discover that you have a loose or damaged alternator drive belt. AutoSite has the ability to keep track of the most commonly investigated problems. How would that look in your case?

You might discover that your clients are more upset about your billing practices than anything else. You might find out that your packaging leaves something to be desired. You might learn that the little rubber feet on the bottom of your electric stapler fall off far more often than the staples get jammed.

Knowledge Base/Chatterbot

The next step up the Customer Interaction Continuum (see Figure 13.4) represents the beginning of some serious investments.

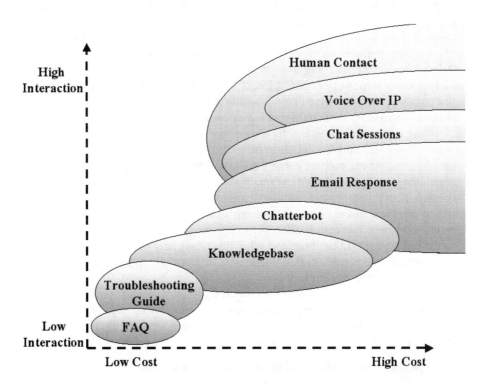

Figure 13.4 The Customer Interaction Continuum leads from the static to the personal.

You could call the information in your Palm or Visor a knowledge base and you'd be right. But typically, a *knowledge base* refers to a large collection of subject-specific information with a natural language front end. People type in a question and the knowledge base comes back with the most likely answer(s).

The most common interface offers up a series of possible questions linking to their answers. If you've ever used a generic system like Ask Jeeves (www.ask.com), then you know the drill. The results vary greatly, depending on how good and how diligent you are at asking questions.

But when these systems are applied to specific realms of knowledge (unjamming a printer, cooking a chicken, or the inhibition of HIV-1 protease by a boron-modified polypeptide), then they become very astute.

Most knowledge base systems provide answers by building rules or keywords. This takes a lot of time to deploy and maintain. A question like "How much does it cost?" could return information on pricing, cost of goods sold, how products are built, and so on.

Newer systems, like the Banter (www.banter.com) Relationship Modeling Engine (RME), maintains and improves its accuracy over time through real-time learning. That is, the system learns, not with keywords or with the complex building of rules, but by employing sophisticated natural language processing. The science behind this stuff gets into the esoteric very quickly, but the back-end results are very informative.

Instead of seeing which frequently asked questions people are clicking on, and instead of seeing which previously asked-and-answered questions people feel most closely match their needs, the Banter system interprets the meaning in their questions, calculates the most likely response, and does the rest.

Humans don't write formulaic questions. They type inquiries like, "Hi there—3 weeks ago I got a confirmation that my books were shipped, and my credit card was charged. It is 22 days later, and still nothing showed up. My Conf number is 2134-656534-294/a. Can you let me know what's up? Regards, John." When faced with such an inquiry, the Banter engine comes up with the most likely meaning (see Figure 13.5).

Besides their Web-based chatterbot interface to knowledge bases, Banter has a system that can answer emails in exactly the same way. What's this about? What's the best answer? Where do I find the details to fill in the blanks?

Email management metrics come into play here as the technology that supports your email agents can measure how much faster those humans can respond to email.

Banter's Reply system obviously can't answer every question—they're just too varied. It's very good at answering 70 percent of the questions with an extremely high degree of accuracy. The rest, it offers up to human agents, along with suggestions on what the question might be about and what the most likely answers might be. The reason the system is so capable is that it learns. It watches which answer the agent sends out and knows better for next time.

Suddenly, you are able to delve into a rich body of customer inquiry information. You can learn not just what people are asking, but how they are asking. You can differentiate between customers who are curious and those who are aggravated. You can track trends on what sort of help people are seeking:

- 68 percent don't understand the assembly instructions
- 13 percent want to know where to buy it

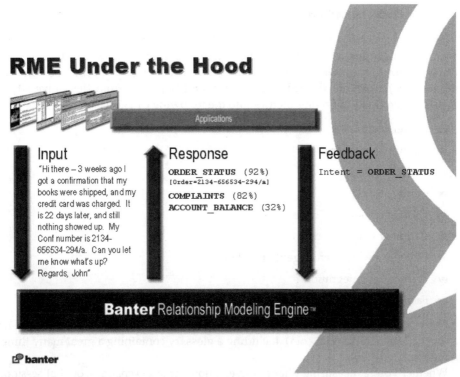

Figure 13.5 Banter thinks this question might be about several issues but calculates an overwhelming likelihood that it's an order status question.

- 9 percent can't get it to turn on
- 6 percent can't get it to turn off
- 4 percent want to know the weather in Seattle

Where should you spend you time and effort? It's pretty clear that the assembly instructions need work.

The next step up after knowledge bases with self-educating auto-response front ends is people.

Human Metrics

Call centers have been a part of our businesses since the telephone. Keeping the costs down and the quality high have been the goals of every call center manager. To understand whether your Web site is doing a good job at servicing your customer and saving the company money depends on whether your people are able to provide better service at a lower cost.

It's time to compare some traditional customer service metrics to some new metrics.

Call-Center Metrics

Purdue University has conducted a nationwide call center benchmark study for the last four consecutive years. These studies allow you to compare your call center performance not only to world-class practices, but also industry-specific, best-in-class metrics. Dr. Jon Anton of Purdue University and Stijn Spit from the University of Maastricht grouped call center metrics into the following categories:

- Center costs
- Performance metrics
- Caller satisfaction
- Center strategy
- Human resources
- Call flow work processes
- Caller knowledge and agent knowledge
- Technology integration
- Facilities

There is a great deal of call center benchmarking information at the Benchmark Portal (www.benchmarkportal.com), including a glossary containing a great many things to measure.

Whether you're measuring phone conversations, email exchanges, or chat sessions, the types of numbers look very much the same:

- Contacts per day
- Contacts per agent
- Call durations
- Abandonment rates
- Contacts per resolution
- Contacts per problem type
- Solution duration
- Average required escalation
- Contact initiation delay (time in queue)
- Savings of contact method vs. telephone
- Agent idle time
- Staff satisfaction
- Customer satisfaction

All of the above, of course, are important not in and of themselves, but in how they change over time. The two important things are to watch the big picture to make sure you are constantly improving, and then to watch for the spikes, which indicate the unusual problems. One manager in a large manufacturing company told me: "I see the metrics on a weekly basis and I look at some of the responses. I adjust a little bit here and there, if there is an issue we see continually. It's the common themes and threads you see throughout the emails, so I try to say, 'Look, we've had twenty-five to fifty emails on this one issue, which is probably enough that it is significant that we have to make a change or an enhancement to the current system to accommodate that specific request.' I look for themes in the messages, but as a project manager I can't take the time to read them all."

Tracking the interplay between your call center staff and your customers may be old hat, but tracking the interplay between your customers is new.

Customer Influence

Measuring the value of viral marketing is interesting, but insider influence is also notable, seldom considered, and may be as bottom-line valuable as getting the word out to new prospects. Insider influencers are people (primarily in the technology sector) who like to help others. They become part of the community we discussed in Chapter 12, "Maximizing Customer Information: The Personalization Continuum." Measuring the impact of specific customers on your support costs has become a science.

First, you need to get a handle on how many people are posting messages to which topics. For that, there are companies like PeopleMetrics (www.people-metrics.com). In addition to providing bulletin board software that can be accessed 24/7 and integrates multimedia, graphics and Web pages, PeopleMetrics provides reports to help keep track of which volunteers are posting how often to which topics (see Figure 13.6).

eFocus Volunteer

Participants	Day 1 Topic #1: Th	Day 1 Topic #2: Th	Day 2 Topic #3: Wh	Day 2 Topic #4: W	Day 3 Topic #5: T	Day 3 Topic #6: Wh	Day 3 Topic #7: Ex	Day 4 Topic #8: L	Day 4 Re:Topic #9:	Day 4 Re:Topic #10	Day 5 Topic #11:	Day 5 Topic #12: T	Day 5 Re:Re:Topic	Total Posts
Alpha	1	1	0	0	0	0	0	1	1	1	1	0	1	7
Beta	1	1	1	0	0	0	0	1	0	0	0	0	0	4
Chi	1	0	0	0	0	0	0	1	0	0	0	0	0	2
Delta	1	2	1	1	1	0	1	1	1	1	1	1	1	13
Epsilon	1	0	1	0	1	1	1	1	0	0	0	0	0	6
Eta	1	1	1	1	1	1	1	1	1	1	0	0	0	10
Gamma	1	2	1	1	0	0	0	1	0	1	0	1	1	9
Iota	1	0	0	0	0	0	0	0	0	0	0	0	0	1
Kappa	1	1	1	1	0	0	0	1	1	0	0	0	0	6
Lambda	1	0	1	1	0	0	0	0	0	0	0	0	0	3
Mu	1	5	1	2	0	0	1	0	0	0	0	0	1	11
Nu	1	6	1	2	0	0	0	0	0	1	0	0	0	11
Omega	0	0	1	2	0	0	0	0	1	1	0	0	0	5
Omicron	2	4	1	2	1	1	1	1	1	1	0	0	1	16
Phi	1	2	1	1	1	0	0	0	0	0	0	0	0	6
Pi	0	0	0	0	0	0	0	0	0	0	0	0	0	0
Psi	2	1	1	0	0	0	0	1	0	0	0	0	0	5
Rho	1	2	1	1	0	0	0	0	0	0	0	0	0	5
Sigma	0	0	0	0	0	0	0	0	0	0	0	0	0	0
Tau	1	0	1	0	0	0	0	0	0	0	0	0	0	2
Theta	1	2	1	1	0	0	0	0	0	0	0	0	0	5
Upsilon	1	1	1	1	1	1	1	1	1	1	1	1	1	13
Xi	0	0	0	0	0	0	0	0	0	0	0	0	0	0
Zeta	2	1	1	3	1	1	1	1	1	1	1	1	1	16
Zu	1	1	1	1	1	1	1	1	0	0	1	1	0	10
Total Posts	24	33	19	21	8	6	8	13	8	9	5	5	7	166
Topic Response Rate	0.84	0.64	0.76	0.6	0.32	0.24	0.32	0.52	0.32	0.36	0.2	0.2	0.28	
Total Response Rate	0.88													

Figure 13.6 This PeopleMetrics report shows Participant Pi was a party pooper and almost everybody was willing to post to Topic #1 on the first day.

QUIQ, Incorporated (www.quiq.com) takes things a step further. Rather than looking at a threaded discussion merely as a way to run an online focus group, they saw companies using it for customer self-service as well. How, then, can you manage and measure the effectiveness of that self-service?

Carrie Alston, director of World Wide Customer Care at Compaq, handles the operation of customer service tools on a daily basis. When she looked at QUIQ's tools she was enthused, but skeptical. She wasn't willing to jeopardize support quality just for a new piece of software. "We need to continue ensuring great turnaround times for new questions. It's important that this is a true support application, not a casual community."

QUIQ offers up a "three-shield" model. First, customers get served from the existing knowledge base. If this doesn't help, the customer can post a new question to all other participating customers. If nobody responds fast enough, questions are brought to the attention of backup Compaq support personnel.

"In the beginning, we were overly conservative," Alston admits. "We had a hard time trusting the user base to provide answers within our timeframe, so we escalated unanswered questions after 4 hours. That's why we initially deployed a large pool of 15 backup Compaq resources. QUIQ did a great job in delivering reporting evidence that convinced us to realize the full potential of its cost efficiencies. Today, over 60 percent of all answers come from the customer base at an average turnaround time of 4 hours [see Figure 13.7]."

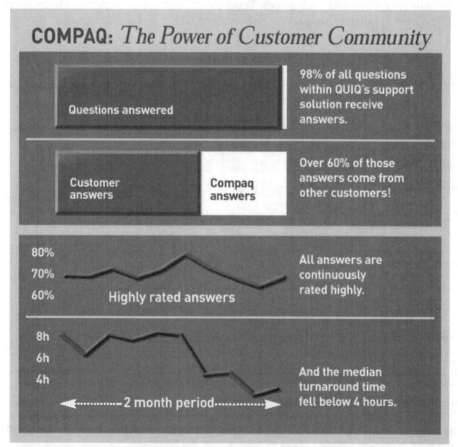

Figure 13.7 Compaq was happy they improved technical support turnaround with QUIQ.

"Now, we only have to use our support personnel when they are absolutely needed, and our level of support quality remains high," says Alston.

That's great, but what about the support that those customers are offering each other? Just how good is it? First of all, people's reputations are made or broken here, so bad advice will likely be rare. But, beyond that, an intelligence agent will constantly listen in and tell you right away if people start giving each other bad advice. QUIQ includes the ability to create intelligent filters that watch for specific phrases that might accompany specific subjects. It can tell right away if people are referring to your packaging as simple, easy, strong, and good-looking, or weak, sloppy, broken, and inadequate.

Finally, how do you motivate people to help each other? First, you have to see who's posting how often. QUIQ divides the participants into three groups: normal users, enthusiasts, and experts. The Executive Performance Report (see Figures 13.8 and 13.9) shows more than the percentage of answers posted by each type of user.

One of the reasons I'm such a QUIQ proponent is the depth of reporting they offer, slicing and dicing statistics on when questions, answers, opinions, and rating were posted, by type of user, with how much time lag between question and answer, within how many sessions, and so on. Lots to sink your teeth into.

As a result, companies know which of their customers are providing the best support and can reward them. Some offer prizes like a new handheld computer. One more technical company got creative and offered a "Meet the CIO" breakfast. They know their audience.

With all of these ways to measure what people are doing on your site by analyzing server logs and watching their behavior, there is one area of measurement that we haven't touched on yet that's fundamental to determining the success of your Web site: Ask your customers for their opinion.

QUIQ Executive Performance Report

"Health Metrics" for week ending	10/20/2001	10/27/2001	11/3/2001	11/10/2001	11/17/2001	11/24/2001
Self-Service Effectiveness						
Ratio of Self-Service Queries to Questions submitted	68	73	68	71	73	73
Mass Collaboration Effectiveness						
Percentage of Answers posted by Experts	39%	59%	61%	58%	53%	49%
Percentage of Answers posted by Enthusiasts (%)	15%	12%	13%	11%	11%	11%
Percentage of Answers posted by Normal users (%)	46%	29%	26%	31%	36%	40%
Percentage of Unanswered questions (%)	2%	1%	1%	1%	2%	3%
Turnaround time distribution						
0-8 hr	47%	37%	43%	40%	37%	36%
8-12 hr	12%	10%	13%	14%	14%	10%
12-24 hr	15%	14%	13%	14%	16%	15%
>24 hr	26%	39%	31%	31%	34%	39%
Community Vibrancy						
Ratio of New Registered Users to Unique Visitors	5%	4%	4%	4%	4%	4%
Ratio of Active Registered Users to New Registered Users	135%	132%	132%	137%	137%	132%
Ratio of Experts/Enthusiasts to Active Registered Users	5%	4%	4%	4%	5%	4%
Nature of Demand						
New Category subscriptions	54	69	95	73	74	69
New Expert subscriptions	3	10	9	13	23	22

Powered by ⊙ QUIQ

Figure 13.8 This generic sample QUIQ report shows how effective the self-service discussion has been.

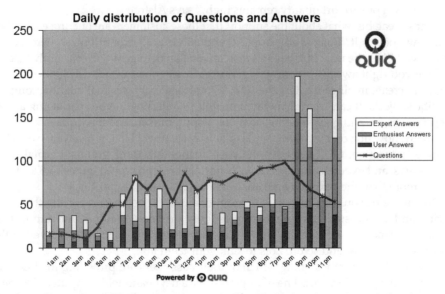

Figure 13.9 Staffing decisions can be made based on the chronological distribution of questions asked and answers posted.

Measuring Customer Satisfaction

As obvious as it may seem, and as important as it is, it is surprising how few companies take customer opinion into account. Jupiter Media Metrix noted this lack of interest in their "Understanding Customer Loyalty" report:

> *Customer loyalty, as many companies currently define it, is a flawed metric: It relies only on easy-to-grasp monetary data such as customers' spending habits and order values. Because most businesses focus on these quantitative measures to identify loyal customers, they too often identify only high-transaction customers as loyal ones. A Jupiter Executive Survey found that 63 percent of Web sites define their loyal customer segments—and the subsequent value they place on these relationships—by customers' spending habits and order values. However, customers tend to be loyal to merchants that win their trust over time via a series of positive events, and many satisfied and loyal customers whose spending is not in the high-dollar category can evade a company's radar screen altogether. To more accurately identify loyal customers, companies need to incorporate rich data that provide a broader view of who their customers are, such as behavioral and satisfaction data; just 13 percent of respondents to the survey said they use satisfaction data when identifying loyal customers [see Figure 13.10]. The incomplete approach to identifying loyal customers companies use currently alienates valuable but lower-spending clients who, through their recommendations to others, may provide a low-cost means of customer acquisition.*
>
> *Understanding Customer Loyalty, Jupiter Media Metrix, 2001*

Most Sites Do Not Look Beyond Monetary Measures to Identify Loyal Customers

Fig. 1   Metrics Sites Use to Identify Loyal Customers

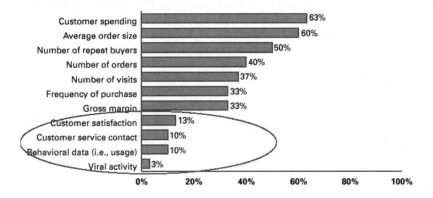

Question asked: What metrics do you use when determining and labeling your most loyal customers?
Source: Jupiter Executive Survey (3/01), n = 30 (US only)
© 2001 Jupiter Media Metrix, Inc.

Figure 13.10   Very few companies are looking at what their customers have to say about offered services.

According to a Modalis Research Technologies (www.modalis.com) study commissioned in August 2001 by WorldCom, 90 percent of U.S. consumers have used the phone for customer service, but only 46 percent gave it an effectiveness vote of "high satisfaction." On the other hand, of the 12 percent of consumers who have used online chat for help, 62 percent were highly satisfied.

While more and more customers are finding Web customer service more satisfying, few companies are asking customers how those services can be made better. Odd. For heaven's sake, *ask your customers what they think!*

How You Are Perceived

Dave Taylor, president and founder of Intuitive Systems (www.intuitive.com), always reminds his clients to get direct feedback about their Web efforts from their customers:

- *Is the site well designed and easily understood?*
- *Are problem reports promptly followed up?*
- *Are problems quickly resolved?*
- *Are customers able to get a high priority when they have a real emergency?*
- *Are customers given training opportunities?*
- *Are they informed of system and product changes—software upgrades, bug fixes, etc.?*

At this point, it's no longer about logs and charts and statistics. It's about perception. If your customers don't feel they're getting the information they need or getting the attention they deserve, it doesn't matter if your logs show more pages viewed this week than last.

So if you *really* want to know what your customers think about your Web site, ask them. You can easily incorporate online surveys ranging from a simple plus or minus on the page to an all-out telephone blitz.

Plus or Minus

There's an interesting feature on the OpinionLab home page. In the lower-right corner, there's a little "[±]" hovering on the page. As you scroll up and down, it floats back to its place in the bottom right corner. When you roll your mouse over it, up pops a very succinct questionnaire (see Figure 13.11).

Pop-Up Surveys

Popping up a survey is a time-honored tradition, and companies like Gomez (www.gomez.com) and BizRate.com are well-known players in that field. They can provide services and aggregated results suitable for benchmarking. Everybody's experience adds to the mix.

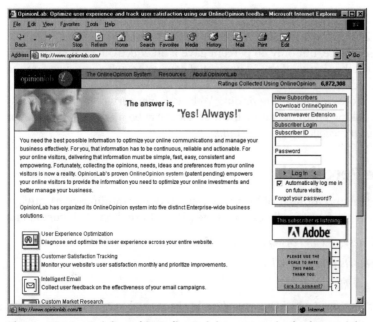

Figure 13.11 OpinionLab's OnlineOpinion system in the lower right corner wants you to rate the page you're on, on a five-point scale.

Steve Robinson from Xerox likes pop-up surveys as a touchstone: "From a metrics standpoint we're trying to gauge usefulness on our driver download capabilities. So what we did is put an online survey on there that asks 'Was the process of download-ing a driver as expected or less than expected or better than expected?' with a simple click-box that they can check off. We also provide a place for them to add text if they feel strongly enough to send us a comment. I surf through them to figure out what kind of enhancements and changes we should think about."

Kris Carpenter at Excite is well versed in the fine art of customer surveys for check-ups: "We have a real-time survey tool that will just pop up and have either one or two quick questions that can be quickly answered, and the idea is we have a way to get some very immediate feedback; we can run it for a couple of hours or a day or a hand-ful of days, whatever we think is appropriate to get enough body of information. Those we use pretty regularly to test new features or to just get quick responses on how sat-isfied you are with our service.

"But we also rely on the third-party research to help us look not just at our own responses collected through direct interaction with our audience, but having a third party ask someone about how they feel about the experience they got on Excite and how it compares to similar sights they've visited and so forth. So, you get another level of detail there . . . . And you know, in every case there's always a little bit of a discon-nect between what consumers say and what they actually do, but given both of those dimensions and the customer responses that we get through email and so forth, we're able to get a pretty good body of data from the consumers themselves."

An e-business director from one energy company told me that they have eight sep-arate surveys on their site, depending on what kind of transaction you perform. But she was more interested in the cross-functional results. "Our research group samples from all of the contacts that we have had with customers by channel, whether it was a Web contact or a call center contact or an office contact. So they standardize that satis-faction questionnaire across the different channels. They are very comparable numbers and the Web site quality numbers are actually slightly higher than the others."

I can hear her smile.

"I think that," she continues, "as good as some of my associates are, you can't qual-ity control that experience as well as you can on the Web site. I think we deliver more consistent service electronically."

Then she told me one of those statistical validations to one of my general, unfounded convictions.

"We did a one-time research study online and we saw a really interesting and statis-tically valid trend. Regardless of what they did on the Web site, if they did anything, they were more satisfied with the company at large. It significantly improved their desire to stay with us. So those are the kinds of things that continue to fuel my funding."

While measuring customer satisfaction is an industry unto itself and it would be silly for me to try and duplicate all of the philosophies and findings here, there are three points I'd like to make before moving on:

1. Ask questions about your questions.

2. Synthesize your answers into business outcomes.

3. Go straight to the horse's mouth.

Ask Questions about Your Questions

I first saw this used at Cisco and then discovered that it's a time-honored tradition. But I was so impressed at the time that I make sure to impress it upon others: When you ask how well things are going, be sure to ask how important it is that things go well.

I recently emailed Dell a tech support question. After the issue was settled, I received an email inviting me to take a survey online that included not only questions about how satisfied I was but also questions about how important it was that I be satisfied (see Figure 13.12).

This gives the organization the ability to determine which things that make customers unhappy are the most important to fix first.

Besides threaded discussion groups, PeopleMetrics does online surveys and they do them very well. After getting his Ph.D., President Sean McDade spent several years at Gallup Consulting Group. What do they do well? Allowing you to analyze the data.

It's nice to know that 65.33 percent of the employees you talk to are satisfied or very satisfied with the company as a place to work. But how do those numbers change when the employee has had, say, more than 6 days of training in the prior 12 months? (See Figure 13.13.)

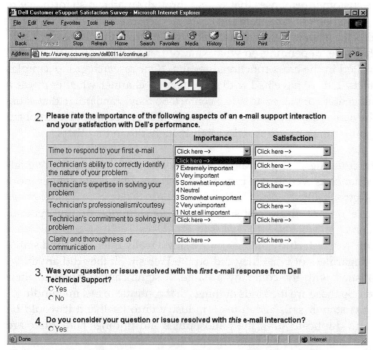

Figure 13.12 Dell wanted to know if the speed with which they answer their email is any more important than their ability to solve my problem.

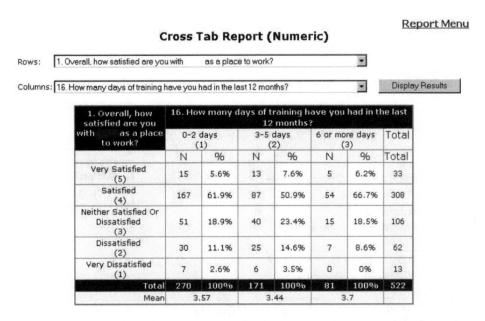

Figure 13.13 PeopleMetrics' reporting lets you slice and dice at will to uncover those counterintuitive insights you might otherwise miss.

Synthesize Your Answers into Business Outcomes

Asking questions and pouring over the answers is interesting, but you can't just hope to trip over a golden nugget, even if they *do* call it data mining. Sean McDade offers some good advice about asking questions: Make sure the answers roll up into something meaningful.

One December morning, over a couple of cups of hot chocolate overlooking the Santa Barbara coast, McDade pulled out an example of an analytical model for a software company. It showed how satisfaction with the sales process was dependent on technical skill, product knowledge, and market intelligence. Product satisfaction was dependent on software performance, ease of obtaining information, and server scalability, and so forth. Here, with a tip of the hat to Sean McDade, is a model of customer satisfaction of a Web site (see Figure 13.14).

This model provides checks and balances to ensure the recording of accurate attitudes. You know what your revenue and profitability are. You know what your retention looks like. Compare those numbers to the way people answer questions about overall satisfaction, but don't stop there. Which of the people/process drivers is having the biggest impact on overall satisfaction? Find out by asking people to rate your visibility, usability, content, and so on. By mixing in and jumping back and forth from questions about your navigation, your knowledge base, your search engine placement, your voice-over-IP services, and so forth, you create a much richer set of verifiable opinions about your site.

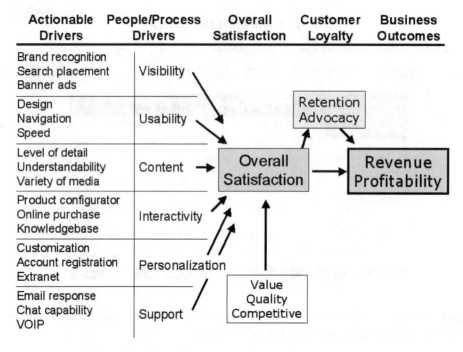

Figure 13.14 Analytical model of Web site satisfaction.

Go Straight to the Horse's Mouth

There is a whole wealth of information to be garnered from people on a one-to-one basis, even if it's over the telephone.

This was brought home to me recently while doing a series of interviews with Web masters. I had retained English & Associates in Nashville, Tennessee, to make the calls, and, as part of their standard practice, they had provided a written transcript and an audio tape of each conversation. While statistical survey results are great for pie charts and bar charts, and a transcript is great for pulling out specific, pithy quotes, the audio tapes were golden. Being able to hear the tenor of people's comments revealed not just what people were saying and what they were thinking, but how they felt. Standard customer satisfaction style surveys are very valuable, but there's nothing better than hearing it straight from the horse's mouth.

Derrith Lambka founded Insights for Action (www.insightsforaction.com) to become a conduit of personal feelings from customers to the companies they buy from. Her team goes to your customers where they live and work to find out how they think and feel. Insights for Action is a trained ear that listens hard to your customers because, as Lambka puts it, "Customers are great at identifying problems. We are great at generating new and innovative ideas to solve those problems. We become 'investigative reporters' about customers. We uncover what they hate, what they see as a minimum requirement, a nice to have, and something you could do that would really 'wow' them."

The result is that they are well equipped to define and design optimal customer experiences that make it easier, faster, and more enjoyable for customers to find and buy products.

"I've seen researchers who knew a lot about customers, but after they'd presented their information and written their report, the binder sat on a shelf and wasn't acted on," says Lambka. "What was missing was putting the insights from the research into a practical application for the customer."

One-on-one customer interviews with a video camera bring faceless customers to life. It's part Q&A, part empathy, and part Web site usability testing. If you're not hearing your customers speak for themselves, you should talk to Lambka.

Bringing It All Together

You've got log files, call center statistics, and customer surveys. You have hard data, a variety of averages, and the somewhat filtered opinions of Web site visitors. The trick is to bring those together in a meaningful way to get the big picture.

At Delta Airlines, Rob Casas, general manager of E-Commerce Development, tells me they've figured out how to do that:

> We have a dedicated, online customer support desk. They take both phone calls and emails, and every week we look at the top ten or twenty issues that are surfacing. For instance, when we introduce a product that perhaps simplifies the navigation experience on the booking site, we go back and compare how effective that was in reducing that category of calls.
>
> If that was one of the top three events happening at the call center, we look at what kind of impact that had. Did fixing it in fact reduce the number of calls on average to that category?
>
> We also have the more traditional surveys and so forth where we take our segment of customers that we communicate with quarterly. We call them "high-value" customers. We ask them questions related to how effective our product development and product offerings are. Every time we launch an initiative we go back and we measure usability. We go out to airports and sit down with customers. You know, the results of these are obviously not as objective as they may be when you measure usability in terms of your server logs, but they still help us get a good indication of where we're going with our efforts.
>
> I don't think you can do one without the other. Hopefully, if you've got good data, they should all be consistent and you should be pointing to some of the same things. But as with everything, you may end up having customers say, "Hey, this is great—I find it a lot more useful," but then your server logs indicate that we have a greater drop-off than we did before the enhancements.

Rob Sherrell, manager of Interactive Marketing at Delta explains: "If our online customer service desk is telling us that the length of the booking process is too long, and we hear that complaint enough, we're going to take action on it. We're going to look back on the server logs and see how much time it actually takes before we made any changes. Then we can set an objective metric in place to reduce it by 30 percent."

Casas spells out on the process: "Within the first week of every product launch we'll not only talk to the customer service group about the calls that came in for that product launch and look at their reports as far as top ten categories coming in, but we'll also compare that to this week's server logs to see if there's any correlation between the two or are there some big discrepancies that may cause us to look a little bit further into it. We do that periodically throughout that initial 3-month launch, and then we'll move on to the next initiative."

Is It Worth the Effort?

The thing PeopleMetrics' Sean McDade really got excited about during our Sunday morning hot chocolate meeting overlooking the Santa Barbara coastline was how good, accurate reports about beliefs and attitudes can pinpoint the areas where a company should focus its time and talent.

"Adding nonlinear analysis reveals refinements in relationships, leading to more optimal resource allocations." It must have been obvious that I wasn't completely in tune with him that morning. He tried again: "Conventional analysis assumes linear relationships between attributes and overall satisfaction."

"Uh-huh. . . ."

"Respondents often respond asymmetrically to various business-related variables such as price, satisfaction, advertising . . . "

"Uh-huh . . . ."

"So," says McDade, doing well at avoiding frustration with the blank stare I'm giving him, "respondents tend to be loss-averse rather than gain-seeking."

My blank stare becomes a frown of understanding. "You mean, after all the studies you've done, you're saying that it's better to fix things gone wrong and get your unhappy people happy than it is to do something special for your happy, but not ecstatic customers?"

"Yes!" and he picks up a pen and goes after his napkin like there's no tomorrow. He can see he's finally broken through and has a new potential convert on the line and makes the mental leap that I am not a statistician.

"So let's say you do several surveys over time asking people how well they like your site, and some questions about how easy the site is to use, and a couple of questions about how fast it is, and a couple of questions about overall satisfaction, that sort of thing. Then you map out their responses and the impact your efforts might have on future responses" (see Figure 13.15).

"In the case of ease-of-use, you want to focus your resources on maintaining midlevel performance and moving low performers into the midlevel performance category, because that's where you're going to reap the biggest payback.

"But over here on the question of speed, you want to focus your resources on enhancing performance and moving midlevel performers into high performance levels because that's what will drive the biggest increase in overall satisfaction."

My frown becomes a smile.

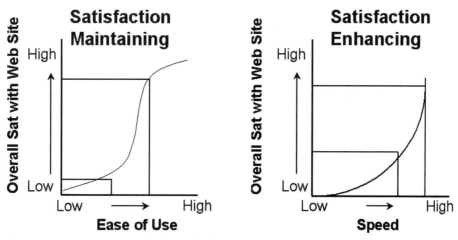

Figure 13.15 Sean McDade draws the line at where to spend your energy.

How Do You *Really* Know You're Doing a Good Job with Customer Service?

Of all the people I spoke with about measuring the value of their online customer service efforts, Kim Seney of the energy company APS came up with the single best answer: "We've actually been able to close offices for walk-in traffic over the year and we are attributing that to an increase in the electronic channel usage. We've closed two offices in the last 6 months or so and we have had fewer than five complaints out of that."

Score one for the Web.

It's obvious that better customer service begets better customer satisfaction. Good customer service can also save money. Once you admit that customer service has a serious impact on the bottom line, you can get serious about measuring it.

Your customer service metrics are going to give you a wealth of information about how well your site is performing and how much people like what you offer on your site. You'll discover how well your goods and services are perceived, and you'll get a unique window into what customers want to talk about on a day-to-day basis and how those topics change over time.

Measuring your online customer service will also improve the ways you measure your standard, call center means of customer service. If nothing else, you'll want to be able to compare the two. But be careful that you don't spend so much time dissecting server logs and survey sheets that you forget the voice of your customer. Listen to individuals as well as aggregate data. Make sure you hear the frustration, delight, and urgency in their tone. Then you'll know which potential projects will have the greatest impact on satisfaction, revenue, and profitability.

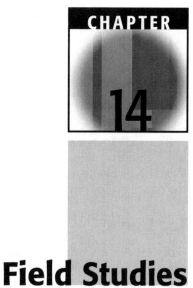

CHAPTER

14

Field Studies

Case studies are usually rigid and controlled, of fixed length, breadth, purpose, and content. The subjects of case studies must exhibit specific attributes, conform to certain provisions, and demonstrate an approach that can be applied in similar facilities.

A field study is a bit different. It's more of a documentary. It's an opportunity for me to satisfy my curiosity rather than fill out a bunch of forms, correlate responses, and dink around with graphs and charts.

As a field-study subject, I found Compaq to be saddled with the common hindrances and liabilities of too much to do and too little time to do it. But what set them apart from all the other companies I looked at was their clear understanding of the need to sift through large data banks of Web information. Compaq is gifted with some rare people and an unusually high organizational understanding of the value of Web metrics. It's a company that's more finely tuned than most. You can feel when your car is just chugging along and when it's well tuned. Compaq has the feel of a high-performance vehicle, fresh from the service bay.

Compaq faces the same problem with data collection, the same conundrum about how to issue informative reports, and the same curiosity about how to turn those reports into positive actions. But they're onto something and they know it. Compaq is at the far end of the Web metrics continuum and the work they're doing is groundbreaking. We'll get to them in a minute. First, a cautionary tale.

Caution: Problems in Mirror Are Closer Than They Appear

On the other end of the Web metrics continuum is one large manufacturer with such a poor grasp of the possibilities and such a poor handle on the realities that I choose to describe its situation in detail, over the ability to disclose its identity. They're doing a lot of the legwork and working hard at it, but their efforts just don't seem to add up.

It's a well-known firm, a household word, and in dire straits when it comes to getting their arms around their Web site. Their biggest problem? The sheer magnitude of their site. So many departments, so many people, so many goals. Their story—an all-too-common one—may sound very, very familiar.

Top Down

Ernest (not his real name) has a lot riding on his shoulders. He is the vice president and general manager of this global manufacturing firm. Ernest wants to summarize what's going on in all the corporate Web sites into an easily readable gauge he can keep half an eye on.

The Dashboard

The easily readable gauge is the dashboard, says Ernest: "The purpose in establishing the dashboard metric was to create a management-by-fact environment within our team and within our company with respect to the Web. The idea was to pick a few key metrics that would, on a week-in/week-out basis, give us a sense of the pulse of the site, its cadence.

"We may end up doing it monthly as some of the figures stabilize. The general notion is to make sure that, out of the universe of tons of things we could measure, we establish a week-by-week or crisis-by-crisis minimal set for just making sure that the patient is healthy or to see if we are continuing to make or not make progress. Just like when you go to the doctor, even if you are healthy, he takes your blood pressure. It's just part of the base lining and to be sure that we keep our eye on the ball.

"The dashboard report serves several functions with different constituencies. We expect to see measurable progress in what we do, and . . . we will celebrate when we see results that are positive and we will ask questions and try to jointly investigate problems when the data looks negative. So, we use it as a way of focusing the attention of the very wide internal team on what is really happening."

It seems that the width of their internal team is the hard part. This is a company with an untold number of business units, product managers, and product lines following some general guidelines and sticking to the rules about look and feel. But when it comes to managing-by-fact, as Ernest calls it, are they all looking at the same numbers? Are they all focused on the same key metrics? Do their definitions hold up across the company, around the world, and across all those disparate servers they run?

"The dashboard itself is an aggregate," responds Ernest. "It basically says the total visitor count, the total page-view count, and the total error rates and things like that.

So it does not provide a weekly document that suggests that this part of the site is working better than another. If we see a spike that is not tied to one of the usual causes, we can then ask a second level of questions to say, 'What was it on the site that was causing that to happen?' And share that either with the source of the good news or bad news on why that was happening."

Good News/Bad News

Ernest seems unusually well informed for a person of his rank. "You have to remember that there are very few metrics except for revenue that are unequivocal good news," he says. "So, for example, we understand that page views going up can either be because there are more people looking for more information or because we made some change that makes it harder for information to find and people are having to do more clicks to find it. We use this information with the internal team as a way of asking those second-level questions and in sending the team to investigate things that look like good news so that we can better understand it.

"The other audience for this is fairly minor—some of the other interested parties in the organization like eMarketing and other partners that are frankly just curious as to what's going on with our site. They just like to see the numbers. And I'm fairly certain that they don't do anything about it, but they're interested, and if we didn't provide them, they would wonder."

That makes me wonder too. How many companies are cranking out reports for internal audiences for no other reason than to placate them? Just to make them feel like they're in the game. What is the cost of delivering data to people who don't use it to make decisions?

"It sounds kind of trivial," Ernest says in self-defense, "but that in fact takes the place of an internal management need. That audience is upper management and we use the reports on an ad hoc basis with senior management in our operations reviews and in our strategy reviews to give them a sense of the evolution of the Web site and to stress the management-by-facts approach. We show upper management that whether it's good news or bad news, we're committed to keeping them in the loop and to, as much as possible, show off the good news. It gives them a sense of security that we're making progress and that we're managing the site on a fact basis."

Fair enough. Keeping the guys upstairs informed is important, even at the vice president level. There's always *somebody* looking over your shoulder. But I wonder if there is an established set of success definitions. Is there some sort of a chart on the wall that determines that they've done a good job for the month?

"No," Ernest answers. "I think last year we tried to set some objectives like that. We sat down with our management to establish how much we would increase traffic or how many visitors we would get to sign up and register and what kind of growth there would be in page views. It was just making stuff up and everyone knew it. Some of them we hit and some of them we didn't, and it was hard to say whether or not it was good or bad. So it turned out to be pretty much folly because no one really knows what to expect in this space and the things that drive Web site traffic are pretty much out of our control.

"When there's good news, site traffic goes up. When there's bad news, site traffic goes up. People look for press releases. It's hard to say that we have control of that. We're still in learning mode in terms of what those values can be and what drives them."

Ernest makes it sound like there's enough measuring going on to begin the process of understanding the finer details. I ask him if anybody in his organization is working on correlating page views to increased revenues or lowered costs.

"No."

But surely, I counter, there must be some attention paid to customer service cost avoidance when customers enter their own orders and solve their own problems online. How else do you determine which project gets funded?

Project Funding Decisions

According to Ernest, "That kind of analysis is done in two ways: The first way we do it is in selecting amongst the proposals the program managers bring forth. We look for business cases, some of which are ROI based, some of which are not, but basically we look for a scenario, a discussion of the value of having a user switch to, for example, doing a change of address request online versus calling up a rep, and some indicators of how many phone calls the company currently gets and how many might switch over and what the savings might be.

"We use that at the front end to judge whether or not we should pursue one program option versus another, and then operations reviews them with our program managers. We don't necessarily have visibility to the cost side to know if the costs are being taken out of the business or not.

"We recently have developed per-unit metrics where we attempted to allocate the costs that are being spent within our team in a logical but not scientific method, because there is only so much effort you want to put into this sort of thing. But we've tried to divide out the costs on a monthly basis that we are putting towards open markets commerce (auctions), versus customer care, versus our extranet activities, versus the steady state of just the site and the browsing and whatnot. We track those costs on an allocated approximate basis, on a monthly basis, and then we divide them by the related metrics. So how many things were downloaded from customer service? How many orders were received over their value in open market commerce?

"And some of these metrics are ugly because certain things are below critical mass but are still an investment area for the company. We're not expecting it to be cheaper than doing it another way for now. That's the brutal reality, and again these metrics make it clear. We have to be in the game to be competitive.

"Commerce is a great example. For a company like ours, which is almost $20 billion, the investment to be able to take orders online is a fair amount. It's a part of our budget and it's difficult to get some of our internal partners to make their products available for sale online as well as to get customers to press the 'buy' button. So our revenues online are far below what we would like them to be and they are below critical mass as the investment per order currently is ridiculous, but it's something that may grow by a thousandfold over the next five years."

At this level in the corporate hierarchy, and at this moment in Internet history, the eyes are on the investment part of ROI.

Says Ernest: "We use the pertinent metrics to be a blood pressure on how are we doing. Are we getting more efficient or are we getting less efficient in the way we do certain activities?"

How Much Do You Invest?

Keeping an eye on things is crucial, of course, but where, I ask Ernest, do you draw the line? Given the cost of collecting the data, the cost of storing it, and the cost of analyzing it—just crunching the numbers—and then the cost of interpreting it, how do you make a determination on how much of an investment to make? How do you decide how much to spend in order to pull the proper metrics out of the system?

"So far we have not had a scientific answer. I guess there are certain things that we felt that we could not live without in terms of reporting. We need to make the investment in the team and the tools to make sure the proper things are measured.

"One of the most interesting elements of that question is the desire for deep, ad hoc metrics. Some of our internal partners will say, 'We're doing an online campaign and we want to know where people come from. We want to know this, we want to know that, and we want to learn all these different things and how long they stay on the site and blah, blah, blah.' Sure, we'd all love to know that, but we don't actually have the tools that are effective in providing that or we are not willing to divert development or resources to customize the tools or customize other code to provide it. It's much easier for people to come up with things they want us to measure. It's another thing to whether or not it is affordable. It is still another thing as to whether or not they will even be used.

"You know, a recent question came up that illustrates this. We rotate ad banners around our home page and several other pages and someone said, 'Okay, thank you for doing that. We appreciate getting some airtime on the site and we understand how many people have clicked over to the related page. But that banner appears in about five other places—it rotates around in different places. How many impressions actually are there on it?' And we have to say, 'We don't know.' We're not Yahoo! Our model is not ad-based revenue. Therefore, measuring impressions of the ads that we use on our own site—internal ads—that's not something that we put any particular energy into. But that is something that people might say, 'You don't have an impressions measure? How can you do an ad campaign internally without measuring impressions?' That's not a bad point, but it's an economic decision. It's a threshold question.

"Of course, if a program manager found twenty-six other program managers who wanted to track impressions, and they could pool some of their project money over to the team, we'd invest it. That kind of give and take happens all the time. Often times people don't understand the opportunity costs. They understand the value to themselves, but they do not understand what doesn't get done. So, the interesting part is when you've been in the room with the people who you are asking to wait a month for what they were hoping to get. The fur begins to fly."

Cost Savings

Ernest says that his company believes in the cost savings of customer self-service: "Those kinds of things generate a lot of calls into call centers. So a lot of people ring in the phone just to have somebody look at a computer screen and look up a date or a number, and it's our belief that those sorts of shifts are the most obvious."

Is there a formula? Is there a standard cost-per-call for the spreadsheets? Every call that comes in that is 5 minutes in length costs the company X dollars, and every time they do it on the Web we can chalk that up as savings?

"We have numbers that we use for that, but no one believes any of them.

"There's always some agenda behind the numbers. The call centers have been a huge win for us as a company. We look at some of the industry benchmarks on how much people think they saved being an online transaction versus a live phone call or in-person transaction. We use some of those numbers, but we know that they need to be used with great delicacy.

"The intuitive element that people believe there is a cost savings is the strongest thing in terms of making the numbers themselves sound somewhat believable. But we all look at the numbers with wariness. One of my partners in Europe and I were look-ing at what they were putting into their business case. They said that taking an order by phone or someone faxing in an order costs something like $6 and it was going to be a tenth of that or something on the Web. And I sort of looked at $6 and thought that couldn't be right, that would be beyond benchmark. Everything that I've heard in terms of orders and who gets them by fax and entering it into the system and all that—the McKinsey numbers or whatever—it can't be right because everyone uses different assumptions in terms of what is really included. I keep a healthy skepticism at what-ever those numbers are because I know that they can be manipulated based on what one chooses to include and what the allocation basis is.

"We know that a lot of it is ludicrous. We've had discussions where people compare making a request for a piece of software via someone calling up, talking to a person, putting a CD-ROM in the mail and mailing it, would be a $20 transaction or more. Two things are ludicrous here. First, that model just doesn't exist anymore. If you are a com-pany that's going to make customers call up and talk to somebody and then send them a CD, you'd be out of business before the month is out. Not only because of the cost, but because of the model, the speed, and the customer satisfaction.

"That is the comparison that people want to see in terms of what the alternative would be. Well, the alternative is being out of business. I wish you could say that the alternative is doing it via a $23 transaction—well, you multiply that by the number of downloads and you have something higher than the gross product of Europe.

"We look for industry benchmarks as a way of using externally validated numbers to provide some validity to these numbers to make them less subject to the manipula-tion that we know people will otherwise suspect that we are doing to prove our par-ticular point. The theme here—back to the why do we do this blood pressure thing—it all really comes back to credibility. We need to make sure that what we're doing is man-agement-by-fact. Making sure that we are being objective wherever we can and mak-ing sure people know that and are using known metrics, known efficiency numbers, to either calculate cost savings or to compare ourselves."

Hands-On Metrics

Having the numbers that make sense is critical. Once you have reliable, meaningful numbers, you can make rational decisions. Not all of them are easy to make and knowing when you are doing something wrong can often be more important than measuring how well things are going. Ernest has some experience in this area.

"We had introduced some new site functionality about a year ago using an external provider. It's something that we thought would build traffic and we looked at the metrics every quarter in terms of what was really happening there and we became convinced that it seemed like a good idea at the time. But it wasn't creating any traffic. So at the end of the earliest point in the contract renewal we told the vendor that we weren't going to renew because it hadn't met our expectations and it was not delivering benefit in proportion to the cost.

"So we do look at metrics, and when we can make those sorts of decisions, we will. It's an important concept to me and I think to lots of other sensible people in this space; you have to be willing to experiment and you have to be willing to act on the results of those experiments.

"You have to take risks. I think it's a cliché from the medical world—the experiment was a success but the patient died. We learned something; it may not be what we wanted to learn. It's the Thomas Edison effect: We now know 4,000 materials that won't make a lightbulb.

"We focus on managing-by-fact and being able to quickly gain consensus with my team on what we should or should not be doing, because we have the metrics and the data to help us with that decision."

Overall, I am left with a feeling of security. There is somebody near the top of the organization who gets it. Somebody who doesn't expect the impossible, doesn't demand the improbable, or count on the unlikely.

It's an old maxim that organizations tend to reflect top management. I was pumped up, ready to interview those who worked closer to the customer in this organization and ready to learn the secrets of their success. But it seems things get a little cloudy as they get closer to the customer. It's hard to detect at first, and unmistakable as the granularity increases.

From the Director's Chair

Frank (also not his real name) is the director of e-Marketing Corporate Strategy. He tells me he is responsible for marketing, branding, advertising, and revenue online worldwide. However, he is quick to tell me that there's not a lot going on in Europe or South America because of budget cuts. But it's true that Frank is interested in measurements:

"I look at metrics beyond measuring page views, site visits, new site visitors, all of these kinds of things. The question is, for every dollar you're spending, what is the return on investment for those dollars that you are spending? And that's a whole different category versus just trying to understand what people are doing on your site and who's coming and all that good stuff.

"I'm going to start off with customer satisfaction. I'm going to start off with the softer things and then I'll get to more of the hard stuff. We look at customer satisfaction both from an end-user standpoint and from a partner standpoint. We look at customer satisfaction from an end-user and an internal customer standpoint in everything we do around online marketing programs. That's the first piece.

"The next piece is, we look into results measures. You try to separate the dollars you spend to enable commerce- versus service-related things. You start to understand: How much commerce are you getting? How many orders are you getting? You base your cost per order and cost per revenue on that. You've got to associate any other dollars, not just what you're spending online, but what offline dollars you are spending to enable that to happen also.

"When it comes to customer care, obviously you are looking at the spend and the kinds of hits that you are getting, be it downloads or anything else. You look at how many of those inquiries you got and then look up the dollar amount that you spent to get some kind of idea around the cost per inquiry. Then it's time for a cost avoidance calculation, since they didn't have to call your call center."

This is starting to sound good to me—right on the money. But Frank starts backpedaling.

"You know, the people that obviously are best at all this are the Amazons and the Dells of the world. They're doing a great job in the consumer space, but in the business-to-business space, there are not a lot of people doing a great job. We haven't gotten to the point where we're really doing cost-benefit on our investor relations pages or employment pages."

Frank reasserts that his job is to watch some things like a hawk: "I have responsibility for everything online around marketing and revenue. So if anything happens where there is a drop-off in traffic, whatever, I am accountable. So I absolutely look at that on a weekly and monthly basis."

That doesn't mean he has the tools to help him see: "I've done lots of programs and initiatives that generate a lot of page views but I couldn't tie them to revenue, leads, or whatever.

"You can clearly associate the increase in revenue that your partners are generating year over year, and you can associate the number of leads that you've driven through your global partners center. But trying to assess the overall impact—that's tough. Now, I get a subset of it. I know how many leads I get; I know the close rate of those leads that we generated through the partner center as an example. I know the revenue associated with that.

"In the end, I have orders and revenue, but I don't know with all the other things we do there—partner training, partner recruitment, all of those additional things—what's the overall business impact of those programs? I'm measuring the hard things there, for example, but it's tough to measure some of the other things."

I find myself confused by the strong vision at the top but a slight slip between intention and implementation. I realize that it's time to head to the source of the Nile. Upstream to the place where the numbers are generated. I go to meet the woman who manages the logs at this unnamed company.

The Metrics Control Center

Hope holds the title Program Director of E-Metrics in the Internet Business Group. That should give one the feeling that this company recognizes the value of metrics and is taking concrete steps to do something about it. The concrete steps are there, anyway. Hope works very hard at her job. She's dedicated. She cares. She gets a lot of it right.

Hope fills the gap between the technical staff and business managers. Her task is twofold. First, she must figure out and implement the best ways to keep track of tens of thousands of daily visitors wandering through tens of thousands of Web pages at www.undisclosed.com. Then, she must field the requests for e-metrics from—and explain the ins and outs of e-metrics to—those employees who want to know about the popularity of their pages, the navigational brilliance of their designs, and the ingenious effectiveness of their promotional efforts.

Hope works in an edifice that was built before the Age of the Cubicle. Her office has one small window looking inward into the hall and three generous windows out into an open atrium between buildings; a corporate greensward with flowering xeriscape bushes, and tree trunks with invisible tops whose leaves' shadows paint a soft, dappled rhythm on the far wall. A small sparrow perches momentarily on her windowsill.

Inside, her bookshelves are home to customer-service awards, product development plaques, peer recognition tributes, and a certificate from a local university identifying Hope as an Internet business specialist. The quality-control handbooks and the multiple dictionaries in multiple languages give way to a large stack of monthly trend reports and key measures reports from Media Metrix, and a *BroadbaseUser Guide* (now part of Kana, Inc. www.kana.com); the first clues that Hope loves to delve into the subtle secrets of Web site statistics.

Keeping an Eye Peeled

Hope is responsible for getting the server to divulge its knowledge but she has to keep her ears tuned to the business side as well. "Why do you want those numbers?" she asks, recognizing that people who don't know what's possible can't ask for the best-possible data.

"On one project in particular," she says, "they came to me with a request for data from seven different sources inside the firewall and outside the firewall, and completely forget to ask for revenue figures. I watch out for things like that."

Hope's squad of half a dozen statisticians and Web charmers churns out a stack of weekly reports for any and all who want to see them. One report draws a graph of site visitors from October 2000 through February 2001. One glance and you can tell there's a severe problem. The graph resembles a seagull sharply shrugging its shoulders. Something went bump in the night at the end of the year.

"In December, we launched version 3 of our corporate site and immediately lost two-thirds of our visitors. It took us 7 weeks to put it right," says Hope, warming to her cautionary tale. "The new site was very sophisticated. We created a content database for each country running in virtual servers, and we designed and tested a new navigation system that was significantly easier to use. But we forgot about the spiders, the external links, and the bookmarks." She shakes her head with twenty-twenty hindsight.

"All of the new URLs were new. All of the search engines had the old URLs. Everybody who wanted a specific page got a 404. We had to create redirects to get people from the old URLs to the new ones, and we kicked off a program of resubmitting our pages to the search engines to get them to reindex our site."

Keeping It Clean

At the same time, Hope had struck a significant blow at the problem of eliminating misleading data from the weekly reports, including spider data. "Some of the services out there used to generate apparent visitors—ghosts—which we took out of the totals for the new site. That was another cause in the drop of traffic; we stopped counting the people who weren't there."

They also stopped counting 404s. Yes, those will show up in your logs if you're not paying strict attention and filtering them out.

The solution Hope came upon was the nonintuitive approach of throwing out the signal and keeping the noise. Repetitive requests made to your server, or those made mere microseconds apart, can be resolved into patterns, or signals. Delete those and what's left (the noise) is your real data.

Explaining It Again

Hope understands the need for standard metrics definitions. "People are always coming to me asking about how many hits they got." She rolls her eyes and bewails in a plaintive tone, "Every time, I have to sit them down and describe the difference between page views and hits and visits and sessions. Since people seem to be stuck on *hits*, maybe we should just declare hits to be page views once and for all and think of the time we'd save!"

Automating the Process

If you want your clickthroughs tracked to specific URLs at this site, or you want to watch the traffic flow from one page to another, the process is automated. Just fill out the Add a Promotion form on the intranet. Name the promotion, the start and end dates, contact information, budget center, whether you're engaging in banner rotation, and the logic rules you'd like to implement, and it all speeds through the intranet to Hope's desk.

The request is handled within hours. The server system they've implemented calls for the assignment of "name value pairs" that identify the country, the language, and the market segment (SOHO or corporate) each page is designed to address.

"It took a bit of explaining to get agreement on why we needed to own the approval of naming URLs, but we got it in the end," says Hope with obvious relief. Without a standardized naming convention, their tracking database is nearly impossible to manage. Efficient software programs thrive on consistency. Tracking requests get batched and are usually in place by the next morning.

From there, it's a simple matter of logging onto the E-Metrics Portal. Available from any intranet connection, the E-Metrics Portal allows interested parties to review the numbers as they happen. "We'll keep Aria (the old analysis system) in place for about a year while we install and bring [Kana's] Broadbase up to speed in stages," explains Hope. "We can't just switch over from one to the other. Well, we could, but training everyone at once would be out of the question."

The weekly report is awash in graphs: visitors by week, page views by week, total online revenues by week, downloaded files by week, viewed FAQs by week, unexpected errors as a percent of total page views by week, and repeat internal and external visitors compared to new visitors by week.

Then there's the Urchin system. "We use this mostly for the daily depth-of-visit report," says Hope, who points out the high numbers at either end. "We start with this huge block of people who look at one page and one page only. That's more than four times the number that look at two pages. Then it diminishes to a very few who look at ten or fifteen. At the moment, this report dumps everybody into this twenty-or-more bucket, so it looks like there's this big block at the end. We don't know what the actual average number of pages is yet. I have this feeling that there's another hill in the graph down at this end, but I'm not sure where. I don't think it just falls away to nothing. I think the numbers might bunch up at twenty-five or something and then fall off. We just don't know yet."

To understand the dynamics of a single page, this firm displays each page by the numbers. A slightly less than life-size Web page is shown, with lines from each of the links on the page to the number of times that link was clicked in a given period and the percentage of clicks it got. Is the search box getting more attention than the promotional banner? Are people more interested in the privacy policy than the copyright notice? They can tell at a glance.

As always, the would-be sleuth of surfing is faced with the challenge of one-sided information. There's no way to tell if those links were each clicked by one passing individual, or if this page was visited 100,000 times by one person with a love affair with the Back button. Given a normalized average number of clicks per link, what happens if you start moving buttons around? Changing their colors? Surrounding them with more white space? Reports like this aren't perfect, but they are what's on the menu and the only thing on the menu.

Integration Indigestion

If you work in a multidivisional, multimarket, multinational company, then you know the pain that comes from trying to bring all the datasets together. Hope knows.

"We started with the U.S. as a template, but every metric that we enable is global. And we are deploying a number of different processes within the U.S. and changing the tools that we have to allow us to have a more comprehensive metric reporting environment. That will enable us to link all the data sources into a different data schema and we'll be able to slice and dice."

Hope faces an overwhelmingly common problem. With so many different departments and divisions using so many different tools and services and collecting so much data, how do you integrate all of it into one standardized global view?

"Some of the things we're reporting today we have to integrate manually—for example, the e-commerce information. We realize that there is this structure between the Web and the back office. So we're trying to automate and integrate the data. Which is—it's a barrier for us right now. The data is not fully integrated in different aspects.

"We approved the purchase of the software tool, which is very significant given the financial constraints of this company at the moment. So the company's really very focused on trying to invest in the Web as a reliable channel. There's enough understanding at the highest levels that this is important and that we should spend the money on it. So that's a major step. That requires a very sophisticated data integration. We've been talking to Broadbase [Kana] and we're deploying the first release in several months. When it's all done, we're integrating the very back-end mainframe database with the billing, with campaigns, promotions, registration—everything.

"That's the plan, but I wouldn't say it's a top priority. In this department, we realize that without measuring what we do and how well we do it, and showing the return on what we're doing . . . it's just no way to function as a business.

"But this company has so many divisions and I can't even tell you how many Web sites we have here. Globally, I think we're not there yet. Just getting Oracle as the one database for the company 3 years ago was a major victory.

"We divided the Web into different applications and we're measuring investment return. For example, we look at the number of clicks and we measure that against dollars invested in operations so we know how much each click costs. We're trying to create the same thing for e-commerce and the same thing for our extranet.

"According to BroadVision, we have a very extensive metrics requirement—it's more than they've ever seen before. It's probably too much, but this company runs by consensus, I think. So we have all the metrics. We have the general requirements for navigation and click analysis, and then we dig into e-commerce—specifically, we dig into shopping cart analysis, we dig into different applications on the extranets, supplies to manager, description manager, registration profile . . . ."

Are Metrics Results Actionable?

The lingering question in all this is how do you make that information valuable? Making it interesting is one thing. There are lots of interesting data about how site visitors use the resource. Do people who come on Monday look at more pages that those who come on Tuesday? Do the visitors who wander in over the weekend wander over a broader range of pages? But how might that information be of value to those making budgetary decisions about the site? "It's a very challenging task," says Hope.

"This year," says Hope, "my goal is really to develop a global measurement and create an intelligent infrastructure so we can capture the metrics and make sure that the objectives of the different business units are met."

I am inspired by the vision at the top, am made wary by the management in the middle, and feel the frustration at the source of all Web metrics data. It's time, finally, to talk to somebody managing a customer-facing Web program.

Segmentation Battle Station

Faith (not her real name) is responsible for personalization, registration, and segmentation for the lower-value, higher-volume, more repetitive purchases.

"People come and learn about our big products, the different specifications, and so on, but it is more likely that they will *purchase* supplies," Faith explains.

"Segmentation is the one area where I use metrics quite often. We did a redesign and moved to a new platform at the beginning of this year. A lot of the concepts are sort of new to us, so we're trying to do different things, test different things with our users, and try out enhancements. Our corporate customer base is quite diverse, but we did some assessments and made a strategic decision to divide our audience up into corporate, small business, and home users. So that's how we build our segmentation architecture.

"This is one area where we look at the metrics on an ongoing basis and try to understand what portion of our customer base views the corporate content versus the home content. We started collecting user profile information through our registration. Of course, we know more about our registered users. That is where the BroadVision database and the logs give us quite a lot of information. Who is coming, what are their areas of interest, and which accounts are most frequently visited?

"We are looking at the user profile information just to get a good understanding of where they fit. Who are the most common visitors? Another metric that I have experimented with is to see where people go from the corporate segments page, and again, trying to identify what sections of the site are most commonly used, most commonly visited, just to sort of target our enhancements or focuses on those areas for future purposes, I guess."

I find myself distracted—not sure if I'm following what Faith is saying. All of this information is very interesting, but how does she actually put it to use? I ask her what changes or decisions she makes based on the results.

"We did quite a number of redesigns trying to put the mostly searched items or the mostly visited items to the higher level. To let the user experience be much more pleasant, giving them what they had been looking for or what they are mostly coming to the site for. So I think it provides us great insight to redesign the site and make more options to the users clearer."

It's obvious she's on the right track.

"We noticed that the small business users and home users index much higher than our organizations' corporate customer base. That would make you think the home segment would be quite an important segment for us on the online channel. We are just getting that profile information and sharing it with other business teams to be used in their targeted marketing campaigns."

So the track is laid and Faith is the engine, but there doesn't seem to be anybody to unload the cargo once the train reaches the station.

"It's more of an organizational thing that not everybody is thinking in the same terms, but, yes, there is quite some sharing of information and some of our businesses have done a much better job than others. I'm just getting that information out of queries based on their criteria—pulling out the targeted customers and sending them email or promotions, etcetera."

It's the very beginning of a Web metrics implementation. Hope is cranking out data and Faith is finding the patterns, but the loop doesn't quite close all the way. There's no connection to all the business units. There are no people on the other end drawing this information out of the metrics team and spinning it into gold. Business unit managers are waiting for the metrics group to provide some of the more obvious answers when it can—such as navigational wisdom.

"We realized early in our process one of the major reasons why users come to our site was to download certain files," says Faith. "Sometimes the link to that area is on the second- or third-level pages, so we put it on our home page. Now that it's easy for the users to find, it increased the traffic four times.

"When you change the navigation, you're trying to change the outcome or the objective. Let's say by hanging the navigation on your catalogues, the objective is basically to drive more people to purchase things from your site. Your ability to define your ROI really depends on tangible metrics. So I simply define it as an increase in my revenues, and that would be the return on my investment. So I think I could define it through some more tangible benefits.

"I'm not exactly sure what the other business teams think—if they're really doing the ROIs. The corporation is going to implement more ROI tools. We actually purchased a new metrics analysis tool, and it will give us more ability . . . to measure the impact of some of these marketing campaigns and do some ROI analysis, but I wouldn't say that we are doing a full-blown job on that."

I'm encouraged that they mean well. I am satisfied that they are working hard. I am confident that given enough time, they will stumble upon that final connection between theory and practice. But I am disappointed that there is no clear line of logic and data flow. I'm wondering if I will ever find a company that connects the reasons for having a Web site with the ability to strictly monitor the results of their efforts.

It turns out I only needed to look a little further.

Goal Orientation: The Secret of Success

"The question, 'How can we make our site better?' will forever be answered with, 'Better at what?' First tell me what are you trying to accomplish and together we'll find politically and technically feasible ways to get there."
Full Sterne Ahead newsletter, November 2001

Compaq headquarters are nestled in a campus carved out of a lush forest on the outskirts of Houston. Profuse vegetation gives way to sleek buildings designed by artist-architects rather than lowest bidders. The twenty-six buildings include:

- Fitness center
- Wellness center
- Numerous cafeteria/food options, from gourmet to health food to pizza—with menus online
- Catering services

- Discounted dry cleaning on premises
- Convenience store
- An employee recreation park with boating, fishing, volleyball, horseshoes (open to employees and their families on weekends)
- On-site Starbucks—for the latté addicted

From the outside, it's a place you'd want to work. On the inside, the feeling is the realization of that desire. People work here. They're focused. They have goals. They have enthusiasm.

I arrived on the day after the HP merger/takeover was announced, so morale was not high. But aside from making for depressed small talk, Damocles' sword and the prospect of changing corporate structures and cultures slipped into the background as the discussion about improving their Web site fired up each individual I interviewed. These people want to win.

Command Center

I got the overview from Seth Romanow, who is (deep breath) director, eMarketing and User Experience eBusiness Systems, Global Business Solutions at Compaq Computer Corporation (and, exhale). Seth made a valiant effort to carve that up into bite-sized chunks for me.

"I sit in our eBusiness Group. We're called eBusiness Systems—Worldwide eBusiness Systems. We're the marketing function of the user experience function within that group. So we work with the PR folks who work with corporate marketing folks. We define the online brand standards; we do customer satisfaction research. We do virtually all the third-party customer-facing research, whether its resellers or obviously end users. We also do human factors work and, you know, a lot of online surveys, and we define the information architecture for the sites worldwide—the guidelines and standards for sites worldwide."

By this time, I had filled a page with circles and arrows and thought of another way to approach this classification problem.

"So what *don't* you do?"

"We don't do any of the back-end work or the middleware work."

"Ahhhh."

"We also don't do any of the demand generation, although we have in the past."

Economies of Scale

Seth's organization was designed to cut costs by centralizing and standardizing where it makes sense.

"Our group, the Worldwide e-Business Systems Group, is really responsible for driving cross-platform (multidepartmental) initiatives. We aim to have a standardized architecture, standardized platforms, and interlaced road maps.

"Economies of scale are in the middle of it all, and in a highly matrixed organization such as Compaq, we found everybody jumped on board the Web as early adopters and did their own thing. Everybody made a thousand Web sites bloom. Bob Napier, our CIO, has woven all that together, and he's done a good job with that."

Roles and Responsibilities

Compaq doesn't earn and save money by controlling everything from a single office. There is a wide distribution of duties.

"The CIO basically said, 'Look, I want you to roll-up the metrics and I want a standard report and I want it now.' There are a couple of things in our favor. First of all, there were a lot of people from different disciplines sitting around the table, so we had the infrastructure people, people like myself who were marketing, people who were responsible for lines of business and looked at margins and sales and that sort of thing.

"We own the home page of Compaq.com. We put in a lot of research in terms of human factors to get it right. We did comparison testing, focus group testing, asking for preferences, and that sort of thing.

"We own the top level for the site and what we call the cross-divisional pages. Our ownership can get down to the third or even fourth level depending on how deep those cross-divisional pages sit. So we own the information architecture. But all the content here is owned by the business units and we work closely with them. They call some of the shots there, but we hold them accountable through our satisfaction and quality measurements."

Regular Reporting

I wanted to know about the reports they produce—and how often they produce them: "We do average daily sales for each of our lines of business as well as for each geography—we have a half a dozen fixed geographies. When I say 'line of business,' that would be government, education, medical, our SMB [small and medium business] store, our consumer store. We have a Compaq factory outlet. We also have kiosks in stores such as Circuit City. We have major accounts extranets, although most of them are migrating to procurement, so that goes down while the procurement goes up as we make that conversion. And finally, Partner Direct.

"So we take a look at all the lines of business and we look at sales on a monthly basis. That way we get to roll them up and double-check them. The data is available on a much more regular basis than that, but the management reports go out on a monthly basis.

"That gives us time to answer questions for some of the data [that] takes a little longer to roll in. We take a look at that versus a year ago."

Promotion Detection

Compaq wants to know which advertising efforts are getting the best results.

"We always take a look at a snapshot of the last 12 weeks. So we kind of do a microscope on that, then we map that information against advertising impressions. We slice that again by brand campaign and demand generation campaign. And we get that information from the ad agency that Compaq uses. We ask them to split the data up in terms of Web-based and non-Web-based, broadcast and non-broadcast. So when we want to slice and dice it, we can.

"We look at the same things on the work panel. We plot it month-to-month and we look at the last 12 weeks. If there's something significant, we know that somebody's done a big blitz , or there's been a big announcement, or a product launch from one of our competitors, then we usually do a callout on the slide.

"So we can say, what's the number one referral to Compaq.com? And we use NetRatings to track our competition on that. We also take a look at our Accrue Hit List from Compaq.com to track visits to the site and then key domains within the site like each of the stores, for example. We plot demand generation against the store traffic so we can see the impact it's had."

Content Contentment

After getting people to show up at the Compaq Web site, making sure that the pages they view are high quality is important to the company.

"We also look at a content error rating on the site. So we comb through . . . just last quarter we combed through 357 pages. We look at the most used pages and develop a criteria set. We have criteria for 17 items and we map the errors on those pages. We actually have people going through all those pages, just eyeballing them.

"We're looking at 404 errors, spelling errors, layout problems, link font—all of it. We automate a lot of it, but we actually go through the top-used pages by hand and sample some other pages against those 17 criteria—everything from part numbers and pricing to whether the nav bar is 175 or 180 pixels. So we bring in employees who are familiar with the site, hire contractors who are familiar with the site, and just have them go through it for about two and a half weeks. Then we come up with an error rating. Our error rating right now is just a few percentage points below our goal."

Navigation Satisfaction

Compaq gets them there, makes sure the pages are good, and then measures site visitors' ability to get around.

"We actually have a scorecard that takes a look at customer experience, among other things. That's the satisfaction levels for different areas within the site. We try to set goals overall as well as for key areas within the site. We look at time to task because satisfaction's not a quality metric, it's a benchmark—it's a result of quality.

"We have somebody go through the tasks of finding a specific kind of driver for a DeskPro and we measure what path they took, how long it took, and their level of satisfaction with that task. We do the same thing for shopping. And we can benchmark that time-to-task for something the customer does and take it from 8 minutes to 6.5 minutes."

Customer Satisfaction

The numbers may show that all is well with the Web site, but Compaq wants to know whether their visitors think so as well.

"We also take a look at customer satisfaction. This information goes up the chain of command—even as far as the CEO. We measure customer satisfaction on a whole bunch of things, including ease of navigation, usefulness of content, is the content up-to-date? That gets reported up the chain on a monthly basis and then we also update it every other week. So we take a look at the month-to-month trend and then we do a drill down, and that's based on our annual goals. We cut that data by location within the site and report out on the same basis, monthly. And every other week we generally have enough respondents to roll up the data so there's statistical significance.

"When you layer that statistical significance with data that reaches back to the second half of 1998, you get historical significance as well.

"We do survey by location and then we do survey by why the visitor is coming to the site. You know, you're here to buy a product, support a product, obtain a driver, get information. Then we use NetRatings' home panel and work panel and we track our traffic versus key competition in terms of unique visitors. We do that monthly and then we compare month over month of the previous year.

"We also started posting our top ten and bottom ten pages in terms of satisfaction. So we have pop-up satisfaction surveys posted in the hundred and eighty areas on the site. We don't change pages instantly when there's a high degree of dissatisfaction. We let it go for two to three weeks to see if it was just one of those things. For example, when we migrated to Titanium from Alpha, the Alpha pages suddenly turned from high satisfaction to horrible. When we went to the customer comments, we realized it wasn't the page they were responding to, it was the announcement. Some people just don't like change.

Total Customer Visibility

Customer satisfaction at Compaq extends beyond the Web site.

"We look at conversion and retention as we go from browse, to the store, to the configurator, into the shopping cart, and to checkout. We're trying to get a handle on how to have an end-to-end view of the customer. Do we have that customer in a certain database that everybody has access to? You know, versus being slotted in a variety of other databases where not everybody has access to it.

"If I'm at a call center, I can access that customer data. If I'm doing data mining, I can access that customer data. Also if I'm running the direct response program, and so forth. So I'm benchmarking around customer relationship marketing.

"There are a lot of questions like, How do you build those road maps? How do you provide the process around that? Who has ownership of it? What's the security behind it? What's the privacy that's wrapped into it? We're beginning to get it under control, but there are many different owners of customers."

Conversion Conclusions

In the long run, the question on everybody's mind is whether the Web site is making sales.

"We know that customers visit an average of six to eleven times before making a purchase decision. They usually go to three sites three or four times before they will make a purchase decision. So we can check whether they've come back or not and what they bought. We can sum all that up, but it's not based on the individual. It's anonymous data, very separate from other behaviors, but we can begin to get kind of an enterprise average picture.

"We're headed toward tracking recency and frequency: This is his fourth visit, but the periods of time between visits are starting to be shorter; therefore we know he is just about to buy so let's make the following offers. What we're getting right now is customer behavior on the site and how they are using the site objectively."

Tools and Techniques

Compaq uses a variety of tools to capture and analyze their Web metrics data.

"We have Vividence (www.vividence.com), so we can actually track how people are using the site and whether the brand improves or doesn't improve and all those sorts of things. We look at customer quality, satisfaction, attitudes and usage, usability, and traffic trends. We use IntelliQuest. We use Survey.com to do tracking on the site. We also measure content quality or site quality on fifteen objective measures. We do a lot of profiling with Keylime. We use a lot of focus groups and one-on-ones. We also use Hit List.

"We go through this data and pull out twenty-five URLs that are bad on a number of areas and work that with the operations team. Then we go back and pull the top twenty-five worst pages in terms of leakage. If people just leave the page, when people leave the site, or dispersion—that's where they are going to too many places from one page and there's not really a focal point to where they go. Sometimes we find out when we go to some pages, that they're partnership pages and you're *supposed* to have leakage, or it's a page with a lot of choices like the enterprise page, where you have services and products and a lot of other things, so high dispersion is okay—like the home page. The home page should have high dispersion.

"So, once we knock those off, we work through the other pages and begin to figure out what's wrong. We may take a whole area into testing if we can't figure it out, but usually we can heuristically say this is what's going wrong and make the changes and see if it improves. If not, then we adjust.

"Every Thursday we sit down and have a SWAT team that works issues on our commercial and our home e-commerce sites. We work specific issues based on the customer intelligence data, and we usually recraft areas within the site to either simplify a process or take a look at the page design or whatever needs to be done."

Automated Inventory Reduction

A Web site that's designed to sell can also be designed to sell different products at different times.

"The gateway page is designed to make traffic flow a little bit more into some designated areas rather than just desktops. We want to direct them into a simplified business process, what we call built-to-order SKUs. We want to focus people on what we have on the floor, ready to go.

"There's a possibility of automating that so that it becomes dynamic. The Web site knows that we happen to have a buildup of these in this particular warehouse, so we'll show you those first. Now, it's a manual decision. It's somebody calling over and seeing what they've got on the floor. Once we build up BroadVision within the site, we'll be able to take a look at in-context bannering and things like that. The online stores have ad managers, so they can program certain things to be in certain areas of the store, but it is not looking at behavior—yet. In time it'll be, here's our catalogue, go ahead and look through. Oh, by the way, you should know there is a special offer on this product."

Trickle Up

Greg Sholene is in charge of strategy and planning. He's the one who makes sure that the CEO and the CIO get the reports they need to run the company. He wastes no time telling me his main purpose: "I'm focused on the revenue side of it. Revenue on the Web."

I ask Greg about the reports that go up into the hallowed halls. I wonder what's on the minds of the executives who have to answer to the board of directors and the shareholders. It turns out Greg has already answered my question. What do the C-level execs want to know about?

"Revenue. Are we growing online revenue as a percentage of our overall company revenue? Senior-level management is interested in daily numbers.

"They are also focused on the satisfaction thing as a key corporate component that profit sharing is all based on. So Web satisfaction is a key component of that. We have targets for our revenue, we have targets for satisfaction, we have targets for traffic as well.

"The report we have today is PowerPoint. We are looking to create a dashboard version, so it's a CEO-type dashboard where they can just see what's going on and see what the numbers are. We're working to automate, specifically on the revenue side, all the different sales sites that we have and the call centers so we can make daily updates in the dashboard format."

Visionary on Board

Between the CXOs and the directors, Marius Haas, vice president of E-Business, listens for shifts in the winds. He gently pulls the strings of those kites that can fly higher and is quick to cut the strings of those that require too much running to keep aloft.

Marius knows what he wants.

Fingers on the Pulse

Marius wants instant, dynamic visibility.

"I want to be able to see—every minute, every day—where we are. And that key metric you talked about—revenue—yes, of course it's one of our leading indicators.

And customer satisfaction is a key path that Seth is embarking down. The other piece is internal efficiencies that we're gaining by implementing some of the automated techniques and/or systems we're putting in place. So those are the three key areas that we are very much focused on. I've got us set at a pace where we're going to be perceived as and/or are an industry leader. And thus far, a lot of it is being measured by revenue per day."

Dollars per Day

Marius wants to know—and publish—just how much money comes in through the site daily.

"We're ramping really quickly. What we're finding, especially with the Hewlett-Packard situation, is that no one counts the same way. I had this conversation with the folks at Giga [Giga Information Group—www.gigaweb.com] because they are anxious to put out e-business, e-commerce revenue targets and are out measuring everybody."

"We've been very conservative with our sales figures compared to some of the competition and published 'unassisted revenue on the Web.' That means there is no intervention from a call center agent. We're measuring both now. We know that almost all of our customers that are especially coming from the SMB space and the consumer space go to the Web first, take a look, save a shopping cart and then they call up the agent. They want to get volume discounts. And then we have a huge number—70 to 80 percent of the customers pick up the phone and say 'I've just saved my cart, but I want number of units and I want a discount.' That *was* being captured as just a call center sale. Soon, we'll be binding those calls to Web shopping and we'll get a better idea of the impact our Web investment is having on sales."

Integration in All Things

My question for Marius is, what's coming? What's over the horizon? What do you want to get out of the Web site? He does not hesitate. He does not disappoint.

"I have a vision. The vision might change based on the trajectory we head down, but I think that there are some real key things that we need to do. The first and foremost is we need a very closely integrated architecture between what we are presenting to our customers on the Web versus the call center agents that are supporting that customer community. That is a very strategic effort to consolidate and integrate all of the data and all of the business processes associated with how we engage with a customer on the Web and how that goes into the different entities."

Marius wants economies of scale, combined with local control over the shifting sands. The pace of his speech quickens. His eyes glow.

"I want to get into a very decentralized development model where I can have collaboration with my geography for them to manage the presentation layer as close to the customer as possible. Do the localization. Do any of the customization they need to have to address any specific marketing.

"A lot of times the investments are coming from the regional sales entities and they have their rollouts scheduled. So I'll succeed as a worldwide team if I deliver to them toolkits at the right time that they can implement when they are ready to do so—obviously, making sure that those are the worldwide standards that we are going to abide by. Ideally, I'd just say boom-implement it now to everybody, because then I'd have my dashboard consistent across the world, but not everyone can make that investment plus the return on investment to do something.

"For example, in Hong Kong right now we might not have the volume to warrant it. But at least there'll be a standard toolkit, and I'll give them a timeline that says this is when I'd like it worldwide.

"I'll be the one providing the core 'service elements'—a taxation module, a language module. The core key elements that are absolutely necessary to run a public, anonymous Web site type of function that I'll leverage across the areas. I'll have my core competencies, then the rest of the world has the ability to move quickly in a manner that is needed for them to address any market shifts that take place."

Closed-Loop Data Sharing

Leads come in through the Compaq Web site, filter through, and end up on a partner Web site. Is the partner going to feed data back to the mother ship?

"There is closed loop. We funnel a lead to a partner all within our system. The partner has a certain time period in which to respond—typically 24 hours—and that means that they have gone into our partner relationship management system and acknowledged that they will take this lead and acknowledged that they will contact the customer and they have to log back in within 24 hours to say they have engaged with the customer, can I officially have the lead?"

Over many generations, Australian aborigines and Tibetan monks have mastered the art of controlled breathing in order to sustain a constant flow of musical sound. Marius Haas has this gift and uses it to talk about e-commerce and customer care.

"If they have not gone into the system and not logged it as their own, that lead automatically goes to the next-most-appropriate reseller to address the needs of that customer. As soon as that lead has been closed, it comes back through the exact same system and the partner has to acknowledge that it has been closed.

"The next step would be to have a transaction engine in this as well so that they'll also place the order and ideally we'll ship directly to the customer. The reseller comes in and records that they installed the system.

"There's a whole knowledge management system being built under this to ensure that we can feed back the kinds of leads we gave them, what they did to them, and the numbers that closed. And here's when you should expect them to buy again. There's also a whole piece, what we call Science of Selling, SOS, that is all of the collateral to sell Compaq solutions. This is what we would like you to present to the customer first—boom, boom, boom—all laid out for them so they really just have to hit the button."

Marius notices the excitement mixed with skepticism in my eyes.

"Hit the button, boom—a presentation pops out, scripts as to what they should be presenting to the customer, all of that. Once you launch a PRM [partner relationship management] environment that's based off of the same database and the same architecture, funneling this to the partner community is a cinch. Every indication we have is that our partners are absolutely just champing at the bit to get this thing rolled out."

Data-Driven Web Development

Marius knows that building and maintaining a Web site by the numbers makes more sense than doing it based on the committee decisions or hot-shot designer intuition.

"We've got to operationalize all the practices that run the analytics in place to make sure that we've got all the numbers and we know exactly what to do with those numbers because we know what they mean. Let's make sure that every day as a development team makes tweaks to the Web site that they are doing it from a data-driven perspective, not from a whim that this might work.

"That is absolutely key across the board, not just on the sales side but also on the support side because we've got a whole customer life cycle that we're taking care of."

The Hard Part: OPEX

People like to tell you about their successes. They love to talk about their vision. I like to ask them about the hard part. I ask Marius. He does not hesitate. He does not disappoint.

His answer, however, is very familiar and has everything to do with the coordination of a large company spread across multiple product lines, multiple functional disciplines, and multiple continents. The hard part is always a simple matter of getting all the different stakeholders on the same page. With that behind him, Marius faces the next problem.

"Now it is purely down to execution. How do you make sure you've got the right funding model? Initially what we do is pull the purse strings—that's what allowed me to have influence over them. But now what you don't want in a very OPEX tight environment—you don't want to have a central group with a huge OPEX bogie."

"OPEX?"

"Sorry, operating expense."

"Thank you."

"You don't want to have a central group that looks like a huge target for reductions. So what you really want to do is have the business sponsors be the ones that are funding the efforts, because they are also the ones that have return on investment in their business cases and their P&L. They care.

"And I want to have a shadow P&L here so that I can assure that work is being done and the business benefits and results are being achieved. That is my next task. Assigning specific targets, holding units accountable, and communicating to staff what we're driving towards.

"So the good news is we've got many deployments already that are showing very positive results. I've got a very solid team, an aggressive group that knows what needs to get done and works real well together. It's been a lot of fun laying the plan out and working with them to say 'Okay, go execute.'"

Social Psychologist

Seth Romanow introduced me to Theresa Doyon as the analyst.

"She really takes a look at our data. She's a statistician. She's a Ph.D. She one of a bunch of rocket scientists who crunch through like a terabyte of data and try to find patterns and do regression analysis and all that sort of stuff. When we get research data on satisfaction she works with the vendor to make sure it's statistically significant. That sort of thing."

Getting Visitors to Speak for Themselves

In person, it's obvious Theresa enjoys her work.

"I actually have a background in social psychology with just an emphasis in quantitative research. And so here I see my role as more of looking at human behavior on the Internet.

"You really do have to do qualitative. It's great to have a number, but the number isn't going to necessarily tell you what's going on. It's like a report card. You're getting an A, B, C, or D. That doesn't tell you what you need to do to get an A.

"You've got to start doing some initial qualitative work, get some feedback. Then, okay, we've got this qualitative work, let's run it through experiments, we'll see grades go up or go down. Then make a change. Then get more feedback—so it's just a constant circle of improvement.

"We run surveys across the board to try and see what people are feeling. We've got our little pop-up survey tagged all over our site—tagged on about 160 to 200 pages.

"We ask every five-hundredth or so visitor how they like Direct Plus Compaq.com. We get about a 5 to 30 percent response depending on the location on the site. We've had increasing problems thanks to X10 (pop-up camera ads). Something pops up—it's like there's an X10 reflex now. Die—die—go away!

"We try to be very polite about it: Please, if you would like to participate . . . And most people seem to see it as a way of getting in touch with us. So they'll comment about everything. They'll comment about our products, about the Web site. People want to help make the place better. We don't offer T-shirts or anything. Before I got here that was a problem apparently, because there was an incentive and that's illegal in Germany. And although we may be the dot-com and the U.S. site, the reality is we have a lot of international traffic. So we don't want to start tangling with governments."

Instead, Theresa likes to tangle with what people are looking at and where they go on the site. She likes to watch. I ask her to describe the Vividence service and the results they get.

"They have a panel of 162,000 people all over the board in terms of market segments and we'll ask them for 200 people per study. We design our own studies to specify what tasks we would like them to complete on the site. So rather than being a Nielsen//NetRatings kind of what are the majority of people out there doing?, it's very specific tests with very specific parameters.

"And on the last survey, questions were: Are you satisfied? Was it easy to navigate? Difficult to find information? We'll ask brand questions and see if the Web site impacts what you think about our products and us as a company. We'll then go back and look at all the clickstream data. Where did people get lost? Where did they backtrack? We can tell you what percentage of users succeeded in their goal. Who failed? What maybe went wrong?

"We have questions as well from our human factors lab. And also we can get an idea of the things for competitors, and get satisfaction with their brand and satisfaction with their site and how people would path through their site to do the same tasks. And are they more efficient than us? Things like how users react to segment links on a home page.

"We have a spreadsheet that says: here are the pages where people backtracked, here are the pages where they disperse off to competitors (which is everyone else on the Internet). Here's their satisfaction. What's in common here? So that's the first step; we're not sure but we're thinking of kind of more elaborate schemes for it. If you go down a specific path, is there a satisfied path to particular pages? Is there a dissatisfied path?

"So we're putting it in context, getting people's behavioral history because it's always kind of a question. If there are five ways to a page and they say they're dissatisfied or they are just neutral on the page, well, might it have to do with how they got there?"

I hit Theresa with the "What's the hard part?" question—only refined to her sphere of influence. What information are you not getting? What do you wish you could measure or count? What do you know is in the data that you can't tease out yet or what data is missing?

"I'm not sure if it's so much missing data. We actually are up to here in data. What I would really like to see is getting more of it together. A familiar part of my background is structural equation modeling, and I kind of did a little step one without the software. But we're trying to get an idea of the quantitative measures of usability that we seem to be getting out of the Vividence work. You know, here's how they all kind of correlate—if we do X to a page we have one impact on usability, one impact on satisfaction, and one on likelihood to purchase. What would you buy? What happened to the conversion?"

Competitive Knowledge

Theresa is also interested in the competitive side of measurement.

"I've been working with NetRatings as they've been developing their tool. With NetRatings I go out to competitors' sites and derive what their unique URLs and sub-domains are. We can look and see the percentage of people who go to Compaq for support this week and what percentage of people go to Dell this week. How many went to Dell for the consumer configurator and we can get a percentage of who bought. I always joke that Dell's made it so nice and so simple with their information architecture structure. There are other sites that drive me nuts, HP is one of them, because it's like someone threw a bomb into their URL's subdomain." She's referring to the clear, hierarchical organization at Dell's site. You can follow a visitor's train of thought, just by reading the URLs as they move from the U.S. home page. . .

```
http://www.dell.com/us/en/gen/default.htm
```

. . .to the desktop/handheld/laptop section. . .

```
http://www.dell.com/us/en/dhs/default_dual_notebooks.htm?rpo=true
```

. . .to the Inspiron notebooks product section. . .

```
http://www.dell.com/us/en/dhs/products/series_inspn_notebooks.htm
```

. . .to the Inspiron 2100 model page. . .

```
http://www.dell.com/us/en/dhs/products/model_inspn_1_inspn_2100.htm
```

. . .to the services and support area on that page (tab top 4):

```
http://www.dell.com/us/en/dhs/products/model_inspn_4_inspn_2100.htm#tabtop
```

The same path at the HP site is not quite as legible, but is still easy enough to follow. . .

```
http://www.hp.com/sbso/index.html
http://www.hp.com/sbso/busproducts.html
http://www.hp.com/sbso/product/notebooks/index.html
http://www.hp.com/sbso/product/notebooks/notebooks_6000.html
http://www.hp.com/cgi-bin/sbso/exit.cgi?goto=support/notebook
```

. . .for a while. Then it looks like the subdomain bomb went off:

```
http://h20000.www2.hp.com/bizsupport/TechSupport/Product.jsp?locale=en_U
S&prodTypeId=68737&prodSubCatId=67919
http://h20000.www2.hp.com/bizsupport/TechSupport/Home.jsp?locale=en_US&p
rodTypeId=68737&prodSeriesId=31762&prodSeriesName=hp+omnibook+6000
```

Competitive Brand Awareness

Theresa isn't just a hard numbers jockey. She pays attention to the soft numbers as well.

"One very interesting thing happed when Dell suddenly had severe server problems during one of our studies with Vividence. It had no impact on people's impressions of Dell. It's almost more important who they were interacting with. Everyone is very forgiving of Dell. They can make mistakes and they frequently do. Their site could crash and it's okay. They can be slow.

"The question's not as simple as, I have a slow modem or somebody hit some network cable out there; they will be more forgiving than they will be of Compaq, HP—any of us.

"We recently had some competitive research from IntelliQuest that shows that in terms of brand here are all of us, we're all average, and then Dell, way up here.

"They can make plenty of mistakes and they're okay. Any of the rest of us—Gateway, IBM, all of us — we can't. We have no leeway at all. The site has to be perfect.

"I've seen Keynote reports. They can tell based on who the backbone provider is out of your city—if it's Sprint, if it's Worldcom—they can tell if that's slowing you down with the particular site. When Sprint has the hiccups out of Saint Louis, we take a hit. Same with a fire in a tunnel in Baltimore."

Flash Is Trash

I have pressed for the moderate use of Flash animations on Web sites for years. When a visitor comes to a Web site and is forced to find the Skip Intro button before being allowed to enter, you're doing a grave disservice to your customers and prospective customers. If you want to use Flash to illustrate a point—show how a part is assembled, show where the leg bone connects to the thigh bone—that's fine. I say use it in moderation or don't use it at all.

This was, of course, all based on personal observation and from listening to thousands of Web surfers over the years. But there's something truly gratifying about having your hunches and impressions backed up with statistical fact. Theresa puts it in scientific terms.

"Flash is bad.

"There are usability experts like Jared Spool and others who will beat to death that flash is bad. We did our own study where we had a bunch of Flash and we discovered that Hit List detects if somebody on a dial-up connection cancels out the window before it's finished downloading all the components.

"We have a conservative estimate of who would leave which Flash. It's very conservative because we can't hit broadband, and what we find is really consistent with Jared: Flash is bad."

Design to Where the Visitor Is Going to Be

Want a sure-fire hint that will stand the test of time? Make sure your content and your visitor end up in the same place. Since you can't control the visitor, Theresa says to be careful about where you put your content.

"Put it at a point where the user expects it and is ready to read. There are pages where people go expecting there to be navigation and they're going to look for a key word on a link to click and go from there. You can put up a sign saying, 'One million dollars,' and they're not going to see it. That's not what they're looking for. That's not what they're paying attention to. It's very much tunnel vision.

"If the link says 'datasheet' or 'white paper,' then I know I'm getting to a leaf. They don't expect content on a home page, unless you're CNN. They expect links. They expect to find a specific link worded the way they expect it to be worded. They'll click on that and then either links or content depending on what exactly their goal is.

Learning from Searching

Navigation numbers tell you whether people are easily finding what they're after, but Theresa knows that how they use the Web site's search tool is a bigger tell-tale.

"The server log give us an idea of what people are searching for. Last week as a matter of fact I was pestering the Keylime people, saying it would be really nice if they could tell us what pages people are entering in specific key words. If we've got 200 people a day entering in iPAQ [Compaq's handheld computer] on a specific page designed for something entirely different, we have a disconnect with our customer. And we have to look at that page and the navigational path to that page.

"Just before I came, everyone realized that the top keyword was *drivers*. Okay, let's try something. Let's put a *drivers* link on the home page. We could tell immediately that searches for drivers plummeted. Fewer people were asking for drivers. They were just finding them.

"While I was here, *drivers* got superceded by iPAQ. We need to have separate links, not just a *handhelds* link. We needed a link that said iPAQ, because the brand has taken over to the point they're just looking for an iPAQ link.

"People like to see that Search box in the top-level navigation bar and they'll go immediately to it even on the home page. Beyond a couple of really simple key words, we find IT professionals don't want to waste any time with navigating. It's just, 'Take me there.' We're trying to improve the search engine and improve all the meta tags sitewide so when the IT professionals come, they get where they want as fast as possible. And also we're gauging the improvement on that using a special, shorter satisfaction survey unique to the search engine."

The Fun Part

The counterpoint to my question about the hard part is the opposite. What's the fun part? Theresa knows.

"Trying to figure out what people do—why they do it. And if you change something, just kind of watching and if it works it's like 'Yeah!' If it doesn't work it's like 'Hmm . . . So we need to run another study here.'"

Bottom Line

Theresa continues, "The real question is, What will it take for people to buy online?"

That's where Abhay comes in.

Customer Intelligence

Abhay Mehta is the senior director of the Customer Intelligence Group at Compaq.

Abhay seemed to be interspersed in and most definitely at the end of every conversation I had with this company: "That's something to ask Abhay."

"Abhay's group is responsible for that."

"You'd have to check with Abhay."

It was time to talk to this walking encyclopedia of Compaq Web metrics. This maestro of measurement. The connoisseur of Web calculations. According to Abhay, "I think my title as it is today is e-business analytics."

Abhay is not focused on himself, but he is definitely focused on his work and his team. "My group analyzes all the clickstream data, combines them with order data, campaign data, and survey data, so we link all of this stuff together. So we get a pretty wide view of what visitors are doing and how they are converting to customers and how they are not converting to customers."

Deep Data

Abhay continues, "We then get all the data and we analyze it, we data mine it, we run statistical models on it, we actually build models of customer behavior, do segmentation and all that stuff. The main idea is we then come up with recommendations and define projects that would then increase the revenue from our site."

At this point, my pupils are dilating and my breathing becomes labored. I have been looking for—hoping for—somebody, somewhere who is performing this level of data delving and is willing to talk about it. I want detail. I want the whole story. I want to reach deep into that vat of rich historical data that this group has been harvesting and aggregating for lo, these many years and lift out complex tapestries of human computer interaction and shopping and buying tendencies that Paco Underhill never dreamed of accessing.

"Well, let me put it this way," Abhay says, letting me down easy. "We've only been doing this for about 6 months now. We went through first the stage of recognizing that we need to get really, really good data.

"At first we decided to go down the log server route. I came across several problems, so this time around I decided not to do it that way. We went with Keylime to give us client-side data from browsers and spent a little bit of time implementing all the pages.

"Keylime gives us two things. One is it gives us some out-of-the-box, off-the-shelf reports on our clickstream data. But more importantly for us, we get an 'x-track' from them which is our entire clickstream data which is coming up on a terabyte now, for the last quarter. And then we do a join with our internal data. The most important, the biggest piece is the order transaction data."

Prioritizing the Seven Fruits

Abhay goes on, "We spent one month analyzing the sales piece. How do we increase the conversion rate? Out of that, I think the real task ahead for us is that there is no shortage of things that one can do to improve the Web site. In fact, there are probably too many things that one can do.

"One of the biggest tasks, first, is to go and define the low-hanging fruit, early on in the curve so you get a large ROI. You need a huge amount of investment, but the jury's still out on the return. The first big task is taking the list of fifty or sixty or seventy possible projects and whittling it down to this smaller list of things that we can actually do and get some leeway on.

"We modeled the behavior of the customer based on what would happen with these customers or this segment of customer if we followed this recipe and made these tweaks to the Web site. So each one of the projects that was on our original list was then quantified and then we came up with the potential increase in revenue for each and every one of them.

"I'm not even trying to put an ROI on the knowledge management aspect—the insights that might lead to other things. Just directly focusing on changes that you can make which then lead to immediate revenues. My goal was to find that low-hanging fruit that can give us those big wins based purely on ROI numbers. Some other techniques might give us better insight, but some of that insight might be difficult to translate into revenue. And these are project recipes where we have a clear path to revenues.

"The seven that I'm mentioning are the ones that made it to the top of the list. And these seven, in our case, total up to 100 percent increase in revenue."

It's very hard to argue with doubling sales.

"We went in and did the analytics and were surprised to find where the low-hanging fruit was. We essentially came up with seven areas:"

1. Optimize Lead Generation
2. Tune Our Pages
3. Optimize Our Navigation
4. Enhance Our Search
5. Optimize Our Merchandising
6. Tune Our Entry Points
7. Analyze Our Sales Funnel

1. Optimize Lead Generation

"The state of the industry is that we put out ads and banners, we put out email campaigns, and then we track the clickthroughs. But then once people enter the site, the site is kind of like a black box. At the end of it, we can find out what kind of orders were made, but we don't have much insight into the different clickstreams that are taken by visitors who came because of different campaigns."

Campaign Consideration

"The first task here was to go in and instrument each of our ads separately. Using Keylime, we are able to instrument them so that we essentially can put tracers on each of these different forces independent of each other. If you click on a Yahoo! ad, then you come in carrying a couple of parameters that are unique to that ad—a unique URL in the parameter field. That tells us what the lead generation source was; an external ad, versus an internal ad, versus an email campaign.

"Once we have the instrumentation in place and these tracers out there, we are able to optimize at the overall campaign levels. Typically, we've got a bunch of campaigns running at the same time. Now we are able to see the performance of one campaign versus another. We also instrumented it so that print ads that have been put out have different vanity URLs with different landing pages, so we can track each one of those independently. Within the first few days of the campaign [we] start seeing what's doing well and what isn't.

"Even this week, when our home page and investor relations numbers are skewed due to the HP announcement, the unique identifiers let us know who came because of advertising."

Predictive Modeling

"Then we have some predictive modeling going on which lets us quickly project out what this campaign is going to do. And that particular model is based on the value proposition of that ad; How large is the ad? What's its position? A bunch of different attributes that you put into a predictive model.

"We predict the lifetime curve of each campaign. A campaign doesn't all come in the first day. It ramps up and then it decays. So we predict the shape of the curve and then what the height is going to be at the max point. Then we drill down to a specific campaign and start looking at how the different ads and the different sources are doing. We also evaluate our internal email campaign list versus our external rented list and all of those things."

Conversion Submersion

"We're comparing clickthrough and click depth and then conversion. So it's really ROI that we are doing this optimization on. We have the cost and we know the revenues that we're generating. You can look at it as an ROI as opposed to a clickthrough, which is sometimes very deceptive.

"We are able to tweak this on a real-time basis. That's something we are implementing as we speak. We've only had a little bit of experience with this, but that little experience has been just phenomenal.

"Let's say we've got ten interactive ads out there for this one promotion. We've got some in Yahoo! Finance and some in Yahoo! News, some in Disney, some in MSN. But we look at all of these different sites or subsites and are quickly able to see the ROI that each one of these is generating. So then we go back and I reduce and increase the number of impressions on the pages that are really working for this campaign."

TIMITI

"We want to get to the point pretty soon where we can actually change the creative during the lifetime of the ad. We're actually requesting our agencies to have multiple versions available so that in fact we can do the swap and then measure the effect in real time. So that's some of the kinds of tweaking that we do. One of the big levers we have is just the number of impressions that we can buy from these different properties. We can also—if some ad is not doing anything at all for us and we're still paying for some impressions there, we might turn that off completely. And we are basically able to rule our portfolio mix, if you will, so that we can optimize our ROI.

"We also can take it all the way down to the performance of each specific ad on a particular day. So we look at it in day increments. We can drill down to a specific ad and see [how] it performed over the last week day-by-day and make some predictions based on that. Is this a good one to reduce? increase? remove? based on the patterns we've seen over the last week.

"We typically give the creative over to the agency, and it is their responsibility to put in the instrumentation. We have our internal marketing people that use this instrumentation. The first few times I had to come and sit side by side with my data miners so that they can actually see it while it's happening and use their marketing expertise. After the data modeling, we go back to the agency and request one of these tweaks that we talked about.

"Let's say a campaign starts over a weekend. Monday, Tuesday, somewhere around then, we do the first pass of the optimization. By Tuesday or so, we will go back to the agency and they will have a couple of days to do simple things like change impressions, change location, all of that kind of stuff. So by the end of that week, which is the second week of the campaign, we've made our first pass at improvement. Then we measure again and we will do this one more pass. In a month-long campaign, we typically tweak it at the halfway point or after 1 week and then again at like week three."

Remember Ron Richards from ResultsLab? Remember how he likes to only change one thing at a time? They understand the importance of Ron's perspective at Compaq.

"We like to do these changes independently. I have one resident statistician on board whose job is to measure the effectiveness on the back end and to remove the complications of one tweak and how they effect another tweak.

"Even more importantly, to take into account macro kinds of attributes, like a merger with HP and what Greenspan might have done to the interest rates and stuff like that. So one of the things that we are introducing is a lot of statistical rigor into the process. At the end of the day we can have actual results with controlled tests as opposed to contextual things."

2. Tune Our Pages

Abhay's team is concerned with pages that work well and those that don't. Which pages have the fastest navigation? Which have the lowest prospect loss? Which have the best conversion rate?

Identifying these pages is the first step. The second is identifying their antipodes. Look at the best, look for the worst, figure out the difference, and apply the best of the best to make the worst better.

What identifies a page in need of a tune-up?

High Prospect Loss

If this was the last page a high number of people look at, what's wrong with this picture? What is it about this page that scares people off? Is there a mislabeled link to this page that brings people to the wrong spot? Is there a navigational error that stops people cold?

High Error Rate

Design, spelling, graphic elements, grammar, server errors—there's no end to the potential problems a page can have.

High Interrupt Rate

Did the user click on something before the page finished loading? If this is a navigational page, that's fine—but its download time deserves some attention. A navigational page may not be among the slowest to download, but if the interrupt rate is high, then the page is loading too slow for its purpose.

High Download Time

A high download time page is likely to experience high leakage. It's certain to harm the brand.

High Help Ratio

If more people hit the Help button on this page than other pages, what's wrong with this picture?

High Dispersion Rates

If people tend to go to the same handful of pages from this one, then it's doing its job. If, however, more people are scattering to the four winds from this page, it implies poor navigation and a general lack of focus. Time to rework the material.

Abhay's team calculates that if they identify these worst-case pages and fix them, they end up with less leakage. Diminished leakage, multiplied by their average conversion rate, translates into hard dollars, the true purpose of the whole Compaq site.

3. Optimize Our Navigation

Individual page tuning is very important, but when individual pages are networked, the problem becomes one of navigation.

According to Abhay, "We have come up with certain models and certain analytics that help us really analyze pages to see how productive they are in converting people. So now . . . for [each] of our products, we've got this matrix of . . . what is the list of most productive pages and what is the optimal path." The same philosophy applies to navigation optimization as page tuning. Find the especially bad navigational pages and fix them. How do you know bad navigation when you see it?

High Backtracking

In a bookstore, it's a normal activity to pick up a book and set it down, then pick up another and set it down. That's what bookstores are for. On a bookseller's Web site, you'd expect the same activity. But at Compaq.com, the expectation is that you will come in looking for something, find it, and leave. Hitting the Back button a few times in the course of a visit is a normal activity and tells you very little about the visitor.

But a single page that experiences an inordinate number of Back button clicks has a navigational problem attached to it somewhere. Why do people look at that page and then back off? What is it about that page that keeps people from exploring further? How can that be fixed?

Short Paths

Short paths are visits that are too short for a visitor to find what they want. They come to the home page, they click, they click again, and they leave. Visits that result from saved URLs like bookmarks or forwarded links don't come into play here. Searches that reveal exactly the right page are not considered either.

In a larger Web site, this short-path behavior from the home page indicates that people are giving up. They are not sufficiently interested in the potential of getting the answer to their question. They are dropouts. By walking through the pages that are most often parts of short paths, Compaq can try to make them more engaging and draw people deeper toward a purchase.

Long Paths

Overly long path visits are rare—or should be. Compaq understands that there are those people, especially technical types, who are problem solvers by nature. They want to dig around a Web site until they have a good feel for what can be found there. That's fine; bonding with the brand is good.

But when visits of fifty and seventy-five pages become a significant percentage of your visits, a few questions pop up. Those pages should also be examined to see if enhancements will speed visitors to their goal.

4. Enhance Our Search

Abhay goes on: "We started analyzing the terms that drove people to us from the outside search engines, but we decided that was not one of our big revenue enhancers. So that didn't make it to the to-do list. We have more control over the *internal* search engine, so that's where we want to spend our time.

"We could take the long approach: Can we make our search engine perfect so that when people search we would give them the right thing? That is the ultimate goal of search, but it would take a long time and we might never get there.

"Rather than that, a quicker approach would be to find those things that people are really searching for on a daily basis. Which one of those search terms result in the most conversions for us? And then, based on a matrix for each one of those terms, which is the most productive page that we should really lead them to?

"We find the most-searched terms in terms of conversion. We calculate how many other people might have bought that product and then relate that to the analysis on productivity of pages and really hardwire those into our best bets set of results.

"Searches also reveal what people cannot find. In fact, failures are the first thing we look at: sessions where people searched over again and/or searched but never clicked on any of the resulting links. This is a sharp signal there are things that are simply too hard to find on the site. Sometimes, people search for things that should be obvious—including product names."

5. Optimize Our Merchandising

"We do a market basket analysis. We find out those items that naturally sell together, and this changes day over day, week over week, so this is a constantly running thing that tells us that item A and item B sell well together. Once we know that, it's a matter of placing those things together either at the configurator page or at checkout or just on the page when they are looking for things. That's the first part of it.

"The second part is we look for and observe and analyze what I would call natural momentum to buy an unrelated product from some other page. And we find this a lot. For example, there might be a natural tendency for people to look at support pages when buying a certain product. Once we find that natural momentum, we try to capitalize on that by really increasing the merchandizing of that product on that path and increasing the conversion rate.

"We see that many people who buy item A end up buying item B as well, so we can capitalize on that. The first is affinity of products to another product and then there's an affinity of pages to products, and that's the other way that we try to optimize the merchandizing.

"Let's say we find people looking at a certain support page. They're looking at technical specifications. It may be that they are looking for specifications for a desktop computer, but we notice that a lot of people who actually see that, for some reason or another, end up buying an iPAQ pocket PC. No direct, logical correlation, but there is a relationship—one we would not have figured out in our minds. Our customers are telling us that there is one. And so that's what I mean by an affinity of seemingly unrelated pages to product.

"The obvious ones, of course, we know about and we do the merchandizing, but these were discovered through our analytics and through looking at ROI calculations on these pages. And we will capitalize on those by putting the right targeted merchandizing on those pages."

6. Tune Our Entry Points

"We can change landing pages internally so we have more control. There are a variety of attributes that we experiment with there. And a lot of these are usability things like how many buttons are there? How compelling is the call for action? Where are the links? Are they above the fold? Are they below the fold? And we do that in a more controlled environment. Only one or two variables at a time so that we can really optimize the ROI."

Abhay produces click density maps that show the preponderance of links on a given page that resulted in sales and those that did not. With a quick glance, you can see a third datapoint—those links that are almost never clicked. The content on the unclicked areas of the page can be upgraded to include more of the types of links that lead to sales. That space may also be given over to promoting special sales or the product configurator.

7. Analyze Our Sales Funnel

"We've broken up our sales funnel into a variety of checkpoints, if you will, in the purchase cycle. We just draw a bar graph of the volume of people that made it to each of those checkpoints:

- People who make it to the home page
- People who make it to the product page
- People who enter the store
- People who use the product configurator
- People who put something in the shopping cart
- People who enter the checkout process
- People who complete the purchase

"We're watching the curve and then breaking it out for different segments of the population. We determine which part of each of those is really a knob that we can turn. Then we determine which one of those knobs is most cost-effective to try and turn."

How can they have an impact on getting more of the right kind of people from stage to stage to stage?

"It's not obvious. You first look at it and you say, 'Well, maybe I just need to get more people to my store.' Is that more important or is it more important to increase the conversion rate from people who have put something in the cart and are checking out?

"So what part of that sales funnel do you focus on? Which segment of the population? We know that people come back multiple times before buying. When they're doing some information gathering, we don't necessarily want to try and convert them then because we might drive them away.

"Depending on where they are in the sales funnel and which knob we want to tweak, we try to do the right things to the right segments of the population to maximize the ROI for that sales funnel."

Measuring for Major Improvements

For each of these seven focal points, the Customer Intelligence Group has calculated the additional traffic, the reduction in errors, and, therefore, the increase in sales: ROI.

If X percent more people can find what they're searching for and they look at Y percent more pages, then the results will be Z percent more sales at an average sales value of $A for a total 7-focus project impact of $B million dollars per period. Their current target, given low-hanging fruit and no changes in the marketplace, *just* changing things on the Web site: 100 percent increase in online sales. Compelling stuff.

The Basic Rules

I can't resist asking Abhay if they've come up with any basic rules. What does he tell the brand-new product manager who wants the very best campaign possible and wants the three most important rules to follow?

Abhay refrains from calling them rules. "They're some hypotheses and we're working on it. It's a big challenge for us. I don't have those for you right now."

Sensing the mathematician speaking, I press him.

"Well, clearly the demographic match. We analyze the value proposition of an ad. We compute the value of that exact configuration of a product in the market by looking at our competitors and everything else out there. And then we compute our differential with the differential of our value versus what perceived value of that configuration is out in the market.

"It turns out that the consumer and the commercial buyer have a very keen sense for what good value is and are able to spot that in the 1 to 2 seconds they're spending on that ad. It's a matter of getting across features per price as quickly as possible.

"I think that that is probably the biggest driver that we're finding, which is unfortunate. If you could find something that was just creative, then we could get by with much less. But no, it turns out that we have to relate this to value."

The Fun Part/The Hard Part

What's the fun part for Abhay?

"I find the marketing campaigns and the behavior of those people coming in through those campaigns the most intriguing, because there are such a lot of different variables and attributes. Depending on how it's structured, you see such a variety of different behavior patterns that I find most difficult to explain and thus the most interesting. I wish I could get the *why* behind the behavior that we've seen. We do see some behavior, we can estimate and guess to a lot of that and we are now being able to put together survey data that people are leaving footprints on our site and combining that to clickstream. But the true reason as to why people do certain things when they did it. I wish I could have that."

When I put my favorite question to Abhay (What's the hard part?) his response echoes the surveys Matt Cutler and I did back at the turn of the century.

"I think probably the most difficult thing is really having to limit what we can do. There's so much data, so much analysis. We're having to limit both from a personal standpoint and for my entire team to keep people focused on just a few big wins and not get cluttered with all of this data. Keeping that focus is the hardest part I would say. Not getting sidetracked."

Then he finishes up with the best advice for any business manager.

"Focus on the one or two metrics that you want to influence. And once you have that, evaluate everything with those one or two metrics and do not get sidetracked by the beauty or intrigued by how detailed or exciting something is. Keep your eye firmly on that ball. In our case that would be conversion rate. There may be a bunch of other projects that might have been considered very interesting in terms of insight, but it doesn't give us the conversion rate, so we wouldn't pursue them."

Making It Work by Bringing It All Together

"One accurate measurement is worth a thousand opinions."
Rear Admiral Grace Murray Hopper

Opinions aren't all bad, but you can't run a company on guesses and experience and gut feel. On the other end of the spectrum, there are lies, damn lies, and statistics, and thank you, Mark Twain. This end of the spectrum is made up of those who would point at the screen and intone, "Because the computer *says* so!"

In a world that relies more and more on spreadsheets, we have faced a unique problem with information: There's just too darned much of it.

Data, Data Everywhere, but Not a Thought to Think

Isn't it wonderful that we are able to collect every bit of information about everything that happens on the Web, at the cash register, in the other processing department, and in the customer service call center? Yes. Undoubtedly.

Wouldn't it be wonderful if we could make sense out of all that data coming from all those places? Yes. Unlikely.

There's just so much data, stored in so many disparate systems, controlled by so many committees, that it costs an inordinate amount of resources (read: money) to get it all in one place.

But Jim, you say, that's just a technical problem. What if you *could* get it all in one place? What if you could build a data warehouse that was properly fed by all those disparate systems and you could slice it and dice it and find all those counterintuitive aha's that would let you trounce the competition?

I used to say such things to myself. You can still catch me at it now and then. It's compelling. It's the logical extreme. It's reassuring that at some point in the future we will have tagged and bagged every known fact and can feed it all into the Deep Thought supercomputer and all will be made clear. (Those of you who said "42," go to the head of the class.)

It's just a technical problem. Get a little senior management support, throw a little money at it, and eventually you have that rich data set that holds the keys to the kingdom. That is, if you don't mind searching for needles in haystacks. Very *large* haystacks.

Data Deluge

Anywhere between 75 percent and 85 percent of your resources will be needed just to prepare the data you have for the analysis you need, in order to get the insights you're hoping for. Why? Because you're trying to build a three-dimensional model of each and every customer based on the data droppings they leave behind with their clicks, calls, and procurements (see Figure 15.1). Bringing all that together is not a simple matter.

With all this data come new types of tools. Tools to help you slice and dice. Tools to help you sort and sift. Tools to help you play "what if?"

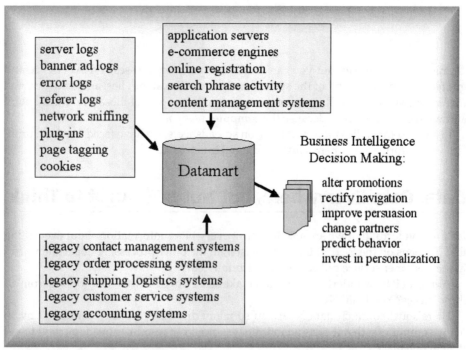

Figure 15.1   Business intelligence comes from all over and requires a healthy amount of integration.

Data Diving

Most people call this data mining, but Neil Raden says allowing your executives to go swimming in a sea of data is akin to letting them go Dumpster diving for lunch.

Raden is president and founder of Archer Decision Sciences (www.archer-decision.com), a consulting company that implements data warehousing and business intelligence and has done so with many of the largest and most prestigious organizations in the world for almost 20 years. He consults, he writes articles, and he holds an audience in the palm of his hand when he's on stage. Lucky for me, he lives in Santa Barbara and likes to have lunch.

It was over several lunches that I began to understand the deep reservations held by this balding and bespectacled guru (which caused me to trust him at once—it was like looking in the mirror).

Raden began by describing the intersection of humans and tools. "Most organizations are constrained by their ability to integrate and understand available, actionable business information. Decision support systems are supposed to improve the decision-making process in an organization by providing timely, reliable information to decision makers. The best decision support systems include the necessary tools to analyze and visualize the information and to provide a means to synthesize information as a result of the analysis. The best of the best are architected to participate in a smooth and seamless flow of information, providing connectedness between all of the steps in the decision-making process.

"Online Analytical Processing (OLAP) is often confused with decision support. At the practical level, OLAP always involves interactive querying of data, following a thread of analysis through multiple passes, such as drilling down into successively lower levels of detail. The information is multidimensional, meaning that it can be visualized in grids. Information is typically displayed in cross-tabs, and tools provide the ability to pivot the axes of the cross-tabulation.

"The problem is that the executives who are given these really cool toys to play with don't understand the underlying structure of the data, and the statisticians who architected the systems don't have any intuition of how the resulting information might be valuable.

"What the 'consumers' of these databases need is reliable, timely, clean, and understandable information that is presented through a medium that facilitates and enhances their ability to perform their jobs."

The big problem is that we have become so attached to our data and we have so much data to become attached to, we have forgotten what we wanted to know in the first place. We have become enamored of the idea of the database as the keeper of secrets, rather than the database as the corroborator of hypotheses.

It's up to us humans to surmise a correlation and go data diving to validate the supposition. If the database tells you that cable modem surfers buy more than dial-up visitors, you have an interesting point and you can praise the database for handing you an all-important fact.

If you surmise that they buy more because the pages download faster, then you can come up with a plan to improve the speed of your site. But if you model that assumption and correlate purchases with attitudes about the speed of your site, you might find a correlation factor of zero: the two have nothing in common. You might build a model that will tell you if the reason more cable modem surfers make purchases is that they enjoy higher incomes.

Rather than depending on the data to divulge heretofore hidden revelations about your Web site and your company, you have two choices. First, go back to your goals and figure out what you are trying to accomplish. Then deconstruct those goals to identify the drivers, and those drivers to identify their respective metrics. Then go looking for ways to capture and calculate those metrics.

The other choice is to let somebody else take a look at your site and render an opinion.

Web Site Critique

I love writing Web site reviews. I spend most of my consulting time giving workshops at large companies, helping them figure out what they've got to work with, helping them figure out what they need to work on, and helping them figure out how they're going to get the job done.

But every now and then, I get to sharpen up the critic in me and have fun playacting the part of the Web site visitor and generally venting my spleen at the whole world of Web site faux pas, failures, and foul-ups.

I always begin my written reviews with something like:

Thank you for asking me to review your Web site. You have shown yourselves to be forward-thinking and brave. You know the value of an outside consultant. I have knowledge of what others are doing on the Web. I have no agenda. I have no stake in the outcome. Therefore, you should take this advice for what it is. Make use of what you find valuable, ignore that which misses the mark, and work hard to make your site a more valuable service for your customers and, therefore, a more valuable asset of your company.

This review concerns your site as it is and as it should be. I start with the assumption that you've worked very hard to get it to this point and for that, I congratulate you. Well done. End of praise.

Time to put on your thick skin and put down your pride of authorship. This document is all about what's wrong and needs to be fixed.

This review is intended to be more of a touchstone than a step-by-step design document. It's intended to give you a look into the mind of a customer.

Shall we?

I have a great job.

Web Site Score Card

The Giga Information Group (www.gigaweb.com) has created a Web Site ScoreCard that was designed to objectively evaluate your Web site strategy and tactics. The plan is to perform enough reviews to establish a benchmark. Then you can compare your site against your competition and other "best of breed" sites.

You pick three other sites, and Giga's consultants start comparing them and compiling a composite of best-practice sites for each category scored. So you might be compared to Amazon.com for online sales, Cisco for customer service, and Compaq for marketing.

The whole point is for Giga to come up with enough recommendations for fixing your site to keep them in consulting contracts for a while. It's a time-honored model of finding the problems in order to recommend solutions. Something they suggest doing every 6 months.

Mapping the Web Genome

If you'd rather do it yourself, there's a company that will gladly scare the bejeepers out of you with a list of Web site items to review. It's appropriately named MuchoInfo (www.muchoinfo.com).

What sets MuchoInfo apart from other Web analytics companies is their Web Genome project to come up with a standard measurement methodology and their effort to use it on as many sites as possible.

First, MuchoInfo created a checklist of site features and functionalities, then they researched the composition of Web sites across various online business categories. The checklist comprises 427 items, including general user tools and traffic boosters (159 items), standard content areas (102 items), online buying, ordering, and selling assistance tools (49 items), Web-site-only revenue streams (32 items), navigation issues (10 items), and industry categories (75 items).

MuchoInfo also defined fourteen metrics to better classify their findings after reviewing almost 1,000 Web sites (see Table 15.1).

Table 15.1 MuchoInfo's Web Genome Definition of Metrics

METRIC	DEFINITION
E-commerce Quotient	Provides score representing the extent to which a Web site is E-commerce enabled. Includes such items as price information or a product/service directory.
Brochureware Advantage	Provides score representing the extent to which a Web site offers brochure-type information or marketing-related content. Shares many of the same items as the E-commerce quotient, such as price information or a product/service directory. Web site is brochureware (not E-commerce) if there are no items checked in Rows 291 through 324.
Browsing Barometer	Provides score representing the extent to which a web site provides navigation, or browsing, tools. Includes such items as text site map, A-Z index of content, and consistent menu/navigation bar.

(continues)

Table 15.1   MuchoInfo's Web Genome Definition of Metrics *(Continued)*

METRIC	DEFINITION
Interaction Indicator	Provides score representing the extent to which a Web site provides interactive communication tools for the visitor. Includes such items as email/message pad for feedback and Internet email.
Customization Quotient	Provides score representing the extent to which a Web site is equipped for customizing the experience for a visitor. Includes such items as personalized greeting and viewing option-simplified/enhanced.
Surfer Incentives	Provides score representing the extent to which a Web site offers incentives that attract visitors and enhance their experience. Includes such items as free E-cards and free newsletters.
Advertising Aptitude	Provides score representing the extent to which a Web site offers incentives that attract visitors and enhance their experience. Includes such items as free E-cards and free newsletters.
Affiliate Equipped Indicator	Provides score representing the extent to which a web site offers information for, and works with, affiliates or partners. Includes such items as affiliate commission/compensation information.
Enhanced Experience Edge	Provides score representing the extent to which a Web site offers tools or features that are specifically designed to enhance the visitor experience. Includes such items as audio and multimedia content.
About the Site & Privacy	Provides score representing the extent to which a Web site communicates information about the Web site and its policy on privacy. Includes such items as Web site rules, terms, and conditions.
Company Information	Provides score representing the extent to which a Web site communicates information about the company. Includes such items as management profiles and company location information.
Jobs & Careers	Provides score representing the extent to which a Web site communicates information and offers tools associated with job and career opportunities. Includes such items as job listings, recruiting events, and career development information.

Table 15.1   MuchoInfo's Web Genome Definition of Metrics *(Continued)*

METRIC	DEFINITION
Investor Relations	Provides score representing the extent to which a Web site communicates investor information and offers tools associated with investing in the company. Includes such items as SEC filings, real-time stock quotes, and calendar of events.
General Help	Provides score representing the extent to which a Web site offers general help tools. Includes only two items: frequently asked questions (FAQ) and glossary/dictionary.

These metrics categories were derived from the 427 items they went looking for, and look they did. The list is too detailed to reproduce in this venue, but here's a taste:

What shopping or buying activities can your visitors participate in?

What best describes your buying or shopping activity?
- *Viewing or reading something about a specific product or service*
- *Viewing or reading something about a specific community host product or service*
- *Browsing or researching general product or service information*
- *Browsing the community host site's product(s) or service(s)*
- *Searching for specific product or service information*
- *Searching for specific community host site product or service information*
- *Reading legal or security information*
- *Viewing information on help or how to buy*
- *Viewing customer service information*
- *Using a customer service feature*
- *Getting ready to make, or actually making, a transaction*
- *Viewing my account information*
- *Communicating with the Web site or another Web user*
- *Entering personal information*
- *Downloading something*
- *Abandoning the buying process*
- *Other*

In what ways can visitors browse your web site?

What best describes your browsing activity?

- *Using a search engine*
- *Using links*
- *Using a site map*
- *Using an index*
- *Using a directory*
- *Browsing the pages*
- *Using the help information or features*
- *Other*

If the Web Genome approach is a little too detailed and numeric for you, there are others who will review your site from afar as well as anear.

Expert Critics

Audit It (www.audidit.com; see Figure 15.2) is co-located in Madison, Wisconsin, and Auckland, New Zealand. When they review your site from afar, they're farther afar than most.

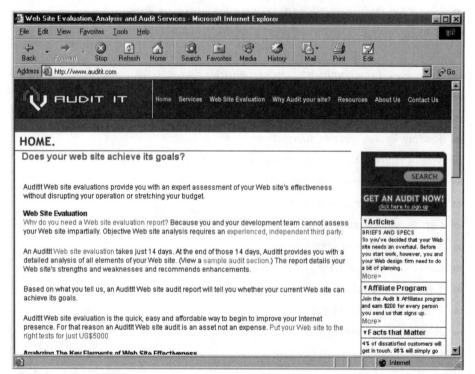

Figure 15.2   Audit It will give your site the once-over by a team of experienced Web marketers and technicians.

It's hard to say if Audit It has 427 items on a checklist, but they *do* identify site strengths and weaknesses grouped into the following fifteen general categories:

Usability. *User interface, navigation ease of use, search engine effectiveness*

Security. *Authentication, encryption systems, certificates, hacker vulnerabilities*

Design. *Screen usage, consistency, professional image*

Visibility. *Search engine visibility, keyword density, search engine optimization*

Performance. *HTML code check, link check, download time*

Style. *Grammar, spelling, punctuation, legibility, consistency of fonts and text layout*

Structure. *Minimizing clicks, user friendliness, navigation, page linking*

Accessibility. *Geographic, language, text-only, device/browser/printer compatibility*

Company/Product Information. *Concise, comprehensive, layout, freshness*

Legal. *Copyright, trademark notices, terms and conditions, privacy policy*

E-commerce. *Trust building content, unique selling proposition, tactics*

Public Relations. *Available contacts for press, +/- Internet newsgroup comments*

Customer Service. *Service standards, feedback policy, Web site value communicated*

Content. *Copy trust building, site freshness, image value, effective interactivity*

Community. *Community building, value-added, functionality*

Large companies in highly competitive markets like retail, travel, or telecommunications will typically engage in customer focus groups and competitive intelligence in order to prioritize future site investments. While focus groups and customer surveys may help make a site easier to use, they will not produce expert insights that would improve marketing, sales, or ROI. For example, few customer groups are savvy enough to suggest ways a retailer could cross-market key products to them in prime screen-real-estate positions or reveal how the company's security vulnerabilities may inhibit customer conversion rates. That requires objective expertise.

A sample of a customer service audit appears on the Audit It Web site and includes the following:

Summary: Yoursite.com offers a basic level of customer service but fails to take advantage of the opportunities for "Wow" customer service that the Internet offers. Attempts to enhance the customer service-related technology on your site offers should be coupled with a concerted effort to add more personality to site and email content. The way your site "talks to" existing and prospective customers will be a key determinant of whether your site makes a connection with them. Remember, customer service will be a key factor in how visitors differentiate your site from its many competitors.

They then dive down into critiques of the "yoursite.com"s email responses, automated responses, communication of service standards, inquiry/feedback policy, use of technology and software, and overall customer experience. With each sting of the lash, Audit It alleviates the pain with recommendations and suggestions.

Most of their audit work is, indeed, done from afar, while some, like a Web site security review, might require a *physical* on-site visit.

Measuring Credibility

Companies like MuchoInfo and Audit It can measure your site's effectiveness, but there's one organization that's determined to determine your site's credibility. Stanford Web Credibility Research (www.webcredibility.org) wants to know why people believe what they see on the Web and how. So they came up with their own checklists (see Figures 15.3 and 15.4).

B. J. Fogg is running this group, which, as they say on their Web site, is dedicated to the following:

Performing quantitative research on Web credibility

Collecting all public information on Web credibility

Acting as a clearinghouse for this information

Facilitating research and discussion about Web credibility

Helping designers create credible Web sites

Stay tuned.

Web Credibility Grid — Examples of elements that <u>increase</u> credibility*

	Presumed Credibility	Reputed Credibility	Surface Credibility	Experienced Credibility
Web Site Provider	The provider is a nonprofit organization.	The provider is recognized as an expert by others.	Users are familiar with the provider outside of the Web context.	Users with questions receive quick and helpful answers.
Web Site Content ·information ·functionality	The site has ads from reputable companies.	The content has been approved by an outside agency.	The site appears to have lots of relevant information.	The site's content has always been accurate and unbiased.
Web Site Design ·aesthetic ·information ·technical	The site was created by an outside design firm.	The site won an award for technical achievement.	The site has a pleasing visual design.	The site is easy to navigate.

*These are working hypotheses. To date, we've studied only some of these variables.

What Variables Affect Web Credibility?   Contact: BJ Fogg (bjfogg@stanford.edu) www.webcredibility.org

Figure 15.3 Who you are, what you've got, and how you look all have an impact on how people perceive your site . . .

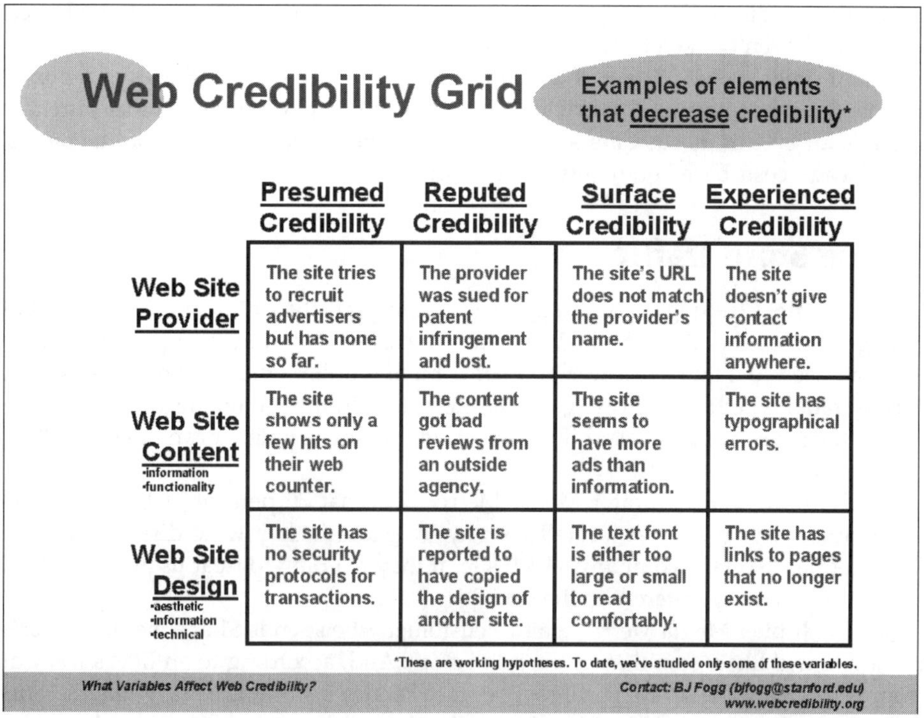

Web Credibility Grid

Examples of elements that **decrease** credibility*

	Presumed Credibility	Reputed Credibility	Surface Credibility	Experienced Credibility
Web Site Provider	The site tries to recruit advertisers but has none so far.	The provider was sued for patent infringement and lost.	The site's URL does not match the provider's name.	The site doesn't give contact information anywhere.
Web Site Content ·information ·functionality	The site shows only a few hits on their web counter.	The content got bad reviews from an outside agency.	The site seems to have more ads than information.	The site has typographical errors.
Web Site Design ·aesthetic ·information ·technical	The site has no security protocols for transactions.	The site is reported to have copied the design of another site.	The text font is either too large or small to read comfortably.	The site has links to pages that no longer exist.

*These are working hypotheses. To date, we've studied only some of these variables.

What Variables Affect Web Credibility?   Contact: BJ Fogg (bjfogg@stanford.edu)
www.webcredibility.org

Figure 15.4 . . . but it's possible to have each of those give your reputation a black eye as well.

The Online/Offline, Cross-Channel, Multichannel, Multivariate Migraine

Please don't stop measuring things at the edges of your Web site. This problem gets more multidimensional at every turn. Those of you with retail outlets need to consider that the Web can either drive traffic to the stores, or it can drive people away from the brand. The Web is a great place to promote offline events. But it doesn't mean it's easy to measure.

Between Two Worlds

META Group Senior Research Analyst Kurt Schlegel is tasked with talking to people and finding out the difference between what they want and what they have. "The Holy Grail would correlate Web data with offline data. I have spoken with very few folks who could say, 'Alright, here is how people are touching our Web site that we're not touching with direct sales or partners or some offline channel.' In fact, to be honest with you, I haven't talked to anybody who can do that."

In their report called "The ROI of Selling Online" (August 2001), Forrester reported that the Sharper Image is, "a striking exception: It compiles cross-channel purchase histories for 80% of its customers, tracks the influence of each channel on the others, and allocates costs based on relative contributions."

Driving Store Traffic

So the leading, bleeding, cutting edge has figured out the online/offline thing. But don't give up on the idea that the Web can turn surfers into store shoppers. As people get more used to a lot of research and some buying online, the line between the two starts to fade. Whether they call, go to the store, buy from a catalogue, or shop online, it's still the same company. And if the experience is suboptimal, it can have a chilling effect on the other channels.

Based on interviews, Jupiter Media Metrix says that 70 percent of U.S. shoppers would spend less money at a retailer's physical store if they were dissatisfied with their experience on the company's Web site. If they're going to treat us poorly online, why would it be any different in the store?

Quoting Jupiter Media Metrix again, a customer who spends $1 at a manufacturer's online site will likely spend $5 at the retail store. And, according to an IBM survey of shoppers by IBM, the average transaction at JCPenney's stores is $122, while the purchase at jcpenney.com is $500. Most interesting is that the average purchase by someone who shops both venues is $1,000.

In 2000, Shop.org, the Online Group of The National Retail Federation (www.nrf.com), produced a study they called "Channel Surfing: Measuring Multi-Channel Shopping." In it, they reported that there was a very strong cross-channel influence on purchasing decisions. I came across their findings in a report by Peppers and Rogers and Institute for the Future called "Measuring the Impact of Consumer Direct: Understanding Cross-Channel Metrics" (see Figure 15.5).

In 2001, Shop.org published "The Multi-Channel Retail Report," wherein they stated that 34 percent of shoppers buy in all three channels:

> Based on more than 48,000 interviews with shoppers in all channels, the study found that store shoppers who also bought online spend an average of $600 more than single-channel shoppers. Shoppers who bought in all three channels now represent 34% of all shoppers. In addition, the study reported that reaching the "Super" multi-channel customer is primary to retailers' success. This is borne out by the fact that online shoppers purchase from a retailer's store 70% more frequently than the average store customer and 110% more frequently from the retailer's catalog.

The "Measuring the Impact of Consumer Direct" report recounts a retail tale that proves the power of multichannel promotions (see Figure 15.6):

*Strong Cross-Channel Influence on Purchasing Decisions
(Percent of customers who looked for or purchased
something previously seen in another channel, where a
retailer offered more than one channel)*

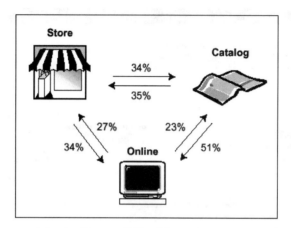

Source: National Retail Federation, *Channel Surfing: Measuring Multi-
Channel Shopping,* 2000.

INSTITUTE FOR THE FUTURE/PEPPERS AND ROGERS GROUP

Figure 15.5 Shop.org found there was no such thing as a single-channel shopper.

Linking the Channels

*We saw one of the most successful examples of cross-channel selling at an apparel retailer.
This retailer used an integrated promotional strategy involving email, catalogs, and stores
to increase sales.*

*The retailer derives a significant amount of sales from the seasonal catalogs it sends out
several times a year. A few days before its catalog mailing, the retailer sends an email to
its customers announcing that the catalog will arrive in a few days (the retailer collects
email addresses via phone, email, mail, and in stores). This retailer has found that these
emails raise catalog sales significantly. Furthermore, the company has found that the catalog mailings coincide with significantly higher store traffic in the days after the mailing.
This effort represents a multiple-channel promotion strategy that has proven very effective in raising sales across channels.*

As marketers get smarter about approaching the Web as simply another communication tool, they are finding it can be just as powerful as direct mail or newspaper ads
for getting people to the mall. Or, as in Crayola's case, into the parking lot.

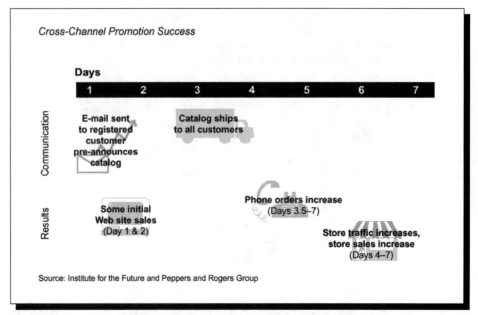

Figure 15.6 Cross-channel promotion success is described by Peppers and Rogers Group and Institute for the Future.

Event Marketing

Gregg Dixon at Binney & Smith was excited about a first-time event they planned around the Crayola brand. "We had a corporate warehouse sale. The first ever. We're a big business in the community locally, and our brand is one of the most recognized brands in the world." No kidding.

"So we thought it would be quite an event. Well, we sent out email to Crayola.com registered users in a 100-mile radius to let them know that we were having this sale and if they brought in their email they would get a special offer. And we would get to test what the actual response would be. It was the perfect test.

"And what was their actual average purchase? Was it greater than a normal person coming to the sale? Was it less? Was it average?

"We ended up with a wonderful turnout. We suspect many more people came as a result of the emailing but did not turn in the coupon and many more word-of-mouth referrals generated visits as well as a result of the email. In total, the email generated about 10 percent to 20 percent of the visits. We also signed up 1,000 people for Crayola.com at the event and realized that many people were already registered. The event was a strong testament to the power of online marketing's effect on offline behavior."

Sure it works if you do it well, and Dixon had a solid, closed-loop way of tracking how well it worked. Had the same offer gone in the local paper or into a direct mail piece, the tracking would have been tricky.

Multicommunication Channel

The words of one senior Web manager were echoed by numerous others: "It's very easy to measure the impact of an online-only program. The difficulty comes when you have an integrated program, which everybody would agree is probably the right approach. When you have an integrated program and you have offline advertising, measuring the specific impacts of those in combination with the online marketing you're doing *can* be done, but it's difficult to do. You're not really looking at actual impact anyway; it's estimated impact. So that's always a difficult challenge."

If you've got a direct mail piece coming out *and* a banner ad, how do you know how much traffic is because one person got one, saw the other, *and* saw the billboard on the highway in the morning? You'll never know.

Another high-level Web executive at a $2 billion manufacturing firm had a quick answer to my favorite question: What's the hard part?

"Getting the full relationship. A Web event is one of many events that result in a sale, and the objective is always a sale. And if we don't tie this thing together, we don't know how effective that is. What we should be trying to do is drive time out of the cycle and drive more value into the face-to-face relationship so that they are closer to the closure point, and that's what we are trying to figure out how to do."

Oracle's vice president of Online Marketing, Rene Bonvanie, tracks a lot, and is on the way to tracking more. "We look at specific pages people look at, certain PDFs they download, event registration—and that includes offline. We take registration for seminars through the same mechanisms. Then when people attend, it goes back into the same system.

"Then we get the feedback loop from the sales side saying this or that company actually did buy. We fan in and then we fan out. We provide the sales full overview of everything that happened to the lead and then when deals get done we actually fan back, which is we look at everything that company did, and figure out what things worked and what didn't work."

Don't for a minute think this is easy, even for a technology company like Oracle.

"Typically, events on the Web site that associate those individuals with that sale run in the hundreds, if not thousands, of interactions, and that," says Bonvanie, looking into the near future, "is an art we are getting to now."

The Multidepartmental Data Dance

It's not only the online/offline struggle keeping Web managers up at night. There are also the marketing/sales struggle and the sales/customer service struggle. National Semiconductor figured out the first one. Phil Gibson's contact management system that displays Web visits as described in Chapter 14 is proof that clear vision and a lot of hard work can get you there. If you're willing to wait, some software vendor might give you a hand.

Such was the case when WebTrends and Siebel systems saw the benefit of teaming up to help their clients alleviate the online/offline customer service struggle (see Figure 15.7).

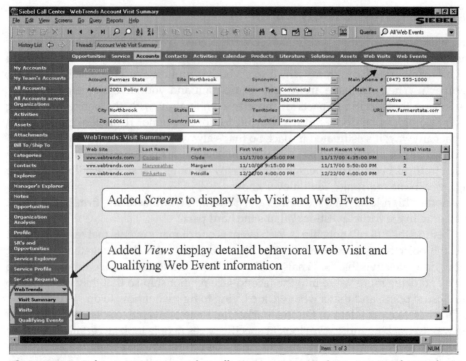

Figure 15.7 Sales or customer service call center representatives can see what Web pages the caller has been looking at.

Barry Parshall is the WebTrends Intelligence Suite Group Product Manager for Siebel *e*Business Applications, and he promises me his title fits on a business card. Parshall described their Conduit for Siebel *e*Business Applications for use with Siebel Call Center as a way to help a call center representative keep an eye on what's been going on online.

Says Parshall: "With the Conduit, users can track behavioral Web data by account name, contact person, visit, or event, and data can be viewed just the way experienced Siebel *e*Business Applications users expect to see it. Users also have the power to query and sort their behavioral customer records at any level, on any screen; export query results for use in spreadsheets, custom reports or other databases; trigger communication based on visit activity with Siebel Workflow; and navigate directly to Account, Contact, and Visit screens via hotlinks."

In other words, when you call in, they know what you did last session.

This integration problem becomes acute for companies that have multiple, separate channels. If their store, their Web site, and their catalogue organizations grew up individually, there'll be a great deal of integration, and it won't be pretty as diagrammed in the "Measuring the Impact of Consumer Direct" report (see Figure 15.8).

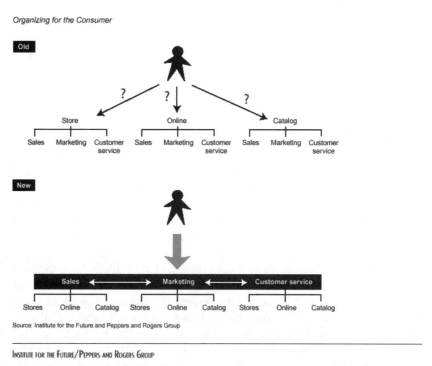

Organizing for the Consumer

Source: Institute for the Future and Peppers and Rogers Group

INSTITUTE FOR THE FUTURE/PEPPERS AND ROGERS GROUP

Figure 15.8 As long as customers feels they are dealing with one organization, there may not be a need for a third level of integration.

Intra-Industry Data Model

Wharton School's Pete Fader likes to think outside the box. Well, outside the company, anyway: "Very different in concept, but very similar in method is going to be looking at behavior across multiple competitors.

"Through Media Metrix we have the click-by-click data down here. We can take a chunk of their behavior and look at Amazon and Barnes & Noble to see how often they actually go from one site to the other within a day or so. Do people tend to be just loyal to one versus the other? So there are really different behavioral issues related to either the incident of their arrival or the rate underlying their arrival. We can learn from their behavior on one Web site and apply it to their likely behavior at a competing one.

"We have some nice results on that. For instance, we can look at people who have never been to Amazon and look at their Barnes & Noble behavior, and then rank-order those people based on how likely they are to visit Amazon. And using the data from this competing Web site, we can make some pretty good guesses—there are some regularities about the site-to-site switching. So it's nice to have that cross-site, cross-channel, cross-competitor data."

Across Industries

In the long run, you get to the point where you're envisioning enough metrics, captured at enough touchpoints, that you can start to build a model of e-commerce as a whole, and then commerce as a whole. And that would be just about the right time to have lunch with Neil Raden again. He'll remind you that keeping it simple to implement, and simple to understand, is akin to keeping it possible.

Connect the Dots

Do not try to measure everything at once and don't expect to measure everything someday.

A small company can't afford the hardware, software, and brainy people to get a handle on complex metrics. Large companies are too complex to bring together all their data silos, normalize all the data, crunch it all in real time, and feed it back to the front lines for instant action. Can't happen.

So I asked Raden about my sweet-spot theory. "Isn't it likely," I wondered, "that a midsized company, with a single product or service, that could afford the latest and greatest tools, but wasn't burdened by legacy mainframe systems or mergers and acquisitions . . . Wouldn't it be possible for them to become a category killer?

"Wouldn't it be possible to use the best tools, capture the right data right off the bat, and create a system that allowed you to control everything at a moment's notice? Wouldn't that company be in a position to scare the bejeepers out of large, lumbering companies?"

"You mean like the dot-coms were going to do because *they* had the Internet?" asked Raden.

"The tide has lifted all boats—even huge, multinational ones," I countered. "We've learned the lesson of overoptimisitic enthusiasm, and we're applying what works and ignoring the exuberance."

"The problem is twofold," he replied. "First, it's a moving target. Building an analytical model of a large financial, or distribution, or marketing system is like medicine. You don't treat a static body. It's always in a state of change. That's why they call it *practicing* medicine.

"The other problem is one of complexity. We are, after all, *modeling* this stuff. We are imitating it inside a computer. Oh sure, you have actual sales figures and actual costs, but then everything else is derivative.

"I had one large client that went through some pretty serious layoffs one year. We were building a data warehouse for them, and the moment came when it was time to set the calculations for cost of goods sold. Now if you talk to the Fortune 500, chances are you'll end up with 495 different ways that they actually arrive at their cost of goods sold figures, so we needed to find out how this multibillion dollar company did theirs.

"There was one guy—*one* guy—who understood the calculation they used and he had taken early retirement. We had to go out to some lake in Michigan to fetch him and hire him back as a consultant."

Spreadsheets are built on assumptions and the data that goes into data warehouses are partly conjecture. So what do you do? You work with finite sets of information and you make sure the data is as clean as can be, the models are as simple as possible (but not more so—thank you, Albert Einstein), and the results are fed back into the business process to close the loop.

Capture and Use Data One Step at a Time

Get a handle on clickstreams, visitors, sessions, and sales first. Then move up to measuring promotional impact and customer input. And finally, when all is well, tackle the multichannel data and the sophisticated, one-to-one customer classification and response systems.

What should you measure at what touchpoint? Institute for the Future has some ideas, as shown in a table in their report with Peppers and Rogers called "Measuring the Impact of Consumer Direct" (see Figure 15.9), and it sorts out measures of cost from measures of value (see Figure 15.10).

A Business Perspective on Consumer Communication: Four Key Roles

Communication Roles	Channels	Measures
Advertising: Brand building, product introduction, identifying potential customers	Mass media, ads	Hits, gross rating points.
Marketing: Providing targeted information	Stores, Web, catalog, magazines, news	References, cross-channel browsing, length of time spent (e.g. number of web pages browsed).
Customer Service: Interactive engagement	Stores, Web, phones, mail	Interactions with consumers, data collected.
Sales: Transactional exchange	Stores, Web, catalogs, mail	Long-term value of the customer.

Source: Institute for the Future

Institute for the Future/Peppers and Rogers Group

Figure 15.9   Each communication channel has its roles and its measures.

Measuring the Impact of Deeper Engagement

Communication Roles	Measures of Cost	Measures of Value
Advertising: Brand building, product introduction	Dollars per impression	Appearances and references on other sites and in other channels.
Marketing: Providing targeted information	Dollars per item	Response rates, additional information requests, or information collected from the consumer.
Customer Service: Interactive engagement	Dollars per interaction	Sales opportunity, dialogue with an interested consumer, feedback from the consumer, complaints satisfactorily resolved.
Sales: Transactional exchanges	Dollars per transaction	Sales and likelihood of future sales (product on hand; needs information collected; efficient delivery; efficient payment system).

Source: Institute for the Future and Peppers and Rogers Group

INSTITUTE FOR THE FUTURE/PEPPERS AND ROGERS GROUP

Figure 15.10   It's one thing to know how you're measuring and another to know what those measurements mean.

Publish Easy-to-Absorb Results

In Chapter 4, we looked at creating a dashboard for executives. The fact is, we all need a dashboard—some simple readout that tells us generally where things stand and is the early warning system when things start going wonky.

Talk to Richard Hunter, managing vice president for Consulting at Gartner E-Metrix, and he'll tell you how hard it is to keep track of too many things at once. "Most people can't monitor 50 things at a time." Those running Web sites need to pare down the overload. "It's better to look at an aggregate metric." That means you need a dashboard of your own.

Oracle's Rene Bonvanie agrees: "The general idea was to selectively elect data that we wanted to keep an eye on and then provide multiple levels of key performance indicators to our management. All the way from Larry Ellison down to individual program managers or people in marketing communications to understand the impact of their marketing program."

Fry Multimedia's Kara Heinrichs agrees as well: "We create data dashboards for us and our clients to look at their site performance defined very broadly over time. And the purpose of that, in addition to being able to allow our customers to see how the site is performing on an ongoing basis, is to help them understand that they don't need to freak about a certain number. Conversion is great, but it moves; every day it is different. And what's really important is the relationship of one curve to another. So if we can help them understand that, they can begin to understand that if they drop an email and it spikes their traffic, but they have to put in an additional ten or twenty servers to support it, maybe it wasn't a net gain for them unless there is some additional lifetime value that they drove there."

The trick is to come up with a display that is easy to understand at a glance. That's one of the strengths of a company called Visual Insights (www.visualinsights.com). In their own words, their company "helps businesses build better eBusiness strategies by providing an immediate and accurate understanding of Web site performance and activity, visitor behavior, and promotional effectiveness." The neat trick is that they've paid a lot of attention to how data is displayed (see Figure 15.11).

A dashboard is more useful when there are large, blinking red lights that let you know you're headed for trouble and large green lights that let you know everything is going according to plan.

The Tragedy of the Feedback Loop Gap

Neil Raden understands the importance of the feedback loop. "One of the industry buzzwords is 'closed-loop decision support,' which is meant to describe the interoperability of analytic processes with operational ones—for example, the ability to explore a customer database to uncover desirable attributes and to immediately dispatch an action, such as creation of a mailing list. In our practice, we consider all decision-support systems incomplete unless they can close the loop. Analysis of sales results is only useful to a point. The engine of value creation in decision support systems is the linking of the analysis to discussion, consensus, action, and results in a systematic way."

But there's a gap.

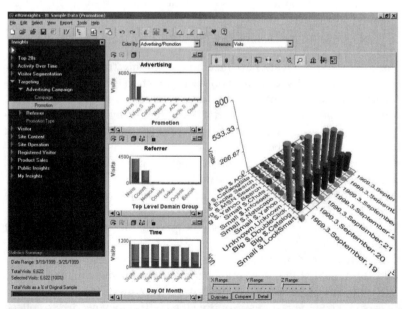

Figure 15.11 Visual Insight understands that some of us prefer getting and manipulating our information visually.

Who works the data? Who chooses and owns the analytical tools? In the case of business intelligence, it's the programmers and the statisticians. With Web data, it's the programmers, the statisticians, and the Web managers. Where are the businesspeople?

In 2000, Matt Cutler and I interviewed twenty-five large-company Web managers and almost all of them said they were drowning in data. One, from a publishing company, told us, "I think working with this volume of data is a bit like being in a canoe in front of a tidal wave—paddling like hell and just hoping it doesn't overrun you."

In 2001, I interviewed fifty Web managers and they had, indeed, made some progress. They had channeled that tidal wave into a culvert and that gave them some semblance of control. Unfortunately, the conversations mostly went like this:

"So you're capturing the server logs and the transactions and filtering out all the extraneous data?"

"That's right. And it took a while, too."

"And you've created some rules by which you pull out the relevant information?"

"Yep—visitors, visits, page views, abandoned shopping carts—the works!"

"And you send that information over to the business side of the house? You let the business unit managers and the product managers know what's going on?"

"Oh no, not yet. First we break it down to a level where they can understand it. We put out one report every week and a whole bunch once a month. We email everybody when the reports are available on the intranet. We make PowerPoint charts and graphs for them so they can see what's going on."

"And then they look over the reports. . ."

"Yep."

". . . and interpret what they mean. . ."

"That's right."

". . . and then tell you what changes need to be made to the Web site to further the goals of the company?"

"Well—not as such. I mean, when the traffic goes down, they want to know why and we usually get a phone call or two."

"Do they work with you to create new methods of driving traffic to the site, or improve navigation, or modify the questions on the registration form?"

"Well, the folks in advertising in each of the business units are supposed to look at the New Visitors reports and decide what to do, if anything. Navigation is our bailiwick and the registration form is managed by the people in customer service. I think they have monthly meetings with the CRM people."

"How do the marketing managers and the product managers and the sales managers know what those PowerPoint reports mean?"

"Oh, we sent out an email explaining everything when we first installed the metrics tools about 18 months ago."

I am reminded why I am a consultant to large companies, rather than a denizen of them.

One enterprising Web metrics team leader of a Six Sigma group in a large, multidivision corporation told me that they sent out a survey to the business managers who had been pestering various departmental Webmasters with requests for more information. The plan was to review the responses, outline the metrics they needed to collect, and then choose tools best suited to the collection and analysis of those metrics.

A BETTER BUT RISKIER WAY OF DETERMINIG CUSTOMER REQUIREMENTS: STOP EVERYTHING AND SEE WHAT CUSTOMERS ASK FOR

Pete was surprised when he took over the finance and planning function of an organization recently. In looking at what the eight people who worked in Finance Planning did, Pete determined that they spent about 80 percent of their time inputting data, summarizing it, and preparing reports of mostly financial information for the rest of the organization. He challenged the need for all of these reports; his team informed him that it had conducted several focus groups and individual interviews to identify the information needs of internal customers. The research revealed that people wanted and needed all of the data they were previously sending out, and a few new reports that they had never done before. The Finance and Planning staff explained that they suspected that they were doing the right things all along, but that this customer requirements research proved it.

Pete was skeptical: "You mean that they said they need all of these reports every single month?" "That's right. We're giving them exactly what they ask for, and always meet deadlines on getting them the information in a timely fashion. " After thinking about the situation for a few days, Pete decided to take a riskier approach to identifying Finance and Planning's customers' requirements. Pete instructed his staff that it was to stop issuing all reports for two months. His team told him he was nuts. "People need these data to run the organization and make business decisions, Pete. The place will fall apart without these data." Pete said he didn't believe it would and he would take the heat for the decision if it turned out to be a bad one. "We'll document it in our meeting minutes that you guys are going along with this experiment under protest."

So for two months Pete's team documented some of its key processes, worked on planning, and kept itself busy doing other things besides cranking out financial reports. What do you think happened during the two months when no financial reports were issued? Paul in Service Operations called a couple of times to get some numbers on his labor costs for the month. A couple of Brand Managers called for some sales figures, and some others called for a few key numbers they needed for their functions. This became Pete's customer requirements needs analysis. The data that people called and asked for turned out to be what they really needed to run their functions. Using the information from this non-traditional approach to needs analysis, Pete was able to reduce the amount of data distributed by his department by about 80 percent and reduce the time his people spent inputting and reporting these data by over 50 percent! So, did Pete lay off half of his staff? Nope. He put them to work helping the organization plan, manage, and control financial performance factors. His people are happier because their work is more challenging and meaningful. Internal customers are happy because they receive only the data they really need to manage their functions, and the overall organization's

(continues)

Perfect! I thought. Finally, somebody is asking the "What do we need to know?" question, rather than the "Here are the logs, what do you make of them?" question. Not only that, there was a business opportunity for me to go in and give workshops if the survey results showed that the managers are way off base—either asking for too much or not knowing what to ask.

Later, I called back to check on the progress.

"Have the surveys gone out?"

"Yes, and response was good. Thirty percent responded."

"Really? That's a lot. I'm surprised. How long will it take to sort through their replies and figure out the next step?"

"No time at all. It was multiple choice so we have our answers already."

"Multiple choice?"

"Uh-huh."

"So . . . you asked them whether they thought page views were important?"

"And whether they'd like session duration information and that sort of thing. Right."

"How did these businesspeople know what they were being asked?"

"Oh, we took care of that up front. We gave workshops and sent out emails explaining all of the possible metrics and the survey was a list of potential data we could offer."

"So you told people what they could choose from?"

"Right. And they mostly wanted average length of time per visit, how many pages per session, most visited pages, and least visited pages."

I was already reaching for the aspirin while contemplating the feedback loop gap (see Figure 15.12).

The technical side of the company doesn't have a view into the business drivers of the company, and the businesspeople don't know (1) what the data mean or (2) what valuable information might possibly be available.

We need to at least educate those controlling the marketing and customer service budgets well enough so they can interpret the data they get. At best, they will understand the metrics reports well enough to make well-informed plans for the next step *and* instrument the execution of those plans so that the right information is gathered with each iteration.

We can hope.

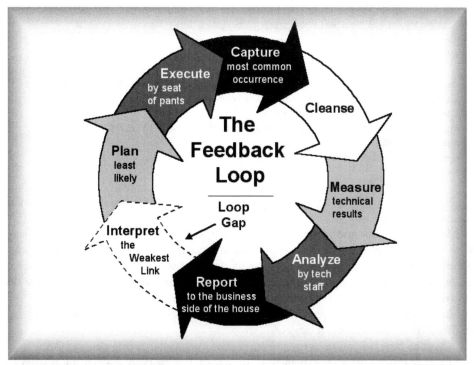

Figure 15.12   The feedback loop gap is the weakest link in the analytics chain.

Customer Success

Tom Peters used the phrase "customer delight" for a while (before he moved on to "customer lust," but this is a PG book, so we'll leave that to Tom). I always liked that phrase and have wondered if it would ever be possible to measure delight.

Every proof-of-concept for delight is anecdotal. Here's a recent favorite, an email from Marnie Wielage at John Wiley & Sons:

```
Subject: Something Kinda Cool!
To: Jim Sterne <jsterne@targeting.com>
From: mwielage@wiley.com
Date: Wed, 30 May 2001 12:01:56 -0400

Hi Jim:
How are you? Something really cool happened today that I thought I'd
share with you . . .
While I was proofing [your book] Web Marketing, 3E, I ran across the URL
for reflect.com and thought I'd take a spin around the site. I played
around for a while and wound up customizing some foundation to see how
the site worked. I bailed before checkout because I never really had any
intention to buy--your description in the book was cool and sparked my
interest.
```

```
That was about three-four weeks ago. Today, I got a nicely packaged
little box from reflect.com with a complementary sample of the
foundation I designed. I immediately thought of everything I'd learned
from your book and thought you'd get a kick out of the story (hmmm . . .
I see the possibilities for a fourth edition!).
Considering how many sites lose customers' interest before checkout, I
thought this was a pretty cool little marketing scheme. . . If I love
the foundation--they've got me!
Anyway, on another note, things are progressing right on schedule for
Marketing, 3E.
Hope all is well, and I look forward to the next one.
Marnie
```

She's delighted. She told me and I'm delighted. I just told about 40,000 people. Go measure *that*.

Mellanie Hills is a good friend whom I've tracked from JCPenney to Dell to Cisco, with time off in between for independent consulting and a couple of pioneering books about intranets. She knows how to make the Internet work inside large companies. I asked her one of those loaded questions. Easy to ask, and hard to answer: "How do you determine the value of spending money on customer-facing features?"

Hills, a master of knowing what she knows and knowing what she doesn't know, replied, "Yep. That's right on target."

"Okay, so how do you measure the success of a customer-facing program?"

"By how much customer satisfaction improved. We measure everything related to customer sat, and a major portion of our pay is based on our customer sat ratings. We set annual goals and we always blow away our goal, and usually exceed our stretch goal."

"There's not an employee at Cisco, even the janitors, that doesn't know that we measure everything by what it does for customer sat. Dixie Garr, our vice president of Customer Success Engineering, says that every employee contributes in some way, even if it's just to not park in the customer parking spaces at the Customer Briefing Center."

I know a number of companies that pay sales bonuses on customer satisfaction. The result is that salespeople refuse to sell to prospects who aren't a good match for the products. Brilliant. But a vice president of customer success engineering? These people are onto something *and* they've figured out how to measure it.

Tomorrowland

We're not taking vacations on the moon or racing around in nuclear-fusion-powered cars like I was promised when I was 9 years old. The New York World's Fair of 1964 is well behind us, but the lesson remains: Feel free to predict the event or the date, but never at the same time.

How are Web metrics going to change in the future?

As processors get faster and data storage cheaper, we'll be looking more and more to predictive tools like those from Genalytics described in the *Calculated Commerce* section of chapter 11. This type of divinatory software will hunt for those counterintuitive patterns for us.

You know that customers of category types 4, 5, and 6 are your prime target (see Figure 15.13), and sometimes you can get types 3 and 7 to show a bit more interest. But you had no expectation that category 9 customers would respond so well.

After that, the sky's the limit. The computer is placed in charge of what sort of offers to make to which sorts of prospects and set whatever marketing budget it feels would yield the best results. It will set pricing lower for overstocked items. It will analyze Web server trends to determine if additional hardware will be needed to keep up with anticipated response to new offers. It will communicate with channel partner systems to determine whether the supply chain can feed sufficient raw materials into the production cycle to keep up with the projected demand. It will talk to distribution systems to see if there are enough trucks available to carry projected shipments. It will calculate executive management bonuses and fold all those numbers back into an ROI number that it will compare to a matrix of strategic objectives to balance short-term tactical goals.

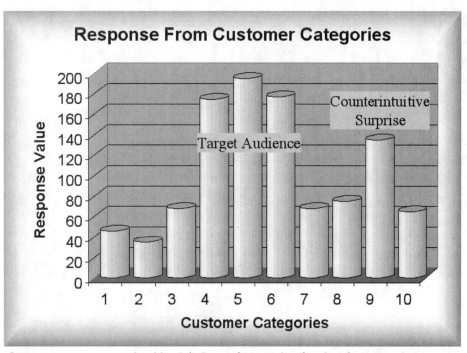

Figure 15.13   A counterintuitive "aha" reveals a previously missed opportunity.

That will all happen about the same time as we vacation in the Hotel Atlantis in General Motors' Futurama's Underseas City from the 1964 World's Fair (see Figure 15.14).

How are Web metrics going to change in the *near* future? They're going to take the strain out of creating a raft of horizontal analytical data models by providing pre-designed, tweakable examples. They're going to take the pain out of sifting through terabytes of server log litter by automatically filtering for the information you want, rather than handing you everything they can. They will be more tightly integrated with offline systems to give you a more three-dimensional picture of your site, your customers, and the interaction between your customer and your company.

Web metrics tools and services are also going to become customized by industry. Web service companies are going to start creating specialized Web metrics reports by industry, as exemplified by this report for B&Bs from Netconcepts and Blizzard Internet Marketing (see Figure 15.15).

Figure 15.14 The Underseas City is coming soon to a seabed near you—just don't hold your breath.

Figure 15.15   Netconcepts and Blizzard Internet Marketing have created a metrics report that goes right to the heart of the hospitality industry.

Having been in the Web design and e-business development business for close to 10 years, Netconcepts President Stephan Spencer laments that traditional traffic analysis software doesn't reveal direct ROI metrics. "Our solution provides all the standard traffic reports, but in addition, it reports on how many reservations and/or reservation requests are delivered by each of the lodging directories, destination guides, and search engines. The innkeeper or hotelier also gets a look-to-book ratio for each referrer and a cost-per-booking, based on what we know to be the average cost of a listing for each lodging/destination site.

"The innkeeper also sees averages of all B&Bs for visitors, bookings, etcetera across categories, such as by state. We monitor all the other steps in the acquisition funnel, such as viewing the rooms and rates page, clicking on the mailto: link, checking room availability, and the like. People who run hotels don't care about server logs. They don't have time. We do all that for them."

And to think that we once measured our success by counting hits. How quaint.

METRIC METER

One single click makes the whole thing tick
When a visitor comes to your site
It's a finger flick that does the trick
But the data keeps you up at night

Do you measure the click? The landing? The hit?
The page? The session? The sale?
There's got to be more to keeping Web score
How do you know you've prevailed?

E-metrics begin to measure the wins
And the losses, the trip ups, and flaws
To point out those sins that cause us chagrin
And give site visitors pause

It can be a short tale from the click to the sale
In a blink from the link to the bank
Or it can take weeks while curiosity peaks
For a sale to be made, let's be frank

Memberships are weighed and gauged
And leads are a good thing to track
But conversion and loyalty
Are the E-metric royalty
These need a new measuring tack

We have been lacking the knack to be tracking
What alters the shape of your funnel
And changes those leads into e-commerce deeds
That light at the end of the tunnel

E-metrics are new, now it's all up to you
To get these e-yardsticks extended
Then you can tell if you've done something well
Something better, or done something splendid

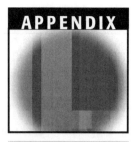

How Interactive Ads Are Delivered and Measurement Implication

Dick Bennett
SVP Audit Svcs/CTO
ABC Interactive
1701 Golf Rd
Tower III, Suite 300
Rolling Meadows, IL 60008
(Reproduced by permission)

Introduction

In order to understand the various ways interactive ads are delivered today and how these different delivery methods affect measurement, CASIE asked Richard (Dick) Bennett of Audit Bureau of Circulations (ABC) to author a paper on this topic. Dick is the Senior Vice President of Audit Services for ABC and ABC Interactive. This paper will describe a number of different approaches of serving online advertisement banners, as well as different technologies which have been developed to deal with the measurement problems caused by caching. While a few definitions of key words have been included in this paper, a full glossary of terms (CASIE Glossary of Internet Advertising Terms and Interactive Media Measurement) is available through the Association of National Advertisers, Inc.

Based on research fielded by ANA and CASIE, the buyers (advertisers and agencies) want accurate and reliable measurement of ads displayed. How that is accomplished is up to the trackers, measurers, and Web publishers, and neither CASIE, ANA, nor AAAA are supporting any specific methodology.

Ad Serving and Tracking

This paper will briefly describe the five most prominent methods of ad serving and tracking that are in use today. They are static ads, insertions, dynamic ads, cache-measured ads, and browser-measured ads. Before we get into the details of these specific ad delivery systems, a gross simplification of the process is as follows:

Step One: User requests a page from content site

Step Two: Content site requests an ad to insert in page

Step Three: Ad is inserted in the page

Step Four: Ad is downloaded to the user's browser

Step Five: Ad is displayed on the user's screen

Step Six: Ad is viewed by the user

All the steps above can be measured except for the last one. Click-rates/click-throughs/click-to-views are certainly indications that the ad was viewed, but there are many ads viewed with no measurable action.

The five techniques which will be described next equate to the steps above as follows:

Step Two: Requests = Cache-Measured Ads

Step Three: Insertions

Step Four: Download = Static Ads or Dynamic Ads

Step Five: Displayed = Browser-Measured Ads

Special Note: The preceding descriptions do not attempt to define whether a given ad is being requested by a "real" visitor interacting with the Web/ad server, or whether the ad is being "pushed" to the browser in some automatic fashion. This concern could be addressed by designating the suggested terms as active or passive.

Static Ads

This approach is characterized by the placement of the ad file name within an image tag inside the HTML page. The user's browser then calls for the image (ad file), after loading the HTML page, which will in turn be recorded as a "hit" in the server's log file. Thus the Web server will have recorded a "hit" for the request for the page as well as a "hit" for the request for the ad. Additionally, the server will also be able to record the successful (or unsuccessful) downloading of the ad file to the browser. This is done via status codes that rely on the underlying protocols of the Internet, TCP/IP, to determine disposition of requests. This technique is used by sites with no ad rotation/server system, or an in-house developed application. [See Figure A.1.] Sites which employ this technique place and rotate ads in batches. For example, they might run a program once per day to tag each page within the site with the appropriate image (ad file) name intended to be displayed on that page. Ad activity recorded for servers using this method of rotation is performed by the web server when the ad file is served. Measurement via this technique would qualify under the IAB's existing definition of an Ad Request.

Caching can have a significant effect on measurement using this technique. Assuming that the site employs little or no cache-busting techniques, this measurement approach understates activity due to caching because any request (for a Web element) which passes through a proxy server that has previously cached that element will most likely not be seen or recorded by the Web server.

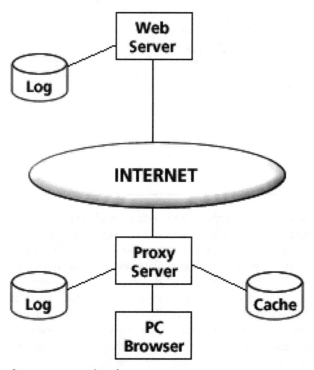

Figure A.1   Static Ads

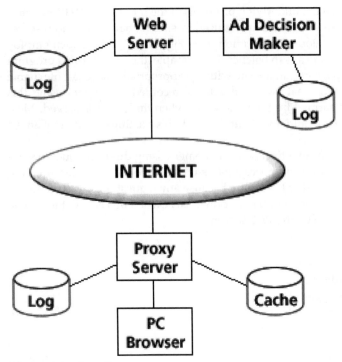

Figure A.2 Insertions.

Insertions

With this technique, an ad server software component (decision maker) is integrated with the Web server software, so that when a page is served to a user's browser, a decision is made regarding which ad to serve the requesting browser, and the HTML code for the chosen ad is "inserted" into the HTML page as it is served. Tracking of ads served in this manner is done at the point where the ad server makes the decision about the ad being served. This method is used by many ad management software products (Accipiter, NetGravity, RealMedia, etc.) currently available and is a normal configuration. This method of measurement is qualified under the IAB definition of Ad Request. However, a significant concern about this technique is that the actual serving (delivery) of ads is not recorded and therefore not measured. [See Figure A.2.]

Measurement of ads using this methodology is subject to several inaccuracies. First, browsers configured to have graphic files turned off are prevented from making the actual request for the ad, and therefore, the user was never exposed to the ad, even though the software recorded and measured the ad request.

Secondly, when a Web site's pages are served from cache, the ad server software has no opportunity to perform the ad insertion, resulting in the display of ads that can not be rotated or recorded by the ad server software. This results in the undercounting of actual ad activity. It also results in unintended ad rotation.

Dynamic Ads

Sites employing this technique embed a tag into an HTML page which makes a generic request for an ad from an ad server. The ad server then determines which ad to display and delivers the ad to the browser. Activity is recorded when the ad is served/delivered/downloaded to the browser. This methodology is used by some ad server service companies as well as some ad management server software. [See Figure A.3.]

This technique is very similar to the approach of using static ads addressed earlier. It differs because the page is served without reference to a specific "ad file," but rather to the "ad server." Thus the number of ads served and measured using this technique should approximate the number of pages served by the server, assuming all pages have ads. When used in conjunction with cache-busting techniques, this method can closely approximate the ads that get displayed on browsers. Although certain "smart" proxy servers have been known to cache ads served in this technique, there are differing opinions as to the number and effect of these "smart" proxies.

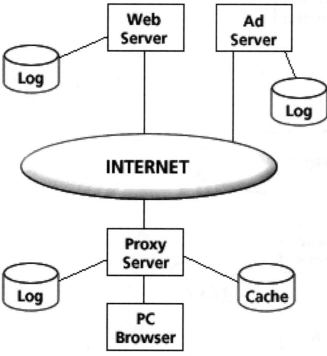

Figure A.3   Dynamic ad.

While ads served this way still meet the IAB measurement guideline, the result can be significantly different measurements than those derived with previously mentioned methodologies (static ads and insertions). Differences relate to the varying degrees of caching of ads as well as the fact that deliveries for actual ads are being measured versus insertions for ad files on pages served. Obviously, the more cache-defeating mechanisms employed by the site, the higher the measurement. The dynamic ad serving methodology also accurately handles the recording and measuring of "gif" file activity where the browser has graphics turned off.

Cache Measured

This method is a modification of the dynamic method. Instead of the ad server returning the ad to the browser, the server delivers a directive, telling the browser the ad to display, and also where that ad is located. The browser then must go out and retrieve the ad. The ad request is recorded at the point that the server makes the ad decision and issues the directive to the browser. [See Figure A.4.]

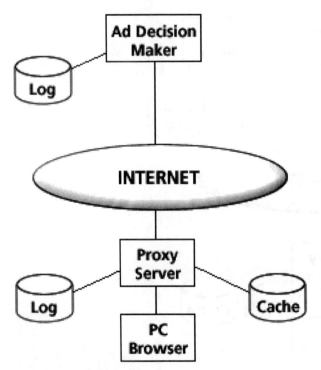

Figure A.4   Cache measured.

This method allows for the approximate measurement of ads stored and provided from cache by the proxy server or the browser, as well as those ads actually provided from the ad server. It does not measure deliveries, but rather requests for the given ad, although somewhat differently than when the insertion method is used.

This measurement methodology provides statistics which are obviously not comparable to most of the above methods unless they are employed with cache-defeating mechanisms. When set up correctly, the cache measured technique accurately deals with browsers configured with graphics turned off.

Browser Measured

This technique allows for the recording of the ad activity via software running on the browser. It employs software which runs on the browser, like Java, which handles the request for an ad from the server, the playing of the ad, recording of the ad played, as well as the transmission of the recorded activity back to some central repository. [See Figure A.5.]

This activity actually is capable of measuring Ad Views/Displays, that is, ads that were actually displayed on the user's screen.

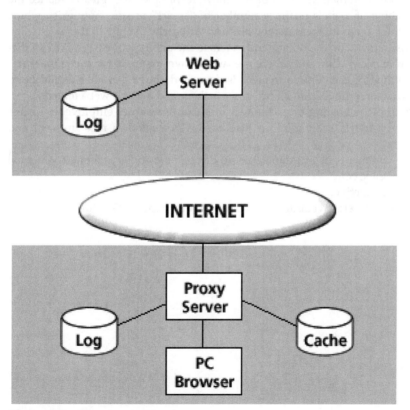

Figure A.5   Browser measured.

How to Control Cache

Additionally, differences between measurements of a similar category can be explained by the degree of caching, cache-busting or cache measurement employed.

"Cache-busting" may be defined as the forcing of a web element (page or ad) across the network to every browser that requests it. Cache-busting can be performed through a number of techniques. Some of the more commonly used cache-busting techniques include [the following]:

1. The site can set the expiration date of the ad to sometime in the past, i.e., January 1, 1990, telling the cache that the ad is out of date, so that the proxy server needs to get a new ad upon the next request.

2. The site can give unique names to each ad that it serves. Since each ad served has a different name, the proxy has problems identifying requests for the same ad, which allows the request for the ad to be passed back to the server.

3. The site can set various other "header" parameters (HTTP file attributes) to request that proxies not cache the ad. Those headers include the pragma, no_cache, and cache-control.

While use of a combination, or all of the above techniques will greatly reduce the amount of caching of a site's traffic, a number of "smart" proxies now exist, which have been trained to ignore these maneuvers and will cache in spite of them.

Cache measurement, on the other hand, refers to the ability to measure activity that was served from cache. Currently there are two known methods for cache measurement. One method of cache measurement is described above. Another would be to obtain the proxy server logs from all proxies which cached a given web element.

Disclosure of cache busting or cache measurement techniques employed by a site would enhance a user's evaluation of the statistics presented in measurement and auditing reports.

If you have comments or questions, please direct them to Dick Bennett via email bennettrp@accessabc.com

© 2001 ABC Interactive.

http://www.abcinteractiveaudits.com/news/white_paper_2332.html

Index